Colleges with a Conscience

81 Great Schools with
Outstanding Community Involvement

Colleges with a Conscience

81 Great Schools with
Outstanding Community Involvement

By the staff of Campus Compact and The Princeton Review

Random House, Inc.
New York
www.PrincetonReview.com

The Princeton Review, Inc.
2315 Broadway
New York, NY   10024
E-mail: bookeditor@review.com

ISBN: 0-375-76480-1

Editorial Director: Robert Franek
Editor: Spencer Foxworth
Contributing Authors: Nicholas V. Longo, Ellen Love, Joshua Stearns, Jenna Alden, and Tom Meltzer
Research Coordinator: Ben Gebre Medhin
Contributing Researcher: Abby Kiesa
Production Manager: Scott Harris
Production Editor: Christine LaRubio

Manufactured in the United States of America.

9 8 7 6 5 4 3 2 1

ACKNOWLEDGMENTS

Elizabeth Hollander and John Saltmarsh helped develop and cultivate the vision for this book. Their work promoting the public purposes of higher education, along with the rest of Campus Compact's staff, made this book necessary. Rob Franek saw the importance of this book and made it happen. Ben Gebre Medhin helped shape the book from the beginning; his passion and commitment to social change is imprinted throughout. Spencer Foxworth was a pleasure to work with and a savvy editor. Josh Stearns, author of the Smart Research section, whose knowledge of admissions and passion for civic engagement that strengthened the book greatly. Abby Kiesa believed in this book and provided timely assistance and fresh ideas. Karen Partridge provided skilled and much-needed editing assistance. Tobi Walker and The Pew Charitable Trusts provided valuable support and resources to high school and college civic engagement, including Campus Compact's Raise Your Voice campaign. Jenna Alden and Tom Meltzer did a wonderful job capturing the spirit of the civic efforts on campuses in the school profiles. Other collaborators included Ben Brandzel, Karley Ausiello, Rick Battistoni, Xavier Benavides, Sherita Moses, Stephanie Raill, Kate Toews, and Erica Carlson. Special thanks to the Campus Compact member institutions, state offices, and the national student organizations that provided the information for this book and who are doing public work so worthy of praise. And thanks, most of all, to our partners, Aleida Benitez and Adam Reich, for their encouragement and loving support.

—Nicholas Longo and Ellen Love

A UNIQUE PARTNERSHIP

The Princeton Review and Campus Compact both care deeply about education. The Princeton Review helps prospective students prepare for and make the right college choice. For this book, The Princeton Review partnered with Campus Compact because Campus Compact is the only national organization whose sole purpose is to advance the public mission of higher education.

Campus Compact is a coalition of more than 900 college and university presidents committed to supporting the public purposes of higher education. Through publications, training, networking, and resources provided through a national office and thirty state offices, Campus Compact helps schools that are committed to social responsibility improve the practice of civic engagement on their campuses. Campus Compact helps students have a meaningful experience once they get into college. All the schools profiled in this book are members of Campus Compact. Membership in Campus Compact shows a commitment to making community and public service part of campus life. To find out more about Campus Compact, including a complete list of member schools, see the Campus Compact website at www.compact.org.

CONTENTS

INTRODUCTION

"Never doubt that a small group of committed individuals can change the world. Indeed, it's the only thing that ever has."

—Margaret Mead

Seeking Social Responsibility

Going to college is a practical way to spend time after high school. In any given year, college graduates earn an average of $14,000 more per year than high school graduates—over the course of a lifetime, that adds up. But finding the right college is about more than putting yourself on the right career track. College is a time of unprecedented personal growth, an opportunity to discover who you are and who you want to become. If you're a student who is active in volunteer or public work, college can be a place to deepen your commitment to community and social change. At the right school, you can find teachers, administrators, and peers to help you connect your desire to learn with your desire to make the world a better place.

True, college can be about getting a job. But college can be much more than that. It can be about getting the knowledge and tools to change the world.

With more than 3,000 colleges and universities in the United States, choosing the right school to meet this greater need may seem like an overwhelming task. You'll have days where you're tempted to take all those glossy college brochures that you keep getting, shove them deep into your closet, and not think about which college to attend—or even whether to attend college—for as long as possible. But if you take a little time to learn about your options, you'll be able select a few good matches and apply to those schools without drowning in information overload or succumbing to stress. The more you know about what to look for in a school, the easier your choices will be.

If you're reading this book, you probably want to dedicate a portion of your time at college to making a difference—volunteering in the community, organizing for social justice, working for political change, or studying social problems by taking action to fix them. *Colleges with a Conscience* will give you what you need to know about socially responsible colleges, and it'll help you sift through all those slick college brochures. It offers detailed information about 81 schools—information that goes beyond raw admissions statistics. Behind a school's average SAT scores are programs and opportunities waiting for students—like you—who want more from their college experience than just academic and job training.

It helps to know that colleges aren't only looking for students with top standardized test scores or class rankings. The schools profiled here believe that education should prepare students to be responsible citizens, so they also want students who will substantially add to the campus and to the surrounding community. Students who care about civic responsibility are assets to these schools; if you genuinely want to make a positive change to your society, they'll want to hear from you.

What Is a College with a Conscience? More than Private Gain, the Public Mission

Higher education in the United States has a long history of serving society. From the creation of land-grant institutions (which gave public lands to each state to create universities which, in turn, served that state's citizens) to the G.I. Bill (which opened college admissions to thousands of returning World War II veterans), the higher education system in the U.S. has long maintained what it calls a "public mission." The public mission is a school's conscience, a set of ideals, strategies, and programs going way beyond affordable tuition and quality education—it's the way a college interacts with its neighbors, the way it contributes to building a vibrant and a just democracy.

A college with a conscience has both an administration committed to social responsibility and an active, engaged student body. Education for these schools isn't only about private gain; it's about the public good.

The schools in *Colleges with a Conscience*—ranging from small religious institutions to huge state universities—care deeply about their public missions and actively encourage students to explore socially responsible work. Many have excellent programs that incorporate community work into academic classes, giving students the chance to learn about social issues through direct experience. Others provide scholarships to students who demonstrate commitment to community service; others offer funding for summer internships with nonprofit organizations. Some schools have exceptionally active student bodies, while others make an institutional commitment to student voice. All of them provide opportunities for students to educate themselves about the world's social and political challenges and to play a role in addressing those challenges.

At these schools, you might be able to take an Urban Studies class that connects academic learning with public work to tackle real-world problems such as poverty, hunger, and homelessness. You could take a Marketing class and volunteer to work on an anti-tobacco campaign with local youth. You might try to get more diverse speakers on campus or serve as a student representative on the Board of

Trustees. This book will help you find which school best meets your desire to learn (and have fun) while offering the support and resources to help make the world a better place.

Apathy? What Apathy?

You probably know all the stereotypes about "young people today"—that they're "lazy," "self-centered," and "apathetic." Nothing could be further from the truth. Martin Luther King Jr. once famously said, "Everybody can be great because everybody can serve." Young people are serving their communities in record numbers: According to a national study conducted by the Higher Education Research Institute at UCLA, 83 percent of entering college freshmen participated in volunteer work during their last year of high school, compared with 66 percent in 1989. And a record high level of freshman say there is "a very good chance" they will continue this community involvement by participating in volunteer activities in college. Next time somebody calls your peers apathetic, ask them where they volunteered in high school.

Not only are students asking for it, but community involvement in college is a sound teaching practice, leading to better student learning inside and outside the classroom. It leads to lower dropout rates. It reduces feelings of isolation on campus. It's even been correlated with a longer lifespan!

For good reasons, colleges are responding to students' desire to have their education in college extend beyond the classroom. One of the most obvious and visible examples of college community involvement has been the growth of campus Community Service or Service-Learning Offices. These offices are centralized places on campus where students can learn how to become involved in socially responsible work, whether through classes, volunteer work, or on-campus student groups. Most offices have a director and a staff of student and/or non-student workers who work to connect their campus with the surrounding community in meaningful and reciprocal partnerships. To give you a sense of recent growth in this field: Today, 83 percent of Campus Compact member schools house a Community Service or Service-Learning Office, up from only 50 percent ten years ago.

Community Service or Service-Learning Offices aren't the only way schools are responding to students' desire to get—and stay—civically engaged in college. More and more schools are offering scholarships and financial support to prospective students for community-service work performed in high school. Like we said earlier, those of you reading this book are the types of students that colleges want to recruit, and they're willing to offer financial assistance to get you into their school.

Once you do get in, colleges also offer financial support to help balance out your civically engaged work with your other college responsibilities. Among other things, colleges offer fellowships for community-based research, paid work-study (or serve-study) positions within the community, AmeriCorps community-service positions that help you pay off student loans, and funds to start a club on campus about an issue you care deeply about.

One of the most important educational trends over the past decade has been the emergence of service-learning. Service-learning combines classroom learning with community-based problem-solving. It puts into practice the idea that we learn best by doing. It also neatly combines teaching course content with meaningful contributions to college communities. For example, an environmental engineering course may have students test and report on a local source of water. Or an English class may have students interviewing and writing the oral histories of local elders.

When you're reading through college course catalogues, note whether any courses have a community component. Ask prospective schools how many service-learning courses they offer. With service-learning, your school's community becomes an additional text; you get credit for service in the same way you'd get credit for reading a book as part of the course (credit reflects your mastery of the course content through this experience, as well as your follow-through on your responsibilities to the community). Instructors, and sometimes student teaching assistants, focus on helping you connect your community experience with classroom learning.

Institutional support for service-learning is increasing widely; 88 percent of Campus Compact member campuses offer service-learning courses, up from 66 percent in 1993. These schools often offer dozens of service-learning courses each semester. Other ways schools support community work—including both service-learning and community engagement in other contexts—include facilitating student-led efforts, offering service awards and scholarships, and managing logistics (like liability and transportation). This makes it more likely that service experiences will be successful.

Who's Doing What

Maybe the best way to understand what service-learning actually looks like is by giving a few real examples from schools profiled in this book:

- At the University of Pennsylvania, students in "Learning Math by Teaching Math" teach a series of hands-on activities to local urban high school students and reflect on their teaching experiences, as well as the math they are teaching, with a faculty member and their classmates.

- At the University of Minnesota—Twin Cities, students in a philosophy class practice the concepts of philosophy by participating in a learning exchange, teaching English to new immigrants and learning about the immigrant experience, at a community-education project called the Jane Addams School for Democracy.

- At DePaul University, entering freshman take a Discover Chicago or an Explore Chicago course during their first quarter. Each course involves a community-service component, which introduces students to the diversity, complexity, groups, organizations, and institutions of a large American city. DePaul also offers a minor in Community Service Studies, which allows students to take a sequence of service-learning courses within several disciplines and perspectives.

- At the University of Massachusetts—Amherst, undergraduate students co-teach an anthropology course that includes an alternative spring break to rural Virginia. During their spring break, students from the class work on a range of development projects within the community, including housing repair and demolition. Student leaders lead the reflection sessions and connect these with some of the themes of the course, such as poverty, racism, classism, community, and power.

- At Portland State University, a school whose motto is "Let Knowledge Serve the City," students take a six-credit, community-based-learning capstone course designed to apply what students they have learned in their major to a real community problem in teams under the guidance of a faculty member.

- At Southwest Missouri State University, political science students serve as special court liaisons to the public and meet with the circuit court judge to review certain cases before the court.

- At Tufts University, in a course entitled "Producing Television Programs for Social Change," students create actual video stories on social issues, learning the skills of camera work, editing, interviewing, production, and publicity by creating socially responsible programs for the public.

Of course, community service isn't the only way that students can get involved. College campuses have a long history of political and social activism. The past few years have seen an increase in political involvement on campus—after many years of decline—along with a broadening of the term "political." While you might think of politics as what someone does in Washington, DC or your state capital, politics encompass the everyday activities you do to make social change. Students have led anti-sweatshop campaigns at schools like University of Wisconsin—Madison and Duke University. They've led fair-trade-coffee campaigns at schools like University of California—Los Angeles, Georgetown, and St. Edwards. They've led voter registration efforts on hundreds of campuses, including University of Montana, San Francisco State University, and Stanford University. They've organized public dialogues on important public issues at campuses such as Macalester College, the University of Rhode Island, and Southwest Missouri State University. Politics, in this sense, is the everyday work of ordinary people creating a public world together.

About This Book

You've probably been using many factors in your search for the right school—factors like cost, size, setting, and academic focus. A school's social conscience is one more important factor. *Colleges with a Conscience* will help you find a school that won't force you to choose between your desire to make the world a better place and your desire to succeed in college.

Your time at college can be civically isolating, without much interaction with the surrounding community or pressing global, national, or local issues, but it doesn't have to be that way. This book will help pop the bubble of isolation and connect you with the issues you care about.

We're also hoping to applaud the good work being done by colleges and give visibility to their civic efforts—public work that's often invisible to people outside of higher education. We hope *Colleges with a Conscience* gives more people on campus the space and opportunities to put their public missions into practice.

Why These Schools?

Sifting through thousands of outstanding colleges and universities across the country for this new book was a difficult task. Colleges and universities have long been hubs for active and engaged citizens determined to make a contribution to their communities. Over the past two decades, these institutions of higher education have refocused on their civic mission by pioneering new strategies for creating more engaged citizens. Recent research has identified innovative methods and highlighted best practices for connecting classroom experience to community engagement.

In identifying schools that have been the most successful at cultivating civic engagement—and to determine our final list of schools for this book—we gathered input from a diverse array of sources. Our process can be broken down into three steps: first, soliciting nominations from experts in the field; second, collecting data from nominated schools; and third, evaluating that data to make our final decisions.

During the first phase of our research, we solicited nominations from dozens of organizations and individuals with expertise in campus community service and student civic engagement (see list on page 10). Care was taken to ensure that responding organizations and individuals had a national perspective. Among these groups were national student organizations focusing on community service, political activism, or advocacy; higher-education associations; national networks of colleges and universities; and higher-education support organizations. Our sample included groups across the political and social spectrum. We also relied heavily on the knowledge of Campus Compact state offices (located in 30 states) and the Campus Compact Consulting Corps, a group of faculty from around the country with expertise in civic engagement and service-learning.

These respondents were asked to nominate schools based on five specific issue areas: 1) engaged student bodies, 2) support for student activism, 3) scholarships and admissions practices that reward students who do community service, 4) support for service-learning, and 5) strong student voice in governance. We tallied the nominations to determine which schools were perceived to be the most civically engaged, and priority was given to schools that were mentioned by multiple sources in multiple categories.

Next we narrowed down the nominated schools to a short list of approximately 100, taking into account the need for diversity in geographic region, campus size, setting (urban/rural), and institutional type (public/private). Through a detailed faculty/staff application and a survey of civically engaged students on each campus, we developed a well-rounded picture of the state of civic engagement on each campus. All told, we received 96 staff surveys and more than 4,600 student surveys.

Selecting the final list of schools wasn't easy. We did our best to manage the complex mix of factors that make each of these schools unique. While we believe that the 81 schools profiled here exemplify the best of civically engaged higher education, hundreds of other colleges and universities may meet your needs. If you're interested in a school that isn't listed in this book, you can still use the information here to guide your search: Why not ask them some of the questions in the "Smart Research" section, for example? They may or may not have all the answers, but you're sure to learn a lot either way. And hey—if they do have all the answers, they may very well be in a future edition of *Colleges with a Conscience*.

The following organizations helped us assemble the list of schools profiled in this book. We've include each organization's website; these groups can help you stay active once you get to college, so when you're checking out schools, see if these organizations have a chapter or local presence on campus. (The selection of the final campuses was done entirely by Campus Compact and The Princeton Review, so responsibility for any omissions lies with us.)

Bonner Foundation: www.bonner.org

Bread for the World: www.bread.org

Campus Greens: www.campusgreens.org

Choice USA: www.choiceusa.org

Circle K: www.circlek.org

Click Back America: www.clickbackamerica.org

College Democrats of America: www.collegedems.com

College Republicans National Committee: www.crnc.org

Feminist Majority Foundation: www.feminist.org

Feminist Majority Leadership Alliances (FMLA): www.feministcampus.org

Free the Planet: www.freetheplanet.org

Global Justice: www.globaljusticenow.org

Habitat for Humanity: www.habitat.org

Hillel: www.hillel.org

Idealist on Campus: www.idealistoncampus.org

National Association for the Advancement of Colored People (NAACP): www.naacp.org

National Student Coalition Against Hunger and Homelessness (NSCAHH): www.nscahh.org

New England Resource Center for Higher Education (NERCHE): www.nerche.org

Oxfam America: www.oxfamamerica.org

Philadelphia Higher Education Network For Neighborhood Development (PHENND): www.upenn.edu/ccp/PHENND.html

Project 540: www.project540.org

Student Empowerment Training Project: www.trainings.org

Student Environmental Action Coalition (SEAC): www.seac.org

Student Public Interest Research Groups (PIRGs): www.studentpirgs.org

Students For Academic Freedom: www.studentsforacademicfreedom.org

Reading the School Profiles

Each of the schools profiled in Colleges with a Conscience makes a commitment to its public mission, and each has its own unique set of strengths. Some of the schools—such as the University of Pennsylvania, Georgetown University, Metropolitan State University, or Portland State University—are committed to creating reciprocal partners with their neighbors. Other schools, such as Harvard University, have less of an institutional commitment to the community, but engaged student bodies at these schools force the college administration to address its public mission. Some schools, such as Antioch College, are committed to student voice in decision-making. Others are committed to service-learning, with schools such as IUPUI, DePaul, and Bentley College offering scholarships for students dedicated to community service. Finally, some schools, such as Rockford College, recruit students who are committed to making a difference.

Each school profile includes school contact information and the contact information of the community-service or service-learning office on campus. Profiles also include sidebars to give you the vital statistics you need to get started, with information about the student body, size, cost, academics, location, and selectivity of each school. Remember, don't rule out schools that don't exactly match your SAT scores or class rank. Grades and test scores are only two of many factors. Your involvement in service during high school will give you an advantage.

The profiles are divided into the following sections:

GETTING INVOLVED

This section lets you know where to go first to get involved on campus. Since it can often take years to find your place on campus, this section is your shortcut to social change. Schools often have activities fairs where student activist and community service groups recruit new members, community-service days during orientation, or other innovative ways to help you get involved in your first year. We'll let you know what each campus does here.

CAMPUS CULTURE OF ENGAGEMENT

One way to take a litmus test of a campus' atmosphere is to check out the campus bulletin boards. If flyers for political lectures, volunteer opportunities, and upcoming protests wallpaper the main campus buildings, you know the student body is active and passionate. Similarly, if there are lots of avenues for incoming students to get involved, there's a good chance that the campus has strong support for students' socially responsible activities. In this section, students give you a firsthand look at the ins and outs of campus culture. They will let you know whether, how, and why students are involved in various activities—and how the campus puts social responsibility into practice.

CONNECTING SERVICE WITH THE CLASSROOM

Imagine planning a community mural for your college art class or testing for lead contamination at a local park in a chemistry class. Students report that the most powerful way to learn about social issues is to approach through both academic texts and personal experience. Many of the schools in this book have excellent service-learning courses in which the syllabus includes both readings and experiential research. These courses require participants to complete a volunteer program or a community research project and to reflect on the connection between these projects and the course content. In these classes, your experiences outside of class form the basis for class discussion and learning.

IMPACT ON COMMUNITY AND STUDENTS

Do a handful of isolated students shout slogans on a corner to no avail? How effective and energetic are the people involved with civic work on campus? This section describes the impact of each school both on campus and in the local community. We'll let you know what programs are well-run and where you can make the most impact.

STUDENT FINANCIAL SUPPORT FOR SERVICES

All of the colleges profiled in Colleges with a Conscience have at least a few opportunities for exceptionally involved student to receive much-needed financial support for their efforts. This support can range from a small stipend for a handful of exceptional students pursuing community service projects to substantial scholarships for students with a history of socially responsible activities.

Keep the following points in mind when you're researching financial support for your civically engaged activities at school:

1. Students who participate in community service will have a much easier time finding financial resources than will students with an interest in political or environmental activism.

2. If you receive a financial-aid package that includes a work-study requirement, ask to work at a nonprofit organization like a domestic-violence shelter or a literacy program instead of the campus café. All colleges and universities in the United States are legally required to place at least seven percent of work-study students at nonprofit, government, or community-based organizations, and many colleges in this book are well above the minimum.

3. In addition to the resources at each school, a range of national scholarships are available for students with a history of community service or civic leadership. Check www.actionforchange.org/getrecognized for a list of scholarships and awards.

Smart Research

This book is a starting point in the college search, but certainly not the end. The "Smart Research" section will guide you through the process and help you to find more information about schools that interest you, including those not in this book. "Smart Research" will provide you with the most up-to-date tips on what to look for on colleges' websites, campus tours, and brochures to find the right school for you.

WAIT! Before You Read Colleges with a Conscience from Cover to Cover...

The first step in choosing a college or university is to reflect on your own expectations and priorities to determine what you want from a college. What do you imagine yourself doing during a typical week at college? What skills and experiences do you want to take away from college? Your process of self-reflection will probably be ongoing—it's rare to know what exactly what you want right away.

Thinking Outside the Book

In addition to reading books like this, it's a good idea to talk to your guidance counselor or check out any number of online resources including those found on The Princeton Review's website (www.PrincetonReview.com).

Think about what type of socially conscious work appeals to you. Are you a political junkie, a dedicated environmentalist, a community-service hero, or something else? The self-assessment guide below will help you determine which types of socially responsible activities and programs interest you, and it'll give you some hints about what you to look for in a college. Once you have a better idea of that, you'll be able to get the most out of this book.

Self-Assessment: Education for What?

Personal reflection is the first and most important step in the process of selecting the right school. Start by asking yourself some of these questions (we suggest using a journal or get together with a small group of friends to discuss these issues).

WHERE I WANT TO BE

- Do I want to go to school in a rural or urban environment?

- Do I want a big or a small school?

- Do I want a public or a private school?

- What am I interested in studying?

HOW I WANT TO MAKE A DIFFERENCE

- What activities, groups, or clubs have I been involved with in high school or in my community?

- Do I want to go to a school that offers similar types of opportunities?

- Did I have courses in high school that included a community-service component?

- Did I have courses that discussed community issues?

- Would I like to take courses like this in college?

- What issues do I care most about?

- What problems in society do I most want to address?

- What communities do I belong to now?

- What communities would I like to stay involved with or become involved with when I get to college? (These may be place-based, issue-based, or identity-based communities.)

- Am I thinking about a specific career goal?

- Can I think of ways that this career affects people's lives?

- What may be some experiences that would develop my ability to connect my career with society?

WHAT TO LOOK FOR

- Do I want to study the issues I care about in class, work on them in my spare time, or both? If you're most interested in class study, pay special attention to the descriptions of majors or departments in the school's literature. If you're interested in taking action outside of class, look for community service and activism clubs in descriptions of student life. If you're interested in combining coursework and action, look for service-learning or community-based education opportunities in course and curriculum descriptions.

- Do I want to be involved in conventional politics, community service, activism, or some combination of the three? If politics interests you, keep an eye out for political campus organizations (College Republicans, College Democrats, Campus Greens), debate clubs, active student government, and democracy-related organizations (such as Democracy Matters). If you're interested in activism, look for issue-oriented organizations or campaigns (such as environmental action organizations, fair-trade campaigns, Students for Academic Freedom, or living-wage campaigns). If you're interested in community service, look for service clubs and Greek organizations to find volunteer, community service, or service-learning offices on campus. If you want to combine the three, seek out a campus with diverse opportunities and a culture that values each type of involvement.

- Am I most interested in international causes or community issues in this country? If you're interested in international service and activism, look carefully at a campus' study-abroad offices and the opportunities they provide; also look for student organizations that address international issues or academic departments that specialize in the issues you care about. For domestic issues, see if a campus has any AmeriCorps positions available and read about the programs at the campus volunteer or community service office.

These questions and tips are only a start. What other questions are important to you in your college decision-making process?

Don't Forget: Organize!

One final piece of advice: No college is going to be perfect. Even the most socially responsible school has barriers to creating change. Overcoming such barriers—or at least learning to deal with them—is part of the growth and learning process in college. In organizing for change, it's often said that until you hear "No," you haven't even started. So whether you're trying to get your school to provide transportation to a volunteer site, a voting booth on campus, or a living wage to its employees, challenging your school to practice democracy—and not just preach it—is part of your great task as a student.

College students have always been on the front lines of social change, fighting for issues ranging from civil rights to equal rights for women to the movement to end apartheid in South Africa. Today's campaigns for social change are no different—students are leaders in activities like the anti-sweatshop and living-wage campaigns, advocates for inclusion and democratic dialogues on campus, and chief organizers in the current community-service movement. But with all of these efforts, at times you must raise your voice not in solo, but as part of a chorus. Being in college is a priceless opportunity to get involved, join others, and organize to make change. The schools profiled in *Colleges with a Conscience* are places where your voice, your ability to organize, and your opportunities to get involved will be nourished and cultivated.

One great resource filled with tools for organizing on campus is Campus Compact's *Raise Your Voice – Student Action for Change* website—*www.action-forchange.org*.

Terms to Know

It's sometimes difficult to track down all the opportunities on campus without knowing the buzzwords. Here are a few common phrases you'll come across in this book and on campuses.

Community Service: action taken to meet the needs of others and better the community as a whole.

Service-Learning: a form of experiential education that includes community work as an additional "text" that can deepen classroom learning through conversation and reflection. Service-learning—in which classes incorporate a community service component—has three basic characteristics:

- It is based on the experience of meeting needs in the community.

- It incorporates reflection and academic learning.

- It contributes to students' interest in and understanding of community life.

Civic Engagement: Project 540, a high school initiative, gives perhaps the most straightforward definition of civic engagement: "Adding one's voice to community conversations. Advocacy on behalf of others. Participation in public life. Encouraging other people to participate in public life. Joining in common work that promotes the well being of everyone."

Smart Research: Seeking Socially Responsible Schools

You'll be doing enough research once you begin college—we want the research you do to get in to be easy, efficient, and smart. The "Smart Research" techniques described in this chapter will provide tools, resources, and guidance on how to find colleges that are committed to community service, activism, and the political life of their students. We'll also set you up with the tools to investigate those colleges and universities you're interested in. So far, you're one step ahead—you're looking in this book.

What Does a College with a Conscience Look Like?

The colleges profiled here give a good picture of what a college with a conscience looks like. But when you look at schools we haven't profiled, what things should you look for? This section provides a list of some of the most important things a campus that honors service and civic engagement will probably have. Look over the list, identify those things that are most important to you, and keep them in mind throughout the rest of this section. The rest of this chapter will give you an idea of where to find the indicators below:

Teaching and Learning: Do courses on campus have a community-based component that adds to the content and subject being addressed (service-learning courses)? Is gaining knowledge through experience (experiential education) accepted and encouraged? Is community-based education only available in one or two majors, or is service-learning available across campus through many different kinds of courses?

A Solid Foundation: Do visible and easily accessible offices, clubs, or people on campus assist faculty and students with community-based teaching and learning or other extra-curricular service experiences?

Support for Student Projects and Clubs: Are there many or few student-led clubs and organizations on campus? How easily can students begin new organizations and obtain funding for these activities on campus?

External Relations: How is the relationship between the campus and the community? Are there projects, activities, or other efforts designed to foster interaction between community members and students or for community building in local neighborhoods? Are campus events and facilities (gyms, libraries, theater) open to community members?

Student Voice: Do students have a voice in campus life and affairs? How active is the student council or student government? What is their role on campus? Are there other modes for student voice: student newspapers, student radio, student television, or campus-supported student websites? Do students sit on any official university committees?

Campus Leadership: Do the president, dean of students, dean of academics, and other campus administrators discuss the civic and economic purposes of going to college? Do they mention service activities in letters or press releases? Are service, activism, or student political activity highlighted in any admissions materials?

Mission and Purpose: Does the college or university's public mission explicitly mention its commitment to the civic purposes of higher education and higher education's responsibility to educate for democratic participation? What aspects of its mission value service or civic activities?

Commitment to Diversity: Does the campus illustrate a clear commitment to diversity on campus and the community? Are diversity and community initiatives connected? Are there multicultural centers on campus?

Mining the College Publications

If you are a high school junior or senior, you're probably being flooded by mail from various colleges and universities. After enough of these pamphlets, postcards, view books, and catalogues, colleges and universities all begin to look pretty much the same. To help you identify campuses that are strong on service and supportive of student activism, gather a list of core values that are most important to you (see the self-assessment earlier in the Introduction). Having that checklist by your side will help you pinpoint them when they appear in college materials. Seek out those important values as you review the college brochures, take notes, and write down questions for use later in the college search.

Where to Look and What to Look For

Some campuses draw a lot of attention to their support for service and activism, featuring these activities prominently in their publications. The ideal campus would feature the issues you care about and examples of how their students are addressing those issues on the front cover of every publication they produce. The academics section would show service-learning classes engaged in coursework and community work. The student-life section would show students raising awareness about pressing community or social issues. The residential-life section would focus on living and learning halls based on service and education. Overall, the publication would highlight how social responsibility is embraced and encouraged throughout all levels of the campus.

However, in most cases—even at very socially responsible campuses—these activities get buried in their promotional materials. When you're reviewing campus publications, look for service-oriented clubs and organizations in "student" or "campus-life" sections. Later, it's a good idea to get in touch with the students running those organizations, especially those that interest you most, and talk about how the campus supports their work.

You'll notice that in the earlier sections of this book, the profiled campuses list offices for community service, service-learning, or community involvement (or something to that effect). Look for references to these specific offices, because like any office on campus, they symbolize an investment in service and a commitment to civic engagement. These offices can be goldmines of information about a campuses social responsibility. If you find one of these on campus, call them up for more information; they'll probably have their own brochures and publicity materials about their programs.

More and more professors are incorporating service into their classes. Chemistry students are doing water testing in local communities. English students are doing literacy work at local community centers. Accounting students are helping non-profits with financial planning. To see if a campus offers these types of opportunities, look in sections on "Academics." Check out the majors that interest you for mention of these types of classes. You may need to look at a master list (a "course catalogue") of all the classes offered at a campus. Classes involving service-learning may also fall under their own category such as "inter-disciplinary," so keep an eye out for those distinctions. Some schools even offer a major or minor in public or community service, peace and justice, gender studies—the list of opportunities goes on and on.

Mining the College Website

By now, you've probably filed about 80 percent of the mail from colleges and universities in the recycle bin, and you're getting a better idea of the schools you're interested in. Keep your list long for now; you have plenty of time, and sometimes schools are better or worse than they appear on paper. Pull out your self-assessment again and get online: College websites can give you a view inside their campus.

The ideal campus website, like the ideal publication, would highlight a diverse set of options and activities that illustrate the importance of society and community to the life of its students. One example of a great college website includes a poll on the front page that gives students a chance to voice their opinion on issues of local community or global concern, photos of students involved in community work, and articles about educating for democracy programs or preparing students as active citizens. Websites often emphasize a wide variety of things; look for these signs, but don't base your entire decision on a school's site. Too often, the people doing the most exciting community work are simply too busy to promote it online.

It's perhaps easiest to begin at the "search" option on a campus website and hunt for the term that best fits your interest: service, activism, civic engagement, community involvement, politics. This broad search will undoubtedly turn up plenty of irrelevant links, but this is also a benefit. Casting a wide net in your initial search will unearth information across the campus, in courses and in clubs, in offices and in residence halls. You'll find interesting connections that never would have surfaced by searching specifically at any one part of the website; you'll also spot references to service, activism, or student politics in campus newsletters or administration speeches.

Once you've tracked down a few of those leads, you can be a little more targeted. The admissions website can be a good gateway to find vital statistics and other information about campus. Start there and get a feel for life on campus. What does the admissions office highlight: the success of soccer team, the new environmental-studies lab, an alternative spring break with Habitat for Humanity? The admissions office tries to present a very specific view of the university, and reviewing their website can provide insight into overall campus values.

Most campuses have a center or an office dedicated to community service (sometimes located within another office like the student-life office, residence-life office, chaplains office, or leadership-development office); the community-service office's website should highlight any activities being sponsored or organized. You'll also get a sense for the school's community-service priorities: Are the bulk of the activities political (like rallies and voter registration), service-oriented (community clean-up or collecting food for a local shelter), focused on fundraising (walk-a-thons, bake sales), or a balanced mixture of all of these? Find a set of activities that are a good match for your interests.

But by all means, don't stop there. Service-learning and activism can sometimes be buried under other programs. Visit the websites of departments and majors you're interested in. Many departments list the courses they're offering—check to see if those courses include service or focus on social issues that you're concerned with (e.g., The Literature of Homelessness, History of Globalization, Computer Science and the Digital Divide). In addition, department websites may give profiles of faculty members. You may be working with these people for four years, so you owe it to yourself to read their bios or personal websites.

The student- or campus-life sections of the website should list campus groups, and many of these groups will likely have their own websites. Again, research these organizations. Do any fit your interests? What activities do they sponsor? If they have websites, send an inquiry e-mail to the student leaders of a particular group and ask them specific questions. Finally, visit the student newspaper online to read up on hot issues on campus.

You might also get a sense for the campus by looking at local websites for the village, town, or city. Check out local newspapers for stories about the campuses impact on the local community.

Other Web Resources

National student organizations and issue organizations related to your interests may recommend colleges that offer outstanding programs in that particular area. Some examples include

- Campus Compact Member Schools: www.compact.org

- Campus Greens: www.campusgreens.org

- Circle K Club Locator: www.circlek.org

- College Democrats of America Local Chapters: www.collegedems.com

- College Republican National Committee Local and State Organizations: www.crnc.org

- Idealist on Campus: www.idealistoncampus.org

- Mother Jones Magazine Top Ten Activist Campuses: www.mother-jones.com

- National Student Campaign Against Hunger and Homelessness: www.nscahh.org

- OXFAM Change Initiative Sites: www.oxfamamerica.org

- The Bonner Foundation Campus Programs: www.bonner.org

- United for Peace and Justice Campuses Who Have Passed Resolutions for Peace: www.unitedforpeace.org

- Young America's Foundation: www.yaf.org

Other more traditional places to find information include, of course, The Princeton Review's website (www.PrincetonReview.com), Atlantic Monthly (www.theatlantic.com), and The College Board (www.collegeboard.com).

Making Contact
THE ADMISSIONS OFFICE

After you have perused the publications and visited a college's website, arm yourself with questions and contact the admissions offices at those schools you're interested in. Contrary to popular belief, admissions offices are your greatest allies in the college-search process. Don't just think of them as the people reviewing your application; think of them as people trying to sell you their university. Admissions counselors tend to know more about the campus than anyone else, and if they don't know something, they'll find the answer.

Begin with a call or an e-mail to the admissions office. Most likely, you'll be connected with an admissions counselor who oversees recruiting in your area. Introduce yourself briefly and talk about your service experience. Make this brief and focused—you want to give them a sense of who you are and what you are looking for, but this isn't the time to detail your entire volunteer history (you can do that on your application). With a little information about your interests, the admissions counselor will be much better equipped to answer your questions and focus their answers to your interests. Use your self-assessment to guide you.

After you have introduced yourself and your experience, ask questions about the campus; again, be as specific as possible. If you're planning on a campus visit, some questions might be better left for your visit. On the other hand, there's almost no such thing as too many questions; admissions counselors appreciate when students are excited and interested in their college or university. You might want to ask an admissions representative some service-opportunity-related questions like:

- What are the service opportunities on your campus? What service organizations are active on your campus? Are most of these student-led or faculty/staff initiated?

- Do you specifically give more weight to prospective students with significant service experiences? Does your campus offer any scholarships for students who have been involved in community service?

- Is your institution a member of Campus Compact or any other organizations focused on service-learning, political, or community engagement?

- How does your campus get along with its surrounding community? In what ways does your campus create partnerships with its surrounding community?

- Are there service activities during school breaks, such as an alternative spring break? If so, are some away from the college or university, or are they primarily focused on the local community?

- Is your campus very political? Are there often student rallies? Are current issues debated in the campus newspaper?

- Do professors use community service as part of their courses? Is there a public-service or community-service major or minor? What departments are most active in the community? Is there an opportunity for me to design my own classes or majors around service-learning or community service?

Keep in mind that if an admissions representative can't readily answer every question on the spot; most will offer to look them up and get back to you. Now is a good time to request any other publications or other materials that would address your specific issues. Some universities keep detailed files of newspaper clippings and other reports that offer specific perspectives on their campus.

Admissions offices can also be matchmakers, putting you in touch with professors and students who share your interests. Ask them to help you make appointments with faculty, staff, and students during your campus visit, or ask them to give your e-mail to possible contacts on campus. At the very least, they'll point you in the right direction.

THE FINANCIAL-AID OFFICE

You or your parents will most likely be in touch with the financial-aid office, either by phone or during a campus visit. Luckily, there are plenty of opportunities for students who are interested in service, activism, and civic engagement to do what they love and help pay for school at the same time. Check out the "Student Financial Support for Service" sections of the college profiles for an idea of how some campuses give financial incentives to students engaged in service and community work. During your visit (or visits) to the financial-aid office, consider asking the following questions about financial support for service that may help you pay for college—and give you an idea of the college's overall commitment to community service.

- Most colleges and university receive federal work-study funds from the federal government to pay for student employees. The law says that at least seven percent of this money must be spent to pay students for community service-related activities. Ask the financial-aid office is there is community-service federal work study available at their campus.

- Some colleges and universities offer scholarships of varying amounts for students involved with substantial community service in high school. Ask the Financial Aid Office if any such scholarships are available at their campus.

- AmeriCorps members receive an education award at the end of their term of service to help pay for college. Some colleges and universities will "match" or double the AmeriCorps education award for students. Ask the Financial Aid Office if their campus will match an education award from AmeriCorps (you can search for these schools at www.life-timeofservice.org, the AmeriCorps alumni page).

THE CAMPUS VISIT

When you talk to an admissions representative, you may want to set up a meeting, interview, tour, or other campus visit. Although they're not necessary, campus visits can be an important—and revealing—part of your college search. Some campuses give one-on-one tours, some will take you around campus in a bus with other families, and others might not offer campus tours at all. Some schools offer individual interviews, some require interviews, and others simply hold information sessions en masse.

If you're planning to do a campus visit, keep some of these tips in mind.

- If you have a full or half-day to spend at a campus, ask the admissions office to set up a classroom visit, preferably with a service-learning class. This is one of the best ways to get a feel for life on campus, because it puts you side-by-side with students and gives you a chance to ask them and professors any questions you might have. If you can't set this up with the admissions office, call the community-service or service-learning office directly, tell them what day you're visiting, and ask to sit in on a class.

- A visit to the community-service or service-learning center on campus is an important step in understanding how a campus supports and encourages student civic engagement. This office can provide you with examples of student- and faculty-led work as well as describe local community organizations that are involved with issues you care about. Also, they may help you visit student groups on campus that are focused on your interests.

- Whether you do an official college tour or not, take an hour to wander through the building where your major interest is housed (e.g., the engineering building or the English hall) and walk through the student center. Here's your opportunity to get a firsthand look at what's happening on campus. Flyers—check dining halls, student centers, mail rooms, bulletin boards, and hallway walls—offer a wealth of knowledge regarding upcoming events, student organizations, and hot issues; check out the speakers coming to campus or service events planned. Also, be sure to pick up a copy of the student-run newspaper, and look for an alternative newspaper. Some admissions offices will have copies of these available; others will hide them away. If you can, give the campus radio station a listen while you're at it.

- The admissions office is a great resource, but they have a certain message they're trying to get across. Now's your chance to seek out a variety of opinions besides those of the admissions office. Talk to the students you meet on your campus visit. Chat with the students working at the mail room, or in the library, or stop people in the hall of the student center. Try talking to a professor or the administrative staff in the department(s) you're interested in. These conversations will give you a variety of perspectives on what campus life is like. Some people will talk frankly about their likes and dislikes; others may not be so willing, but it's worth it to try.

- If time permits, explore the surrounding town. Eat a meal off campus. Talk to the people shopping or working in local stores about the role the college or university plays in the town. Do people in the community have positive associations? Or are there negative feelings towards the campus and the students? It's also worth asking at the admissions or service office about area alumni who are working at local nonprofits or involved in other civic work in the local community. As people who've been exposed to the campus from both sides, they can offer a unique perspective on the campus' support of students and community.

PLANNING YOUR TRIP

If you have a half-day to visit:

- Go to the admissions office and get a campus tour.

- Spend some time walking around campus and talk with students.

- Stop by the community service office.

If you have a full day to visit:

- Go to the admissions office, have an interview, and get a campus tour.

- Spend some time walking around campus, hang out in the students' union, and talk with students.

- Make an appointment to talk with staff at the community-service office.

- See a service-learning class in action.

- Spend some time checking out the neighborhood around campus.

If you can visit overnight:

- Go to the admissions office, have an interview, and get a campus tour.

- Spend some time walking around campus, hang out in the students' union, and talk with students.

- Make an appointment to talk with staff at the community-service office.

- See a service-learning class in action.

- Spend some time checking out the neighborhood around campus.

- Sit in on another, more traditional class in your interest area.

- Consider setting up an overnight on campus with a student leader if the admissions office will help.

And if you can't do a campus visit:

- Explore the school's websites.

- Set up some time for a phone interview with the admissions office.

- Ask them to connect you with a professor who teaches service-learning or teaches in the department you are interested in.

- Ask if a student who works in the admissions office would be willing to talk.

- Contact the community-service office and talk to a staff person there.

SO YOU'VE BEEN ACCEPTED...

For many students, the real college search happens between March 1st and May 1st, when acceptance letters are sent out and it's time to make the final choice. Admissions offices want the students they accept, and they're sometimes willing to work to get you there. Look for activities planned specifically for accepted students—these "open houses" are often in-depth and aimed at showing both the academic and the extra-curricular sides of campus.

With that letter in your hand, you might have a different perspective on things. Once you know they want you, you can ask the tough questions and start looking at the entire campus through a magnifying glass. These tough questions shouldn't be sole deciding factors for any college or university, but they're telling indicators of a campus' level of commitment to social responsibility, both globally and in its own community. You'll probably have to seek out sources beyond the admissions office to get answers; where applicable, we've tried to identify who, besides the admissions office, might be able to answer these questions.

- Throughout the 1990s, college students around the country rallied to get their campuses to stop putting their name on sweatshop-produced clothing. Campus bookstores and athletics departments across the country changed their buying practices to meet the demands of students. Does the campus you're considering still support sweatshop labor by selling clothes made in unjust labor conditions? Talk to the bookstore or check out the Workers Rights Coalition (www.workersrights.org) or United Students Against Sweatshops (www.studentsagainstsweatshops.org).

- In the 1980s, a major student movement arose to stop campuses from investing in companies that supported apartheid in South Africa. Many campuses hire investment firms to handle their endowments; this money is often invested in a wide range of companies involved in unjust labor practices, weapons manufacturing, and unsustainable environmental practices. Does the college or university invest its money in socially responsible companies? Are there socially responsible investment options for faculty and staff or for alumni who wish to donate? Ask around at financial or bursars offices on campus, the benefits office, development office, or the alumni and parent-programs office.

- Universities are often exempt from paying property taxes for the land they own. Therefore, in many places both urban and rural, massive swaths of land owned by the campus reduce the amount of possible money provided to local secondary schools, social agencies, and police, fire and rescue organizations. By way of contributing to the local economy, some campuses voluntarily pay taxes on some of their land. Does the university pay property taxes? Are there other ways that the campus supports services in the local community? Does the university fund community programs like local charter schools or a community health center? Ask financial or bursars offices on campus along with local town or city budget offices.

- Historically, campuses have been prized as spaces for open and informed dialogue on some of the most pressing issues of the time. Does the campus offer space for local community groups to meet? Has a diverse group of speakers visited campuses from different political, ethnic, and cultural backgrounds? Ask the student-activities coordinator, the director of the student union, or inquire at the community-service office.

GLOSSARY OF HIGHER EDUCATION

Many incoming students arrive on campus with little or no knowledge of how a college or university works, the power dynamics at play, or who does what. By the time most students have really learned to navigate the campus, knowing how to leverage support and create change, they're often juniors and seniors.

Language will always be a powerful ally. With this glossary, we hope to arm you with the information needed to identify your comrades—and challenges—early on in your college career. You'll benefit not only from understanding the different structures and organizational roles on campus, but by using a common language, you'll speak on equal turf as college staff, presidents, and faculty.

The Glossary, while short, is split up into two sections: People and Places. More detailed definitions to many of these words—and sources from which these definitions were drawn—can be found at Campus Compact's Glossary (www.compact.org/aboutcc/glossary/glossary.html).

GLOSSARY: PLACES

Admissions Office

The admissions office often becomes irrelevant to most students after they've been accepted. However, since no other office is quite so image-conscious—with service-learning being added to many college-ranking lists—it's a good place to find out exactly which service-learning activities a campus offers.

Community-Service / Service-Learning / Community-Based-Learning Office

A person, group, or office on campus specializing in coordinating partnerships and activities between campus and community. Traditionally, these offices were defined by which part of campus they resided in (student activities versus academic affairs). Some campuses have two such offices, one on either side of this divide. The staff at these offices can aid in nearly every aspect of your college search.

Multicultural Office

Many campuses have dedicated offices that act as centers for issues surrounding race, ethnicity, and diversity. These hubs are important to helping all members of the campus community participate fully in civic and community life.

GLOSSARY: PEOPLE

Board of Directors / Trustees

The decision-making group in charge of general management at a college or university. Often composed of high-profile national leaders, alumni, and other university-connected people, they're often tapped for their experience and leadership in management or fundraising. Boards may have one or two student representatives (who may or may not have voting power).

Board of Regents

A group which governs the state university system, vocational-technical centers, community colleges, and—in some states—other programs relating to postsecondary education. Members are appointed by the governor and confirmed by the state senate. Students target this group at times in their efforts to change in overall policy, such as sweatshop-labor issues or living-wage campaigns.

Chief Academic Officers (CAOs)

Also known as Provost, Academic Dean, Dean of Faculty, or Vice-President of Academic Affairs, the CAO is the primary administrator in charge of a school's academic core. CAOs and their staff oversee department chairs; approve new classes, minors, and majors; and review cases of academically struggling students. They're instrumental in implementing change in the educational structure of a course, department, or campus. CAOs commonly have discretionary funds—private budgets which they can distribute for any project they deem worthy.

Community-Service Director / Service-Learning Director

Community-Service Directors (CSDs) are full- or part-time coordinators for community involvement by students, faculty, and other campus members. CSDs sometimes work out of a dedicated office; other times, they're housed within a major or other center on campus.

Dean of Students

The Dean of Students is the primary administrator in charge of a school's student-life side. Contemporary colleges and universities are split between student affairs and academic affairs—and odd division, considering that students rarely draw a line between their academic lives and their personal interests. It's useful to understand which departments answer to which dean—the Dean of Students or the CAO (or Academic Dean). Community-service offices are often under a Dean of Students' jurisdiction, whereas service-learning offices are the responsibility of academic affairs.

Department Chair

A tenured faculty member who has taken a leadership role in a department. The department chair approves department courses, manages the department budget, supervises other faculty members' workload, and ensures that the department's activities are consistent with university requirements.

President (or Chancellor)

College and university presidents have a wide variety of roles, and how much emphasis is placed on which roles depends on individual presidents. A president's major responsibilities include representing the university, fund-raising, and overall decision-making for the campus. The president reports to the Board of Trustees.

Attending a College with a Conscience

As you enter college, you're joining millions of students across the nation who view college as much, much more than a mere rung on the career ladder. American higher education has a long radical and revolutionary tradition of educating people for the good of society. Congratulations on your choice to seek out a college that lives up to this tradition. If you follow your heart, you'll find a great match and make the most of your college years.

COLLEGES WITH A CONSCIENCE:
THE SCHOOLS

ALLEGHENY COLLEGE

OFFICE OF ADMISSIONS, ALLEGHENY COLLEGE, MEADVILLE, PA 16335

ADMISSIONS: 814-332-4351 • FAX: 814-337-0431 • FINANCIAL AID: 800-835-7780

E-MAIL: ADMISSIONS@ALLEGHENY.EDU • WEBSITE: WWW.ALLEGHENY.EDU

CAMPUS LIFE

Type of school	private
Environment	rural

STUDENTS

Total undergrad enrollment	1,929
% male/female	48/52
% from out of state	34
% from public high school	83
% live on campus	75
% African American	1
% Asian	3
% Caucasian	93
% Hispanic	1
% international	1
# of countries represented	31

ACADEMICS

Calendar	semester
Student/faculty ratio	12:1
% profs teaching UG courses	100
% classes taught by TAs	0
Most common reg class size	10-19

MOST POPULAR MAJORS

biology/biological sciences
political science and government
psychology

Getting Involved

One Allegheny student gives a friendly warning: "No matter who you are, Allegheny is going to pull you into some kind of activism role—be it community service, civic engagement, or leadership."

The school's service structure makes for unity and cooperation, with all civic-engagement programs under an umbrella organization called the Coordinating Council for Civic Engagement. Programs within this "central clearing house" include the Center for Political Participation (dedicated to fostering democracy), the Center for Economic and Environmental Development (committed to boosting awareness about environmental sustainability), the Community Service and Service-Learning Program (coordinator of Allegheny's community partnerships) in the Allegheny College Center for Experiential Learning (ACCEL), and the Values, Ethics and Social Action (VESA) minor. The Writing at Allegheny Program encompasses a variety of campus publications which address civic engagement. *French Creek*, one of those publications, is "the only national journal for undergraduate environmental writers."

The Allegheny College Center for Experiential Learning (ACCEL) is the locus of service-learning at Allegheny. "Students don't have to try hard to find something to be involved in. If they want to help but just don't know where, they can head to the ACCEL office and get matched up with an organization."

In general, students agree that "for a campus of less than 2,000 students, Allegheny offers an amazing variety and number of opportunities. The college strives to make service-learning fit into any schedule and any set of interests." "The amount of funding and the support of the faculty and staff at the school are big plusses."

Campus Culture of Engagement

Students report that "all you have to do is have your eyes open and you'll find something that interests you." "Incorporating civic engagment into the classroom from the first year familiarizes students with the process and gives them the confidence to seek service-learning on their own in later years at Allegheny." Service opportunities also travel readily by word of mouth, ominipresent posters, and an electronic mailing list. According to one student's slightly oxymoronic metaphor, "like a good disease, it spreads."

Engagement is the norm—or, according to one student, "definitely a really cool thing to do." "From the day I set foot on campus, I knew this campus was very involved in the community and in society in general, by just meeting other people. Offhand, I can't think of one person that doesn't do some kind of civic engagement." Another explains that "Allegheny is not a self-centered campus like some of the schools I've been to and seen. Instead, Allegheny is a humble instituition that breeds open-mindedness and unity."

Connecting Service with the Classroom

"The beauty of Allegheny College is that service work and civic engagement are built directly into the class. From the initial First-Year Seminar up to 500-level classes, Allegheny professors strive for students to make a difference in the College and city-wide communities."

The administration reports that in the last two years, 38 service-learning courses were taught by faculty from 15 different departments. The Values, Ethics, and

Social Action (VESA) minor, supported by faculty from the Departments of Psychology, Philosophy and Religious Studies, and Economics, particularly aims to strengthen "the curricular layer of Allegheny's commitment to the local community," connecting the dots between classes and service. "In the introductory VESA course, students contract for 24 to 36 hours of service. In the capstone seminar, students do approximately 12 hours of community service plus an activism project." A student participant explains, "Civic engagement as my minor (VESA) has opened me up to a whole new way of learning. It had shown me issues that I never knew existed nor could ever imagine that I, my own individual self, could make an impact [on] in anyone's life."

Other academic departments provide additional opportunities for experiential learning. The Psychology department offers experience-based internships working with inmates in a minimum-security prison, and the Geology department offers students the opportunity to teach science to local middle schoolers. "The Theater/Communication Arts outreach program has sponsored student-made documentaries for Women's Services of Crawford County, for the Association of Retarded Citizens, and about children from Meadville's low-income neighborhoods for the United Communities Independence Programs (UCIP)."

Impact on Community and Students

"Almost all of the nonprofit orginizations in town have some sort of student participation," reports one student, "from the women's shelter to Tamarak Wildlife Rehabilitation to Bethesda Youth Center." Service takes place "all over campus, all over the town of Meadville and all over the country."

The administration cites the Center for Economic and Environmental Development (CEED) as an indicative reflection of student involvement with the surrounding community. "CEED has more than 250 community partners and has held workshops (largely prepared and organized by students) that have reached more than 15,000 people. A modest sampling of current and past internships include Creek Connections, where interns helped develop learning modules that focus on watershed awareness for local middle and high schools; the Arts & Environment Initiative, where interns created artwork for the Green Room at Crawford County Industrial Park and for two projects at PennDOT (Signs & Flowers and Read Between the Signs); and the Meadville Community Energy Project, where interns promote energy sustainability and education in the community through various activities and presentations."

As one student says, "Allegheny has given me the opportunity to really understand what I want to contribute to in my life and how I can go about doing just that."

Student Financial Support for Service

Allegheny provides the necessary funds to support its stated commitment to community service. The George J. Barco Student Aid Fund provides financial assistance to students "with demonstrated qualities of high moral character and genuine interest in service to the community and others."

The Betsy Dotson, Esquire '74 Experiential Learning Fund assists students involved in experiential-learning opportunities in the Washington, DC area."

The Alyson M. Lawendowski '93 Community Service Fund helps provide scholarships to students "to enable them to participate in national or statewide conferences on community service, service-learning and civic engagement. In addition, this fund provides an annual award to a student who has made outstanding contributions to community service."

And finally, The AmeriCorps Bonner Leader program "mobilizes up to 20 student service leaders who each complete 900 hours of service over a two-year period, including at least one summer. These students are compensated for their service through the Corporation for National and Community Service, federal work-study funds, and a summer stipend from Allegheny College."

SELECTIVITY

# of applicants	3,279
% of applicants accepted	74
% of acceptees attending	27
# accepting a place on wait list	122
% admitted from wait list	4

FRESHMAN PROFILE

Range SAT Verbal	550-650
Range SAT Math	560-650
Range ACT Composite	23-28
Minimum Paper TOEFL	550
Minimum Computer TOEFL	213
Average HS GPA	3.74
% graduated top 10% of class	43
% graduated top 25% of class	72
% graduated top 50% of class	94

DEADLINES

Regular admission	2/15
Regular notification by	4/1
Nonfall registration?	yes

FINANCIAL FACTS

% frosh rec. need-based scholarship or grant aid	72
% UG rec. need-based scholarship or grant aid	72
% frosh rec. need-based self-help aid	58
% UG rec. need-based self-help aid	60
% frosh rec. any financial aid	98
% UG rec. any financial aid	96

ALMA COLLEGE

614 WEST SUPERIOR STREET, ALMA, MI 48801-1599

ADMISSIONS: 989-463-7139 • **FAX:** 989-463-7057 • **FINANCIAL AID:** 989-463-7347

E-MAIL: ADMISSIONS@ALMA.EDU • **WEBSITE:** WWW.ALMA.EDU

CAMPUS LIFE

Type of school	private
Environment	rural

STUDENTS

Total undergrad enrollment	1,214
% male/female	42/58
% from out of state	4
% from public high school	93
% live on campus	84
% African American	2
% Asian	1
% Caucasian	94
% Hispanic	1
% international	1
# of countries represented	7

ACADEMICS

Calendar	4-4-1
Student/faculty ratio	15:1
% profs teaching UG courses	100
% classes taught by TAs	0
Most common lab size	10-19
Most common reg class size	10-19

MOST POPULAR MAJORS

business administration/management
education
psychology

Getting Involved

Alma College's nexus of civic engagement is the Service Learning Office, which supports most of the campus's prominent programs: AmeriCa Reads/AmeriCa Counts Tutoring, Community Service Work-Study, Service Week, Service Learning House, Student Community Action Network (through Michigan Campus Compact), and the Tutoring Network.

The Discovering Vocation Internship Program, which offers students "the opportunity to work in congregations, mission agencies, and nonprofit organizations," promises to help "all members of the college community discover their calling"—with a distinct focus on "populations or specific issues of public concern." The program delivers students to nonprofit institutions according to their areas of interest then matches them with supervising professional staff members who are "prepared to mentor and supervise throughout their career exploration." Placement sites include Hands to Honduras, The Society for Protecting the Rights of Children, and Texas Rural Legal Aid.

Honors courses and the McGregor Program highlight the potential for civic awareness within "the values of a liberal arts education." The McGregor preterm institute "brings the top first-year students together with a team of three faculty and three Alma College seniors for a dialogue-based institute aimed at examining some of society's most pressing questions." Each year, the institute addresses a theme of pressing social relevance, such as AIDS/HIV, bio-terrorism, human cloning, and global warming; "recent honors offerings have explored issues like the science of environmental politics and liberal education in a complex world."

Campus Culture of Engagement

According to students, Alma's spirit of social responsibility brings the campus together "in a united front of civic duty." Civic engagement opportunities are "incredibly diverse for a small campus" and "service groups are well supported, well attended, and well financed."

Upon arriving at Alma, students are introduced to service opportunities through a Volunteerism Fair and Service Week. Continued awareness of options comes easily: "Not only are there posters everywhere, but the school is small enough and people are friendly enough that they come and seek you out."

Student service organizations abound. "There are very few groups on campus that do not raise money for a philanthropy or work to educate the campus on the issue that they are most dedicated to," and groups do "a wonderful job of making sure that the message that they are trying to spread reaches the whole campus, not just those who are already interested in the issue." Student organizations that actively engage in service and civic engagement include Alpha Phi Omega, Amnesty International, Chemistry Club-Future Generations, Habitat for Humanity, and Students Against Sweatshops. In addition, "many of the Greek social organizations have active philanthropic initiatives."

For students particularly interested in making service a part of their everyday lives, the Service Learning House houses seven students each year and provides space for meetings and service events. Students can also participate in "Alternative Break," during which they travel to different parts of the country to pursue service initiatives.

Connecting Service with the Classroom

Approximately 10 to 19 academic service-learning courses are offered each term, with over 580 students participating in these courses each year. Well over half of the past six graduating classes have participated in at least one service-learning course and just under half of Alma College faculty incorporate service-learning to some extent.

The Service Learning Office provides support for sixteen disciplines with service components, ranging from Chemistry, to Dance, to Environmental Studies. Students report a wide range of experiences made possible by Alma's service-learning classes: "visiting an elderly widow to make a memoir of the life she and her husband had together," traveling to Mexico "to research the status of the environment," and serving "in a church in downtown Detroit working at their soup kitchen/outreach program."

Impact on Community and Students

According to students, there's "a very close feeling between the community and Alma College." "Instead of being surrounded by the typical scene of college students all of the time," says one, "our service projects allow us to become part of the community and get to know people younger and older than us."

Alma College maintains community partnerships with various nonprofit, service constituencies, and a partnership with the Alma Public Schools has flourished over the past six years: "We have moved from a few volunteer tutors in the Middle School homework help room to expanding tutoring opportunities through AmeriCa Reads/AmeriCa Counts, mentor and leadership positions with the Explore After-School Program, community service work-study positions related to education, and academic service learning courses providing service in recreation, science, music, and other related disciplines. Alma College has been awarded a two-year AmeriCorps VISTA position to begin July 2005. This position will focus on strengthening service experiences and opportunities for college students while promoting the formal service network in partnership with the Alma Public Schools and their programs."

The Pine River Superfund Citizen Task Force is "recognized by the Environment Protection Agency as the official Community Advisory Group overseeing the superfund site and supporting the clean-up of the Pine River. Faculty and students from various disciplines, including biology, chemistry, economics, geology, political science, public affairs, and theater, have been intricately involved in various aspects of this Community Advisory Group (CAG) and its Technical Advisory Group (TAG)." Student engagement projects include community interviews, economic research, educational outreach to special populations, and analysis studies on the contamination in the Pine River.

In addition, prior McGregor-funded initiatives have resulted in a "program grant to implement a campus-wide Aids Awareness campaign. The Michigan AIDS Walk is now an annual event for Alpha Phi Omega."

Student Financial Support for Service

Alma offers one service-related scholarship: The Mary Jansen Opra Memorial Endowed Scholarship, given annually to a junior or senior who is "caring, compassionate, friendly and helpful." The Service Learning Coordinator and the Service Learning Task Force co-chairs coordinate the selection of the student recipient. "In addition, Alma College has participated in the Michigan Service Scholars Program [since] October 2004. Students completing 300 hours of service in youth organizations or with nonprofits through the strengthening of volunteerism are eligible to receive a $1,000 AmeriCorps education award."

ANTIOCH COLLEGE

795 LIVERMORE STREET, YELLOW SPRINGS, OH 45387

ADMISSIONS: 937-769-1100 • FAX: 937-769-1111 • FINANCIAL AID: 800-543-9436

E-MAIL: ADMISSIONS@ANTIOCH-COLLEGE.EDU • WEBSITE: WWW.ANTIOCH-COLLEGE.EDU

CAMPUS LIFE

Type of school	private
Environment	rural

STUDENTS

Total undergrad enrollment	488
% male/female	39/61
% from out of state	71
% live on campus	95
% African American	3
% Asian	1
% Caucasian	49
% Hispanic	2
% Native American	1
% international	3

ACADEMICS

Calendar	trimester
Student/faculty ratio	11:1
% profs teaching UG courses	100
% classes taught by TAs	0
Most common reg class size	<10

Getting Involved

Civic engagement is not so much a choice at Antioch as it is a prerequisite, with more than 80 percent of the student population performing service in return for financial aid. Before arriving at Antioch, many students learn that they have been chosen to participate in the Community Responsibility Scholars program or the Bonner Scholars Program, through which they receive funding in return for completing hours of community service. At orientation, they get acquainted with the Center for Community Learning, the "central resource area for any student, faculty, or staff interested in community service opportunities, service-learning, and the Bonner Scholars program." While some students express frustration with the Center's chronic "lack of funding" and understaffing, the general sentiment is positive: The Center is "staffed by amazing people that not only hook us up with awesome community service," but also "get to know us and make sure that we are applying what we learn from community service in the classroom and vice versa."

Orientation provides ample introduction to service opportunities available and creates a dynamic of "mentorship between first years and older students." The best way to find out about service opportunities is by talking to other students on the close-knit campus, whether through conversation, electronic mailing lists, flyers, mealtime announcements, or at the weekly community meeting.

Campus Culture of Engagement

There's no doubt about it: Antioch is a campus of activists whose strong convictions—for better and worse—dominate the tenor of the environment. One student surmises, "I don't think there is a single Antioch student whose education hasn't been shaped by the ideals of service and engagement." "Community service is everywhere," according to another student. "You can't miss it." Says yet another: "From the time that a student begins his or her education at Antioch, they discover that service and civic responsibility are held in high esteem by the entire community."

Community Government is a good venue for students to integrate progressive values into all aspects of Antioch existence. "Students have voting seats on all college legislative committees, and Community Government is responsible for the large majority of social and cultural aspects of the college." It allows students to work side-by-side with faculty and staff with responsibilities ranging from "hiring decisions, to implementing the socially responsible investment policy, to making the difficult decisions involved in creating the college budget."

Antioch is ripe with opportunities for civic engagement on campus and in local areas. When not fulfilling service requirements off-campus as part of the celebrated "co-op" program, many students find themselves "working at a daycare, in the Antioch garden, visiting elders of Yellow Springs, Ohio" or at "local radio stations, art museums, and the alternative library." Many students find themselves working "five to ten hours a week helping out or running offices."

Connecting Service with the Classroom

According to the administration, "service-learning is bound in with the college's mission," and "virtually all students at Antioch do at least one four-month cooperative education experience in a nonprofit organization," leading one student to call the school "a boot camp for nonprofits." In order to earn their degrees, Antioch students must complete five term-long co-ops ("full-time work/service experiences") in conjunction with their coursework—usually entailing nonprofit or activist labor: "Unions, Quakers, human rights work, organic farming, you name it." For at least one of these co-ops, students must pick up and move to another part of the country or world, a process that can be both exhilarating and exhausting. "It looks like a hippie-dippie school, but it requires intestines of steel and absolute fearlessness to hurl yourself into the unknown, find a job, find a place to live, make friends, and move back to Ohio four months later. It's hard. It's intense."

In the fall of 2006, Antioch will introduce "a new curriculum, which will draw all first-year students into Experiential Learning Communities. 60 students taking the equivalent of three classes together, drawn around a common theme, will be able to do significant fieldwork related to the learning community's topic."

Impact on Community and Students

Students praise Antioch's service requirements for taking them "outside the realm of the theoretical" and exposing them to communities far less privileged than their own: "Education ceases to be a silly game played in a bubble of wealth and privilege when it starts to engage the real world." Antioch "has over 150 community partners with which students work" with types of organizations including "literacy, environment, arts, homelessness, hunger, community renewal, alternative media, and domestic violence prevention."

The administration cites: "One first-year student worked with Love Makes a Family during his work semester as a grant writer and liaison to other nonprofits. Another student performed service at a local domestic violence shelter, educating school-aged children on violence prevention, staffing the hotline, and working with clients. The shelter has since hired her."

Students express overall satisfaction with the strength of the service programs, but concede that "it is difficult to build continuity with people coming and going all the time," and "there are so many different sites to volunteer at that it's less organized than it could be." The school's passionate service-oriented climate can be divisive: "When there are differing opinions on campus, it can get ugly. We take our stands very seriously." Political conviction "tends to define our friends and foes."

Student Financial Support for Service

The majority of students at Antioch receive service-related financial aid. According to Antioch, The Community Responsibility Scholars are selected from the incoming class each year based on past demonstration of community involvement. In exchange for a $5,000 to $10,000 renewable annual tuition reduction, recipients commit to 50 hours per term of active participation in the college's governance system, select work-study positions, and/or other local community agencies.

The Bonner Scholars Program selects ten students per year from the incoming class to receive a service scholarship which includes $1,050 per semester for academic expenses during study semesters and a total of $5,500 for up to three off-campus service jobs (co-ops). In addition, students receive a $1,600 loan reduction if they complete all of their requirements. Bonner students perform 140 hours of service (predominantly off-campus) during study semesters and around 500 hours during co-op terms. The Bonner Scholars are selected (from very low-income families) for their interest in service.

In addition, Antioch administers half-time AmeriCorps service terms through the Bonner foundation. Nine hundred hours of service over two years is awarded with a $2,362.50 Education Award, which can be used to pay higher-education tuition or loans.

SELECTIVITY

# of applicants	458
% of applicants accepted	59
% of acceptees attending	34

FRESHMAN PROFILE

Range SAT Verbal	550-670
Range SAT Math	490-620
Range ACT Composite	21-26
Minimum Paper TOEFL	525
Average HS GPA	3.10
% graduated top 10% of class	18
% graduated top 25% of class	29
% graduated top 50% of class	63

DEADLINES

Regular notification by	rolling
Nonfall registration?	yes

Augsburg College

2211 Riverside Avenue South, Minneapolis, MN 55454

Admissions: 612-330-1001 • **Fax:** 612-330-1590 • **Financial Aid:** 612-330-1046

E-mail: admissions@augsburg.edu • **Website:** www.augsburg.edu

CAMPUS LIFE

Type of school	private
Environment	town

STUDENTS

Total undergrad	
enrollment	2,720
% male/female	43/57
% from out of state	10
% live on campus	33
% African American	5
% Asian	3
% Caucasian	68
% Hispanic	2
% Native American	1
% international	1
# of countries represented	33

ACADEMICS

Calendar	semesters;
weekend college is on trimesters	
Student/faculty ratio	16:1
% profs teaching	
UG courses	99
% classes taught by TAs	0
Most common lab size	10-19
Most common	
reg class size	10-19

MOST POPULAR MAJORS

business administration/management
communications studies/speech
communication and rhetoric
education

Getting Involved

The Center for Service, Work, and Learning (CSWL) supports civic engagement at Augsburg with two staff members devoted exclusively to service-learning and community involvement. One student praised the "dedicated staff" that is "always able to match students up with internships that connect their academic internships and a service-learning component. They know the city very well and thus are able to find great opportunities."

Service is a requirement during students' first year at Augsburg: "All first-year students participate in a community-service project as part of first-year orientation in order to learn about the city of Minneapolis and as a way to help students understand Augsburg' Macalester Colleges motto, 'Education for Service.'" During the first-year, in a half-semester course known on campus as "Aug Sem," students work in groups of 15 with a faculty member and a student-orientation leader. They travel to specific service sites including "homeless shelters, nursing homes, schools, a community radio station, and a variety of other community organizations." Augsburg maintains over 50 long-term community partnerships, "most of which are in our immediate neighborhood."

Campus Culture of Engagement

Students find service opportunities "readily available" and "well-run," and they tend to agree that "making community service a requirement for the liberal arts is a real strength" of Augsburg.

Students learn about service opportunities through "the traditional recruitment methods such as the activities fair and flyers," but more often "find out about student groups and service activities through social networks." Student organizations actively recruit for their efforts: Augsburg Community Link is a student-led community service organization that "connects the students of Augsburg College to the community in which they live, locally, and nationally," coordinating volunteer programs within the Twin Cities and coordinating excursions to national leadership conferences.

The Coalition for Student Activism (CSA) is based on the idea that "before becoming active, one must first be truly educated on the topic," and so brings "speakers and activities about social justice, racism, environmental issues" to the Augsburg Campus. In 2003, in response to the Iraq War, the group "organized a walk-out, protest, and teach-in," and "promoted discussion activities the entire year to get the word out and provide a place for people to discuss their views." The group also sponsors a day of "social-justice celebration" each year.

Connecting Service with the Classroom

Augsburg is a national leader in service-learning and offers service-learning courses in every discipline: "Each semester, 20 to 25 Augsburg courses include a service-learning component that offers students in the course the opportunity to participate in a service experience. Sites are carefully selected by the coordinator of the service-learning program in conjunction with faculty members to help connect community service experiences to classroom learning." More than 500 students per year participate in a service-learning course. Example courses include Journalism (students each have a social-issue "beat"—such as homelessness, literacy, or domestic abuse—that they follow throughout the semester by working with an organization that addresses the chosen issue), Research Methods (students do a research project for a nonprofit organization; "a project done by an Augsburg student for Habitat for Humanity became a national model"), Environment and Behavior (students subsidize courses with work at environmental organizations such as Citizens for a Better Environment, Clean Water Action, and MPIRG), and History of Social Movements (students work "in women's organizations, peace and justice organizations, and environmental groups in order to understand how the current issues relate to past struggles").

Impact on Community and Students

While Augsburg's proximity to low-income areas might make it less desirable to some students, those actively engaged with service see it as a boon: "I believe that Augsburg has access to some of the best internships and volunteer opportunities because of its inner-city location. Not only does the mission of the school promote involvement, but the location facilitates it."

One student reported a diverse service itinerary: "My freshman year, I went to a inner-city puppet theater and helped to clean up the theater and learned the history of the building. I just took a class that required work and study in one of the neighborhoods in Minneapolis to find out what forces change the community. In one of my other classes, I worked for a nonprofit peace-focused organization (where I will have an internship next year), helping them organize peace rallies and communication during the start of the war."

Through the Campus Kitchen Project, a popular group with an outpost on the Augsburg campus, "volunteers prepare meals on campus, then deliver them to agencies and individuals in the community." Volunteers also teach "basic food preparation and culinary skills to unemployed and underemployed men and women" through the Culinary Arts Job Training Program, a subsidiary of the CKP.

More than 100 Augsburg students each semester tutor children and adults at public schools, literacy centers, and neighborhood organizations in Minneapolis. A particularly "strong partnership has developed between a new K–10 public charter school and Augsburg college." Cedar Riverside Community School "is located in a low-income high-rise three blocks from campus" and has attracted Augsburg student involvement in fields such as Graphic Design, History, and Information Systems. Through the Music department, 18 children "came to campus once a week for private piano lessons and group discussion. The school had no music program prior to this partnership."

Student Financial Support for Service

The Marina Christensen Justice Award is given at commencement each year to "one senior who represents Augsburg's motto, 'Education for Service,' and who has demonstrated a dedication to the kind of community involvement and professional life exemplified by Marina Christensen Justice, a 1965 alumna." Augsburg also offers a Community Scholars Program (CAPS) and a $5,000-per-year scholarship for anyone in the country who is a graduate of AmeriCorps*VISTA.

SELECTIVITY

# of applicants	954
% of applicants accepted	79
% of acceptees attending	48

FRESHMAN PROFILE

Range SAT Verbal	490-610
Range SAT Math	485-605
Range ACT Composite	20-25
Minimum Paper TOEFL	550
Minimum Computer TOEFL	213
Average HS GPA	3.26
% graduated top 10% of class	16
% graduated top 25% of class	36
% graduated top 50% of class	68

DEADLINES

Regular admission	8/15
Regular notification by	as soon as app recv'd
Nonfall registration?	yes

FINANCIAL FACTS

Annual tuition	$20,260
Room and board	$6,080
Books and supplies	$1,000
Required fees	$498
% frosh rec. need-based scholarship or grant aid	65
% UG rec. need-based scholarship or grant aid	56
% frosh rec. need-based self-help aid	52
% UG rec. need-based self-help aid	53
% frosh rec. any financial aid	90
% UG rec. any financial aid	76

BATES COLLEGE

23 CAMPUS AVENUE, LINDHOLM HOUSE, LEWISTON, ME 04240

ADMISSIONS: 207-786-6000 • **FAX:** 207-786-6025 • **FINANCIAL AID:** 207-786-6096

WEBSITE: WWW.BATES.EDU

CAMPUS LIFE

Type of school	private
Environment	village

STUDENTS

Total undergrad enrollment	1,743
% male/female	49/51
% from out of state	88
% from public high school	55
% live on campus	90
% African American	2
% Asian	4
% Caucasian	83
% Hispanic	3
% international	6
# of countries represented	72

ACADEMICS

Calendar	4-4-1
Student/faculty ratio	10:1
% profs teaching UG courses	100
% classes taught by TAs	0
Most common lab size	10-19
Most common reg class size	10-19

MOST POPULAR MAJORS
economics
political science and government
psychology

Getting Involved

The Center for Service-Learning is where much of Bates' socially-conscious action happens. The Center, which was established eight years ago "to integrate service into the intellectual and academic life of the College," reflects what the administration cites as its guiding humanitarian philosophy: "Since the College's founding in 1855 by abolitionists, values of egalitarianism, service, and social justice have been central to Bates' mission. The connection of learning to action and the connection of the intellectual life to the world beyond Bates are a part of that mission." Students applaud the Center's powers that be: "The strengths of the civic engagement efforts on the Bates Campus are the people who head the Center for Service Learning," says one student. "They are very dedicated individuals, and their dedication has drawn in some amazing students to lead projects and to further promote the programs."

Though Bates already offers an array of service-learning and civic-engagement opportunities, the future promises to get even brighter. One student cheerily reports that the college has received funding to consolidate and expand its civic-engagement efforts in order to "build stronger and closer bridges between scholarly and student research, community-service learning, and students and community members." This newly endowed Harward Center for Community Partnerships will serve as an umbrella organization for Bates' connections with the Lewiston-Auburn community.

In addition to the service-learning coordinated by the center—which tends to outshine other avenues of civic engagement by most student accounts—the college offers a Student Fellows Program "run exclusively by student leaders selected to work with the community to develop volunteer opportunities" and to "coordinate volunteer fairs and a two-day, pre-orientation community service project for incoming first-year students."

Campus Culture of Engagement

Bates may be a high-ranking school populated by the standard fare of ambitious achievers, but its students are about more than just pulling all-nighters in the library: "Batesies are busy people—academically, athletically, socially—but make time to do service and be involved in the community they call home for four years."

The opportunities for civic engagement, service, and activism at Bates College are "endless," "inspiring," and "extremely powerful." Reports one impassioned student, "Bates will provide you with the cognitive and social tools to change your life and the world around you for the better. You will learn to take action and make effective and meaningful change. Along the way, you will establish great relationships with other dedicated students, staff, professors, and community members."

In addition to the school's service-learning program, student coalitions flourish. "There are very active social justice groups on campus such as the New World Coalition, Environmental Coalition, Friends of Fair Labor, The Women's Resource Center, OUTfront, and many other multicultural organizations." On- and off-campus student-led projects include "voter registration, homelessness advocacy, solidarity economics, anti-capitalist creative economy work, soup kitchens, community gardens, community bike workshops, and the list goes on and on."

Connecting Service with the Classroom

At Bates, "the willingness of the professors to begin conversations or projects which encourage civic engagement is a major strength." One student even says "I learned more out of school than in the classroom."

The administration reports that "over half of our student body has participated in some type of service project" through classes offered by many different departments and programs, with projects ranging from coursework to independent study abroad to senior theses. In addition, "community-based research opportunities with faculty are available," and "we offer a variety of funding sources for summer service-learning research and projects, which students can design and use anywhere in the world."

By way of example of Bates' classroom/community-service synergy is this student's experience: "My freshman year in college, I took a course called 'Fieldwork in American Cultural Studies.' I chose to research the life of low-income single mothers, and so aside from writing my term paper with library resources only, I inserted several diary entries and critical analyses of my experience working with my mentoree. This not only strengthened my arguments, but it also deepened my understanding of and augmented my interest in the welfare state."

Another student reports, "In the Psychology department, seniors are encouraged to conduct service-learning theses in which they can work with local citizens. This includes working with the parents of an autistic child to come up with strategies to improve their child's behavioral skills at home. After engaging and completing such a huge project, the student masters the issue under study (i.e., autism), the broader issues that surround it (i.e., family distress, money), and contributes to the solution."

Impact on Community and Students

Bates' spirit of engagement has a profound influence on-campus and off. Students appreciate the ways in which their classes provide context for their work. "Before I enrolled at Bates, I was always involved in my community. I worked at soup kitchens, ran can drives, but I never really stopped to think about the broader, ideological issues behind why there was poverty in the first place and what I could do to fix the problem rather than just assuage it. Bates did that for me."

Bates maintains "a sincere and committed relationship" with surrounding Lewiston Auburn. Last year, Bates students worked with over 175 community organizations and service learning institutions extending from surrounding neighborhoods to Cape Town, South Africa. One example is the partnership with the Lewiston Housing Authority, which "presents opportunities for students to undertake volunteer and service-learning projects with a neighborhood health clinic, an after-school program for children, a family literacy program, and a program to prevent child abuse."

One student "will be teaching elementary school in New York City next year, a decision that was inspired by my extensive service-learning experiences with children while enrolled in classes such as advanced developmental psychology, where we were required to conduct extensive evaluations of Head Start childrens' social, cognitive, and emotional development and triangulate and discuss our findings with the classroom teachers."

Student Financial Support for Service

Though Bates does not have specific scholarships set aside for service-oriented students, it is dedicated to funding students' service projects: "Bates has grant money available on a competitive basis to support students as they undertake summer service-learning and research projects, which can be local or global in scope. During the academic year, students who are eligible for federal work-study funding can apply to earn money working for community nonprofit organizations of their choice."

SELECTIVITY

# of applicants	4,098
% of applicants accepted	30
% of acceptees attending	38
# accepting a place on wait list	1,055
% admitted from wait list	10

FRESHMAN PROFILE

Range SAT Verbal	630-710
Range SAT Math	670-710
Minimum Paper TOEFL	200
% graduated top 10% of class	65
% graduated top 25% of class	92
% graduated top 50% of class	100

DEADLINES

Regular admission	1/15
Regular notification by	4/1
Nonfall registration?	yes

FINANCIAL FACTS

Books and supplies	$1,750
% frosh rec. need-based scholarship or grant aid	40
% UG rec. need-based scholarship or grant aid	40
% frosh rec. need-based self-help aid	37
% UG rec. need-based self-help aid	39
% frosh rec. any financial aid	40
% UG rec. any financial aid	40

BENTLEY COLLEGE

175 FOREST STREET, WALTHAM, MA 02452-4705

ADMISSIONS: 781-891-2244 • **FAX:** 781-891-3414 • **FINANCIAL AID:** 781-891-3441

E-MAIL: UGADMISSION@BENTLEY.EDU • **WEBSITE:** WWW.BENTLEY.EDU

CAMPUS LIFE

Type of school	private
Environment	village

STUDENTS

Total undergrad enrollment	4,250
% male/female	58/42
% from out of state	45
% from public high school	71
% live on campus	80
% African American	4
% Asian	7
% Caucasian	69
% Hispanic	4
% international	8
# of countries represented	61

ACADEMICS

Calendar	semester
Student/faculty ratio	16:1
% profs teaching UG courses	100
% classes taught by TAs	0
Most common reg class size	20-29

MOST POPULAR MAJORS
accounting
finance
marketing/marketing management

Getting Involved

Civic engagement is—pardon the phrase—the wind beneath Bentley College's wings. The school's deeply revered service-learning program, which has been recently ranked among the 20 best (by a certain annual report from an unnamed source), is one of its main attractions, and the administration allocates staff-and-funding resources accordingly.

The Bentley Service-Learning Center was established in 1990 "to lay the foundation for our students' long-term civic engagement." The center encompasses the school's academic service-learning initiatives as well as its non-academic community-service programs including the scholarship program, the Student Steering Committee, and the Community Work Program. Students report that the "service-learning organization is very vocal and visible" and—with admirable chipperness—"the people that run the office could not be any better!"

Other campus institutions contribute to its service-oriented infrastructure: The Bentley Alliance for Ethics and Social Responsibility—which encompasses the Center for Business Ethics, Cyber Law Center, and the Institute for Women in Leadership—aims to align Bentley's service organizations with "greater awareness of and respect for ethics, service, and social responsibility." Bentley's Spiritual Life Center staff co-sponsors the Alternative Spring Break Program, through which students and faculty embark on annual service-oriented excursions.

Campus Culture of Engagement

While well known for developing future business leaders, the spirit of service at Bentley looms large among students: "Service-learning occurs in so many places I couldn't begin to name them all." Students readily learn about new opportunities through orientation, ever-mentoring upperclassmen, and dedicated staff. "I found out about the service-learning program from my freshmen seminar facilitator, who is a junior at Bentley. My first visit to the office to check out the program was amazing; the head of the program was so enthusiastic and interviewed me on the spot for a position. Her enthusiasm rubbed right off on me." When programs aren't pre-existing, initiating new ones is a cinch: They are "constantly being developed from scratch." One student reports, "I mentor a group of junior high students who participate in an adventure leadership club I started two years ago. Many of my friends have started their own programs and work on a daily basis in the local community."

The student social fabric is woven around service, not just because "many strong friendships are found through engaging in service" and Bentley's sororities and fraternities share a philanthropic mission, but also because students play "a critical role" in the leadership of the Service-Learning Center. Each semester, approximately 35 student "project managers" coordinate community partnerships and help develop new programs.

Connecting Service with the Classroom

Bentley's service-learning projects cross all disciplines in business, arts, and sciences. In the 2003–2004 academic year, about 400 students were engaged each semester in service-learning for credit. According to one student, "the greatest strength of service-learning at Bentley is its diversity and independence. Participation could be anything from tutoring, reading, or math on a weekly basis to helping elderly learn how to use computers." Students can determine the extent to which they want to commit themselves to service and shape their curriculum accordingly. They tend to agree with one student's assessment that "service-learning has been the biggest part of my college education."

Bentley divides its service-learning program into three primary formats. When service-learning is "embedded" within a course, its professor assigns projects in conjunction with a community partner, and students work in groups to address problems faced by the organization. "Fourth-credit format" gives students the option to undertake a 20-hour service project as an additional assignment within a three-credit course. Lastly, through three-credit service-learning internships, students work full time over the course of a semester or summer with an instructor and community partner on more intense—and personalized—service-learning projects. According to one student, "a major strength is our reflection session, which is held to make sure students are making the connection between the academic side of the program and the work they do."

Impact on Community and Students

Bentley students agree that they have "a huge presence" and "wonderful reputation in the greater Waltham community," thanks to the school's intense involvement with approximately 50 off-site services. Bentley's programs give students experience as community leaders: "The communication skills that are gained through the experiences are endless. I'm always trying to get into touch with various heads of programs, teachers, principals, and students. Especially in my role in the elementary school, being a positive role model at all times is key."

Bentley classifies its community projects in four "clusters": technology, skills development, business enhancement, and business and the arts. Noteworthy projects include "working with retired seniors at Brookhaven to teach them the use of e-mail so that they could communicate with their children living in distant locations"; conducting marketing research for the YMCA; and, through the Voluntary Income Tax Assistance program, offering "free assistance in completing income tax returns for individuals who would not otherwise be able to afford to pay for such services."

Student Financial Support for Service

Bentley puts its money where its mouth is, providing substantial financial support for students willing to commit themselves to civic engagement. With one of the oldest and largest service-learning scholarship programs, they currently support eighteen service-learning scholarship students at $5,000 a year, and they plan to have increased that number for the incoming class of September 2004.

Scholarship recipients serve as "the student voice of service-learning across the campus, meeting with faculty both in large group sessions and in individual departments, mentoring students new to service-learning, and developing their own service initiatives. As a condition of the scholarship award, scholars are asked to sign the 'scholarship agreement,' which requires that, by the end of their sophomore year, they will have either developed and implemented a new program for the Bentley Service-Learning Center or assumed responsibility for an already existing service-learning program and enhanced it." In addition, each student scholar is required to take on a 180-hour, three-credit service internship project during their junior or senior year.

SELECTIVITY

# of applicants	5,865
% of applicants accepted	45
% of acceptees attending	36
# accepting a place on wait list	936
% admitted from wait list	2

FRESHMAN PROFILE

Range SAT Verbal	540-620
Range SAT Math	580-660
Range ACT Composite	23-27
Minimum Paper TOEFL	550
Minimum Computer TOEFL	213
% graduated top 10% of class	35
% graduated top 25% of class	76
% graduated top 50% of class	97

DEADLINES

Regular admission	2/1
Regular notification by	4/1
Nonfall registration?	yes

FINANCIAL FACTS

Annual tuition	$25,330
Room and board	$9,860
Books and supplies	$920
Required fees	$214
% frosh rec. need-based scholarship or grant aid	53
% UG rec. need-based scholarship or grant aid	48
% frosh rec. need-based self-help aid	48
% UG rec. need-based self-help aid	48
% frosh rec. any financial aid	75
% UG rec. any financial aid	70

BEREA COLLEGE

CPO 2220, BEREA, KY 40404

ADMISSIONS: 859-985-3500 • **FAX:** 859-985-3512 • **FINANCIAL AID:** 859-985-3310

E-MAIL: ADMISSIONS@BEREA.EDU • **WEBSITE:** WWW.BEREA.EDU

CAMPUS LIFE

Type of school	private
Environment	rural

STUDENTS

Total undergrad	
enrollment	1,514
% male/female	41/59
% from out of state	64
% live on campus	84
% African American	19
% Asian	1
% Caucasian	69
% Hispanic	2
% Native American	1
% international	7
# of countries represented	71

ACADEMICS

Calendar	4-1-4
Student/faculty ratio	11:1
% profs teaching	
UG courses	100
% classes taught by TAs	0
Most common	
reg class size	10-19

MOST POPULAR MAJORS

business administration/management
family and consumer
sciences/human sciences
industrial production
technologies/technicians

Getting Involved

Berea College's dedication to civic engagement has distinctively utopian roots: The college was established in 1855 by radical abolitionists who envisioned "a community where blacks, whites, men, and women could learn together as equals." Since then, the college has been committed "to serving African Americans and people from southern and central Appalachia who could not otherwise afford a college education."

The Center for Excellence in Learning Through Service (CELTS), which coordinates service and service-learning efforts to connect Berea College to the Appalachian Region (and beyond), was founded in 2000 as part of a strategic plan called "Being and Becoming."' The center incorporates three components: "student-led community service through the Labor Program," "service-learning in the curriculum," and "educational opportunity and regional outreach." Students applaud "the great support from the college and its faculty" and advise, "If you want to do something meaningful in your life, go to the CELTS office as soon as you arrive."

Campus Culture of Engagement

Though the CELTS support staff earns high marks from Berea students, students emphasize that service is "student-guided and initiated." "Be prepared. Berea is not just a place to attend on a free academic scholarship, have your own laptop, and earn a paycheck to shop with at Richmond's or Lexington's malls, but an institution in which people work hard every day in educating their minds, fulfilling their personal selves with compassion, commitment, and love through service, labor, and civic engagement."

Berea College "admits only students with high academic potential and limited resources, providing them with the equivalent of a full-tuition scholarship. Every student is required to work at least ten hours per week on campus or in the community." Because community service is built into the labor program, students arrive at Berea expecting intense community involvement. One student engaged in 20 hours of community service per week reports: "When I first received information about Berea College, I was very well informed of the college's impacts on the community and its programs. That's how I decided to come to this school and get involved."

Student-led service programs include Students for Appalachia, Bonner Scholars, Habitat for Humanity, and People Who Care. Though students acknowledge occasional tension surrounding "activism that seems unappealing to the conservative Christian population"—such as abortion rights—campus activism unites more often than it divides. Students recount a recent controversy when "Fred Phelps, a preacher who preaches 'God hates fags,' was due to come here" and "the students organized not a protest, but a love fest the weekend before his arrival. The local churches came out to support this effort, community members came out, and college students came together to reflect the true spirit of a community that bonds together with a common heart and soul." To many students' glee, Phelps ultimately decided not to show.

Connecting Service with the Classroom

Students find no shortage of service opportunities at Berea: "Everything is at your fingertips; just reach out for a taste. You can incorporate service in your classes, participate in internships, study abroads, or independent studies in whatever area interest you have; you can begin new programs if they are not already in place."

Service-learning programs are growing rapidly and include Entrepreneurship for the Public Good (EPG), a two-summer program in which students learn about community development in Appalachian communities. "During the first summer, students attend an eight-week institute on entrepreneurship and leadership, which are taught in part through service-learning. During the second summer, students complete a ten-week entrepreneurial internship with a nonprofit or for-profit business. The goal of the EPG program is to prepare students to use their skills and talents to create a better future for Appalachia and beyond."

Sustainability and Environmental Studies (SENS), a multidisciplinary program including an academic minor, also offers opportunities for civic engagement. "One of the most unique is the Eco-Village, a residential community designed according to principles of sustainability. As residents in the SENS House, students offer environmental education to the campus and community."

One student whose life "has been centered around dealing with hunger and homelessness" dedicates her "academic studies to reasons for poverty, understanding the impoverished family, giving a 'hand up, not a hand out,' as Habitat for Humanity advocates." Through a Berea education, she attests, "we are taught to be reformers."

Impact on Community and Students

Because so many of Berea's students come from the Appalachian region and because the school's mission is explicitly aligned with community betterment, CELTS has developed a close relationship with the surrounding area. Berea maintains about 30 partnerships in the Appalachian region, most of which are located in its home base of Madison County. "Service takes place on and off campus and can take the form of implementing after-school programs about service, driving senior citizens without cars wherever they need to go, or offering free babysitting."

Students' labor requirements—a component of their scholarships—often bring them in close contact with the community. Each year, 15 first-year Bonner Scholars, led by upper-class coordinators, "work in teams to run three of the Boys & Girls Club national after-school programs throughout the year. Each of these programs takes place two afternoons per week at CELTS, on the Berea College campus." Positions vary from ten to 15 hours of commitment a week.

The 10x10 Campaign, an offshoot of the Student Environmental Action Coalition (SEAC), is dedicated to conserving energy on-campus and off. "This program is unique in that it connects concrete steps that students can take with an institutional goal that will benefit the environment for the entire college and surrounding community. It also addresses the Appalachian issue of coal mining that harms the environment, depletes resources, and enriches corporations not based in Appalachia."

Student Financial Support for Service

Berea College is one of 25 colleges with a Bonner Scholars Program which offers "access to education and the opportunity to serve for 60 Berea College students. Bonner Scholars receive funding for summer internships and service trips." The scholarships, which reflect a "special commitment to Appalachian and African American students with limited economic resources," send a powerful message to students who might otherwise feel socially powerless: "As a college that is for students who are from lower incomes and therefore less inclined to participate in the political process, Berea makes many efforts to engage its students."

SELECTIVITY

# of applicants	2,108
% of applicants accepted	27
% of acceptees attending	71

FRESHMAN PROFILE

Range SAT Verbal	490-615
Range SAT Math	510-615
Range ACT Composite	21-26
Minimum Paper TOEFL	500
Minimum Computer TOEFL	173
Average HS GPA	3.40
% graduated top 10% of class	27
% graduated top 25% of class	64
% graduated top 50% of class	92

DEADLINES

Regular admission	4/30
Regular notification by	rolling
Nonfall registration?	yes

FINANCIAL FACTS

Annual tuition	$21,600
Room and board	$4,980
Required fees	$516
% frosh rec. need-based scholarship or grant aid	100
% UG rec. need-based scholarship or grant aid	100
% frosh rec. need-based self-help aid	100
% UG rec. need-based self-help aid	100
% frosh rec. any financial aid	100
% UG rec. any financial aid	100

BRANDEIS UNIVERSITY

415 SOUTH STREET, MS003, WALTHAM, MA 02454

ADMISSIONS: 781-736-3500 • FAX: 781-736-3536 • FINANCIAL AID: 781-736-3700

E-MAIL: SENDINFO@BRANDEIS.EDU • WEBSITE: WWW.BRANDEIS.EDU

CAMPUS LIFE

Type of school	private
Environment	village

STUDENTS

Total undergrad enrollment	3,158
% male/female	44/56
% from out of state	75
% from public high school	70
% live on campus	82
% African American	3
% Asian	8
% Caucasian	67
% Hispanic	3
% international	7
# of countries represented	54

ACADEMICS

Calendar	semester
Student/faculty ratio	8:1
% profs teaching UG courses	100
% classes taught by TAs	0
Most common reg class size	10-19

MOST POPULAR MAJORS

computer and information sciences
and support services
political science and government
psychology

Getting Involved

Brandeis University, "the only non-sectarian institution in higher education sponsored by the American Jewish community," is a sparkplug of social activism. Founded in 1948 "at a time when racial, religious, and ethnic quotas and restricted policies barred talented students from many universities," the school attributes its social conscience to the fact that many of its early founders and faculty were refugees from persecution in Europe. Students attest to the reality of this lofty ideal: The school consistently "attracts speakers, professors, and students interested in challenging the status quo and ruffling a few feathers."

Ask any Brandeis student about civic engagement on campus, and they'll send you to the Waltham Group, "the largest club on campus—which says a lot about the student body and the value it places on action and activism." The campus service organization was founded in 1966 by student leaders affiliated with tenant's rights issues at the Waltham Prospect Terrace Public Housing. The Waltham Group now serves as Brandeis' center for service with over 30 volunteer student coordinators. "Through its tutorial, recreational, and mentoring programs, it responds to the needs of children in the community and assists all community members through volunteer placements in social-service agencies." Students call the group "well-funded and well-organized" and applaud its "incredibly diverse array of opportunities." "Empower yourself," they say, "and the university will back you up."

Campus Culture of Engagement

Brandeis students wear their civic engagement like badges of honor. The student experience is based not just on ubiquitous community service, but also on a propensity for debating issues relating to social justice—and then debating them and debating them again.

Any student "will find it difficult to attend Brandeis and not find out about the numerous activist causes and service opportunities available on campus. Flyers cover lightposts, and community message boards dot campus. It is incredibly easy to get involved with causes for social justice because it is always at the forefront of students' consciousness." The Activities Fair during the first week of orientation is likely the best way to find out about all that is happening on campus: "It's just a fun, crazy scene."

Lively political discourse on the "extremely informed, active, and passionate campus" makes social activism the norm. "I was never really very politically or socially active before college," says one student. "Now I'm a board member for a very active feminist organization that raised $10,000 to send 150 students to the recent March for Women's Lives in DC"

Campus discord does sometimes result from the climate of perpetual ideological discussion: "Racial issues are big here" and were particularly enflamed recently when a student recently wrote "a hurtful racial remark in the student newspaper. There were protests, open forums in which the president of the school and other faculty spoke about the incident and ways to battle future incidents. Three students resigned from the newspaper."

Connecting Service with the Classroom

Service-learning at Brandeis, which spans the disciplines, is supported by academic departments "where social justice and civic engagement is the central mission." The International Center for Ethics, Justice, and Public Life teaches ethical responses to conflict and injustice through on-campus conferences such as "Justice Across Cultures" and a series of annual seminars. The Alan B. Slifka Program in Intercommunal Coexistence, a branch of the Center, offers a master's program in Coexistence and Conflict; an undergraduate minor in Peace, Conflict, and Coexistence Studies; and research and outreach with partner organizations in Sri Lanka and the Middle East. Students also have access to classes at the Heller School of Social Policy and Management, a graduate school and research institution dedicated to studying community needs and social policy.

Undergraduate disciplines embrace service as part of their curriculum. "Just today, for a Visual Culture class I am in, I went with other members of the class to a local middle school to work on art projects with them. Every week throughout this semester we have gone and tried to implement what we learned in the classroom into the art projects." In the Social Change in American Communities class, students embark on a spring semester of "general analysis of social movements and change, combined with research into specific communities across the Eastern U.S., followed by a month-long 'bus trip' in June to these communities. In the following fall semester, students complete research projects and also convene events on campus to share their learning and collective experiences."

Students can also take an intensive seminar called Internships for Community Action and Social Justice, through which they initiate community action projects in Waltham and greater Boston area.

Impact on Community and Students

The Community Service Department maintains partnerships with about 40 community organizations in Waltham and the greater Boston area. Groups include public schools, the Salvation Army, domestic violence organizations, and tenants' organizations. "Brandeis' civic engagement has made me want to learn more for the sake of helping the world more. Students seek solutions and want to give back to the world."

Through the Companions to Elders Program, led by student coordinators at the Waltham Group, volunteers pay weekly visits to private residences and nursing homes. The Big Sibling program, also a part of the Waltham Group, is a community-based mentoring program. "Brandeis student volunteers are matched with children from kindergarten to 6th grade for long-term supportive relationships. The matches visit once a week during the academic year and stay in touch during the summer and winter breaks. Some big siblings have continued to mentor their little siblings through high school and college, and they have even been in attendance at each other's weddings."

The ESL Learning Initiative began in the 2001 with the intention of teaching English to non-native speakers working within Brandeis' food service and facilities. Students tutor campus employees in English so as to prepare them for equivalency diplomas and citizenship.

Student Financial Support for Service

At the time of admission, up to ten merit-based Deans' Awards are given to incoming students who have demonstrated a commitment to service within their communities while in high school. Through the Ethics and Coexistence Student Fellowship Program, sophomore and junior fellows can receive a $3,500 stipend to cover living expenses during an ethically responsible summertime internship. Brandeis also holds an annual awards ceremony, through which more than 50 students receive "prizes ranging from $150 to support of their financial-aid packages for tuition" as reward for their contributions in Leadership and Community Service.

SELECTIVITY

# of applicants	5,831
% of applicants accepted	40
% of acceptees attending	33
# accepting a place on wait list	874
% admitted from wait list	4

FRESHMAN PROFILE

Range SAT Verbal	630-720
Range SAT Math	630-720
Range ACT Composite	28-33
Minimum Paper TOEFL	600
Minimum Computer TOEFL	250
Average HS GPA	3.85
% graduated top 10% of class	71
% graduated top 25% of class	89
% graduated top 50% of class	100

DEADLINES

Regular admission	1/31
Regular notification by	4/15
Nonfall registration?	yes

FINANCIAL FACTS

% frosh rec. need-based scholarship or grant aid	56
% frosh rec. need-based self-help aid	46

BROWN UNIVERSITY

Box 1876, 45 Prospect Street, Providence, RI 02912

Admissions: 401-863-2378 • **Fax:** 401-863-9300 • **Financial Aid:** 401-863-2721

E-mail: admission_undergraduate@brown.edu • **Website:** www.brown.edu

CAMPUS LIFE

Type of school	private
Environment	town

STUDENTS

Total undergrad	
enrollment	5,806
% male/female	46/54
% from out of state	96
% from public high school	60
% live on campus	85
% African American	6
% Asian	13
% Caucasian	51
% Hispanic	6
% Native American	1
% international	6
# of countries represented	72

ACADEMICS

Calendar	semester
Student/faculty ratio	8:1
% profs teaching	
UG courses	100
% classes taught by TAs	13

MOST POPULAR MAJORS

biology/biological sciences
history
international relations and affairs

Getting Involved

Envision your average Ivy League university, and you're likely to picture a campus of go-getters studying around the clock, fueled by ambition and more than just a little narcissism. But things don't work that way at Brown University, and that's why the school has long held its reputation as the most socially aware of the Ivy bunch. According to one student, "the fact that civic engagement is a part of most of the students' lives and not just a few makes Brown's civic engagement really stand out."

The Swearer Center for Public Service is the nexus of community involvement on the Brown campus. Within its confines, students can find resources related to community partnerships, academic initiatives, and funding. Most of the center's programs share a common structure: They are facilitated by a student coordinator and a group of volunteers, who are in turn organized into "learning communities" that encourage critical inquiry alongside civic engagement. The center provides "training and orientation, opportunities for collaborative teaching, and a forum for formal and informal evaluation." In addition, its University/Community Academic Advising Program "offers incoming students the opportunity to think explicitly about connecting the classroom with the community."

Peer leadership is key at the Swearer Center. Student coordinators work with full-time staff in an apprenticeship model and praise the "excellent support network" available to them. "You don't have to be a super self-starter to get involved (though most Brown students are). Just go to the Swearer Center and tell someone about your interests—they can help match you up with a program."

Campus Culture of Engagement

Brown students learn about "countless volunteer opportunities" through activity fairs, where most programs run through the Swearer Center "give information about their programs and recruit potential participants." In addition, "for students of color, there's the Third World Transition Program (TWTP) that supports freshmen Getting Involved in service and activism."

Campus-wide political fervor contributes to a push for civic engagement on campus. "People are always staging demonstrations that have follow-ups with political organizations," and the campus enjoys an avalanche of "public forums around community issues" in the form of "on-campus speakers and dialogues and public art or protests on the main campus green area." When the campus recently witnessed a hate crime towards a gay student, "students in the LGBTA organized protests and wrote letters and columns in the student newspaper" and ultimately met with Brown's president to explore how the administration could have handled the incident more effectively.

Connecting Service with the Classroom

While a range of academic programs do offer opportunities related to social justice and Brown classes often "encourage students to draw together their academic work with their community commitments," the administration states that "service-learning is not an ideology that has been embraced by Brown." One student explains, "I know of a few classes that have community components, but most of the civic engagement on campus takes place removed from [academic] learning, within the Swearer Center."

The school cites the Learning Communities program as a prime example of its civic engagement education: "Learning Communities are different from academic seminars. They emphasize the learning and teaching responsibilities of all participants and do not privilege the expertise or organizational responsibility of any one member. Learning communities meet every week for 90 minutes and draw upon experience, readings, exercises, presentations, site visits, and discussion."

According to one student, "the learning communities provide a great space for lively discussion amongst other students involved in community service. As a student coordinator, I often take back what I pick up in learning community to my volunteers."

Brown emphatically encourages students to design their own socially conscious curriculum. "My primary academic interests are affordable housing and urban poverty, and at Brown, one can create their own course—so I have just created a course on Brown's relationship to the city of Providence: politically, economically, socially, spatially. To me that is the perfect intersection of civic engagement and academic learning."

Impact on Community and Students

The Swearer Center maintains relationships "with nearly 200 community-based agencies," and Brown students take full advantage. "Having the opportunity to get off campus and experience the happiness and hardships of the children I work with has enriched my time as a young adult in college. I would have felt too isolated on College Hill had I not had the opportunity to work weekly with people in the Providence community."

The Swearer Center's community programs are divided into the categories of Art and Society; Health and Development; Language and Literacy; and Youth Development and Education. Examples include Space in Prison for the Arts and Creative Expression (SPACE), a partnership with the Women's Division of the RI Adult Correctional Institute (ACI) through which teams of student volunteers conduct evening workshops in creative writing, movement, and theater with local inmates. The AIDS Oral History Project "seeks to preserve the stories and memories of Rhode Islanders living with HIV/AIDS through audio-taped interviews and collaborative writing." Let's Get Ready! provides free SAT test preparation for college-bound students in under-served communities.

One student involved with Rhode Island Jobs with Justice and a community organization of low-income workers reports having "found my calling through this work, and I have learned a great deal about the complexities of social and political change, which is really what I am most interested in. While I value the education I receive in the classroom, I would give it up far more quickly than I would my community activism."

Student Financial Support for Service

Brown provides a variety of fellowships for students interested in engaging in independent, service-oriented projects. The Arthur Liman Public Interest Program at Yale Law School offers summer internships to students who aspire to work in public interest law. The CV Starr National Service Fellowship Program rewards students exhibiting "a demonstrated pattern of service" with the resources to design a project relating to public issues. The Howard R. Swearer Public Service Fellowship is a full-time summer fellowship providing up to $3,000 to junior and senior students who want to spend the summer pursuing international service work with priority given to students receiving financial aid. In addition, each year the Royce Fellowship Program awards merit scholarships of up to $4,000 to 25 outstanding student interested in completing extra-curricular projects.

Students appreciate having access to "lots of funding opportunities to explore academic interests in the real world. For example, the career center awarded me a stipend to work with an organization that was studying occupational health in factories in Honduras. I used the information I gathered for my senior thesis."

SELECTIVITY

# of applicants	15,157
% of applicants accepted	16
% of acceptees attending	60
# accepting a place on wait list	1,200

FRESHMAN PROFILE

Range SAT Verbal	650-750
Range SAT Math	650-750
Range ACT Composite	26-32
Minimum Paper TOEFL	600
Minimum Computer TOEFL	250
% graduated top 10% of class	87
% graduated top 25% of class	95
% graduated top 50% of class	100

DEADLINES

Regular admission	1/1
Regular notification by	4/1
Nonfall registration?	no

FINANCIAL FACTS

Annual tuition	$29,200
Room and board	$8,100
Books and supplies	$2,300
Required fees	$900
% frosh rec. need-based scholarship or grant aid	39
% UG rec. need based scholarship or grant aid	37
% frosh rec. need-based self-help aid	38
% UG rec. need-based self-help aid	39

CALIFORNIA STATE UNIVERSITY—MONTEREY BAY

100 CAMPUS CENTER, SEASIDE, CA 93955-8001

ADMISSIONS: 831-582-5100

E-MAIL: ADMISSIONS@CSUMB.EDU • **WEBSITE:** HTTP://CSUMB.EDU/

CAMPUS LIFE

Type of school	public
Environment	town

STUDENTS

Total undergrad enrollment	3,535
% male/female	42/58
% from out of state	3
% from public high school	44
% live on campus	70
% African American	4
% Asian	6
% Caucasian	47
% Hispanic	28
% Native American	1
% international	1
# of countries represented	38

ACADEMICS

Calendar	semester
Student/faculty ratio	25/1
% profs teaching UG courses	95
% classes taught by TAs	0

MOST POPULAR MAJORS

liberal studies

Getting Involved

Civic engagement at California State University—Monterey Bay (CSUMB) revolves around the Service Learning Institute (SLI), which serves as "an instructional unit, an academic resource center, a center for developing community partnerships, and the home of the Student Leadership in Service Learning (sl)^2 Program." (sl)^2 trains and employs students to provide direct support to faculty and community agencies involved in service learning and social justice "by sponsoring campus and community initiatives that respond to community needs and concerns." Student leaders then serve as classroom facilitators and liaisons at key community sites.

In addition to providing leadership for the campus' service-learning program, the SLI supports numerous civic-engagement initiatives, such as Hunger and Homelessness Awareness Week, Food and Clothing Drives, and Day of Silence. It's also the academic home of the minor in Service Learning Leadership, "a degree program that provides students with the knowledge and skills necessary to become leaders in the field of community service and social action."

Students agree that the SLI is where it's at: "As for a first-year student, I would suggest going to our main office, or the 'One-Stop Shop.' They have all the information concerning all of the activities and programs on this campus." They also salute the potential for participation within the SLI. "CSUMB is a fairly new school, less than ten years old, so students have more of a say in how things are run and have more opportunities in shaping the campus."

Campus Culture of Engagement

Attitudes towards service run the gamut at CSUMB, but all students agree that Getting Involved is easy—or rather, unavoidable: "This school is very well connected. You get e-mails all the time informing you about what's up and asking for participation. Profs are very active and want to get you involved, so they keep you posted as to what is up as well. There are bulletin boards everywhere, always with new info." If all that doesn't do the trick, "probably the easiest way is through the service and pedagogy class of Service Learning 200," one of the school's many available service-learning courses.

Required service-learning is a topic of debate at CSUMB. On the one hand, the campus's service-oriented population gives its policy glowing reviews: "Activism and service are part of the heartbeat of this school," and, "for the most part, people are very open-minded and want to participate to make a difference!" But the jaded masses have their gripes. Because it's mandatory, "you will find that some people don't really care; they are just doing it for the grade." Says another, "I think a lot of students feel forced into doing service-learning and go in with that kind of attitude." Ultimately, students can meet in a middle ground. "Many students at first feel like service-learning is a joke until they actually see the impact they are able to have in the surrounding community" and, in the end, "people that choose not to engage at this school often transfer or drop out."

For the activists in the bunch, the intimacy of the 3,500-student campus is a boon. "On some college campuses, no matter how hard you rally, your voice never really gets heard. It's not like that here."

Connecting Service with the Classroom

CSUMB is one of the few public universities in the country where service-learning is a graduation requirement. "Each year, nearly 50 percent of CSUMB students take service-learning courses, contributing tens of thousands of hours of service annually to local community organizations, schools, and government agencies." Service-learning at CSUMB consists of two components: All lower-division students must take a course called Introduction to Service in Multicultural Communities in order to meet the school's general-education requirement in Community Participation. "Each section addresses a specific community issue, such as Hunger and Homelessness, Educational Equity, Community Health, Women's Issues, Men's Issues, or Youth and Elders." In their majors, students take a second service-learning course relating to their particular field of study.

Says one participant: "I have been involved in a service-learning project that allows me to work with the Special Education teachers and their aides. I developed an orientation handbook for the aides which provide them with pertinent information about the way the school that they are working at operates and some general guidelines about working in mainstream classrooms and special ed kids. Since I plan on becoming a Special Ed teacher, I learned a lot about the field through observations and interviews."

Impact on Community and Students

CSUMB works in conjunction with a core group of 40 partner organizations in the surrounding Monterey Bay and Salinas Valley region. Together, they offer a range of opportunities consistent with the school's Vision Statement, which emphasizes "serving the diverse people of California, especially the working class and historically undereducated and low-income populations" and examining "the underlying root causes of the region's most difficult social problems."

One student confesses, "I do not think I would have had the motivation to study at all if it were not for all of the civic activities that I have participated in. I served at an AIDS project, a teen pregnancy-prevention program, in student government, and started a club. All the principles and theories discussed in class were visible when doing my work. I was able to conceptualize much better and put my knowledge to use."

Through the Monterey County AIDS Project (MCAP), "students are trained to provide AIDS-prevention information and materials to marginalized communities throughout the region." Through the After School Collaborative, student leaders help design arts, music, and service-based curriculum modules for local after-school programs, and then provide mentorship and supervision at program sites.

Students are also active in the Return of the Natives Restoration Education Project (RON), a community- and school-based environmental education project that includes "school-based native plant gardens, nature areas, and greenhouses, as well as large-scale habitat restoration and native-plant landscaping projects in parks and open spaces in the Monterey Bay Area."

Student Financial Support for Service

While CSUMB does not offer merit-based scholarships aimed specifically at service-oriented students, its $(sl)^2$ program employs many of the campus's student leaders. The school also offers a range of scholarships to students demonstrating general merit and/or financial need.

SELECTIVITY

# of applicants	7,069
% of applicants accepted	60
% of acceptees attending	16

FRESHMAN PROFILE

Range SAT Verbal	200-790
Range SAT Math	200-740
Range ACT Composite	10-30
Minimum Paper TOEFL	525
Minimum Computer TOEFL	197
% graduated top 10% of class	10
% graduated top 25% of class	32
% graduated top 50% of class	73

DEADLINES

Regular admission	none
Regular notification by	3/15
Nonfall registration?	none

FINANCIAL FACTS

Annual tuition	$2,761
Room and board	$6,691
Books and supplies	$1,200
Required fees	$427
% frosh rec. need-based scholarship or grant aid	5
% UG rec. need-based scholarship or grant aid	38
% frosh rec. need-based self-help aid	6
% UG rec. need-based self-help aid	49

Clark University

950 Main Street, Worcester, MA 01610-1477
Admissions: 508-793-7431 • Fax: 508-793-8821 • Financial Aid: 508-793-7478
E-mail: admissions@clarku.edu • Website: www.clarku.edu

CAMPUS LIFE

Type of school	private
Environment	town

STUDENTS

Total undergrad enrollment	2,075
% male/female	39/61
% from out of state	63
% from public high school	70
% live on campus	77
% African American	3
% Asian	4
% Caucasian	65
% Hispanic	3
% international	7
# of countries represented	56

ACADEMICS

Calendar	semester
Student/faculty ratio	12:1
% profs teaching UG courses	100
% classes taught by TAs	0
Most common lab size	10-19
Most common reg class size	10-19

MOST POPULAR MAJORS
biology/biological sciences
political science and government
psychology

Getting Involved

The Community Engagement and Volunteering Center (CEV) is where most of Clark's service and service-learning opportunities are born. The center promotes volunteerism through information tabling and its website and offers walk-in hours during which students can browse a searchable database of service programs. It also supports faculty in the development of service-learning courses and "coordinates on-campus community service events, such as an annual Volunteer Fair, Presidential and Student Dialogues about important community issues, and an annual Student Service Day."

Students praise the center for offering "endless!!!!" opportunities. "I cannot say enough about the CEV on Clark campus," says one enthusiastic proponent. "They have a great relationship with our community and work very closely with those who are also trying to make a difference. They have done so much for me since I have been here and have supported me in anything I wanted to try."

Campus Culture of Engagement

"I knew about how strong Clark was with volunteerism and activism the second I stepped on campus and even previously when I visited the school as a prospective. There are always events and programs, followed by flyers and posters, that let us all know what's going on in the school, the community, the country, and even the world."

"When you first come to Clark, it may seem overwhelming, but go to three or four first group meetings just to see what's out there. You may end up doing things that you never expected to."

Clark students attest to a widespread spirit of civic engagament, with claims that "just about everyone is involved in civic engagement in at least one way" and that Getting Involved is easy because "if there isn't a group, it is easy to start one, and you can find plenty of people to help you." Students describe their campus as being "quite liberal" and praise some memorable activist efforts in recent years: "Many Clark students recently organized themselves and took a trip to Washington, DC to participate in the March for Women's Lives," and there was "a benefit concert on campus to sponsor students who travel to Nicaragua over spring break to work in communities over there building homes."

Connecting Service with the Classroom

Though service-learning at Clark does not enjoy the same prominence on campus as extracurricular volunteer opportunities, some faculty do use the classroom as a bridge to the Worcester community. According to the administration, approximately 15 percent of Clark undergraduates perform course-related community service at some point during their college careers.

The emphasis of many service-learning classes rests on urban affairs, particularly "the inner city and the search for solutions to its problems." The Urban Development and Social Change concentration "enables students to use Worcester as a laboratory for studying industrialization, immigration, and the architectural landscape," and "our Hiatt Center for Urban Education enables students to experiment with innovative teaching strategies inside the Worcester public schools."

The Human-Environment Regional Observatory (HERO), a program within the Geography Department, sends students into the community to conduct site research on environmental problems affecting the lives of residents. The All Kinds of Girls program, created and supervised by our Women's Studies faculty, is run mainly by undergraduate women students. One volunteer explains, "the goal of the program is to help girls maintain a strong voice, which will aid them in their adolescence. It is a fantastic program."

Impact on Community and Students

Clark partners with about 40 local organizations. "Our presence in the greater Worcester community is immense," says one student. "Clarkies go everywhere from schools to Community Centers and YMCAs to shelters." Says another student, "being in a large city like Worcester, there are a lot of people and programs out there that need help, and we're just a campus waiting to serve."

The pinnacle of Clark's community involvement is the University Park Partnership (UPP), a grassroots effort established more than 15 years ago in collaboration with the Main South Community Development Corporation (CDC). The Partnership has recently been awarded "one of seven $8 million grants by the Carnegie Corporation to scale up our success in University Park to a system-wide reform of secondary education in Worcester."

The UPP has made particularly great strides in the realm of education. With help from Clark's Hiatt Center for Urban Education and the Worcester public schools, it helped spawn "the creation of the University Park Campus School, a neighborhood school for seventh to twelfth graders where Clark students serve as tutors and mentors, and Clark faculty teach seminars and courses." The Partnership also provides training for current public school teachers, a free summer recreation program for neighborhood children, and free tuition at Clark for neighborhood residents who meet Clark's admissions and residency requirements. In addition to these initiatives, the UPP "has successfully renovated over 200 residential properties and 20 storefronts," and embarked on "a $30-million project to create more than 100 new units of housing, a new Boys and Girls Club, and new athletic facilities for use by Clark and the community."

Clark students also participate in the ROTARACT Partners in Community program, through which neighborhood residents are paired with students "who visit weekly to provide companionship, help with yard work, snow shoveling, and other jobs." One student leader reports, "I am president of the ROTARACT Club on campus, second year running. Just being able to use my drive and enthusiasm for volunteerism and getting the word out there has allowed me to turn the club from a 15-active-member organization to a 50-member organization in just one year."

Student Financial Support for Service

"Each year, Clark University offers 20 admitted students a $44,000 four-year Making a Difference Scholarship in recognition of their outstanding commitment to community service. The students also receive $2,500 stipends "to support projects they may undertake in the Worcester community during the summer following their sophomore or junior year." Additionally, the annual John W. Lund Community Achievement Award "is given to a student, faculty member, or staff person who has done outstanding work in the Worcester community."

Aside from those scholarships offered specifically to service-oriented students, Clark offers fellowships and grants that allow students "to apply their classroom and research experience in the greater global community."

SELECTIVITY

# of applicants	3,950
% of applicants accepted	63
% of acceptees attending	22
# accepting a place on wait list	160
% admitted from wait list	5

FRESHMAN PROFILE

Range SAT Verbal	550-660
Range SAT Math	540-640
Range ACT Composite	22-27
Minimum Paper TOEFL	550
Minimum Computer TOEFL	213
Average HS GPA	3.41
% graduated top 10% of class	30
% graduated top 25% of class	69
% graduated top 50% of class	96

DEADLINES

Regular admission	2/1
Regular notification by	4/1
Nonfall registration?	yes

FINANCIAL FACTS

Annual tuition	$26,700
Room and board	$5,150
Books and supplies	$800
Required fees	$265
% frosh rec. need-based scholarship or grant aid	60
% UG rec. need-based scholarship or grant aid	60
% frosh rec. need-based self-help aid	56
% UG rec. need-based self-help aid	56
% frosh rec. any financial aid	80
% UG rec. any financial aid	83

CLEMSON UNIVERSITY

105 SIKES HALL, BOX 345124, CLEMSON, SC 29634-5124

ADMISSIONS: 864-656-2287 • FAX: 864-656-2464 • FINANCIAL AID: 864-656-2280

E-MAIL: CUADMISSIONS@CLEMSON.EDU • WEBSITE: WWW.CLEMSON.EDU

CAMPUS LIFE

Type of school	public
Environment	rural

STUDENTS

Total undergrad	
enrollment	13,808
% male/female	55/45
% from out of state	33
% from public high school	89
% live on campus	47
% African American	7
% Asian	2
% Caucasian	82
% Hispanic	1
# of countries represented	83

ACADEMICS

Calendar	semester
Student/faculty ratio	17:1
% profs teaching	
UG courses	95
% classes taught by TAs	7
Most common lab size	20-29
Most common	
reg class size	20-29

MOST POPULAR MAJORS

business administration/management
engineering

Getting Involved

Just about every university in the book plays up the "one-big-happy-family" angle in its promotional literature. If they were all telling the truth, our world would be united by a chain of campuses holding hands and singing "Kumbaya." The strange thing is that at Clemson University, the claim actually rings true.

Clemson's campus community appears to be sincerely built on a foundation of volunteerism and self-sacrifice. One student explains, "here at Clemson, we have a 'One Clemson' iniative which focuses on bringing the Clemson family closer. It fosters collaboration between student groups and the inclusion of each and every student on campus to make them feel like part of 'the family.' So service learning happens everywhere on the Clemson campus."

Civic engagement originates at the Community Service Office, which "maintains a database of local agencies and their volunteer needs, as well as a calendar of service events, which students can access through the internet." The office also advises the student-service club, Tigers Who Care, which sponsors the annual Volunteer Fair, weekly service trips, and Hunger Awareness Week each November. Students explain that the office is still in its growth stages, but report that "it is extremely easy to become involved with service organizations at Clemson."

Campus Culture of Engagement

Clemson is populated by people who "are passionate about each other and the community" and "who dedicate enormous time and energy to making our world a better place." Asserts one service-oriented student: "We are not just a bunch of college kids partying and having a good time." Students often learn about volunteer opportunities "the day before classes begin, at the Welcome Back Festival." There they encounter a smorgasbord of student organizations whose "efforts are full-throttle"—including a campus chapter of Habitat for Humanity, Big Brother/Big Sister, and Best Buddies. "Religious clubs, such as Fellowship of Christian Athletes or the Baptist Collegiate Ministry, also offer service opportunities, including alternative spring break service trips."

The campus Greek community—including Alpha Phi Omega (a national service fraternity) and Gamma Sigma Sigma (a national service sorority)—"engage constantly in community service in the community and those surrounding it." "I am involved with Alpha Phi Omega," says one Greek student, "and we do approximately ten to 12 service projects each semester. These projects include two blood drives, one of which is the largest blood drive in the state of South Carolina, book drives, and working with foster children. Next year we are starting a fund to help raise funds for multiple sclerosis research."

Connecting Service with the Classroom

Through the Communication Across the Curriculum program, "each of Clemson's five colleges offers service-learning courses in a number of disciplinary areas. For example, in the College of Agriculture, Forestry, and Life Sciences, service learning is used in Food Science & Human Nutrition courses. In the College of Arts, Architecture, and Humanities, courses in English and Planning & Landscape Architecture utilize service-learning."

Professor Mary Haque has offered a Horticulture class in which "students teamed up with students from three other departments to design outdoor learning environments for elementary schools across the state. The students presented their designs to school officials and parent groups using sketches and posters. Haque's students also created landscape plans for a Habitat for Humanity home built by Clemson students and faculty."

A Parks, Recreation, and Tourism Management (PRTM) professor named Gina McLellan has instituted a program called Traveling Trash Bash, which takes recycling education into local schools. "Students taking Professor Morgan Gresham's Technical Writing class developed a 12-page booklet on recycling, composting, and other environmental issues for the program. PRTM students took these booklets to five schools this year and plan to eventually reach every school in Pickens County."

Impact on Community and Students

Clemson enjoys more than 50 partnerships with various service agencies in the tri-county area, and service takes place "all over the state of South Carolina and sometimes even around the world." "Through volunteering, I have gotten to meet people and do things that I never would have been able to otherwise."

The school's relationship with the Pickens County Habitat for Humanity affiliate is particularly strong: "Each year since 1994, Clemson University student volunteers have built a Habitat for Humanity house on Bowman Field alongside the traditional floats and displays as part of the university's annual homecoming celebration. After Homecoming, the structure is moved from campus to a permanent site in the nearby community, where the house becomes a home for a local family. In 2001, the popularity of this homecoming tradition led to Clemson University students spearheading the nation's first student-led Habitat for Humanity Blitz Build, an accelerated house build that begins with just a foundation and ends with a complete house in a matter of weeks. For two weeks, university and community volunteers worked side by side with future Habitat homeowners to build five Habitat houses. Work on the houses continued for another four weeks after the initial blitz ended in early March, and college students from across the nation came to Clemson during their spring breaks for the opportunity to be a part of the 'ultimate service-learning project.' By the project's end, approximately 4,000 volunteers had participated."

Other community partners and projects include Sprouting Wings, an after-school program for children that uses the South Carolina Botanical Garden to teach about nature and nutrition, and the Clemson Elementary Outdoors program, through which 1,500 Clemson students have participated alongside faculty and other community members in designing and building "outdoor learning areas" for elementary school students.

Student Financial Support for Service

Clemson University offers two scholarship/grant opportunities for students to perform community service. The Clemson University Campbell Scholars Program awards up to $6,000 per year to a small number of students to "perform at least ten hours of community service per week in a designated elementary or middle school and work for six weeks with compensation at a residential youth-related summer camp during at least one summer during their college career," in addition to tutoring throughout the year.

Clemson University also offers a financial aid program called the Clemson Community Service Grant, which is awarded to 500 to 700 students a year according to financial need. In exchange for the grant, students serve the community through volunteer activities for a minimum of 20 hours each semester.

The Clemson University Community Scholars program, slated to begin operation in 2005 and still in the development stage, will also "provide scholarship assistance to students while providing them with the opportunity to gain knowledge through research and service to surrounding communities."

In addition, the Clemson University Career Center helps subsidize internships with local nonprofit agencies.

SELECTIVITY

# of applicants	10,620
% of applicants accepted	69
% of acceptees attending	42
# accepting a place on wait list	129
% admitted from wait list	15

FRESHMAN PROFILE

Range SAT Verbal	540-640
Range SAT Math	570-660
Range ACT Composite	24-28
Minimum Paper TOEFL	550
Minimum Computer TOEFL	213
Average HS GPA	3.90
% graduated top 10% of class	42
% graduated top 25% of class	72
% graduated top 50% of class	92

DEADLINES

Regular admission	5/1
Regular notification by	rolling
Nonfall registration?	yes

FINANCIAL FACTS

Annual in-state tuition	$7,840
Annual out-of-state tuition	$16,404
Room and board	$5,292
Books and supplies	$798
Required fees	$234
% frosh rec. need-based scholarship or grant aid	13
% UG rec. need-based scholarship or grant aid	18
% frosh rec. need-based self-help aid	25
% UG rec. need-based self-help aid	29
% frosh rec. any financial aid	86
% UG rec. any financial aid	81

CONNECTICUT COLLEGE

270 MOHEGAN AVENUE, NEW LONDON, CT 06320
ADMISSIONS: 860-439-2200 • **FAX:** 860-439-4301 • **FINANCIAL AID:** 860-439-2058
E-MAIL: ADMISSION@CONNCOLL.EDU • **WEBSITE:** WWW.CONNCOLL.EDU

CAMPUS LIFE

Type of school	private
Environment	village

STUDENTS

Total undergrad enrollment	1,796
% male/female	40/60
% from out of state	76
% from public high school	52
% live on campus	99
% African American	4
% Asian	4
% Caucasian	71
% Hispanic	4
% international	7
# of countries represented	39

ACADEMICS

Calendar	semester
Student/faculty ratio	11:1
% profs teaching UG courses	100
% classes taught by TAs	0

MOST POPULAR MAJORS

English language and literature
political science and government
psychology

Getting Involved

Connecticut College boasts the rare wonder of a civic-engagement program that is heavily trafficked without being required. The Office of Volunteers for Community Service (OVCS) is the center of the action. Armed with a posse of faculty and community partners, the OVCS reports that it works with over 500 students on an annual basis providing training and orientation, maintaining lines of communication with the New London community, and evaluating service projects. The office also runs three vans that transport students to their community sites free of charge.

Students praise the office emphatically for its "very accessible programs" and "the wonderful staff behind the scenes that ensure that everything can be done." "There is a lot of constant support, and opportunities are really endless, from swimming with belugas at the Mystic Aquarium to working at a New London special-education school to leading tours in our arboretum."

Campus Culture of Engagement

Upon arriving at Conn College, getting involved comes naturally. "There is information everywhere! Just to name a few, students can find out during orientation, at activities fairs, at multiple highly-publicized meetings held year-round, from other (usually very vocal) students, and hundreds of e-mails and voice mail messages about engagement, service, and activism opportunities." Word travels fast: "For every one student who has a positive experience interning or volunteering with an organization, three more hear about that one positive experience and sign up for the next semester."

Because Conn College's population includes more than just liberal activists, political dialogue is inevitable. "Many student organizations bring speakers and lecturers to campus to engage and inform the campus commuunitity. Sometimes the speakers are controversial and really rile up the student body. In the fall, the College Republicans brought right-wing politicians and thinktanks to campus. The entire campus got into a heated debate over the issues."

Students cite an "ongoing dialogue about racial issues" and explain that in the aftermath of "a few bias incidents on campus, the college has really been stressing diversity. After each incident, the campus is very aware of the problem and student organizations, leaders, and professors open up and think of ways to educate people about the issue."

Connecting Service with the Classroom

Conn College students praise its faculty, whose members "are actively involved with many of the groups on campus and help to spread awareness on a variety of issues." Service-learning opportunities are offered in 30 classes from departments ranging from Botany to Hispanic Studies, with about 45 percent of students participating.

The Holleran Center for Community Action and Public Policy, an interdisciplinary academic center, houses many of the university's service-learning programs. Its most celebrated component is the Program in Community Action (PICA), a certificate program that Conn College students from any major may apply to enter during their sophomore year. "PICA scholars select core courses from a variety of disciplines that connect to their area of interest, complete leadership workshops such as negotiation and community organizing, complete a funded internship in their junior summer, and complete a senior integrative project. PICA scholars have worked to advance human rights in the United States and abroad, completed health care reform and improved public health programs, worked for educational equity and enhanced resources for public schools, and strengthened environmental ethics and sustainability."

One student reports, "beyond the literal—it funded my internship of direct service work with refugees in Minnesota—PICA has had a profound influence on my ability to merge my academic and activist interests. It is by far the best thing I did in college." Another student's PICA experience "definitely complemented my interest in the psychological and sociological reasons that juveniles commit crimes" by providing "opportunities for me to work with such youths and to design a three-year project focusing on this topic."

Impact on Community and Students

"My participation in the community has made my career path clear. I am going to graduate school next year for social work, and my experience in the New London community with professionals and clients has prepared me for future jobs and has given me the interpersonal skills I need to work with diverse populations. I have worked at an HIV/AIDS social service, delivered meals to terminally ill members of the community, served as an ESL volunteer at a social service for Hispanic immigrants, and now have an internship with a licenced clinical social worker at Head Start."

Conn College maintains 21 community partnerships with organizations including the aquarium, public housing authorities, and Head Start. According to one student, "much of the volunteering is done at local public elementary, middle, and high schools as well as alternative educational and after-school programs." Another student reports, "my friend and I began an after-school enrichment program in New London for middle-school students through the guidance and funding of the school. We serve 15 middle schools and their familes and plan to expand the program."

Project KBA (Kids, Books, and Athletics) is a partnership with the New London Public Schools which aims "to improve health and wellness, reduce obesity, and foster the love of reading with elementary and middle school." Through the program, Conn College students travel to schools and after-school programs where they teach both physical exercises and multicultural reading curriculum in alternating sessions.

Through the Healthy Trail project, students work with professionals and organizations to "research, design, develop, and implement a walking trail through the urban center of New London. The trail will highlight local historical sites, provide fitness information, and improve the urban landscape."

Student Financial Support for Service

Conn College's Holleran Center for Community Action and Public Policy provides a $3,000 summer scholarship for students enrolled in its Program in Community Action. "This scholarship is given to students during the summer between their junior and senior year as they complete their community/public service connected to their senior integrative project. The college's career services and its other academic centers also provide this summer scholarship for students who do community/public service in international settings and in environmental projects." Beyond this scholarship, the "OVCS hires, trains, and places 120 [work-study] students each year to run service programs and to work at community non-profits including schools, clinics, museums, and hospitals."

SELECTIVITY

# of applicants	4,503
% of applicants accepted	34
% of acceptees attending	32
# accepting a place on wait list	973
% admitted from wait list	5

FRESHMAN PROFILE

Range SAT Verbal	620-700
Range SAT Math	630-700
Minimum Paper TOEFL	600
Minimum Computer TOEFL	250
% graduated top 10% of class	55
% graduated top 50% of class	99

DEADLINES

Regular admission	1/1
Regular notification by	4/1
Nonfall registration?	yes

FINANCIAL FACTS

Room and board	
Books and supplies	$800
Required fees	
% frosh rec. need-based scholarship or grant aid	38
% UG rec. need-based scholarship or grant aid	42
% frosh rec. need-based self-help aid	37
% UG rec. need-based self-help aid	40

DARTMOUTH COLLEGE

6016 McNUTT HALL, HANOVER, NH 03755

ADMISSIONS: 603-646-2875 • **FAX:** 603-646-1216 • **FINANCIAL AID:** 603-646-2451

E-MAIL: ADMISSIONS.OFFICE@DARTMOUTH.EDU • **WEBSITE:** WWW.DARTMOUTH.EDU

CAMPUS LIFE

Type of school	private
Environment	rural

STUDENTS

Total undergrad enrollment	3,996
% male/female	50/50
% from out of state	96
% from public high school	63
% live on campus	83
% African American	7
% Asian	13
% Caucasian	58
% Hispanic	6
% Native American	4
% international	5

ACADEMICS

Calendar	quarter
Student/faculty ratio	9:1
% profs teaching UG courses	100
% classes taught by TAs	0
Most common lab size	10-19
Most common reg class size	10-19

Getting Involved

Dartmouth College may be home to legions of superarchievers, but this Ivy League school doesn't just train its undergradate population to pontificate—it provides a solid education in "battling the complacency demons," thanks to an impressive civic-engagement program.

The Tucker Foundation is the campus umbrella organization for community service on campus. "Approximately 60 percent of the student body participates in Tucker Foundation-sponsored community-service activities annually," the school tells us. "These include sustained weekly local commitments, ten-week internships and fellowships, alternative spring breaks, one-time events, and Cross Cultural International Study and Service trips." In addition, Tucker's Civic Intern program hosts 20 outreach internships each year. One student assures us that "anyone with interest can just wander in there and find tons of information and numerous staff members, deans, and student interns who are there to help students find something that fits their needs and wants."

The Rockefeller Center is another locus of civic engagement on campus. The public policy center "strives to be a gathering place where students can explore divergent views, deliberate about public issues, and gain the skills and understanding to be energetic and thoughtful participants in democratic politics." It sponsors co-curricular programs, hosts a minor in public policy, funds 60 internships a year, and supports an array of student-led, politically focused, weekly discussion groups.

For the post-college minded, Career Services at Dartmouth offers the Careers for the Common Good (CFCG) initiative, with a mission "to empower and support students in the pursuit of values-driven work opportunities in the not-for-profit, public, and private sectors."

Campus Culture of Engagement

Civic engagement is, according to one student, "one of the essential components of being a Dartmouth student." Says another, "We are smart, organized, and task-oriented students with idealism that translates into action. Students are mobilized at Dartmouth to change the status quo."

Starting out is easy—"I got involved with the mentoring program that I now chair by getting information at the Volunteer Fair"—and students stress that further involvement often comes naturally because community consciousness is a "social norm." Dartmouth promotes "an environment in which civic engagement is viewed as cool, and inspires people who might not normally join to try it out."

Campus groups represent a spectrum of political views, from the Coalition for Life and the College Republicans to the Dartmouth Civil Liberties Union and Dartmouth Students for Reproductive Rights. Students can also locate service opportunities through the Greek system at Dartmouth. "In the academic year 2002–2003, the Coeducational Houses and Fraternity and Sorority Communities raised over $30,000 in their philanthropy efforts and performed over 31,000 community service hours."

Connecting Service with the Classroom

Like other Ivy League schools, rather than implementing a curriculum of service-related class work, Dartmouth more often encourages students to design independent internships and research projects related to service-learning. "Faculty or students working with faculty who wish to incorporate a service-learning portion into any class find funds available in the Dean's Office—as long as the professor feels the project has intellectual merit."

The Cross Cultural Education and Service Program (CCESP) at the Tucker Foundation currently includes two service-abroad options. The Nicaragua program consists of "a two-week service project focused on healthcare, construction, agriculture, or a combination of the three." The Belarus CCESP travels to Poland and Belarus and enables students to study "the moral and spiritual challenges created by the Holocaust," culminating in a work project that renovates abandoned Belorussian Jewish cemeteries. Of the Nicaragua trip, one student reports, "Personally, this program changed my life. I am significantly more passionate about developement issues in underdeveloped countries and on-site active engagement with communities who have as much to teach us as we have to teach them."

The John Sloan Dickey Center for International Understanding offers additional opportunities for global civic engagement. Its War and Peace Studies minor and War and Peace Fellows program immerse students in studies of conflict and conflict resolution, and its Undergraduate Internships for International Understanding support students who want to spend a term abroad studying with international governments or humanitarian organizations. "Typically the center funds between 25 to 30 undergraduates who travel to almost as many different countries."

Impact on Community and Students

Students salute projects ranging from "meeting famous journalists for dinner, to creating a model sustainable residence hall room, to making t-shirts for the clothesline project for sexual assault awareness" as escape valves from "the bubble of the Ivy League world where the majority of us lead fairly privileged lives." Dartmouth Community Services (DCS) at the Tucker Foundation maintains "over 40 local outreach relationships within a 30-mile radius of the campus" with over 1,500 students engaging annually. Each year, the Foundation supports five Alternative Spring Breaks. "Past trips have included constructing houses with Habitat for Humanity in North Carolina, working in food kitchens in Washington, DC, constructing a medical clinic in Costa Rica, and delivering computers to schools in the Mississippi Delta region." Other community outreach programs include Food Security, which works with "a coalition of local farmers, caterers and community partners" to provide free meals, the Bildner Urban Summer Internship, which connects participants with "multi-racial, multi-ethnic, and economically diverse urban communities through work at the Boys & Girls Clubs of Newark," and Student Teachers in the ARTs (START), which pairs Dartmouth students with a teacher and classroom of children in the region surrounding the college and allows them to teach weekly arts and/or cultural lessons of their own design.

Student Financial Support for Service

Dartmouth provides more fellowships and grants that we have room to print here. Most public and community-service grants award up to $2,500 "to facilitate a ten-week off-campus service experience." A sampling includes Tucker Fellowships, Rockefeller Center Public Policy Internships, Dickey Center for International Understanding Internships, and the Nancy Boehm Coster Public Policy Career Encouragement Fund, which provides support for students who wish to explore public-service career options. The Olga Gruss Lewin and Richard Lombard Post Graduate Fellowships grant $8,000 to $10,000 to very recent graduates pursuing strong fellowship or internship opportunities with domestic or international nonprofit organizations.

One student offers a ringing endorsement of Dartmouth's financial support: "I completed a Dartmouth Partners in Community Service Internship the summer after my freshman year at a nonprofit environmental law foundation. As a financial-aid student, I would not have been able to take this unpaid, full-time position without the funding from Dartmouth. I am very grateful and as I graduate and move on to my job as an environmental consultant, I look at this experience as a key stepping-stone to my future career."

SELECTIVITY

# of applicants	11,855
% of applicants accepted	18
% of acceptees attending	51
# accepting a place on wait list	1,296
% admitted from wait list	4

FRESHMAN PROFILE

Range SAT Verbal	660-760
Range SAT Math	670-770
Range ACT Composite	
Minimum Paper TOEFL	600
Minimum Computer TOEFL	250
Average HS GPA	3.66
% graduated top 10% of class	84
% graduated top 25% of class	97
% graduated top 50% of class	100

DEADLINES

Regular admission	1/1
Regular notification by	4/10
Nonfall registration?	no

FINANCIAL FACTS

Annual tuition	$30,279
Room and board	$9,000
Books and supplies	$1,122
Required fees	$186
% frosh rec. need-based scholarship or grant aid	47
% UG rec. need-based scholarship or grant aid	47
% frosh rec. need-based self-help aid	45
% UG rec. need-based self-help aid	48
% frosh rec. any financial aid	48
% UG rec. any financial aid	50

DEFIANCE COLLEGE

701 NORTH CLINTON STREET, DEFIANCE, OH 43512-1695

ADMISSIONS: 419-783-2359 • **FAX:** 419-783-2468 • **FINANCIAL AID:** 419-783-2376

E-MAIL: ADMISSIONS@DEFIANCE.EDU • **WEBSITE:** WWW.DEFIANCE.EDU

CAMPUS LIFE

Type of school	private
Environment	rural

STUDENTS

Total undergrad	
enrollment	918
% male/female	45/55
% from out of state	21
% live on campus	50
% African American	4
% Caucasian	92
% Hispanic	3
# of countries represented	3

ACADEMICS

Calendar	semester
Student/faculty ratio	13:1
% profs teaching	
UG courses	100
% classes taught by TAs	0
Most common lab size	10-19
Most common	
reg class size	10-19

MOST POPULAR MAJORS

business administration/management
criminology
early childhood education and teaching

Getting Involved

It comes as no surprise that the students at a college called Defiance are a socially conscious bunch. While the school is not necessarily the bastion of political dissent that its moniker implies, its firmly established service-learning program guarantees a constant level of civic engagement on campus. "Service is an everyday part of life at DC," says one student, "from the classroom, to the sports field, to the extracurricular meetings."

Outside of the required service-learning seminar that students take in their first year, Defiance students encounter "excellent" and "endless" civic-engagement opportunities through the Office of Service Learning and at the McMaster School for Advancing Humanity. "The strengths of the efforts are the support of faculty, staff, and administration" who "work right alongside students when doing service." "If you can think of a project to do, people are extremely willing to help make the opportunity possible."

The Presidential Service Leader program is one of the strongest initiatives on campus. Each year, the program recruits "up to ten incoming students to become Service Leaders and function as liaisons between faculty and staff and other students. Besides assisting faculty with developing service opportunities for their courses, this team of 40 students works closely with community agencies on a weekly basis." They also help "to organize and operate local and national service projects such as Relay for Life, Red Cross Blood Drive, Make a Difference Day, United Way Day of Caring, Join Hands Day, WalkAmerica, and many more." One student offers a ringing endorsement of the program: "DC service leaders rock!"

Campus Culture of Engagement

"Starting with their very first trip to the admissions office, a first-time student is sure to hear about what is going on on campus. It just builds from there."

Students explain that, following the freshman seminar class, "where they are expected to commit 12 hours out of the first semester to serving the community," the "small size of Defiance College" guarantees a steady stream of service talk and strategizing. "I believe it is very important, if living in the residents halls, to keep your door open. Talk to other people. Make friends. See what they like to do and what they are involved with."

One student emphasizes that "the active role played by the Defiance service leaders cannot be missed as we have weekly commitments to which we normally invite other students to participate." And yet others lament that "sometimes it does seem that the service leaders are the only ones who are engaging in civic efforts," and they express frustration with efforts "to get all students to stay active in service beyond their freshman year and the classes that require it."

Connecting Service with the Classroom

"There is a huge excitement about what the service-learning program is doing," reports one student. Another earnestly commends the program for "upholding our school motto: To Know, To Lead, To Serve, To Understand."

In addition to being a requirement of the Freshman Seminar and Life in Society courses, service-learning is offered as a component of 36 courses and is a part of the curriculum of 14 majors.

The McMaster School for Advancing Humanity is a particularly powerful force of service learning on campus. "The mission of the School is to educate students for responsible citizenship and to produce committed global citizens and leaders who understand the importance of individual liberties in improving the human condition worldwide." Each year, the school sponsors up to ten undergraduate students who display academic promise and a commitment to community service. "The program involves designing and proposing one's own research project, traveling nationally or internationally to perform the service and research the needs of that particular location, and returning to the campus to present their findings in the form of symposiums, class presentations, and papers of publishable quality. They are also expected to mentor the next class of McMaster students and assist with continuing campus activities focused on advancing humanity and improving the human condition."

Impact on Community and Students

Defiance students are proud to report that "the service program is well established within both the college and the community," and that its service-centric reputation "has caused the number of service opportunties to drastically increase."

The college maintains partnerships with 37 service agencies in and around the Defiance area. Many of these agencies are, in turn, partners with the Volunteer Connection of Defiance County, which works to promote and coordinate local volunteerism.

Local partnerships include the annual Lowe's Heroes Day, when small groups of first-year students visit homes of the elderly. "The goal is for students to provide service in the homes for half the morning and then spend the other half of the morning visiting with and getting to know the seniors."

Defiance also works in conjunction with the AmericaReads program, "which links Defiance College students with children in need of reading improvement from the four local elementary schools. The goal of the program is to ensure that all of the youth are reading at their class level by the time they leave the 4th grade and enter middle school."

Campus Student Leaders are presented with a range of additional national and international service opportunities. "In May, following graduation, the freshman, sophomore, and junior Service Leaders—along with interested faculty, staff, and invited community supporters—take a week-long domestic service trip to an underprivileged and impoverished area of the United States. The urban setting is Detroit, Michigan; the suburban site is Back Bay Mission in Biloxi, Mississippi; and the rural location is the Oglala Lakota Indian Reservation in Pine Ridge, South Dakota. Senior Service Leaders engage in an international service trip to Jamaica over the Christmas break where they construct houses for the homeless in partnership with Christian Service International."

Students credit Defiance's service programs with some significant life epiphanies: "Volunteering at various elementary schools has given me the opportunity to gain valuable experience for my future career as a teacher"; "As an aspiring lawyer, I have decided to dedicate my life to serving others in whatever way possible."

Student Financial Support for Service

"Each year, up to 40 students (ten per class) with established records of service to their school and community are offered an $8,500 renewable scholarship to continue their commitment to service throughout their years at Defiance College." Qualifications to apply for the Presidential Service Leadership Award (PSLA) include a strong academic records and a history of school and community service.

SELECTIVITY

# of applicants	940
% of applicants accepted	73
% of acceptees attending	36

FRESHMAN PROFILE

Range SAT Verbal	440-580
Range SAT Math	450-580
Range ACT Composite	19-24
Minimum Paper TOEFL	550
Minimum Computer TOEFL	213
Average HS GPA	3.14
% graduated top 10% of class	15
% graduated top 25% of class	36
% graduated top 50% of class	65

DEADLINES

Regular admission	8/25
Regular notification by	rolling
Nonfall registration?	yes

FINANCIAL FACTS

Annual tuition	$17,780
Room and board	$5,590
Books and supplies	$600
Required fees	$450

DENISON UNIVERSITY

Box H, Granville, OH 43023

Admissions: 740-587-6276 • **Fax:** 740-587-6306 • **Financial Aid:** 800-336-4766

E-mail: ADMISSIONS@DENISON.EDU • **Website:** WWW.DENISON.EDU

CAMPUS LIFE

Type of school	private
Environment	village

STUDENTS

Total undergrad enrollment	2,198
% male/female	44/56
% from out of state	58
% from public high school	69
% live on campus	98
% African American	5
% Asian	3
% Caucasian	83
% Hispanic	3
% international	5
# of countries represented	31

ACADEMICS

Calendar	semester
Student/faculty ratio	12:1
% profs teaching UG courses	100
% classes taught by TAs	0
Most common lab size	10-19
Most common reg class size	10-19

MOST POPULAR MAJORS

communications and media studies
economics
English language and literature

Getting Involved

Recently at Denison University, "the entire campus rallied together to help make over 800 peanut butter and jelly sandwiches for the homeless." Heartwarming stuff, right? It's that kind of place.

Most civic-engagement opportunities at Denison originate at the John W. Alford Center for Service-Learning, which supports curricular service-learning, the Denison Community Association, Big Brothers/Big Sisters, and America Reads, among others. The Director of Curricular Service-Learning handles the academic side of things—helping to develop new courses and host workshops and lectures—while the Director of Community Service oversees the Denison Community Association (DCA). "DCA is the largest student organization on campus (500+ members) and is comprised of 30 committees that work with community partners on a wide variety of issues."

Thanks to a "generous endowment," the Alford Center is able to provide transportation to and from service venues, as well as funding for visiting speakers and students and faculty who wish to attend off-campus conferences. "For example, students have attended national Alternative Break schools and faculty have participated in national service-learning conferences across the country."

Students report that it is "so easy and rewarding to get involved on campus." "The people that keep the Denison Community Association going do a fantastic job. They make sure the chairs of all of the many (and continually growing committees) have everything that they need. They will help in any way that they can."

Campus Culture of Engagement

In addition to holding an involvement fair to incoming students, Denison offers an orientation option designed specifically for students who have expressed an interest in community service. The Denison Service Orientation (DSO) trip unites up to 32 first-year students with a small group of faculty and upper-class leaders. "Students first spend a day on campus getting to know each other and researching various social-service agencies and issues. The next five days are spent in Washington, DC performing community service for local food kitchens, homeless shelters, and social-service agencies. Evenings are spent together in structured reflection sessions. Typically, these DSO students become future leaders in the Denison Community Association."

Students applaud the DCA for its strong presence on campus and are grateful for the sense of community it creates. "A major strength is the closeness among the students who do service—the bond that we all share as service-oriented students." They urge, "Denison is a small campus and thus there are many opportunities to become a leader—take advantage of them!"

Connecting Service with the Classroom

The John W. Alford Center for Service-Learning works to develop "reciprocal working relationships" between its surrounding community, the Denison Community Association, and class curriculum.

"Five to 12 different courses are offered each semester in a variety of disciplines. For example, courses have included Homelessness and Theology; Second-Hand Lives; Critical Pedagogy in U.S. Education; Families, Sexuality, and the State;Drawing II; Microeconomic Analysis; and Human Anatomy and Physiology." Within the past year, the center appointed a tenured faculty member as the Director of Curricular Service-Learning, with a mission of "increasing the number of service-learning courses in each academic department and establishing a mentoring relationship between seasoned faculty who offer service-learning courses and other faculty who want to develop courses."

The education department requires its students to participate in a tutoring program alongside their coursework. "Students tutor kids who have been through the juvenile court system or kids living in foster homes. This has allowed me to broaden my horizons and help students that have different backgrounds than myself."

Impact on Community and Students

"Many students at a small, private, secluded college such as Denison are sheltered, and civic engagement forces them out of their comfort zone." Students are grateful that Denison's service organizations help establish "direct personal contact with people in need."

Among its 30 community partners, the DCA works with 12 county schools, supports Habitat for Humanity trips, and "has a staff position on campus to recruit, train, and mentor Denison students" as Big Brothers and Big Sisters for local children. All told, DCA students spend over 13,000 hours in the community each academic year.

Through a program called HOPE for Autism, 33 students are specially trained to work with young children with autism within the community. "DCA student volunteers are able to give the enormous amount of time (20 to 30 hours per week) required for the treatment to each child. HOPE for Autism committee members not only work in the community with children throughout the year but held a full-day workshop for parents, community educators, and students."

Through DCA's Helping Hands program, Denison students work with building an organic community garden with girls who've been in the county juvenile system. "The Denison students serve as mentors as well as supervisors as the girls learn about gardening from the initial clearing of land to harvesting the produce." After their produce is harvested, it is donated to a local food pantry.

Students credit their community service with some major life epiphanies. One student who "went on a trip during winter vacation that focused on HIV/AIDS" was able "to realize that this is an area that I would like to specialize in after medical school." Another credits her work with kids at a local domestic-violence shelter with providing "some of my best memories of college. I had the chance to lead my organization for two years, link my own committee with the philanthropy of my sorority, and form connections both on- and off-campus. Combining service with my phenomenal academics has helped me realize my calling of a lifelong commitment to service, my upcoming year of service with AmeriCorps, and my future academic goals of working towards my Masters in Public Policy."

Student Financial Support for Service

The John W. Alford Center for Service-Learning offers Ashbrook scholarships to students for summer research. "The Ashbrook scholarships," says the school, "are designed to foster and promote research and educational cooperation between faculty and students in exploring ways to improve the political and economic betterment of underprivileged residents in our home county. Students are given free room and board and a stipend." Past projects have included a Homeless Management Information System and the development of a settlement house for at-risk youth in the county.

DePaul University

1 East Jackson Boulevard, Chicago, IL 60604-2287

Admissions: 312-362-8300 • **Fax:** 312-362-5749 • **Financial Aid:** 312-362-8091

E-mail: ADMITDPU@DEPAUL.EDU • **Website:** WWW.DEPAUL.EDU

CAMPUS LIFE

Type of school	private
Environment	town

STUDENTS

Total undergrad enrollment	14,239
% male/female	42/58
% from out of state	13
% from public high school	68
% live on campus	18
% African American	9
% Asian	8
% Caucasian	50
% Hispanic	11
% international	1
# of countries represented	85

ACADEMICS

Calendar	undergrad & graduate/quarter; law/semester
Student/faculty ratio	16:1
% profs teaching UG courses	100
% classes taught by TAs	0
Most common lab size	<10
Most common reg class size	20-29

MOST POPULAR MAJORS
accounting
business administration/management
general studies

Getting Involved

What's the greatest strength of service at DePaul University? "The fact that you rarely run into a student who is not participating in civic-engagement efforts on campus." Although DePaul is a Catholic university, its student body maintains diverse political viewpoints—making for a student life as colored by community service as it is by activist rabble-rousing. DePaul was founded by a religious order deriving from the work of St. Vincent de Paul and has committed itself ever since to working with "the poor and the disadvantaged." Its efforts are advanced by The Irwin W. Steans Center for Community-based Service Learning (CBSL), whose core purpose is to develop service-learning courses at DePaul. The center employs 24 students as community liaisons and houses the academic Community Service Studies Program (CSS). In addition, it funds community-service internships, runs the community work-study program, and administers three scholarship programs.

University Ministry Community Service also advances DePaul's commitment to civic-engagement programs through its thirteen Service Immersions—opportunities for students to participate in one –to –two week-long "service and justice experiences" nationally and internationally—over winter and spring breaks. University Ministry also houses the DePaul Community Service Association, the umbrella organization for DePaul's student-led service and justice organizations.

Campus Culture of Engagement

At DePaul, "information about how to get involved is all over the place." "At the beginning of the year, there is something called an 'involvement fair.' Practically every student stops by for a little while. E-mail lists are formed, meeting information is disseminated, and everyone has a blast." From that point on, "our student center is always loaded with student orgs promoting their events." Campus participation in civic engagement tends to be "very passionate" and widespread. Annual community-wide community-service days—during which university volunteers perform approximately 7,000 hours of community service "in anything from protest to building projects to peer mentoring"—"are fun and almost seen as social events." Students with particularly strong service yearnings can gather in Amate House, a faith-based residential program for ten undergraduate students who volunteer for six to ten hours each week in addition to enrolling in "an experiential learning class which focuses on Catholicism and social action." Students report that "because the campus is so diverse, there is a lot of social activism happening all the time" in addition to constant "debates and conversation." Student-led activist groups include Amnesty International, DePaul Students Against the War, Concerned Black Students, and DePaul Students for Latino Empowerment. Their messages come "in the form of protests, petitions, lectures, debates, organizing efforts, films, spoken-word venues, and fundraisers."

Connecting Service with the Classroom

DePaul students praise their "like-minded, conscious professors who utilize our urban environment to 'teach' our students about the world." In collaboration with the Steans Center, faculty in over 25 departments and programs offer more than 100 service-learning courses each academic year. Upon entering DePaul, freshman students are required to take one of two service-learning classes—"Discover Chicago" or "Explore Chicago"—which both involve "a day of service or a service component" meant to introduce students to Chicago's diverse groups and organizations. From there, "a sophomore multicultural seminar involves students in deep discussion about the ways in which many groups have enriched our common life," and "junior-year students may elect a service-learning course as one way to fulfill the Experiential Learning requirement." Service-oriented academic programs include the Environmental Studies major, the Peace, Conflict Resolution, and Social Justice minor, and the Religious Studies Concentration in Ethics and Social Justice. Community Service Studies "combines courses from several disciplines that provide a framework for viewing community service from the perspectives of theory, ethics, and group dynamics." Study-abroad opportunities include "Bringing It Home," a program which aims to place domestic issues in international perspective. "One example of such an experience is the El Salvador December study-abroad course. During class meetings prior to the December trip, students are introduced to and begin working with community organizations in the Chicago area that focus on immigrants' issues and rights, including work with survivors of war and torture. Students travel to El Salvador for two to three weeks, after which they return to the community organizations during the winter quarter to carry out a project or some other work that they have negotiated with the organization."

Impact on Community and Students

DePaul's service opportunities tend to take place "in parts of Chicago that are under-resourced, under-represented, and under-served." The university maintains 13 local, domestic, and international community partners through its Immersion Program, and "varying degrees of partnerships with more than 100 community-based organizations in the Chicago area."

In the 2003–2004 academic year, DePaul students contributed approximately 6,400 hours of service to The Inner Voice, an organization that serves the homeless in Chicago. "DePaul students have served as tutors for children at one Inner Voice transitional shelter, developed a documentary video that Inner Voice uses as a promotion and information tool, taught parenting classes to parents in the transitional shelter, assisted with grant writing through a grant-writing course, and hosted a holiday party for the families of several of the shelters."

Other partnerships include the Gary Comer San Miguel Middle School, where DePaul students organize projects promoting ecological and neighborhood awareness in order to counteract some of the social issues "ranging from unemployment to illegal gang activity" in the school's Austin neighborhood. At the Theresa House, a transitional family shelter on Chicago's South Side, students from the DePaul group Students Against Hunger and Homelessness (SAHH) mentor children and help with weekly dinners.

Student Financial Support for Service

To be eligible for the Community Service Scholars program, applicants must "demonstrate a significant commitment to community service, declare a Community Service Studies Minor, and complete 30 hours of community service per academic quarter for a total of 12 quarters. Twenty to 25 scholars each year receive $5,000 per year for up to four years."

In addition, the Joan and Richard Meister Community Service Scholarships grant $1,000 to students "whose commitment to community engagement is exemplary," and the McCormick-Tribune Community Internships award $1,000 to students "who have established relationships with community organizations and intend to complete a project that the organization finds beneficial."

Additional scholarships—of which there are several—include the 36 $1,000 to $3,000 University Ministry St. Vincent de Paul Community Service Scholarships for DePaul Community Service Association coordinators, Amate House need-based scholarships for volunteers, Mayor's Leadership Scholarships for Chicago residents with exceptional records of civic activity, Monsignor Egan Hope Scholarships for service-oriented students from Chicago's urban and inner-city communities, and the Vincentian Endowment Fund (VEF), which supports "student-led initiatives and faculty-student initiatives that have a direct community service or social justice objective."

SELECTIVITY

# of applicants	10,087
% of applicants accepted	69
% of acceptees attending	33

FRESHMAN PROFILE

Range SAT Verbal	520-620
Range SAT Math	500-610
Range ACT Composite	21-26
Minimum Paper TOEFL	550
Minimum Computer TOEFL	213
Average HS GPA	3.30
% graduated top 10% of class	19
% graduated top 25% of class	43
% graduated top 50% of class	75

DEADLINES

Regular notification by	rolling
Nonfall registration?	yes

FINANCIAL FACTS

Annual tuition	$19,700
Room and board	$9,307
Books and supplies	$1,000
Required food	$65
% frosh rec. need-based scholarship or grant aid	54
% UG rec. need-based scholarship or grant aid	52
% frosh rec. need-based self-help aid	56
% UG rec. need-based self-help aid	54
% frosh rec. any financial aid	65
% UG rec. any financial aid	68

DUKE UNIVERSITY

2138 CAMPUS DRIVE, DURHAM, NC 27708

ADMISSIONS: 919-684-3214 • FAX: 919-681-8941 • FINANCIAL AID: 919-684-6225

E-MAIL: UNDERGRAD-ADMISSIONS@DUKE.EDU • WEBSITE: WWW.DUKE.EDU

CAMPUS LIFE

Type of school	private
Environment	town

STUDENTS

Total undergrad enrollment	6,066
% male/female	52/48
% from out of state	85
% from public high school	66
% live on campus	82
% African American	10
% Asian	12
% Caucasian	60
% Hispanic	7
% international	5

ACADEMICS

Calendar	semester
Student/faculty ratio	8:1
% profs teaching UG courses	96
% classes taught by TAs	4
Most common lab size	10-19
Most common reg class size	10-19

MOST POPULAR MAJORS
economics
psychology
public policy analysis

Getting Involved

"When I came to Duke, I thought location was a disadvantage—it's not a major city and I always thought that's what I wanted. It turns out that Durham has so many opportunities for Duke students to be part of an exciting, changing community and to put their skills to use for positive change. The location is really an attraction to students who want to learn about civic engagement in a firsthand way."

Duke University's tight relationship with Durham stems from a strong institutional dedication to service and service learning. The Community Service Center (CSC) is the nexus of campus-outreach efforts, serving as the meeting ground for student-service clubs and leading faculty efforts to integrate service learning into school curriculum. The center also promotes campus literacy initiatives and coordinates community-based service internships for work-study students. The Office of Community Affairs provides additional opportunities through an umbrella program called the Duke-Durham Neighborhood Partnership "whose goal is to improve the quality of life in the 12 neighborhoods and seven public schools closest to campus."

According to a Duke student, "The program is well designed to first get people interested and then to guide students to the resources that will enable us to make substantial changes to the community." The CSC "is really well run and has a great influence and presence."

Campus Culture of Engagement

First-year students meet "countless opportunities" upon arriving on campus, thanks to the CSC's efforts to "involve freshman very early on." "During orientation week, they have a program called 'Into The City' in which students are brought into Durham to see what the major problems are and places where they can help." Additionally, "freshman-year dorms usually have a year-long community-service project, such as volunteering at a local grade school."

Service thrives on a social level because students maintain a "constant dialogue about Duke's involvement in the community." "If you can't find an established program that you're interested in, it is not uncommon or difficult to start your own group on campus. Just this semester, undergraduates have started Duke chapters of Operation Smile and Physicians for Human Rights on campus."

Duke activists aren't shy about speaking out. Recent controversies have involved the University Health Care System's outsourcing of laundry services to company that employed "union-busting tactics": In addition to presenting a petition to the administation containing 1,000 signatures and publishing editorials in the campus newspaper, "students organized a protest that involved dropping dirty laundry at the administrator's office!"

Connecting Service with the Classroom

Duke students report that service-learning programs are "widespread and growing." They first encounter Research Service Learning (RSL) through "more than sixteen introductory or 'gateway' research service-learning courses in the humanities, social sciences, and natural sciences. Gateway courses require 20 hours of service per semester with one of the program's community partners—primarily social services agencies and public schools—as well as ethical inquiry reflection sessions and an introduction to field-based research."

The Hart Leadership Program also offers Service Opportunities in Leadership

(SOL) through the Terry Sanford Institute of Public Policy. This "intensive 12-month leadership program for Duke undergraduates combines academic study, community service, mentoring, and leadership training. It includes a half-credit course in the spring, a community-based internship in the summer, and a research seminar in the fall. Interns work with community-development initiatives, organizing efforts, refugee and immigration issues, clinical-health programs, and a range of service projects."

One student testifies, "My work as a volunteer tutor at a local elementary school began during my first semester as the service-learning component to course work, but I have continued this work independently throughout my time here. This has provided the chance to learn about educational equity issues and also a greater understanding of the community dynamics of Durham, my temporary home."

Impact on Community and Students

"Durham is a great place to get your hands a little dirty." "Because of our location, there are many opportunities for inner-city work or for migrant-farm worker collaboration nearby."

"In addition to the 27 social service agencies and public school partners in RSL gateway courses," says the school, "the Duke-Durham Neighborhood Partnership includes formal partnerships with eight schools, 12 neighborhood associations, eight faith-based organizations, and 14 nonprofits." The Project Child tutoring program annually delivers about 80 first-year Duke students to public schools and community centers, where they volunteer twice a week for a semester and meet biweekly in reflection sessions. Through Duke's Project HOPE, first-year students devote themselves to an "after-school program for at-risk students who live in Duke's partner neighborhoods." The program recently received a $2.25 million grant from the Kellogg Foundation.

"Civic engagement has changed the way I view my education in a way I never would have imagined when I came to Duke my freshman year. That first year, I joined a community-service group that tutored in a local community center based in a housing project. When I got to this community center and met all of these wonderful, bright children with so few resources, it hit me like a ton of bricks how easy I had had it in terms of my education and how much easier it had been for me to succeed and come to Duke than it could be for these kids. Both of my parents have law degrees, and many of their parents did not graduate from high school. My mother stayed home with me and made me do my homework every night; many of their parents worked two jobs just to stay afloat. Now I am working towards my elementary-education certification, and I've become very involved in service-learning on campus as the student coordinator for LEAPS. Through LEAPS, I hope to help other people have the same kind of profound experience that I had."

Student Financial Support for Service

The Robertson Scholars Program "awards full scholarships to 15 students who spend the summer after their first year doing a community-service internship in the southeastern United States. The summer after their sophomore year, they go abroad, focusing on community service and crossing cultural boundaries in an international setting." The Lars Lyon Memorial Endowment is given annually to a full-time undergraduate student in recognition of volunteer community service. The Reginald Howard Memorial Scholarship Program provides five scholarships annually "to first-year students of African American heritage who demonstrate evidence of serious commitment to a life of service to others." The Benjamin N. Duke Leadership Scholarship Program "recognizes ten of North and South Carolina's brightest and most highly motivated student leaders who are devoted to community service. These students complete a service-based internship in North or South Carolina after their freshman year."

SELECTIVITY

# of applicants	13,976
% of applicants accepted	26
% of acceptees attending	44
# accepting a place on wait list	1,648
% admitted from wait list	6

FRESHMAN PROFILE

Range SAT Verbal	650-740
Range SAT Math	670-770
Range ACT Composite	29-34
% graduated top 10% of class	90
% graduated top 25% of class	98
% graduated top 50% of class	100

DEADLINES

Regular admission	1/2
Regular notification by	4/1
Nonfall registration?	no

FINANCIAL FACTS

Annual tuition	$28,475
Room and board	$8,205
Books and supplies	$910
Required fees	$820
% frosh rec. need-based scholarship or grant aid	37
% UG rec. need-based scholarship or grant aid	36
% frosh rec. need-based self-help aid	33
% UG rec. need-based self-help aid	33

ELON UNIVERSITY

100 CAMPUS DRIVE, ELON, NC 27244-2010

ADMISSIONS: 336-278-3566 • **FAX:** 336-278-7699 • **FINANCIAL AID:** 336-278-7640

E-MAIL: ADMISSIONS@ELON.EDU • **WEBSITE:** WWW.ELON.EDU

CAMPUS LIFE

Type of school	private
Environment	village

STUDENTS

Total undergrad enrollment	4,622
% male/female	39/61
% from out of state	69
% from public high school	70
% live on campus	59
% African American	7
% Asian	1
% Caucasian	86
% Hispanic	1
% international	1
# of countries represented	40

ACADEMICS

Calendar	4-1-4
Student/faculty ratio	16:1
% profs teaching UG courses	100
% classes taught by TAs	0
Most common lab size	20-29
Most common reg class size	10-19

MOST POPULAR MAJORS

business administration/management
education
mass communications/media studies

Getting Involved

Elon University credits its hardcore service ethic to the United Church of Christ, which shaped its founders' vision of "an academic community that transforms mind, body, and spirit and encourages freedom of thought and liberty of conscience."

Elon walks the walk as emphatically as it talks the talk, thanks to a broad civic-engagement support system. The Kernodle Center for Service Learning is the architectural heart of the mission, and the Coordinating Council for Civic Engagement oversees several campus programs that promote civic and social responsibility. According to students, "This school provides you many opportunities to take hold of leadership roles." Elon Volunteers!, a program run by 60 student volunteers, helps to match students with community-service needs. The Isabella Cannon Leadership Program is a four-year program encompassing workshops, retreats, and seminars which culminates in a final capstone project about student responsibility and systemic community change. Elon also benefits from its role as the founding host campus for North Carolina Campus Compact (NCCC)—a relationship that keeps students and staff connected to service on a statewide level.

Students report that "opportunities to get involved in any way are enormous" and compliment the "very involved" staff for its readiness to "give the students the feedback they need."

Campus Culture of Engagement

The "best" first-year engagement opportunity is arguably the Service Learning Community. The SLC—designed primarily for first-year students and run with the help of small number of sophomore mentors—is comprised of 41 students who are selected prior to arriving at Elon. They arrive on campus early for a special orientation, and then, "throughout the year, the students create a structure of committees to plan and implement monthly activities for themselves." They also enroll in a core service-learning course and a winter-term service-learning excursion, often in Washington, DC. "Students learn about service opportunities, the social issues that plague America, what our government is or isn't doing about it, and they get to work towards the cause."

Service at Elon isn't just for the SLC elite, of course; says the school, "88 percent of graduating seniors have participated in at least one service project during their time at Elon." "I have never been part of community that dedicates so much time to others, and I wouldn't have it any other way." "We have groups that go and help those that have AIDS or HIV, we help build houses, get clothing or toys for children and adults, do blood drives, and it is all over campus and in the community. It is very public and welcoming."

Elon students note that "we are not particularly politically active here," and "activism needs help." "However, steps are being taken to ensure this improves—[like] registering students [to vote], political forums, and speakers."

Connecting Service with the Classroom

Elon's professors are "very active and encourage engagement, service, and activism."

In the 2003–2004 academic year, Elon "offered 35 service-learning courses, which involved approximately 600 students in an estimated 15,000 hours of service to the community."

Project Pericles is one of the most celebrated sites of service-learning on campus.

The national program selects 44 Elon sophomores each year to be Periclean Scholars and gives them the opportunity to "take a series of courses (one per school year) culminating in a class project of global social change." "The first group of scholars was selected for the fall of 2003 and chose to focus on the pandemic of HIV/AIDS in Namibia. Members of the class spent time in Namibia to learn about the social structural causes of the problem and then wrote and received a grant to return to Africa and develop an educational video about HIV/AIDS."

The Elon Institute for Politics and Public Affairs educates students about public policy and civic leadership through "real-world problem-solving" with public, private, and nonprofit organizations. "Elon students recently surveyed neighborhoods in Greensboro, NC, plotting a map of library branches to show which branch needed language materials or services for the deaf."

The Washington Center provides its own opportunities for civic engagement: "For each of the past eighteen years, 20 students have participated in seminars on the presidency and the media, featuring high-profile speakers and visits to important sites in the nation's capital. About ten to 15 students intern each year in the White House, executive agencies, Congress, the judiciary, political parties, interest groups, and think-tanks." One student reports that because of these kinds of civic opportunities, "I am a much better citizen, I have registered to vote, and I pay a lot more attention to the political atmosphere, issues, campaign, and debates."

Impact on Community and Students

Through the Kernodle Center for Service Learning and Elon Volunteers!, Elon works with more than 40 community organizations. These include soup kitchens, the Women's Resource Center, and the Red Cross. According to one student, "Through doing service work for the past two years, I was motivated enough to start my own organization on campus dealing with service projects and awareness campaigns dedicated to stopping sexual assault, dating violence, and sexual harassment."

Elon is "the first college in the nation to commit not only to building at least one Habitat for Humanity house each year, but to raising $30,000 needed for each project." "Each year, students participate in spring break trips with Habitat in locations such as Florida, Alabama, and the Dominican Republic. During winter term, students travel to Guatemala to work with Habitat as part of a service-learning four-credit course." A student explains, "On any given week, I am giving much of my energy to Habitat—whether we are preparing to work on the roof of the house, making spaghetti at a fundraiser, or talking about poverty awareness by making shacks for an event called Shack-a-thon."

Other community partnerships include Elon Cares, an on-campus HIV/AIDS awareness group that sponsors the AIDS Walk and a monthly lunch for people who are HIV positive, and Family Abuse Services, an agency that provides services to victims of family abuse. "Students volunteer weekly in a childcare program while the parents are in support groups," and "individual volunteers are paired with children to serve as their advocates in the courtroom during their court cases."

Student Financial Support for Service

"The Kernodle Center for Service Learning is endowed and provides $2,500 scholarships for three students who are the top student leaders coordinating service programs and student volunteers. Two other endowed programs require students to complete service: Eight Watson scholarships of $5,000 are awarded annually to first-year North Carolina students with high financial need; four Isabella Cannon Leadership Fellows scholarships are awarded annually based on leadership experiences. These scholarships continue over the students' four years, contingent on meeting program requirements. Each program requires a minimum of 20 hours of service."

FLORIDA STATE UNIVERSITY

2500 UNIVERSITY CENTER, TALLAHASSEE, FL 32306-2400

ADMISSIONS: 850-644-6200 • FAX: 850-644-0197 • FINANCIAL AID: 850-644-0539

E-MAIL: ADMISSIONS@ADMIN.FSU.EDU • WEBSITE: WWW.FSU.EDU

CAMPUS LIFE

Type of school	public
Environment	village

STUDENTS

Total undergrad enrollment	29,820
% male/female	43/57
% from out of state	15
% from public high school	89
% live on campus	14
% African American	12
% Asian	3
% Caucasian	73
% Hispanic	10
% international	1
# of countries represented	134

ACADEMICS

Calendar	semester
% profs teaching UG courses	100
% classes taught by TAs	32
Most common reg class size	20-29

MOST POPULAR MAJORS

criminal justice/safety studies
finance
psychology

Getting Involved

Florida State University's service and service-learning initiatives take place "at a little house on campus": the Center for Civic Education and Service. This hub earns high marks from participating students who encourage incoming enthusiasts to "drop by. The staff there is extremely helpful and knowledgeable about service both on an off campus." There, "they work to tailor service to each individual" thanks to "working relationships with a myriad of not-for-profits related to hunger and homlessness, AIDS/HIV, FCAT mentoring, [and] Florida Reads."

It is important to note that although we all know that truly virtuous acts of service are those performed without self-advancement in mind, it is worth mentioning that the Center also purportedly does "an excellent job tracking each student's service." Its ServScript program allows students to record service hours to their transcripts as they are performed.Other FSU service coordination sites include the Institute of Science and Public Affairs and the Office of K–20 Initiatives, which "promotes assistance to public education in Florida and currently catalogs over 70 distinct partnerships." The Florida Alliance for Student Service (FASS)—a coalition of statewide service programs—and the FSU Service Corps provide additional opportunities for civic engagement.

Campus Culture of Engagement

"Outreach Projects" provide a particularly convenient introduction to community involvement. "These happen on a regular basis (each project happens one or two times a week on a set day). The center provides a van and a team leader who is familiar with the community agency where the service will be taking place. A student who is interested in a certain outreach project need only drop by the center or call and have his or her name added to the signup list for that week. All the student then must do is drop by at the set time, and the team leader will take care of the rest."

Unfortunately, FSU may not scream "civic engagement" to those outside of the know: " The school is known more for its football players than for it's volunteers. Yet students insist, "we have a number of registered student organizations whose sole purpose is to serve the community (like Project FSU, HELP, SPEAK, and CHICS). In addition, our SGA and Greek systems help spur these initiatives by using their already assembled groups to help out." "By being involved, you feel a sense of 'family' at FSU."

Students describe the FSU campus as being "very politically active"—especially via "the strong organizations of Student Goverment, the Black Student Union, and the Greek system, just to name a few"—but also note that the realm of political activism tends to remain "separate from service." "I mention this only to caution students who assume that activism and services necessarily equal politics—this is not the case."

Connecting Service with the Classroom

FSU currently offers service-learning courses in 29 departments ranging "from Art Education to Information Studies to Meteorology to Social Work to Urban and Regional Planning." In fall of 2003 alone, the 76 service-learning course offerings included "Art in Community Service" and "Family Problems and Social Change." Courses exist at the undergraduate, graduate, advanced graduate, and professional levels.

"I am a Psychology major," attests one student, "and I have gotten involved with America Reads (a program that helps low-[SES] children learn to read). I am now pursuing an Honors Thesis in how children acquire reading skills."

Says another, "I've painted houses in New Orleans for a low-income housing project, I've helped build a school for a rural community in the Republic of Panama, I've listened to activist speakers, and I've been able to help serve different needs of the community. All of these experiences have help to broaden my understanding of the world around me and the issues that need to be worked with. I have been able to see firsthand the issues of inequality and development that I learn about through lectures and books."

Impact on Community and Students

FSU maintains relationships with a whopping "200 community-based agencies, nonprofits and governmental (city, county, and state), plus many more school sites at the elementary, middle, and high school levels." "Since we're the capital of Florida, a lot of people work with legislators and lobbyists. There is also a lot of opportunity for outreach in Leon county and the surrounding counties, especially in working with the homeless and with migrant workers."

Noteworthy programs include the student organizations Community Medical Outreach and International Medical Outreach. "Founded by pre-med students within the last five years, CMO and IMO students interested in health professions have provided hundreds of hours in medical assistance to those in need in rural Florida and Caribbean nations." FSU also maintains a strong relationship with the United Way of Big Bend, "infusing all 45 of its affiliated nonprofit agencies with service-learning students from public administration, MIS, business, and marketing to further their mission and support their staff in the delivery of support services to citizens in our community."

FSU's ties to local public schools are particularly strong, thanks to an office dedicated exclusively to cultivating K–12 partnerships. America Reads involves nearly 500 FSU students a year in reading tutoring for first-graders in nearby schools." One student reports, "I volunteered at a local elementary school through the America Reads program which tutors first graders who are at risk for falling behind their peers with regards to reading. It has helped me have hands-on experience with students and the school system."

Student Financial Support for Service

"The Service Scholar Program, established in 1997, is designed to recognize students with an outstanding record of service and to promote service as an integral part of the liberal arts education at FSU. Each year, a minimum of 12 scholarships are awarded to incoming freshmen who have demonstrated excellence in service to the community and who have an interest in continuing to enhance their learning through community service while attending Florida State. Service Scholarship awards are valued at $2,000 per year and may be renewed for up to four years by meeting published criteria." Scholars perform 75 hours of service per semester and attend monthly leadership seminars.

"As a Service Scholar at FSU, I have dedicated at least 75 hours of community service a semester to the area. In addition, my service alongside numerous students who are leaders in other facets of campus has spurred me to found my own student-service organization on campus, SPEAK, which is dedicated to starting and maintaining speech and debate programs at the local high and middle schools in the area."

SELECTIVITY

# of applicants	22,127
% of applicants accepted	65
% of acceptees attending	44
# accepting a place on wait list	300

FRESHMAN PROFILE

Range SAT Verbal	530-630
Range SAT Math	540-630
Range ACT Composite	22-27
Minimum Paper TOEFL	550
Minimum Computer TOEFL	213
Average HS GPA	3.73
% graduated top 10% of class	55
% graduated top 25% of class	93
% graduated top 50% of class	100

DEADLINES

Regular admission	3/1
Regular notification by	11/1, 12/15, 2/1, 3/1, 4/1
Nonfall registration?	yes

FINANCIAL FACTS

Annual in-state tuition	$2,290
Annual out-of-state tuition	$14,796
Room and board	$6,488
Books and supplies	$800
Required fees	$748
% frosh rec. need-based scholarship or grant aid	29
% UG rec. need-based scholarship or grant aid	31
% frosh rec. need-based self-help aid	25
% UG rec. need-based self-help aid	32

GEORGE WASHINGTON UNIVERSITY

2121 I STREET NW, SUITE 201, WASHINGTON, DC 20052
ADMISSIONS: 202-994-6040 • FAX: 202-994-0325 • FINANCIAL AID: 202-994-6620
E-MAIL: GWADM@GWU.EDU • WEBSITE: WWW.GWU.EDU

CAMPUS LIFE

Type of school	private
Environment	town

STUDENTS

Total undergrad enrollment	9,953
% male/female	43/57
% from out of state	98
% from public high school	70
% live on campus	68
% African American	5
% Asian	9
% Caucasian	65
% Hispanic	5
% international	5
# of countries represented	101

ACADEMICS

Calendar	semester
Student/faculty ratio	15:1
% profs teaching UG courses	67
% classes taught by TAs	3
Most common lab size	10-19
Most common reg class size	10-19

Getting Involved

Most civically engaged schools can boast of strong relationships with their surrounding communities. But rarely do we stumble upon one whose setting is so central to its student character as that of George Washington University, whose Washington, DC, location is a principle draw for students interested in social change. "Just walk down the street and you will see eight posters, three chalk messages, and get handed a flyer by a variety of activist groups," says one GW student. "Everyone who comes to DC has some sort of political interest, so nearly every cause imaginable is loudly championed by someone on campus. This is the activists' mecca." Activism may trump less-politicized forms of volunteerism on the GW campus, but the University's Office of Community Service (OCS) runs a tight and effective ship. Housed in the Student Activities Center, the OCS coordinates opportunities for "one-time, ongoing, volunteer, internship, and federal work study community service and service-learning opportunities in over 40 different community agencies in all eight wards of the District of Columbia." Its programs include Alternative Spring Breaks, Community Building Community (for incoming freshmen), DC Reads, Jumpstart, and the Neighbors Project. The Community Living and Learning Center (CLLC) provides additional support for service-learning initiatives within residence halls. "GW puts a large amount of money into its budget for community-service projects. Unlike high school, where everything is done with volunteers' resources, students can skip the internal-fundraising and work towards very solid, well-planned, and well-funded community service activities."

Campus Culture of Engagement

"Service and activism opportunities practically fall into your lap at GW," explains one student. "A student comes face-to-face with the various service/activist groups the very first day of school orientation, months before classes start. There are representatives on campus handing out pamphlets, hosting panels, and roaming the streets, looking for students with whom they can talk. Once classes begin, the fervor intensifies, and it becomes quite impossible not to become involved in various activities."

Students can't rave enough about the level of civic engagement on campus, describing the student body as "politically obsessed" and "passionate." "The DC atmosphere breeds a sense of power and efficacy that is contagious." The action takes place "everywhere: in the Marvin Center, in Kogan Plaza or the Campus Quad, on any sidewalk on campus, through workshops and meetings, at Homeless Shelters across DC—anywhere there is room, there is something going on." Students have recently participated in the March for Women's Lives, protests against the World Bank/IMF, and sit-ins against sweatshop labor.

GW supports "more than 300 registered student organizations, many of them dedicated to civic engagement"—including the GW Votes Program, Students for Fair Trade, Progressive Student Union, Habitat for Humanity, Help Initiate Peace, and Books for Africa. "While I haven't agreed with all of the causes, just the experience of having anti-abortion rallies or Howard Dean endorsing John Kerry in the middle of campus, or having the politically charged 'CNN's Crossfire' held in a classroom building is exciting and really drives students to learn more about the events. Since these events are very visible and noticeable, you are likely to have three or four conversations about them with different students or professors, which really gets you thinking and motivated to either get involved or take a solid position on whatever the issue."

Connecting Service with the Classroom

In the 2003–2004 school year, more than 400 students participated in service-learning classes spanning the departments of Human Services, Sociology, Spanish, Women's Studies, and the Medical School. The Human Services Program is a service-learning major or minor with the long-term goal of preparing students for leadership roles in nonprofit organizations. Through the program, "advanced students work directly for small, start-up service organizations. Seniors and juniors who have already volunteered for well-established nonprofit organizations participate in program development, evaluation, and grant writing at organizations still in need of stabilization." In turn, these organizations offer students the opportunity to put their nonprofit management knowledge into practice. Other service-oriented academic programs include the Hamilton Fish Institute on School and Community Violence, which works closely with the DC public schools in developing and testing violence-prevention strategies. The Interdisciplinary Student Community-Oriented Prevention Enhancement Service (ISCOPES) project, a collaborative effort between George Washington University Medical Center and George Mason University, "is dedicated to improving community healthcare through service learning" in areas with deficient public-health education and promotion.

GW students appreciate that their professors "always encourage out-of-class assignments to use the resources available in the DC area" and applaud the many opportunities to link classroom learning with external internships. "One semester, I was taking Legislative Politics on Tuesday and Thursday, and on Monday and Friday I interned with Congressman Greenwood. The city allows your education to come to life."

Impact on Community and Students

"To get connected, DC is the place to be." "I am a member of Student Global AIDS Campaign, and through them, I've learned about the nature of collective activity and participated in things I wouldn't have done otherwise, like lobbying Congress or organizing a teach-in."

GW's community partnerships "include educational institutions, hospitals, clinics, shelters, advocacy and public policy organizations." A group called FRIENDS—a partnership with residents of the Foggy Bottom area—has been meeting for two years to discuss ways in which the university and its surrounding neighborhood can better collaborate.

The Neighbor's Project is GW's oldest, largest, and most prominent volunteer placement program. Its nine undergraduate Service Coordinators each work with four to five agencies and are responsible "for recruiting, orienting, and tracking student volunteers at their agencies." Partnerships within the program include National Student Partnerships, "which assists homeless and low-income clients with finding employment opportunities, literacy programs, affordable housing, healthcare, and drug treatment," and Second Chance Employment, through which students provide one-on-one employment assistance to battered and abused women.

Other programs include DC Reads, which pairs GW tutors with public after-school programs. Jumpstart at GW "pairs approximately 40 GW federal work-study students with pre-school children struggling in Head Start programs at three sites in the District in order to prepare them to enter school at or above grade level."

One student reports, "through mentoring programs, I realize the need for qualified teachers in public schools. I will be joining Teach for America because of my undergraduate community-service experience."

Student Financial Support for Service

GW's awards and honors for community and public service include the Manatt-Trachtenberg Prize for social conscience, the Martin Luther King, Jr. Medal for Service and Social Justice, the Baer Award for Individual Student Excellence, and the Dorothy M. and Maurice C. Shapiro Fellowship to be used for public service. "There are also scholarships for Student Leadership Development, Awards for University Service, and faculty awards for Service, Teaching, and Research."

SELECTIVITY

# of applicants	20,159
% of applicants accepted	38
% of acceptees attending	35
# accepting a place on wait list	1,601
% admitted from wait list	11

FRESHMAN PROFILE

Range SAT Verbal	590-690
Range SAT Math	590-680
Range ACT Composite	25-30
Minimum Paper TOEFL	550
% graduated top 10% of class	58
% graduated top 25% of class	87
% graduated top 50% of class	99

DEADLINES

Regular admission	1/15
Regular notification by	3/15
Nonfall registration?	yes

FINANCIAL FACTS

Annual tuition	$30,790
Room and board	$10,210
Books and supplies	$850
Required fees	$30
% frosh rec. need-based scholarship or grant aid	38
% UG rec. need-based scholarship or grant aid	37
% frosh rec. need-based self-help aid	34
% UG rec. need-based self-help aid	35

GEORGETOWN UNIVERSITY

37TH AND O STREETS, NW, 103 WHITE-GRAVENOR, WASHINGTON, DC 20057

ADMISSIONS: 202-687-3600 • **FAX:** 202-687-5084 • **FINANCIAL AID:** 202-687-4547

E-MAIL: GUADMISS@GEORGETOWN.EDU • **WEBSITE:** WWW.GEORGETOWN.EDU

CAMPUS LIFE

Type of school	private
Environment	town

STUDENTS

Total undergrad enrollment	6,282
% male/female	46/54
% from out of state	98
% from public high school	45
% live on campus	78
% African American	7
% Asian	10
% Caucasian	69
% Hispanic	6
% international	4
# of countries represented	81

ACADEMICS

Calendar	semester
Student/faculty ratio	11:1
% profs teaching UG courses	100
% classes taught by TAs	0
Most common lab size	<10
Most common reg class size	10-19

MOST POPULAR MAJORS
finance
international relations and affairs
political science and government

Getting Involved

Georgetown University "educates women and men to be reflective lifelong learners, to be responsible and active participants in civic life, and to live generously in service to others." It strives to locate "the glory of God and the well-being of humankind" through strongly established service and service-learning programs. According to one student, "Georgetown's Center for Social Justice program and the religious groups on campus are the heart and soul of the student body." The Center for Social Justice Research, Teaching, and Service is home-base for community-based research, teaching, and service. It operates the Office of Volunteer and Public Service (VPS)—an umbrella organization for 28 student-run social-justice groups. One student describes the Center as "very involved. You can find a program for almost any type of service, and if it doesn't exist, you can initiate one with the school's full support."

The Center for Public and nonprofit Leadership, a part of the graduate program at the Georgetown Public Policy Institute, "provides education, research, and training dedicated to the development of public, nonprofit, and philanthropic leadership." Georgetown is also part of the Community Research and Learning (CoRAL) Network, an umbrella organization that coordinates partnerships with community groups and research institutes for all local universities within the greater DC metropolitan area.

Campus Culture of Engagement

Exposure to engagement opportunities begins with lots of posters and "the big fair in September, at which both service-focused and activist groups are well-represented." "Additionally, the campaigns and events that groups publicize draw in freshmen, whether it be a panel discussion on AIDS, peace activism on Iraq, or a feminist speaker series. Special events such as the recent groundbreaking festivities for Georgetown's own Habitat for Humanity House naturally draw more students to what is happening."

Students attest to the omnipresence of service on campus, reporting that "many people participate, and it is a significant part of campus life." "It is literally impossible not to be affronted with some kind of plea for service work from an organization that really fits you personally."

The character of activism at Georgetown may be shaped by what one student describes as a "very bright, very motivated, and very conservative" student body— "as a very liberal California Democrat, I was hard-pressed to find activism activities at Georgetown to get involved in." Yet the lower percentage of radicals does not necessarily make for a dearth of speak-outs, and some students argue that political diversity leads to more active dialogue on campus. "When Paul Wolfowitz came to speak on campus, students loudly and roundly criticized Wolfowitz, both through demonstration outside the venue and through asking questions and making comments critical of his department's policies. His speech, as well as his defensive responses to the questions and comments, was broadcast internationally. The resulting debate among student groups and in student publications was heated but demonstrative of the strong opinions and positions of students across the political spectrum."

Connecting Service with the Classroom

"As of summer of 2003, we could document 20 SL courses taught in six different departments in Georgetown College of Arts and Sciences, one in the School of Business, and seven in the School of Nursing and Health Studies (SNHS). In addition, we had eleven 'Service-Learning Credit' courses—an extra credit based on 40 hours of service/justice work, three short papers, and three discussion sessions that are attached to a regular three-credit course."

The Department of Sociology/Anthropology offers a Social Justice Concentration, which focuses on community-based work and works with the Office of International Programs and the Center for Social Justice to offer "social-justice practicum" in six study-abroad locations. Other options include the Program on Justice and Peace, an undergraduate minor/certificate requiring community-based work in one of its six courses. The Office of Public Interest and Community Service—a division of Georgetown's Law Center—is a "pro bono program that encourages all law students to perform volunteer work while they are at the Law Center." The School of Nursing and Health Studies offers service-learning opportunities to work with Milagros: The Center of Excellence in Migrant Health.

Impact on Community and Students

Students find that "Georgetown's location in Washington, DC, adds a strong support to various civic-engagement efforts." Some students "want to get directly involved in serving the DC community and find themselves leaving campus to do so, some run for election in local politics, and many work for or intern at nonprofits and NGOs headquartered in Washington."

For the not-necessarily-politically-inclined, "service takes place at various sites around the city—vans dropping off soup and fruit to homeless people in the parks, tutoring in the projects, GED preparation in the prison, and classroom aid in the public schools. Georgetown students are sent out as ambassadors to every needy facet of the city."

Georgetown maintains a strong partnership with the Calvary Bilingual Multicultural Learning Center (CBMLC), a community center in the working-class neighborhood of Columbia Heights focusing on child and family development. "Every Saturday, about 30 Georgetown volunteers teach English to about 100 adult learners, using Calvary's facilities. In addition, the program provides free meals to the learners while Calvary provides child care and tutoring for the learners' children."

Georgetown's Center for Minority Educational Affairs (CMEA) has developed a particularly strong relationship with the local Ronald H. Brown Middle School in the far northeast DC community, "selected because of its grave economic, social, and educational challenges." The CMEA has "developed a six-year-long enrichment program, aimed at assisting kids in getting access to resources and improving opportunities to enter college. The program provides many services, including math, science, and English classes, recreational activities, mentor and peer counseling, career internships, community-service projects, college planning, and many other varied experiences that have helped formulate their college and career plans. More recently, CMEA has leveraged additional human resources from GU, by having two Georgetown classes (one Biology and one Sociology) taught as community-based learning courses and working in collaboration with students and faculty at Ron Brown Middle School."

Student Financial Support for Service

Georgetown annually offers 20 Landegger Service Awards, valued at $2,500, to "outstanding undergraduate students for their deep commitment to and work in volunteer service to the community."

SELECTIVITY

# of applicants	14,855
% of applicants accepted	22
% of acceptees attending	47
# accepting a place on wait list	1,901
% admitted from wait list	1

FRESHMAN PROFILE

Range SAT Verbal	640-740
Range SAT Math	640-730
Range ACT Composite	27-32
Minimum Paper TOEFL	200
% graduated top 10% of class	90
% graduated top 25% of class	98
% graduated top 50% of class	100

DEADLINES

Regular admission	1/10
Regular notification by	4/1
Nonfall registration?	no

FINANCIAL FACTS

Annual tuition	$29,808
Room and board	$10,554
Books and supplies	$960
Required fees	$355
% frosh rec. need-based scholarship or grant aid	42
% UG rec. need-based scholarship or grant aid	37
% frosh rec. need-based self-help aid	37
% UG rec. need-based self-help aid	37
% frosh rec. any financial aid	44
% UG rec. any financial aid	43

HAMPSHIRE COLLEGE

Admissions Office, 893 West Street, Amherst, MA 01002

Admissions: 413-559-5471 • **Fax:** 413-559-5631 • **Financial Aid:** 413-559-5484

E-mail: admissions@hampshire.edu • **Website:** www.hampshire.edu

CAMPUS LIFE

Type of school	private
Environment	rural

STUDENTS

Total undergrad enrollment	1,344
% male/female	43/57
% from out of state	84
% from public high school	70
% live on campus	93
% African American	3
% Asian	4
% Caucasian	72
% Hispanic	5
% international	3
# of countries represented	26

ACADEMICS

Calendar	4-1-4
Student/faculty ratio	11:1
% profs teaching UG courses	100
% classes taught by TAs	0
Most common lab size	<10
Most common reg class size	10-19

MOST POPULAR MAJORS

liberal arts and sciences/liberal studies
social sciences
visual and performing arts

Getting Involved

Hampshire College is a rebel of a school, eschewing conventional academic structures like majors and grades in favor of student-guided, student-initiated projects. Its civic-engagement programs fit right into the mold. While the school was one of the first liberal arts colleges in the United States to implement a universal community-service requirement for graduation, the ways in which students incorporate service into their educations is highly flexible. One student explains that "because this school is self-directed, community service can take any form, look like anything that students want it to."

Many service efforts stem from the Community Partnerships for Social Change (CPSC) Office, which "recruits, trains, and places over 300 students—or more than a quarter of the Hampshire student body—each year in a wide range of short- and long-term, academically focused, co-curricular service internships at community organizations." One student applauds the office's service-based internship program: "I believe that the CPSC office does incredible outreach. Much of student engagement means making the decision to work with people off-campus. When people do make that decision, the CPSC is very supportive."

Hampshire's other service-learning sites include advocacy and policy institutes like the Civil Liberties and Public Policy program, "a national reproductive-rights advocacy and education organization" and the Center for Innovative Education. These institutes serve as sites of research and coordination for students' off-campus internships. One students adds that "the Lebron-Wiggins-Pran Cultural Center does amazing work as well, working with international students, students of color, and mixed heritage students for art events, institutional support, and get-togethers."

Campus Culture of Engagement

"A certain type of person is attracted to Hampshire: the radical, liberal kind." So it comes as no surprise that activism looms large. "Many students come already involved in activist work and start organizing actions and protests as soon as they get here. Others connect with these students and older organizers on campus in the dorms, at the dining hall, on the lawn." Additionally, "we have special days called 'Hampfest' where all the student groups can set up a table and spread the word."

Students report "lots of protests, sit-ins, and 'making public statements.' It occurs everywhere." "There are about 100 student groups on campus, and a lot of them are dedicated to progressive social causes. Food Not Bombs, Student Action for Radical Change, the Fresh Food Project, Hampshire Anti-Hunger—it's easy to join these groups and get involved." Students most recently rallied around the cause of campus "re-radicalization," seeking "to overhaul the new first-year plan and reinstate independent work as the centerpiece of our curriculum. We had a sit-in this week which was well received."

Connecting Service with the Classroom

A Hampshire student's education consists of an "individualized, interdisciplinary program of study" developed "in close collaboration with faculty mentors." The school strongly emphasizes the importance of independent research: "Every student does project-based work while at Hampshire, and approximately 40 percent to 50 percent of the students design community-based learning projects or research."

This free-wheeling academic system is more than just idealistic jargon. A student attests, "One of my most meaningful experiences in college was an independent study where I designed a curriculum to teach photography and writing as a way of fostering self-confidence and identity development. I then started a program in two different community centers during my last two years at Hampshire, following the curriculum I designed. It was an amazing experience."

Each year, five to ten Community-Based Learning (CBL) courses are offered to help students learn how to incorporate community involvement into their independent research. Examples include Agriculture, Ecology, and Society, a "course comparing conventional and sustainable agricultural practices" through research with area farmers, and Children and Their Cultural Worlds, a social-psychology class through which students complete internships with community agencies serving children or adolescents in order to explore "how children from a range of world cultures understand and make sense of the societies around them."

Courses often lead to long-term scholarly commitments: "I did my senior thesis on a project that I worked on with EARTH. I created tools for student activists who wanted to start a campaign to get their schools to use 100 percent recycled paper. I toured all over the U.S. encouraging other schools to start similar campaigns, and I have made several friends along the way. My life has taken a new turn because of my work with EARTH."

Impact on Community and Students

Hampshire maintains ten core community partnerships within a network of 50 to 75 local organizations. These partnerships range from Capacidad, a "multi-cultural, anti-bias after-school program for ages five to 12," to Enchanted Circle Theater, a multi-ethnic theater company that addresses educational and social themes.

One of Hampshire's proudest partnership is with Nuestras Raíces (NR), a grassroots organization founded by a Hampshire student in 1991 which promotes economic, human, and community development in the post-industrial city of Holyoke through urban agriculture. "Programs include the start and maintenance of community gardens, youth and elder programming, educational workshops, the building of a community agriculture center and entrepreneurial development." NR has been incorporated into Hampshire's programs in Film Studies, Sustainable Development, Environmental Studies, and Urban Studies—whose combined efforts have resulted in documentary footage of the garden's development, a mural project, and a bilingual newsletter.

Hampshire works closely with the other colleges in its Five College Consortium (Amherst, Mt. Holyoke, Smith College, and University of Massachusetts at Amherst) as part of the Holyoke Planning Network. This cross-college coalition "kicked off its work by hosting the 2002 National Planners Network conference entitled 'New Visions for Historic Cities: Bridging Divides, Building Futures.' Over 400 participants from around the country participated in the conference including local residents, urban planners, community organizers, academics, leaders of nonprofits, city officials, and students."

Student Financial Support for Service

Second- and third-year financial-aid students can compete to win Social Justice Scholarships, which provide funding for nonprofit internships. The Global Migrations Program funds student internships with "nonprofit, non-governmental organizations that work with refugees, migrant workers, new immigrants, and other displaced persons, and which are concerned with transnational migration, human rights, and other social-justice issues." In addition, "community service and activism play a role in qualifying students for a number of Hampshire's merit-based scholarships, including the A Better Chance Scholarship, Jane Clark Carey Scholarship, Arturo Schomburg Scholarship, and Surdna Foundation Scholarship." Hampshire is also "the first college or university in the country to offer matching grants to students with National Service Education Awards (AmeriCorps)."

SELECTIVITY

# of applicants	2,180
% of applicants accepted	59
% of acceptees attending	26
# accepting a place on wait list	436
% admitted from wait list	20

FRESHMAN PROFILE

Range SAT Verbal	610-700
Range SAT Math	550-660
Range ACT Composite	25-29
Minimum Paper TOEFL	577
Minimum Computer TOEFL	233
Average HS GPA	3.28
% graduated top 10% of class	26
% graduated top 25% of class	33
% graduated top 50% of class	88

DEADLINES

Regular admission	1/15
Regular notification by	4/1
Nonfall registration?	yes

FINANCIAL FACTS

Annual tuition	$30,418
Room and board	$8,113
Books and supplies	$500
Required fees	$560
% frosh rec. need-based scholarship or grant aid	60
% UG rec. need-based scholarship or grant aid	56
% frosh rec. need-based self-help aid	60
% UG rec. need-based self-help aid	56
% frosh rec. any financial aid	70
% UG rec. any financial aid	61

HARVARD UNIVERSITY

BYERLY HALL, 8 GARDEN STREET, CAMBRIDGE, MA 02138

ADMISSIONS: 617-495-1551 • **FAX:** 617-495-8821 • **FINANCIAL AID:** 617-495-1581

E-MAIL: COLLEGE@FAS.HARVARD.EDU • **WEBSITE:** WWW.FAS.HARVARD.EDU

CAMPUS LIFE

Type of school	private
Environment	town

STUDENTS

Total undergrad enrollment	6,649
% male/female	53/47
% from out of state	84
% from public high school	65
% live on campus	96
% African American	8
% Asian	18
% Caucasian	42
% Hispanic	8
% Native American	1
% international	7

ACADEMICS

Calendar	semester
Student/faculty ratio	8:1
% profs teaching UG courses	100
% classes taught by TAs	0
Most common lab size	<10
Most common reg class size	<10

MOST POPULAR MAJORS

economics
political science and government
psychology

Getting Involved

Civic-engagement opportunities may not be the primary reason most students attend Harvard University, but nearly two-thirds of the student population is involved in public service at some point in their careers, and half of those students are actively, continuously engaged. One reports, "Anything in the world you want to do—from pet therapy [for nursing-home residents], working with immigrants, reading to the elderly, theater for hospitalized children—we have it. We have so, so many programs."

The Phillips Brooks House is where most service begins, coordinated by the two groups contained within: the student-led Phillips Brooks House Association (PBHA) and the university-administered Public Service Network (PSN). The former is an independent nonprofit organization consisting of 77 student-led programs, including "12 community-based summer camps serving the children of Boston and Cambridge, the only student-led homeless shelter in the country, ESL instruction for recent immigrants, and legal advocacy for low-income residents."

The Public Service Network (PSN) "supports and fosters public service at Harvard through ongoing collaboration with" PBHA and other groups; the PBHA is also the umbrella organization for the 40 independent (non-PBHA) student-led public service programs on campus. PSN oversees The Center for Public Interest Careers, helping Harvard undergrads locate paid summer internships and year-long postgraduate fellowships in nonprofit organizations. Students applaud the PSN for making "lots of financial resources available to student groups" and cite "great organization at the top levels."

Campus Culture of Engagement

Students report swift initiation into the world of service at Harvard. "The First Year Urban Program is an excellent orientation program that also provides first-years with a direct 'in' to the service and activist communities at Harvard. Besides FUP, the Phillips Brooks House Association fair is a great place to find out about the various service/advocacy organizations on campus." If that doesn't suffice, "there will be posters everywhere advertising Harvard's millions of service groups."

According to students, service maintains a high profile: "Everyone I know does at least one program; it's not frowned upon as uncool." "Those who partcipate in programs of civic engagement are passionate about what they do and constantly strive to do better."

Harvard students know how to speak out. "A few years ago, Harvard launched a campaign to get low-paid service workers better wages. They raided University Hall, the President's office, and had a sit-in for several weeks while others camped out in Harvard Yard and refused to go to class. As a result, wages were raised. This campaign had a ripple effect across the nation; other schools started to copy us."

Connecting Service with the Classroom

According to Harvard's administration, "service-learning is not part of the core mission at Harvard University. Individual professors may connect students' service involvement with a particular component of the class; however, there are no requirements for professors to incorporate service-learning into the curriculum. However, one of the many issues under consideration during the current comprehensive curriculum review is the possibility of connecting community issues to classroom learning."

In spite of this caveat, Harvard does offer opportunities for "students to explore community issues and reflect on their public service." In the ten-week, student-initiated Education for Social Action (not-for-credit) class organized by PBHA, students link community and advocacy research with outside service work. One student explains, "the aim of E4SA is to educate students more deeply about the issues (education, prisons, and immigration) they work on and the neighborhoods (Dorchester, Roxbury, South Boston) where they do this work." During the annual, three-day Public-Service Summit, students come together to discuss their civic-engagement experiences. "To help students connect their service and academic interests, the PSN annually compiles the Focus on Service, a listing of university classes that incorporates a practical component so as to make connections between academic work and public service."

Impact on Community and Students

At Harvard, "every public-service student group is connected with at least one community partner." PBHA's Chinatown Committee, for instance is "a collaboration of six student-led programs that serve Boston's Chinatown, the oldest Asian-populated neighborhood in New England. Chinatown After-School provides enrichment and tutoring for 60 children in grades one through six; Chinatown Big Sibling is a one-to-one mentoring program; Chinatown Citizenship teaches basic America history and government to residents who are preparing to become naturalized U.S. citizens; and Chinatown Teen provides after-school program focused on group interaction and community exploration. More than 200 Harvard undergraduates volunteer with PBHA Chinatown programs."

Project HEALTH connects 120 Harvard volunteers with staff from local community and medical centers—including the Boston Medical Center and the Children's Hospital—in order to study, design, and implement "innovative programs in children's health" in accordance with its mission, "to break the link between poverty and negative pediatric-health outcomes and provide children living in the inner city with an equal opportunity to lead healthy lives." Students help run five advocacy programs, intended to connect community groups with government resources, and four after-school programs intended to provide health education and physical exercise for children suffering from asthma, obesity, and sickle-cell disease.

Additional programs include the PBHA Summer Urban Program (SUP), a student-run organization through which "approximately 150 college students live in and run ten summer camps in various communities in Boston and Cambridge" during the summers. The program combines "classroom-based enrichment activities" with field trips around Boston. Alternately, CityStep provides volunteer opportunities during the school year, bringing a curriculum of dance and other creative activities to after-school programs for kids in fifth through seventh grade. "CityStep volunteers teach, compose music, choreograph, handle publicity, and raise funds. The year culminates with a gala spring performance that showcases the children's dance abilities for parents, teachers, and friends at Cambridge Rindge and Latin High School."

Student Financial Support for Service

One student exclaims that "it is wonderful to attend a school where grant money for your service projects is so readily available!" In addition to stipends granted on a case-by-case basis, the Stride Rite leadership program "provides work-study wages and intensive leadership development for up to 40 students involved in community programming. Stride Rite Scholars are selected for their dedication to year-round service and financial need." Federal work-study-eligible students can earn additional funding tutoring children in reading and math through the America Reads and America Counts programs.

SELECTIVITY

# of applicants	19,609
% of applicants accepted	11
% of acceptees attending	79

FRESHMAN PROFILE

Range SAT Verbal	700-800
Range SAT Math	700-790
Range ACT Composite	30-34
% graduated top 10% of class	90
% graduated top 25% of class	98
% graduated top 50% of class	100

DEADLINES

Regular admission	1/1
Regular notification by	4/1
Nonfall registration?	no

FINANCIAL FACTS

Annual tuition	$26,066
Room and board	$8,868
Books and supplies	$2,522
Required fees	$2,994
% frosh rec. need-based scholarship or grant aid	47
% UG rec. need-based scholarship or grant aid	48
% frosh rec. need-based self-help aid	34
% UG rec. need-based self-help aid	41

HOBART AND WILLIAM SMITH COLLEGES

629 SOUTH MAIN STREET, GENEVA, NY 14456

ADMISSIONS: 315-781-3472 • **FAX:** 315-781-3471 • **FINANCIAL AID:** 315-781-3315

E-MAIL: ADMISSIONS@HWS.EDU • **WEBSITE:** WWW.HWS.EDU

CAMPUS LIFE

Type of school	private
Environment	rural

STUDENTS

Total undergrad	
enrollment	1,825
% male/female	46/54
% from out of state	53
% from public high school	65
% live on campus	90
% African American	4
% Asian	2
% Caucasian	87
% Hispanic	4
% international	2
# of countries represented	18

ACADEMICS

Calendar	semester
Student/faculty ratio	13:1
% profs teaching	
UG courses	100
% classes taught by TAs	0
Most common	
reg class size	10-19

MOST POPULAR MAJORS
economics
English language and literature
history

Getting Involved

The powers that be at Hobart and William Smith Colleges understand the value of civic engagement: The colleges' President, Mark D. Gearan, is a former Director of the Peace Corps. One student gushes, "our president is the best thing our school has to offer—he truly believes in the impact service-learning can have on students."

HWS' community-service efforts are supported by the Public Service Office, recently renovated and relocated to what one student describes as "much more prominent space where students will find it." The new office supports the colleges' service-learning curriculum, community-service work-study programs such as America Reads and Jumpstart, student groups, and "regular office-sponsored service programs such as Alternative Spring Breaks, blood drives, and the annual Holiday Project."

The president's office also contributes to campus engagement through its President's Forum series, which "has brought a number of prominent public figures to HWS, many of whom have spoken about service and civic engagement." Past speakers have included Senator Hillary Rodham Clinton, Peace Corps Director Gaddi Vasquez, Save the Children Foundation President and CEO Charles MacCormack, and author Jonathon Kozol.

Campus Culture of Engagement

Students report that "civic activisim begins right at the start" with an orientation that matches students with their area of community interest, as stated on summer surveys. "During orientation, students travel with their groups to different places in Geneva, performing some sort of service at each site. Some groups paint, some do yard work; I spent my orientation service working at a local school."

According to one student, "I would say that 80 percent of students are in some way involved with civic engagement and actually enjoy it." Another proposes, "civic engagement that goes on at this school looks like a giant web—so many people, organizations, and support all interweaving."

Involvement comes easily because "if there is something they are interested in that is not offered on campus, it is very easy to create a club or organization on campus. In my first semester, I started up my own chapter of a national reproductive-rights organization." Student groups include "Habitat for Humanity Campus Chapter, Geneva Heroes, Rotaract, Celebrate Service, Celebrate Geneva, Day of Service Committee (an annual day when volunteers from campus and the greater Geneva Community gather to work on service projects throughout the area), Make-A-Wish Club, AIDS Awareness Club, Progressive Student Union, and Campus Greens." Service-oriented students can choose to live in the Community Service House, a residence for 20 students who are "required to complete five hours of service per week to remain in the house and sponsor campus-wide service activities."

Connecting Service with the Classroom

Students report that "during service, it is common to find faculty, students, and community members working side-by-side in efforts towards a common goal." Service is a "very visible component of our education."

HWS offers approximately 20 different service-learning courses annually, with between 300 and 350 students enrolling each year. Service-learning classes span departments and programs from Africana Studies to Peer Education in Human Relations, with requirements ranging from "approximately 30 hours per semester working with a specific partner to project-oriented experiences where students may develop an activity or workshop to share with an outside group." Courses include "Contexts for Children in a Changing Society," "Morality and Self-Interest," and "Economics of Caring."

The colleges offer an interdisciplinary Public Service minor, which "consists of five service-learning classes distributed across the divisions, plus a culminating service experience in a senior seminar or independent study." One student minoring in Public Service tells us that "this experience has made me who I am and focused me on what I want to do for the rest of my life."

Impact on Community and Students

"Service-learning and civic engagement take place throughout the Finger Lakes region and within the Hobart and William Smith Community. It takes every appearance, from environmental activism to woman's rights work, from trail-building to team-building at the local high school and junior high. It's working with preschool students at Jumpstart to being a companion to an elderly man or woman at the local community center." "Our school is proud of their meaningful connections with the outside community and eager to help in anyway we can."

HWS maintains approximately 60 community partnerships and works with about 25 of those intensely. Students are encouraged to continuously develop new initiatives: "An HWS student originated Geneva Heroes Youth Service Corps, a mentoring program for area eighth graders. HWS students meet with the eighth graders for approximately ten Saturday-morning sessions and work together at area sites."

One major partnership is with the local Boys & Girls Club. "HWS students are a major factor in the success of the Club's 'Power Hour,' where members receive tutoring and homework help after school before they are able to participate in other activities. Our students have served as one-on-one tutors, developed programs such as international cooking and an Earth Day clean-up at Seneca Lake for the members, and developed manuals and programs for computer use."

HWS maintains a strong commitment to literacy programs: "HWS was one of the first institutions with an America Reads program and now places approximately ninety-five students per semester in six different schools and three school districts to help second and third graders. Each is overseen by one or two student coordinators who are trained to assist the tutors and serve as the administrator and liaison for each site." Through the Jumpstart program, students work with area preschoolers on social and literacy skills. "It has been amazing working with kids from all types of backgrounds—socially, racially, and economically. I would like to become a secondary mathematics teacher, and I really feel fortunate that I was able to be part of a town that was very much unlike my own."

Student Financial Support for Service

Presidential Leader Awards "are merit-based and look at a student's leadership and community-service activities. They range from $3,000 to $12,000 and approximately 100 are awarded each year." There are also several need-based "Named Scholar Awards," which have a community-service component and are offered in consultation with the PSO. The Bowman Award for Leadership and Civic Engagement provides stipends for unpaid summer service internships. "Past recipients have received awards to work for Labor of Love, a disaster-relief youth program associated with the Episcopal Church, teach English in Thailand, work in a U.S. senator's office, and attend the Institute on Philanthropy and Voluntary Service."

SELECTIVITY

# of applicants	3,266
% of applicants accepted	63
% of acceptees attending	23
# accepting a place on wait list	338
% admitted from wait list	7

FRESHMAN PROFILE

Range SAT Verbal	540-630
Range SAT Math	545-640
Range ACT Composite	
Minimum Paper TOEFL	550
Minimum Computer TOEFL	220
Average HS GPA	3.23
% graduated top 10% of class	31
% graduated top 25% of class	55
% graduated top 50% of class	95

DEADLINES

Regular admission	2/1
Regular notification by	4/1
Nonfall registration?	no

FINANCIAL FACTS

Annual tuition	$30,076
Room and board	$7,987
Books and supplies	$850
Required fees	$567
% frosh rec. need-based scholarship or grant aid	59
% UG rec. need-based scholarship or grant aid	61
% frosh rec. need-based self-help aid	48
% UG rec. need-based self-help aid	53
% frosh rec. any financial aid	74
% UG rec. any financial aid	64

HUMBOLDT STATE UNIVERSITY

1 HARPST STREET, ARCATA, CA 95521-8299

ADMISSIONS: 707-826-4402 • FAX: 707-826-6194 • FINANCIAL AID: 707-826-4321

E-MAIL: HSUINFO@HUMBOLDT.EDU • WEBSITE: WWW.HUMBOLDT.EDU

CAMPUS LIFE

Type of school	public
Environment	rural

STUDENTS

Total undergrad enrollment	6,450
% male/female	46/54
% from out of state	4
% from public high school	79
% live on campus	20
% African American	2
% Asian	2
% Caucasian	46
% Hispanic	6
% Native American	2
# of countries represented	21

ACADEMICS

Calendar	2 semesters plus summer term
Student/faculty ratio	18:1
% profs teaching UG courses	100
% classes taught by TAs	0
Most common lab size	20-29
Most common reg class size	20-29

MOST POPULAR MAJORS

art/art studies
biology/biological sciences
liberal arts and sciences/liberal studies

Getting Involved

Students with green thumbs—and green hearts—should feel at home at Humboldt State University, where social justice, service, and environmental responsibility go hand in hand. One of the school's most distinctive programs is the Campus Center for Appropriate Technology (CCAT), a "demonstration home and educational center for sustainable living" where three students live on site. The administration explains, "CCAT hosts hundreds of visitors from around the world each year and holds ongoing workshop series for students and the community, compost education, and appropriate technology classes—including bio-diesel making, solar technology, and pond building."

The Service Learning Center (SLC) houses many of the school's other civic-engagement programs and supports faculty across the disciplines. It places a strong emphasis on training student leaders: "This spring, the Service-Learning Student Interns sponsored the month-long Raise Your Voice: Month of Dialogue on Civic Engagement with a program of workshops, film series, discussions, speakers, and town-hall meetings." Because Humboldt serves as the Northern California Regional Center for the Study, Promotion, and Documentation of Student Civic Engagement, the Center also helps coordinate retreats for student service leaders in Northern California and Oregon. One student announces, "here at Humboldt, we are really lucky to have a president, faculty, staff, and students who all really care about the public mission of education."

Campus Culture of Engagement

Humboldt students report "a really strong campus committment to civic engagement"— "Returning students involved with service and activism are incredibly engaged with the student body through media such as weekly HSU e-mails, campus-wide booths which advertise organizations, flyers posted in accessable areas, and of course, word of mouth through informal class discussions." "Just hanging out on the quad is a great way to find out what is going on service-wise and how you can help."

Student engagement stems from a "wonderful organization" called the YES (Youth Educational Services) House. YES is the umbrella group for student-directed nonprofit organizations and volunteer groups. "Student-initiated pilot programs frequently act as catalysts for stable, far-reaching, and professionally staffed efforts. Some spin-off programs include "CCAT, the Multi-Cultural Center, Campus Recycling Program, and 4-H Trail (outdoor experiences for physically-challenged youth). YES has 180 students per semester involved in community volunteering." According to one student, "the YES house is well-known in the area and on campus."

Connecting Service with the Classroom

"I am a graduate student in Environment and Community, and it has connected me with local agencies. Rather than sitting in a library studying about 'those people out there,' I am meeting them, talking to them, asking questions, and learning from human exchange."

Service-learning classes span the Humboldt curriculum, particularly in the areas of education, environment, health, social services, and political activism/community organizing. Last year students spent a total of 13,500 hours on course-related service.

Service-learning classes include Intercultural Communication, "an upper-division class with service-learning that is usually taken by Environmental Science,

International Studies, Communication, and Education majors." Its professor, Dr. Armeda Reitzel, has received a Cesar Chavez Day of Service and Learning grant three years running. With the help of the grant, she and her students have worked intimately with children in the K–12 system and local tribes in order to pass along the values of Cesar Chavez, with a focus on "environmental awareness and respect." "My students planned and coordinated a Cesar Chavez Celebration on Cesar Chavez Day at the Indian Education Resource Center, Hoopa Elementary School, and Hoopa High School in Hoopa, CA. The K–12 youth learned about Chavez, worked in the community garden, made and distributed organic seed packets, made and distributed Cesar Chavez 'respect for life' bookmarks, and interviewed my students about Chavez and local environmental issues for newspaper articles and for broadcast on a radio show that they put together on the tribal radio station."

Other service-learning classes include the Economics Department's "Sustainable Economic Development in Humboldt County," through which students are paired with community partners for research projects on local sustainable economic development. The economics department encourages further field research and civic engagement through a variety of offered internships.

Impact on Community and Students

The Service Learning Center works with over 200 partners, with a particular emphasis on environmental sustainability. "In the College of Natural Resources and Sciences, there is a 'memo of understanding' with the Natural Resources Conservation Service for cooperative work. That college has informal and ongoing relationships with Redwood Community Action Agency, Humboldt County, Redwood State and National Parks, local interest groups (e.g., Freshwater Group and the Lindsey Creek Watershed group), and virtually all of the other office-of-natural-resources agencies at the local, state, and national levels."

The administration calls the Humboldt Language Academy for Children "a point of light in our department and in our college." "It was founded in the fall of 2000 and offers French, German, Japanese, and Spanish language classes to approximately 40 children between the ages of eight and eleven. Classes take place on several Saturdays throughout the semester. This year, approximately 30 to 40 HSU students assisted either as aides in the Saturday Academy or in the Morris Elementary School's bilingual immersion program in McKinleyville."

The Humboldt Students in Action Addressing Hunger and Food Insecurity is a recently developed student initiative. "This two-year project will link academic course work with community-based projects and activities that support a healthy regional food system. Our local food bank, Food for People, Retired Senior Volunteers Program, local church groups, parents, municipal entities, social-service agencies, and nonprofits will be an integral part of the planning and service as co-educators and mentors to students. Service activities will be promoted on and off campus: food drives, service days, community-garden projects, fundraisers, and forums."

Student Financial Support for Service

Humboldt State University offers approximately 30 scholarships per year "to reward and encourage ongoing community-service activities and to raise awareness on campus about community service." The awards are $500 per semester "sponsored by the HSU Associated Students." The Women's Enrichment Fund Board offers some financial support to women "engaged in projects that positively impact the campus community and residents in the region." Through a partnership with the North Coast Small Business Development Center, the HSU Faculty-Initiated Economic Development Project Fund awards grants to faculty "for involving their students in a wide variety of projects directly related to local business and economic development."

SELECTIVITY

# of applicants	5,521
% of applicants accepted	67
% of acceptees attending	24

FRESHMAN PROFILE

Range SAT Verbal	470-600
Range SAT Math	470-580
Range ACT Composite	18-25
Minimum Paper TOEFL	550
Average HS GPA	3.18
% graduated top 10% of class	14
% graduated top 25% of class	41

DEADLINES

Regular admission	varies
Regular notification by	rolling
Nonfall registration?	yes

FINANCIAL FACTS

Annual in-state tuition	$2,046
Annual out-of-state tuition	$3,768
Room and board	$6,861
Books and supplies	$1,050
Required fees	$493
% frosh rec. need-based scholarship or grant aid	43
% UG rec. need-based scholarship or grant aid	47
% frosh rec. need-based self-help aid	37
% UG rec. need-based self-help aid	45

Indiana University—Purdue University Indianapolis

Indianapolis, IN 46202

Admissions: 317-274-4591 • **Fax:** 317-278-1862 • **Financial Aid:** 317-274-4162

E-mail: apply@iupui.edu • **Website:** www.iupui.edu

CAMPUS LIFE

Type of school	public
Environment	town

STUDENTS

Total undergrad enrollment	20,844
% male/female	41/59
% from out of state	2
% live on campus	2
% African American	11
% Asian	2
% Caucasian	80
% Hispanic	2
% international	2

ACADEMICS

Calendar	semester
Most common lab size	<10
Most common reg class size	20-29

MOST POPULAR MAJORS

business administration/management
elementary education and teaching
nursing - registered nurse training
(RN, ASN, BSN, MSN)

Getting Involved

IUPUI's strong reputation for civic engagement rests not only on its wide variety of service and service-learning programs, but also on a strong commitment to funding student projects through the Sam H. Jones Community Service Scholarships Program. One enthusiast attests, "It can't be said more strongly: The people [and] the program directors are exceptional, talented, and full of endless energy. And although it doesn't sound as altruistic, money in the form of scholarships is very important."

The IUPUI Center for Service and Learning (CSL), which "provides centralized support to faculty, students, and staff for curricular and cocurricular involvement in the community," consists of four offices: The Office of Service Learning, the Office of Community Service, the Office of Community Work Study, and the Office of Neighborhood Partnerships. IUPUI has declared an increased commitment to service-learning with its recent "Civic Collaborative," a multi-year plan that pledges $700,000 new base funds to double student participation in the community through service–learning courses, volunteer activities, and community work-study programs.

Campus Culture of Engagement

As one student recommends, "the best thing a prospective student could do is apply for a scholarship that requires community service or civic engagement. This way you get to know other people in the university as well as stay motivated to be involved in the community." One former Freshman Service Scholar reports, "I worked with the Center for Service and Learning all year long and had a great experience volunteering my time at a community school." Civic engagement provides the necessary social glue among students: "Considering it's such a large commuter school, it was an excellent way for me to meet students and remain involved in service."

IUPUI students find no shortage of service spirit: "Service-learning and civic engagement are all over this campus. It comes in the form of involvement with student government, fraternities, scholarships, university-organized philanthropic projects, and outside-community-organized philanthropic projects."

Student organizations include a chapter of Alpha Phi Omega, which "sponsors campus blood drives, volunteers at local parks and homeless shelters, and participates as a team in many of the IUPUI Days of Service." College Mentors for Kids!, another student organization, "pairs children from an Indianapolis public school with IUPUI student mentors in campus settings to engage in activities focused on college, community service, and culture and diversity."

Connecting Service with the Classroom

"My service-learning experience was in my First-Year Experience class. It was a group effort, and we had to research the organization we served at and then present a final reflection paper on what we learned. This benefited me so much by giving me a first look into group work as well as giving back to the community."

During the 2002–2003 academic year, 57 faculty from nine schools offered 42 service-learning courses which resulted in 15,758 hours of service at 128 community sites. Courses span the campus's schools, including Art, Business, Dentistry, Education, Liberal Arts, Medicine, Nursing, Public and Environmental Affairs, and Science.

In conjunction with the Center for Earth and Environmental Science (CEES), the Department of Geology displays a particularly strong commitment to service-learning courses. Through its curriculum, science lectures are supplemented with community field projects: "Service-learning opportunities available to students at several community environmental sites include native-species plantings, flood-plain reforestation maintenance, and natural area clean-ups."

Impact on Community and Students

Students report "close ties with the community" and appreciate that "we are in a large city with so many opportunities." "As a future physical therapist," says one student, "I have had ample opportunites in such places as outpatient physical therapy, a specialized rehab hospital, a clinic for children with disabilities, the National Institute for Fitness and Sport, and many more."

The CSL maintains partnerships with 58 community sites (including "Boys and Girls Clubs, community centers, medical facilities, public schools, museums, and environmental organizations"), and IUPUI maintains a strong relationship with George Washington Community School (GWCS), a grade six-through-12 community school in the Indianapolis Public Schools. With the help of a Community-Higher Education School Partnership grant (CHESP), the Office of Neighborhood Partnerships has "assisted in implementing service learning into their curriculum and instituted a Nutrition Project, a Youth Service Day, and a neighborhood needs assessment. In 2002–2003, over 1,000 students at GWCS participated through eight IUPUI programs represented by four campus units and departments."

Other community programs include Aftercare in Mentoring (AIM) Program, a tutoring and mentoring program that connects IUPUI's Criminal Justice students with juvenile offenders. "AIM pairs IUPUI service-learning students and community volunteers with young men who will soon be released from the facility. Students serve as mentors offering advice on job opportunities, health, education, social skills, and money management." Since its inception at IUPUI, the AIM program has blossomed at nine other correction facilities and three support centers across the state of Indiana.

Student Financial Support for Service

Service is a component of all scholarships given at IUPUI. "Since 1994, the Sam H. Jones Community Service Scholarship Program has recognized students for previous service contributions to their high school, campus, or community. It is one of the largest service-based scholarship programs in the nation. In 2004–2005, $192,000 of campus scholarship funds will be awarded through this program." Available scholarships include the Freshman Service Scholarship ($2,000 to eighteen Service Scholars); Community Service Scholarship ($3,000 to sixteen Service Scholars); Community Service Associate Scholarship ($1,500 to $3,000 to nine Service Scholars); Service Learning Assistant Scholarship ($750 to $1,500 to 30 Service Scholars); and America Reads/America Counts Scholarships ($2,000 to ten Service Scholars). "As part of the scholarship program responsibilities, some students take a service-learning course, contribute four hours of weekly service in the community, or organize and lead campus service activities or a social-advocacy project."

SELECTIVITY

# of applicants	6,078
% of applicants accepted	73
% of acceptees attending	61

FRESHMAN PROFILE

Range SAT Verbal	440-550
Range SAT Math	440-550
Range ACT Composite	18-23
Minimum Paper TOEFL	550
Minimum Computer TOEFL	180
% graduated top 10% of class	11
% graduated top 25% of class	31
% graduated top 50% of class	70

DEADLINES

Nonfall registration?	yes

FINANCIAL FACTS

Annual in-state tuition	$4,526
Annual out-of-state tuition	$14,346
Room and board	$2,554
Books and supplies	$840
Required fees	$573
% frosh rec. need-based scholarship or grant aid	32
% UG rec. need-based scholarship or grant aid	35
% frosh rec. need-based self-help aid	26
% UG rec. need-based self-help aid	38

JAMES MADISON UNIVERSITY

SONNER HALL, MSC 0101, HARRISONBURG, VA 22807

ADMISSIONS: 540-568-5681 • **FAX:** 540-568-3332 • **FINANCIAL AID:** 540-568-7820

E-MAIL: ADMISSIONS@JMU.EDU • **WEBSITE:** WWW.JMU.EDU

CAMPUS LIFE

Type of school	public
Environment	rural

STUDENTS

Total undergrad enrollment	14,677
% male/female	40/60
% from out of state	29
% live on campus	39
% African American	3
% Asian	5
% Caucasian	97
% Hispanic	2
% international	1
# of countries represented	53

ACADEMICS

Calendar	semester
Student/faculty ratio	18:1
% profs teaching UG courses	100
% classes taught by TAs	1
Most common lab size	20-29
Most common reg class size	20-29

MOST POPULAR MAJORS
communications studies/speech
communication and rhetoric
marketing/marketing management
psychology

Getting Involved

When we asked students about service learning at James Madison University, hyperbole poured forth: "We have one of THE best service-learning offices in the country"; the student body consists of "really incredibly friendly and wonderfully caring, loving people"; "the program seems to attract amazing individuals." Why all the superlatives? JMU has some genu-ine award-winning programs in its roster.

Most projects originate in the Community Service-Learning (CS-L) office, a program of JMU's Student Success initiative. CS-L supports service-learning courses "through placement and reflection services as well as support and development of service-learning faculty. CS-L coordinates 100 community partnerships which involve JMU students through service-learning courses, individual volunteerism, and Special Projects geared towards student clubs and organizations." America Reads/Community Work Study "are CS-L programs where illegible students are placed in community schools and organizations rather than working on campus for their financial-aid awards." Each February, CS-L holds the annual JMU Service Fair, featuring such organizations as the Peace Corps, AmeriCorps, Jesuit Mercy Corps, and Teach for America. Last but not least, CS-L coordinates the beloved annual Alternative Spring Break (which one student describes as a "huge deal at JMU"): "Each year," says CS-L, "JMU students travel to 25 domestic and international locations to dedicate their spring break holiday to service to these communities. In 1999, JMU's program was selected by BreakAway [a nonprofit that supports alternative break programs] as the model program for the nation."

One student offers, "My advice is to go to the CS-L department, describe your interests and history, and let them help you find the perfect fit for you. It truly is a life-changing experience." Another gushes, "the CS-L department is extremely organized, helpful, active, and involved in everyday life at JMU."

Campus Culture of Engagement

Entering freshman can get a taste of JMU civic-engagement opportunities through Freshman Service Trips before the beginning of fall semester, or at the annual Student Organization Night, which presents "every possible student-driven activity." One student explains, "The vast majority of clubs and organizations offer numerous volunteer opportunities. Fraternities, sororities, choral groups, large organizations, and even the more obscure ones (like Breakdancing Club) are all largely rooted in the volunteer aspects."

Participants applaud the student-run nature of many of JMU's programs: "We have a strong and loud voice that is able to reach more students and groups than a professionally run staff." Campus discourse thrives, thanks in part to The OrangeBand Initiative—a group founded by undergraduate students "in response to a perceived lack of civic engagement and open dialogue exhibited on their campus." The OrangeBand runs two-week Action Campaigns, during which the community focuses on a chosen issue through a schedule of speaker forums and video screenings.

Students cite a strong current of activism on campus. "Mother Jones magazine ranked James Madison University as the 'Sixth Most Activist College/University' in the world for their 2003 rankings. We have a very engaged student body and an organization representing virtually every major politcal issue or ideology." Students recently fought for their rights when "emergency contraception was banned from being distributed by the Heath Center by the Board of Visitors." "Almost immediately, the student body signed petitions and passed an SGA senate bill that stated the students' feelings that this was the wrong decision. The students refused to let this issue rest, and in January, ECP began to be distributed again and the BOV decided to leave medical decisions to medical professionals."

Connecting Service with the Classroom

Student empowerment may be key at JMU, but "professors are usually highly involved too. They provide you with great opportunities if the school doesn't." Each year, JMU offers around 40 service-learning classes in conjunction with 100 community service agencies.

The Institute for Innovation in Health and Human Services (IIHHS) in the College of Integrated Science and Technology offers partnerships with community health and human-service agencies. The Institute declares a mission to "foster a culture that values cross-disciplinary interaction, communication, and collaboration to enrich teaching, learning, research, and service delivery in the area of health and human services." Organizational partnerships include the Blue Ridge Area Health Education Center, Community Health Interpreter Service, Teen Pregnancy Prevention program, and the Caregiver's Community Network. "All of the partners embrace the mission of the IIHHS to involve students in real-life experiences that not only meet the needs of their organization but meet course objectives."

Impact on Community and Students

Service at JMU has a contagious effect: "Before college, I had never worked in any community-service atmosphere, and I'm now working at least three days a week at the SPCA and can't imagine my life without it." JMU's community partnerships, which total more than 100, give students ample opportunity to find organizations that suit their needs within the Shenandoah Valley. "CS-L is an active member of community networks such as Healthy Community, Hispanic Services Council, Rockingham County Partners for Student Success, and Valley Volunteer Forum."

The Migrant Education Program aims "to ensure that all migrant students reach challenging academic standards and graduate with a high-school diploma or complete a GED that prepares them for responsible citizenship, further learning, and productive employment." Through the program, JMU students provide English-language tutoring to eligible students—from pre-school to the age of 22—and assist them with their post-high-school career goals. They also serve as interpreters within the school system, in order to improve communication between parents and the administration.

The Alternative Break Program is another hallmark of JMU's service outreach—in 2003-2004, the program offered over 20 different trips in the United States, Dominica, Jamaica, Bahamas, Dominican Republic, and Mexico. Alternative Breaks can take place over any of the JMU academic breaks, with each service trip consisting of 12 members and two student leaders. One student testifies, "I went on an Alternative Spring Break two years ago because it was a cheap option to Cancun or the Bahamas, and I fell in love with the people I met. I worked in an AIDS hospice and realized that I was so caught up in my own world that I had no idea what was going on around me. I changed my career goal from English teacher to being a social worker. I currently coordinate the ASB program with one other student and I have learned more from the program, the trips, and the people involved than I have in any class."

Student Financial Support for Service

JMU does not currently offer service-based scholarships to its students, but students eligible for federal work-study can choose to be placed as an America Reads tutor in a local elementary school or as a student worker in a local community agency.

JOHNSON & WALES UNIVERSITY—RHODE ISLAND

8 ABBOTT PARK PLACE, PROVIDENCE, RI 02903-3703

ADMISSIONS: 401-598-2310 • **FAX:** 401-598-2948 • **FINANCIAL AID:** 800-342-5598

E-MAIL: ADMISSIONS@JWU.EDU • **WEBSITE:** WWW.JWU.EDU

CAMPUS LIFE

Type of school	private
Environment	town

STUDENTS

Total undergrad enrollment	9,145
% African American	11
% Asian	3
% Caucasian	71
% Hispanic	6
% international	4

ACADEMICS

Calendar	quarter

SELECTIVITY

# of applicants	13,495
% of applicants accepted	76
% of acceptees attending	23

Getting Involved

Johnson & Wales University bills itself as a "career university"—one that provides "valuable, experiential, 'real-life' education opportunities to its students" in addition to classroom learning. Its service-learning program fits right into this mission, incorporating an element of practicality often missing from community-service programs: "Students are given opportunities to develop their career skills at community sites and are encouraged to think about future opportunities to contribute to the community throughout their career." One student explains, "Giving back to the community is a very big part of going to JWU." It is, in fact, a requirement for graduation.

The Feinstein Community Service Center (FCSC)—located on J&W's Providence campus—is the most visible hub of civic engagement, coordinating service and service-learning initiatives across the University's colleges/schools of Culinary Arts, Hospitality, Business, Technology, and Arts & Sciences. According to one student, "the office is team-oriented and fully committed to the surrounding community. The staff does a great job of keeping volunteers updated with future events."

Community Leadership programming is a particularly strong focus of J&W, consisting of three primary academic components: an online service-learning course, a one-term community service-learning experience, and a leadership course. "The University supplements this basic program with enrichment, co-curricular, and selective programs that help interested students become more deeply engaged in the life and growth of their communities"—from volunteer opportunities to credit-bearing programs such as Community Leadership: An Applied Sociology and a new statewide Philanthropy course.

Campus Culture of Engagement

"Community service opportunities are posted everywhere," says one enthusiastic student. "They bombard you with opportunities to get involved, and service is also talked about within the classroom" since community service-learning is a graduation requirement. In addition to opportunities built into the curriculum, students can get involved "by stopping by the Feinstein Center and asking a [service-learning coordinator] about volunteering. They should mention any particular interest or field they plan on helping out in. For example, I'm interested in helping women, so the representative helped me find a position at a battered-women's shelter."

Service delivers a sense of cohesiveness that might otherwise be lacking at the university: "We really don't have a centralized campus, so it's difficult to find people who all have a centralized theme to their upbringing. But if you get involved with the civic-engagement or other clubs, you end up with a lot of networking opportunities and find friends who have similar passions."

Predictably enough, the mandatory service-learning requirement inspires hot debate among students. One proponent explains, "I'm glad civic learning is mandatory. Too many young people my age take their lives for granted. We need to see the other side." Meanwhile, a skeptic grumbles, "I love doing community service, but I hated doing my mandatory [service-learning requirement] because of all the paperwork that was associated alongside of it. If I want to be involved within civic engagement, let me be involved and have my own personal satisfaction."

Connecting Service with the Classroom

"I like how this school ties in community service-learning with our other classes. It introduces to students [the idea] that in the business world, it is still important to volunteer your time, and it gives student a chance to do service which makes them feel good and want to do more."

At J&W, over 70 courses offer a service-learning option, and almost 100 professors use Community Service Learning (CSL) to some extent in their classes. "Students may choose to complete their CSL through a course in their major field (like a business student working on a business plan for the local Latino business empowerment initiative, or a culinary student helping educate schoolchildren about basic cooking and nutrition), through selected internship/practicum programs, or through a general-studies course ([for example], a science class participating in a service project at a local community farm)."

Students can choose to specialize in Leadership Studies. All students must complete "SL1001, a one-credit, online course in social responsibility, corporate citizenship, and community leadership" and "SL2001, an experiential service-learning requirement through an academic course or internship," which "allows students the opportunity to gain valuable experience and make lasting contributions to the community-based organizations that serve as placement sites."

Impact on Community and Students

J&W maintains partnerships with over 100 community organizations in Southeastern New England. "The food drives, Save the Bay (conserving the little nature we have left), tutoring younger children, giving out meals (clothing and food drives for the homeless), and teaching our senior citizens about the changing environment: We do so many things that better our community."

The John Hazen White School of Arts & Sciences recently partnered with Mary Fogarty Elementary School in South Providence, RI. "J&W faculty members brought their students to Fogarty to work with the younger students, and J&W students participated in leadership and reading programs, poetry lessons, enrichment programs, nutrition programs, and acted as classroom assistants at Fogarty. This partnership grew each trimester and during the spring term, there were 45 students assisting in programs and classrooms throughout the elementary school."

J&W has also partnered with the Rhode Island Community Farm (RICF) in nearby East Greenwich, Rhode Island. "This site grows fruits and vegetables that are donated to member agencies of the Rhode Island Community Food Bank for donation to low-income families who do not have consistent access to fresh produce. In the fall and spring terms, J&W science students, FCSC staff members, and a J&W science faculty member visit the farm and partake in a CSL project—in the fall, students harvest the crops and in the spring, students prepare the fields for planting." Last fall, J&W students harvested 600 pounds of food.

Student Financial Support for Service

J&W offers a range of scholarship programs. "The primary service-based scholarship is a $2,000 Community Leader scholarship, which is renewable for four years. Approximately 140 Community Leader scholarships were awarded last year. The Gaebe Eagle Scout scholarship is a $1,000 scholarship awarded to incoming freshmen who have earned the designation of Eagle Scout through their scouting and community-service work. Approximately 12 of these scholarships were awarded last year. In addition, J&W participates in the RI Campus Compact AmeriCorps Scholarship for Service Program, in which 12 students are given educational awards for their service work in the community."

FRESHMAN PROFILE

Range SAT Verbal	420-530
Range SAT Math	410-540
Average HS GPA	2.90
% graduated top 10% of class	4
% graduated top 25% of class	19
% graduated top 50% of class	58

DEADLINES

Regular admission	
Regular notification by	rolling
Nonfall registration?	yes

FINANCIAL FACTS

Annual tuition	$19,200
Room and board	$7,545
Books and supplies	$825
Required fees	$900
% frosh rec. need-based scholarship or grant aid	63
% UG rec. need-based scholarship or grant aid	49
% frosh rec. need-based self-help aid	69
% UG rec. need-based self-help aid	59

Lewis & Clark College

0615 SW Palatine Hill Road, Portland, OR 97219-7899

Admissions: 503-768-7040 • **Fax:** 503-768-7055 • **Financial Aid:** 503-768-7090

E-mail: admissions@lclark.edu • **Website:** www.lclark.edu

CAMPUS LIFE

Type of school	private
Environment	village

STUDENTS

Total undergrad	
enrollment	1,845
% male/female	39/61
% from out of state	78
% from public high school	74
% live on campus	70
% African American	1
% Asian	5
% Caucasian	67
% Hispanic	4
% Native American	1
% international	4
# of countries represented	42

ACADEMICS

Calendar	semester
Student/faculty ratio	14:1
% profs teaching	
UG courses	100
% classes taught by TAs	0
Most common lab size	20-29
Most common	
reg class size	10-19

MOST POPULAR MAJORS

English language and literature
international relations and affairs
psychology

Getting Involved

Ah, the Left Coast: Haven of coffee shops, organic vegetarian restaurants, and—most importantly for our purposes—activists by the bushel. Lewis & Clark College, located in Portland, Oregon, fits right in. Consider one emphatic student endorsement: "You can serve, you can protest, you can hold teach-ins, you can hear from experts on a variety of current issues. Creating a thinking and progressive citizenry seems to be what this school is all about."

The school sponsors civic-engagement efforts through its Office of Student Leadership and Service, previously a part of the Center for Service and Work (CSAW). The office connects students with a variety of volunteer programs, sponsors Alternative Spring Break trips, and provides socially-conscious campus programming (like AIDS education). One student describes the office as "a very visible and accessible center for volunteering. It's really easy to participate in civic-engagement events, and it's easy to find other ways to connect with the Portland community by asking people at the office."

Lewis & Clark prides itself on the strength of its Student Academics Affairs Board (SAAB), which provides students with the resources to design socially-conscious projects. "Students are able to apply for grants to attend conferences, do research projects usually in other countries, bring speakers to campus, and a variety of other academically related projects." Thanks to a proposal developed by LC undergrads, the school now offers Journey to Democracy Dialogues—a series of symposiums about socially-responsible citizenship.

Campus Culture of Engagement

"There is an activities fair at the beginning of the semeseter, but it is more likely that students find out about activism on campus via word-of-mouth or the thousands of flyers that pepper the walls over the course of the semester. If anything, Lewis & Clark students are proactive learners, and the campus is small enough that this results in students quickly digging into issues of their choice."

Students cite "omnipresent civic dialogue among students" and praise each other's abilities to "raise challenging questions and produce thoughtful responses." "Having transferred here from another school," says one student, "I can honestly say that the civic engagement here on campus at LC continously amazes and impresses me. Students have an idea, discuss it, study it, and then mobilize to act on it."

Student-initiated groups include Students Allied in Democracy, Amnesty International, Students Engaged in Eco-Defense, Organization for Peace and Politics, and the Black Student Union. Student Voter Action, a student group dedicated to educating peers about voter registration and political issues, has succeeded in making voter education a permanent component of LC's curriculum. Justice for Janitors has worked to educate immigrant employees of off-campus housekeeping services about union membership and initiated a student-run shuttle service to help workers circumvent the inefficient community bus system.

Students report that their school is "a home for controversy." "Every three years, the Zero Awards are put out. These are awards given (with a great deal of sarcasm) to academic departments who have no tenured faculty of color. Posters around campus listed the departments who received the 'award' as well as departments who were praised for their successful efforts to increase their ethnic diversity."

Connecting Service with the Classroom

The administration is the first to admit that "service-learning is a 'new' concept at Lewis & Clark." While one student concedes that "our academics and our civic-engagement experiences are not solidly integrated," another points out that "there is a growing body of students, faculty, and staff working hard to bring civic engagement to LC and to make it a central part of the academic curriculum here."

Students can locate departments and classes with stated commitments to civic engagement. Environmental Studies, a popular interdisciplinary field at Lewis & Clark, "integrates scientific study of ecosystems, pollution, climate, energy, and other environmental and natural resource matters on a global, regional, or local scale, with policy-related study of environmental ethics."

The Sociology/Anthropology department "believes the local community is an active learning laboratory for Lewis & Clark students" and so offers field projects such as that for the Crime and Punishment class for which students "visit local penal institutions to observe the nature and effects of punishment and rehabilitation methods used in our society." In the Education and Modern Society class, students do fieldwork in public schools and then gather to discuss issues facing Oregon's K–12 school system. And in an economics class called Pacific Northwest Policy Issues, students work in teams to research and interview community organizations about "alternative policy issues."

Impact on Community and Students

Lewis & Clark students can't praise their home city enough. "The greatest resource we have is Portland, where the energy of involvement makes it hard not to want to change things one sees as problems. The college has developed many relationships with organizations in the Portland area, so it is very easy to make connections if one takes the first step."

Lewis & Clark maintains 35 community partnerships, primarily consisting of nonprofit organizations and public schools. Dignity Village, one of LC's partners, is a "homeless tent city" in Portland, Oregon. "Dignity Village is used as a service work site for various weekend projects, such as building or weatherizing structures. Members of Dignity Village also participate in campus events and serve on panels to talk about issues of homelessness in Portland." Students have organized clothing and food drives for the community and have attended City Council meetings to support its goal of finding a permanent location.

Start Making a Reader Today (SMART) is the largest partnership in which Lewis & Clark College students are involved. Each year, about 60 students volunteer an hour a week to read with children in local low-income elementary schools. "One area which we have improved this relationship is to provide training for new volunteers on campus, which makes it more accessible to students and also helps us to recruit new volunteers for the program."

Student Financial Support for Service

Leadership and Service Scholarships "recognize students who have demonstrated outstanding academics combined with exemplary leadership and/or service in their school or community." The scholarships are worth $5,000 per year and are renewable for three additional years based on continued leadership and/or service combined with academic success.

LOUISIANA STATE UNIVERSITY—BATON ROUGE

110 THOMAS BOYD HALL, BATON ROUGE, LA 70803

ADMISSIONS: 225-578-1175 • **FAX:** 225-578-4433 • **FINANCIAL AID:** 225-578-3103

E-MAIL: ADMISSIONS@LSU.EDU • **WEBSITE:** WWW.LSU.EDU

CAMPUS LIFE

Type of school	public
Environment	town

STUDENTS

Total undergrad enrollment	25,849
% male/female	48/52
% from out of state	12
% live on campus	23
% African American	9
% Asian	3
% Caucasian	81
% Hispanic	2
% international	2
# of countries represented	119

ACADEMICS

Calendar	semester
Student/faculty ratio	21:1
% profs teaching UG courses	89
% classes taught by TAs	14
Most common lab size	10-19
Most common reg class size	20-29

MOST POPULAR MAJORS

biological and biomedical sciences
general studies
psychology

Getting Involved

Large research universities tend not to have the best reputations for community building. Yet at Louisiana State University, the administration tackles the polarizing possibilities of its 30,000-plus student body with one of the most thoroughly-integrated curricular service-learning programs we've encountered—one that brings students closer to one another and to their Baton Rouge environs. "There are so many organizations that help out our community," one student explains, "and living in Louisiana, we somehow always find a way to make these events fun. That is our culture."

The Center for Community Engagement, Learning, and Leadership (CCELL) is the umbrella organization for service-learning on campus, bringing together academic programming, community partnerships, and faculty training. "It links service-learning to the Honors College, Learning Communities, and Residential College(s)" and offers Student Leadership Development programs to train emergent student mentors. The office works in conjunction with the Career Services Experiential Education Office (providing a volunteer-placement database and coordinates nonprofit internships), the Center for Student Leadership and Involvement (coordinating student organizations), and the Office of Community Design and Development (supporting community-outreach opportunities within the fields of Interior Design, Architecture, and Landscape Architecture.)

The Community University Partnership Office further works to insure that LSU uses its "extensive resources" to combat "economic, environmental, and social challenges," with a particular focus on Old South Baton Rouge and the neighborhoods immediately north of LSU's campus. The office has received a Community Outreach Partnership Center Grant from the U.S. Department of Housing and Urban Development to support its efforts towards neighborhood revitalization.

Campus Culture of Engagement

"Students can find out about activities and organizations on campus through a thorough and fun-filled orientation experience. During this time, orientation leaders share their personal experiences of involvement, and the students have the opportunity to go to a student organization fair. They are also mailed information on attending a program called STRIPES (Student Tigers Rallying, Interacting, and Promoting Education and Service) that teaches them about the history and traditions of LSU and provides sessions on student involvement." "As a pilot member of the STRIPES program, I can testify that its influence had a direct reflection on my four years of experiences at LSU. It was and still is a growing program, producing alumni who remain just as dedicated and involved as the current students."

Students describe "a definite philanthropic presence on this campus." "It is everywhere!" says one ebullient student. "From deep within the universtity to worldwide programs sponsored by student organizations, it becomes a way of life and a call of duty to some." A small sampling of the 300 student-led organizations include Africa Initiative, American Red Cross Club, Habitat For Humanity, Men Against Violence, and Student Leadership Network for Children. The students also have their own Service-Learning Advisory Council, which plans projects and events and works with the LSU Student Government to link service organizations with the service-learning program.

Connecting Service with the Classroom

Service-learning is LSU's bread and butter—the administration boasts that "LSU is one of the few research-extensive universities with strong student-based outreach and leadership programs." Service-learning classes are offered in 137 sections in 35 departments each year, "many of which offer deliverable student-produced projects, such as grant writing or landscape designs, in addition to more traditional placements at agencies."

Students report varied experiences: "In Horticulture classes, we help elementary through high schools in coastal Louisiana to save the wetlands with nursery projects;" "I took an English class that was a food, culture, and literature class. Our service-learning was to volunteer at the Greater Baton Rouge Food Bank."

The administration offers another sampling of available opportunities: "veterinary medicine, kinesiology, chemistry, and theater students worked in inner-city classrooms to reinforce K–12 institutional standards. Biological-engineering students collaborated with elementary-school students to design and construct environmentally-sensitive playgrounds and butterfly gardens. Social-work and communication students contributed to programs that support battered women, neglected or abused children, and family development."

One student explains, "I think the buzz about service-learning is growing. In my service-learning class on the first day, the teacher asked who had participated in service-learning before, and half of my class raised their hands. This blew me away, that so many students came back to have another service-learning experience—and now having experienced it, I can see why."

Impact on Community and Student

LSU partnered with 80 agencies and community groups during the 2003–2004 school year. "Service-learning can take place anywhere in the Baton Rouge community. Students are assigned to various locations, such as soup kitchens, homeless shelters, or elementary schools, based on which course they choose to take that has a service-learning component."

The Volunteers in Public Schools (VIPS) and LSU Service-Learning Partnership pairs education, math, and English students with area schools for one-on-one mentoring and extracurricular projects. "One professor has committed herself and her students to 'building a safe and attractive playground for every public school in the city.' Thus far, her biological-engineering students have designed and built playgrounds for five schools." The partnership has also entrusted undergraduate students with classroom demonstrations—such as Entomology students presenting insect collections and theater and drama classes writing scripts for elementary-school students.

The MLK Day of Service, sponsored by the Dr. Martin Luther King, Jr. Commemorative Committee, also provides service to the Baton Rouge public-education system. In 2003, 221 students, faculty, and staff traveled to local elementary, middle and high schools to promote the theme of "The MLK Blueprint: A Design for Peace, Justice and Equality." Schools created a "wish list" of projects "that would greatly improve the learning environment," and the Day of Service committee went to work—distinctly "with, rather than for" the members of the community they served.

Student Financial Support for Service

"Approximately 100 Chancellor's Leadership Scholarships, each valued at $1,000 for one year, are available. To be considered for this award, applicants must demonstrate excellent leadership skills, possess commendable high-school academic records, and be recommended by their high-school principals. Extensive community service is a major criteria in the selection process." Additionally, the Partner Liaison Program recruits work-study students to serve as liaisons on-site at schools.

SELECTIVITY

# of applicants	11,077
% of applicants accepted	78
% of acceptees attending	66

FRESHMAN PROFILE

Range SAT Verbal	520-630
Range SAT Math	530-640
Range ACT Composite	22-27
Minimum Paper TOEFL	550
Minimum Computer TOEFL	213
Average HS GPA	3.42
% graduated top 10% of class	23
% graduated top 25% of class	50
% graduated top 50% of class	80

DEADLINES

Regular admission	4/15
Regular notification by	rolling
Nonfall registration?	yes

FINANCIAL FACTS

Annual in-state tuition	$2,855
Annual out-of-state tuition	$9,655
Room and board	$5,882
Books and supplies	$1,000
Required fees	$1,371
% frosh rec. need-based scholarship or grant aid	43
% UG rec. need-based scholarship or grant aid	37
% frosh rec. need-based self-help aid	22
% UG rec. need-based self-help aid	28
% frosh rec. any financial aid	94
% UG rec. any financial aid	85

LOYOLA UNIVERSITY CHICAGO

820 NORTH MICHIGAN AVENUE, CHICAGO, IL 60611

ADMISSIONS: 312-915-6500 • FAX: 312-915-7216 • FINANCIAL AID: 773-508-3155

E-MAIL: ADMISSION@LUC.EDU • WEBSITE: WWW.LUC.EDU

CAMPUS LIFE

Type of school	private
Environment	town

STUDENTS

Total undergrad enrollment	7,320
% male/female	34/66
% from out of state	34
% from public high school	38
% live on campus	29
% African American	8
% Asian	11
% Caucasian	67
% Hispanic	11
% international	1

ACADEMICS

Calendar	semester
Student/faculty ratio	13:1
% profs teaching UG courses	97
% classes taught by TAs	0
Most common lab size	10-19
Most common reg class size	20-29

MOST POPULAR MAJORS
biology/biological sciences
nursing
psychology

Getting Involved

Loyola University Chicago bills itself as a Jesuit Catholic university "that prepares people to lead extraordinary lives." Students insist that "there's something for everyone, religious or not—and it's easy to get involved." For the more secularly inclined, the school's location in bustling, service-hungry Chicago is key.

Service has several homes at Loyola. The University Ministry, Center for Service and Justice, Office of Student Activities, and Division of Academic Affairs all commandeer different service and service-learning projects on campus. The Magis Initiative is, however, "the main center for community and civic engagement." Through Magis, "students are engaged in courses and programs that emphasize and foster their leadership role in a participatory democracy, in critical thinking about civic responsibilities, and in their commitment to citizenship, service to others, and social responsibility. Magis Scholars are students who take this idea seriously and want to gain recognition for it." Participating students partake in three community-based service-learning classes, three community engagement activities in the community, and three leadership activities on campus.

One student reflects, "Last year, I went to a small college; I transfered to Loyola so that I would have more opportunites to get involved in the community, and I hoped that Loyola would offer more hands-on experiences in my major. In only the first year of being a student at Loyola, I have volunteered with a commissioner and have set up an internship for next year. Loyola has not only met my expectations but has amazed me by the commitment they have to the students."

Campus Culture of Engagement

"A student doesn't have to go looking" for service opportunities at Loyola—"every campus group is involved, and there are posters everywhere," not to mention "students sitting at tables begging for help for projects."

There are over 100 student organizations on campus, with plenty of focus on service and civic engagement. Groups include Big Brother Big Sister, Colleges Against Cancer, and the Volunteer Action Program, in addition to cultural organizations such as the Council of Pan-Asian Americans, Minority Men United, and Rainbow Connection. Political and social organizations include Amnesty International, Campus Greens, College Democrats, College Republicans, and Loyola Students Against Sweatshops. One student assures, "Loyola will foster and support your interests. There's a lot of liberalism and conservatism on campus, but both coexist peacefully and very actively."

While one student explains that students on campus tend to "agree to disagree," "the school's diversity ensures that most controverial issues popular in politics today are presented in one way or another on campus. Issues such as the war, homosexual marriage rights, and abortion are brought up through posters and open forums on campus."

Connecting Service with the Classroom

"Our education focuses not just on developing intellect but also character," declares one service-learning devotee. The aforementioned Magis Initiative is a strong force of service-learning on campus. Each semester, there are a minimum of 35 service-learning classes offered for students, with over 700 students involved on an annual basis. Service expectations range from a minimum of 12 hours per semester in some classes to over 100 hours of community work in some internship programs.

Service-learning classes—which gain this designation by meeting a set of engagement criteria developed by Magis—can be found throughout the College of Arts and Sciences, School of Education, School of Nursing, School of Business, and joint programs with the professional Schools of Social Work and Law. "Some of the available classes are 'Restoration Ecology' (Biology), 'Free Speech vs. Hate Speech' (Communication), 'Internship in Adult Literacy' (English), 'Action and Values: Ethics for Teachers' (Philosophy), 'Chicago Politics' (Political Science), 'Global Inequalities' (Sociology), and 'Moral Problems: Urban Issues' (Theology)."

Students can also pursue service-learning through Loyola University Chicago's Center for Urban Research and Learning (CURL). "CURL is a non-traditional university research center which places strong emphasis on research that addresses community needs and involves the community at all levels of research." CURL's partnerships include Early Childhood Advisory Network, The Enterprising Kitchen, Families Together Cooperative, Friends of Battered Women, Greater Chicago Food Depository, and the Peace Museum.

Students also have access to service-learning opportunities while studying abroad. Through a partnership with the University of Alberto Hurtado in Chile, they can choose to work with local community-development organizations as part of a course on Poverty and Development. One participant reports, "During my semester abroad in Santiago, Chile, I worked in a community center with teenagers, playing soccer and teaching English."

Impact on Community and Students

"Because Loyola is in Chicago, a great deal involves service to the city. Students often help out right in the Rogers Park neighborhood by volunteering at the literacy center, teaching English to immigrants, [or doing] Rogers Park clean-ups. Others choose to volunteer with nonprofits located in the city, and still others serve the campus community. You can generally find a group of Loyolans at every major service event in Chicago."

The Loyola Partners is a new project coordinated through Magis, serving as a bridge between Loyola and seven core community organizations. The groups involved include Centro Romero ("providing adult educational opportunities, women's programs, legal assistance, youth education, and leadership programming for the Latino community"), Enterprising Kitchen ("offering job, business, and life skills training to women by teaching them how to make and market fine-quality soaps"), and Residents for Effective Shelter Transition ("running shelters, case-management services, a housing program, and many programs for substance abusers").

The administration cites a "special community partnership" with the Devon-Sheridan senior residence, home to "a large number of Russian Jewish residents." "Through the partnership, students help at the computer center, translate letters and forms, and teach English. Each semester, the Hillel students also host celebrations of holidays, such as Sukkot, Hanukkah, and Purim." Through another recently-developed partnership with Chicago's Streetwise newspaper, students in Magis Scholars English composition classes assist homeless Chicago residents in writing and editing resumes and cover letters.

Student Financial Support for Service

Loyola offers a range of religious and non-religious scholarship programs. "The Jesuit, BVM, [and] Sisters of Christian Charity Presidential Scholarships are given to a student who attended a Jesuit or BVM High School. Students receive a half-tuition scholarship and are required to perform 20 hours of service per semester." The Gannon Scholars Leadership Program rewards "young women who have displayed outstanding contributions to the schools and communities." Last but not least, Magis Leaders scholarships award "a limited number of scholarships to incoming students who show need as well as commitment to collaborative leadership, community engagement, diversity, and global perspectives."

SELECTIVITY

# of applicants	11,009
% of applicants accepted	82
% of acceptees attending	21

FRESHMAN PROFILE

Range SAT Verbal	540-640
Range SAT Math	510-630
Range ACT Composite	22-27
Minimum Paper TOEFL	550
Minimum Computer TOEFL	213
Average HS GPA	3.53
% graduated top 10% of class	28
% graduated top 25% of class	66
% graduated top 50% of class	93

DEADLINES

Regular notification by	rolling
Nonfall registration?	yes

FINANCIAL FACTS

Annual tuition	$21,780
Room and board	$8,824
Books and supplies	$800
Required fees	$560
% frosh rec. need-based scholarship or grant aid	74
% UG rec. need-based scholarship or grant aid	73
% frosh rec. need-based self-help aid	63
% UG rec. need-based self-help aid	64
% frosh rec. any financial aid	74
% UG rec. any financial aid	75

MACALESTER COLLEGE

1600 GRAND AVENUE, ST. PAUL, MN 55105

ADMISSIONS: 651-696-6357 • **FAX:** 651-696-6724 • **FINANCIAL AID:** 651-696-6214

E-MAIL: ADMISSIONS@MACALESTER.EDU • **WEBSITE:** WWW.MACALESTER.EDU

CAMPUS LIFE

Type of school	private
Environment	village

STUDENTS

Total undergrad enrollment	1,867
% male/female	44/56
% from out of state	75
% from public high school	66
% live on campus	68
% African American	3
% Asian	6
% Caucasian	73
% Hispanic	3
% Native American	1
% international	14
# of countries represented	86

ACADEMICS

Calendar	semester
Student/faculty ratio	11:1
% profs teaching UG courses	100
% classes taught by TAs	0
Most common lab size	<10
Most common reg class size	10-19

MOST POPULAR MAJORS
economics
English language and literature
political science and government

Getting Involved

Nestled in Minnesota's Twin Cities, Macalester College boasts not only a strong academic reputation, but also an uncommonly unified spirit of social and political awareness. One student explains, "People who come here have a purpose. They know how to commit to a community and engage themselves in meaningful work. The school does not preach volunteerism—it does not need to."

The Community Service Office (CSO) serves as the campus's catalyst for civic-engagement efforts, coordinating community partnerships, three leadership programs, and service-learning initiatives. The CSO employs four professional and 12 student employees, each of whom is responsible for an issue area such as "Arts for Social Change," "Economic Justice Issues," or "Immigrant and Refugee Resources." Says the school, "The students act as liaisons with the community organizations working on their issue, they educate the campus and generate dialogue about their issue, and they recruit and support student volunteers." The Leaders in Service Program provides additional opportunities for 40 student leaders to collectively wrestle with issues of social concern and engage the campus for community causes. Student participants also attend two retreats and monthly training workshops.

The CSO will keep growing bigger and better, thanks to a plan to launch a new and improved Center for Global Citizenship in the fall of 2005. "The center will bring together all of the college's research, curricular, cocurricular, and institutional initiatives related to educating global citizen-leaders."

Campus Culture of Engagement

Macalester's adminsitration states that 80 percent of students participate in some kind of service before they graduate. One student explains, "There is basically no way for students to miss out on becoming involved. The very first week, there's a student-org fair that attracts tons of students. First years have already done a day of service in the small first-year class groups, so in just a few days, they learn about off-campus and on-campus opportunities. Also, within the first three weeks of school, over 40 community partners set up tables for 'A Taste of Service' to recruit even more students."

The nearly 80 student organizations on campus provide for plenty of opportunities for student-initiated service work, especially through groups such as Maction, Amnesty International, and Habitat for Humanity. However, the student body is not just devoted to community service, but also to political outspeak: "Macalester is a high-energy, highly-motivated, and very socially-conscious campus;" "issues are actively debated and people really make a difference—they go out and do it and don't just talk." Student organizations include MULCH (Macalester Urban Land and Community Health), Mac CARES (Mac Conservation and Renewable Energy Society), Mac Peace and Justice, and Mac SLAC (Student Labor Action Coalition). One student sums up the political tenor of campus discourse: "Sometimes there is a tiny bit of tension between the liberals, the über-liberals, and the anarchists."

Controversy thrives at Macalester. "Gender-blind housing, the Coca-Cola boycott, and need-blind admissions are all big topics on campus right now. A new alternative to our weekly newpaper has sprung up (partly) as a response to some of these topics as well as to create a place to discuss radical politics."

Connecting Service with the Classroom

Macalester recently encouraged its faculty to attend a three-day workshop on civic engagement. The outpouring of responses reflected what one student describes as "a genuine commitment among many faculty to recognize students who do this work and encourage it."

Each year, between eight and 12 different courses with civic-engagement components are offered in a variety of fields. "Psychology courses in 'Developmental Psychology' and 'Family, Children, and Public Policy' have required students to volunteer each week at nonprofit children's sites; political science courses in 'Public Policy and Affordable Housing' and 'Legislative Politics' have utilized internships in governmental organizations, nonprofit organizations, and for-profit organizations to help students learn about public policy from a variety of perspectives." One student attests to how community involvement opened up her eyes: "The concepts of my sociology class were really supplemented by the service component: I tutored American Indian children."

Service-learning and action research projects have also been integrated into many urban studies and geography courses, whose projects include "mapping the community resources of neighborhoods, researching the history of urban communities, and designing Geographic Information System (GIS) mapping projects that support the work of community partners." The Environmental Studies, Women and Gender Studies, and American Studies programs require nonprofit internships for all of its majors.

Impact on Community and Students

The Community Service Office maintains files on over 300 local and national nonprofits, schools, and community organizations. Community partnerships encompass "immigrant and refugee resources, children and tutoring, the arts for social change, peace and justice, women and gender issues, public policy, economic justice, international-speakers program, health, senior citizens, AIDS, and environmental issues."

The English Learning Center for Immigrant and Refugee Families, a nonprofit organization in Minneapolis, offers English-language classes, computer-literacy classes, and children's tutoring programs—all of which have attracted the participation of Mac students. As part of the "Lives of Commitment" program, first-year students plan and teach weekly English language classes. Students also enjoy a partnership with the Jane Addams School for Democracy, "a program that supports intercultural English-Spanish, English-Hmong, and English-East African learning circles." "Students in an education class successfully applied for a Raise Your Voice grant through Campus Compact to bring representatives of the Jane Addams School to campus for a public dialogue on immigration and citizenship," and an anthropology class partnered with the Jane Addams School to interview immigrants and refugees.

Student Financial Support for Service

Several of Macalester's scholarship programs have a community-service requirement as part of the eligibility for the scholarship. They include the Destination 2010 Scholarship, requiring 40 hours of tutor/mentoring in local urban schools; the Alan Page Scholarship, awarded to students of color who must tutor children ages five through thirteen; and the Phillips Scholarship, which gives $14,000 for student-designed major service projects.

In addition to these academic scholarships, the alumni-endowed Action Fund offers resources to support students' community-based service projects with up to $500 grants. The Lilly Grant funds six students completing summer internships with nonprofit organizations, allowing them to reflect on issues of work and ethics. Macalester also offers the Off-Campus Student-Employment program, which gives students the option of fulfilling their work-study requirements at local nonprofit organizations; Macalester pays their entire work-study wage, rather than asking the community organization to partially fund the students.

SELECTIVITY

# of applicants	4,341
% of applicants accepted	44
% of acceptees attending	27
# accepting a place on wait list	249

FRESHMAN PROFILE

Range SAT Verbal	650-730
Range SAT Math	620-700
Range ACT Composite	28-31
Minimum Paper TOEFL	570
Minimum Computer TOEFL	230
% graduated top 10% of class	71
% graduated top 25% of class	96
% graduated top 50% of class	100

DEADLINES

Regular admission	1/15
Regular notification by	4/1
Nonfall registration?	no

FINANCIAL FACTS

Annual tuition	$28,474
Room and board	$7,858
Books and supplies	$805
Required fees	$168
% frosh rec. need-based scholarship or grant aid	72
% UG rec. need-based scholarship or grant aid	69
% frosh rec. need-based self-help aid	72
% UG rec. need-based self-help aid	69
% frosh rec. any financial aid	76
% UG rec. any financial aid	73

MARQUETTE UNIVERSITY

PO Box 1881, Milwaukee, WI 53201-1881

Admissions: 414-288-7302 • Fax: 414-288-3764 • Financial Aid: 414-288-7390

E-mail: admissions@marquette.edu • Website: www.marquette.edu

CAMPUS LIFE

Type of school	private
Environment	town

STUDENTS

Total undergrad	
enrollment	7,709
% male/female	45/55
% from out of state	58
% from public high school	56
% live on campus	55
% African American	5
% Asian	4
% Caucasian	85
% Hispanic	4
% Native American	0
% international	2
# of countries represented	80

ACADEMICS

Calendar	semester
Student/faculty ratio	14:1
% profs teaching	
UG courses	77
% classes taught by TAs	
Most common lab size	10-19
Most common	
reg class size	10-19

MOST POPULAR MAJORS

business administration/management
nursing - registered nurse training
(RN, ASN, BSN, MSN)

Getting Involved

In the spirit of its Jesuit tradition, Marquette strives "to develop men and women for others, who practice a faith that seeks justice." A student sampling attests, "The core of my Marquette experience has been service; it is emphasized by everyone from the president of the university, to the newest students here."

The Center for Community Service within the Office of Student Development coordinates many of the school's community partnerships and advises student organizations devoted to service. The Center works in conjunction with University Ministry, which coordinates the Marquette Action Program. Since 1977, this program has enabled students to participate in winter and spring break service trips to 11 different sites in North America.

Other service-oriented campus institutions include the Les Aspin Center for Government, which strives to prepare students for ethical lives in the public sector: "Since 1984, the Center has educated more than 1,100 students who have interned in nearly 100 congressional offices, the State Department, the Food and Drug Administration, U.S. Secret Service, the White House, and the Federal Communications Commission." The Marquette University Institute for Transnational Justice and the Institute for Urban Life also work to promote a civically-engaged student body.

Campus Culture of Engagement

"We have an introductory leadership program called Students Taking Active Roles (STAR), which does an excellent job of bringing in prominent university people to give talks about issues and student groups. It is a great way to get in touch quickly and efficiently with the actively-minded mainstream during your freshman year." In addition to STAR, students find service opportunities at the multi-day Community Service Fair and through Urban Connection, a one-day service event for new students.

Students describe an earnest and widespread spirit of civic engagement on campus. "I think that it is amazing that about 85 percent to 90 percent of students report that by the time they graduated, they had performed some type of community service." "The people who volunteer do so because they want to, not out of obligation."

Student-led organizations include Supporting Special Olympics (Marquette was the first college in the country to have its own Special Olympics chapter); Best Buddies of Marquette; Circle K International; Gamma Sigma Sigma; Habitat for Humanity; and JUSTICE (Jesuit University Students Together in Concerned Empowerment), "a student organization that challenges the administration to make decisions that are congruent with the Catholic, Jesuit nature of the university and uphold principles of fairness and justice."

While service looms large at Marquette, students report that activism tends to be less prevalent—partially because "the university has a very stringent policy on public demonstrations." There's still room for debate, however; says the school, "Recently, the College Republicans were given a voice in the national Democratic Presidential Debate hosted on campus."

Connecting Service with the Classroom

The administration reports that since its inception ten years ago, "the Service Learning Program has grown from ten courses and 160 students to 50 to 60 courses and 700 to 900 students each semester. There has been at least one course in every college at the university."

Marquette's diverse range of service-learning opportunities include the Marquette University Legal Clinic, where Marquette University law students provide free legal information and referral services, and the College of Nursing's USAID-funded programs to train health care workers in Africa, through which "nursing students and faculty travel to Kenya to train health care providers in providing care to patients with HIV and AIDS." Engineering and other students participate in HEILA (Health, Environment, and Infrastructure in Latin America), in which students "perform two-week service-learning projects in countries such as El Salvador, Guatemala, and Honduras while learning about the region's history, culture, and politics."

The School of Education and its branches—the Education Resource Center, the Hartman Literacy and Learning Center, and Teachers for Social Justice—are particularly active in the realm of service-learning. One student reports, "In my Child Developmental class, I worked at a day care for low-income families, with a focus on children with disabilities. This opportunity opened my eyes to the need for good education for children of all types and economic backgrounds."

Impact on Community and Students

Marquette maintains community partnerships through multiple service sites on campus: The Center for Community Service sends volunteers to 42 agencies each semester; the Service-Learning Program has relationships with over 130 schools and agencies; and a program called Midnight Run sends volunteers to eleven shelters throughout Milwaukee each day.

The Campus Kitchen Project at Marquette "brings students, on-campus dining service professionals, and community organizations together to combat hunger in Milwaukee." In addition to providing food to underserved populations, the program offers tutoring, counseling, and culinary training. The Hunger Clean-Up is "the largest one-day community-service project at Marquette—for approximately three hours on a Saturday in April, volunteers work at sites including homeless shelters, elementary schools, community organizations, and many more." Each year, more than 1,500 students, staff, and faculty participate.

Marquette's Service Learning Program has also worked extensively with Journey House community center providing Spanish courses to assist with ESL and GED tutoring and business students to help with employment and HR skills. One of the Journey House programs, an adolescent support group called Girls in the House, has attracted students from Psychology, Sociology, Criminology, and Social Welfare and Justice classes, who have helped to co-facilitate the group.

Marquette's service also extends far beyond Milwaukee, thanks to the International Marquette Action Program in Jamaica and other service programs in Guatemala, Honduras, South Africa, Kenya, the Dominican Republic, and El Salvador annually. One student reports, "This past Christmas, I participated in a trip to Kingston, Jamaica, for two weeks where we taught, worked with the elderly, and worked with kids with AIDS and kids with physical and mental disabilities."

Student Financial Support for Service

The Burke Scholarship is a four-year, full-tuition scholarship "awarded annually to up to ten academically talented Wisconsin high-school seniors who exhibit leadership in a manner that reflects exceptional commitment to community." Recipients are expected to perform 300 hours of meaningful service and participate in a seminar and lecture series each academic year. The Trinity Fellows Program is a fellowship "dedicated to developing urban leaders with a commitment to community service. Fellows participate in a 21 month study/work program while earning a master's degree in one of nine fields of study." Lastly, the Companions in Leadership Undergraduate Leadership Internship Program funds juniors and seniors interested in pursuing year-long internships with local agencies and schools.

SELECTIVITY

# of applicants	10,206
% of applicants accepted	67
% of acceptees attending	26

FRESHMAN PROFILE

Range SAT Verbal	530-640
Range SAT Math	540-650
Range ACT Composite	24-28
Minimum Paper TOEFL	520
Minimum Computer TOEFL	190
% graduated top 10% of class	33
% graduated top 25% of class	64
% graduated top 50% of class	93

DEADLINES

Regular notification by	1/15
Nonfall registration?	yes

FINANCIAL FACTS

Annual tuition	$21,550
Room and board	$7,890
Books and supplies	$900
Required fees	$382
% frosh rec. need-based scholarship or grant aid	51
% UG rec. need-based scholarship or grant aid	53
% frosh rec. need-based self-help aid	49
% UG rec. need-based self-help aid	51
% frosh rec. any financial aid	88
% UG rec. any financial aid	85

MERCER UNIVERSITY—MACON

ADMISSIONS OFFICE, 1400 COLEMAN AVENUE, MACON, GA 31207-0001

ADMISSIONS: 478-301-2650 • **FAX:** 478-301-2828 • **FINANCIAL AID:** 478-301-2670

E-MAIL: ADMISSIONS@MERCER.EDU • **WEBSITE:** WWW.MERCER.EDU

CAMPUS LIFE

Type of school	private
Environment	town

STUDENTS

Total undergrad enrollment	4,561
% male/female	32/68
% from out of state	22
% live on campus	65
% African American	29
% Asian	3
% Caucasian	60
% Hispanic	2
% international	2
# of countries represented	37

ACADEMICS

Calendar	semester
Student/faculty ratio	18:1
Most common lab size	20-29
Most common reg class size	10-19

MOST POPULAR MAJORS

business administration/management
communications, journalism, and related fields
engineering

Getting Involved

Mercer University makes it easy for students to get their feet wet in the waters of service-learning: It is a required facet of students' first year on campus. Of course, this "highly motivated bunch of students, speakers, and faculty" needs little incentive to engage with its surrounding community.

Mercer is a Baptist-affiliated university with campuses in Macon and Atlanta, but undergrads are taught primarily on the Macon campus. The Mercer Center for Service-Learning and Community Development supports a full-time Director of Service-Learning, who works with faculty and student groups to integrate volunteerism into campus life. The MCSCD also promotes community outreach, through programs "aimed at neighborhood revitalization and University research on issues of social, educational, and economic improvements in the Macon community." The center focuses primarily on the strengths of grassroots leadership. The President's Task Force for Civic Engagement, established by the University Commons and the MCSCD, brings together representatives from all ten of Mercer's schools and colleges "to act as an advisory group for President R. Kirby Godsey and to engage students, faculty, staff, and administrators in meaningful dialogue about the civic mission of the University."

Many students' first exposure to service-learning comes through the popular first-year seminars (FYS/X), a two-semester series of seminars intended to introduce students to the realm of service-learning. The College of Liberal Arts also offers a service-learning-based concentration in its Program in Leadership and Community Service.

Students report that "opportunity is everywhere" at Mercer, but do caution that it is "not publicized enough," so "you must take the initiative in order to take advantage" of the school's offerings.

Campus Culture of Engagement

"Service-learning and civic engagments begin in the very first week that new students arrive, with an 'Into the Streets' program during Fall orientation. This civic engagement is then carried over to the entire first year in a class called First-Year Seminar." "Engagement, service, and activism" are, therefore, "an integral part of a first-year student's experience here at Mercer," and many "continue their involvement throughout their time here."

One student enthusiastically reports, "I have personally been involved in campus clean-ups, Habitat for Humanity, and different fundraisers held on campus that raise money for different charitable organizations. Every week, there are a number of service opportunities at Mercer. Even if you don't intend to, at one point or another, you will have done some sort of service for others at Mercer!"

Mercer's student ministry groups (Baptist Student Union, Catholic Newman Ministries, Fellowship of Christian Athletes, Reformed University Fellowship), athletic teams, and Greek organizations all support a variety of service activities. Student groups promoting civic engagement include Bear Buddies (supporting Big Brothers and Big Sisters); Circle K (supporting Macon Community Food Bank); Habitat for Humanity; Students for Environmental Action; and Up 'til Dawn (supporting St. Jude Children's Research Hospital with more than $10,000 raised annually).

Connecting Service with the Classroom

Students report that "support from faculty is a major strength and valuable asset in civic engagement." Approximately 20 to 25 undergraduate service-learning courses are offered in a given academic year, and additional community-related internships and research projects are encouraged by the schools of Business, Education, and Engineering. Each year, about 20 percent of the undergraduate enrollment participates in some kind of service-learning.

The aforementioned First-Year Seminar (FYS/X) program, instituted in 1969, leads to an annual contribution of more than 3,500 hours of tutoring in Macon elementary schools. Each semester of the Seminar is devoted to a theme—most recently "Composing the Self" and "Engaging the World." "Both topics explore texts from traditional and modern literature, philosophy, religion, history, and political science, complemented by speakers and other events outside the traditional classroom. The seminars explore questions of individual identity, civic duty and citizenship, and social justice in connection with community involvement. Students in the specially designated experiential sections tutor one hour weekly at neighborhood elementary schools and participate in community-service projects such as Habitat for Humanity, the Boys and Girls Club, and Rebuilding Together."

The Program in Leadership and Community Service in the College of Liberal Arts—a concentration or "enhanced major"—provides additional service-learning opportunities for Mercer students, aiming to prepare liberal-arts students for civic leadership through public-service placements. "The curriculum is also designed to prepare students to work in a number of different fields, combining a practicum and elective tracks in public policy and planning, psychology, environmental policy, social work, or nonprofit management, with core courses ('Education for the Common Good,' 'The Literature of Social Criticism and Change,' 'The Origins of Our Institutional Models,' and 'Social Ecology')."

Impact on Community and Students

Mercer's service-learning program "assists in creating an incredible community feeling on campus and in the surrounding area." "It is everywhere, from cleaning up trash beside the road to cleaning up around the river in Macon. People help build houses, tutor inner-city children, and help renovate schools."

The Mercer Center for Service-Learning and Community Development (MCSCD) is a strong nexus of community partnership on campus, focusing on developing "sustainable grassroots leadership in a 120-block neighborhood of Central South Macon." "Central South, the core area of downtown Macon, has suffered two decades of population decline and the loss of jobs and services." The MCSCD program provides neighborhood organizations with "logistical support, training activities, and connections to university and community resources" and places federally-funded student workers within the community, primarily as tutors for local area schools. To date, "seventeen classes in Marketing, Law, Technical Communication, History, Political Science, Sociology, Education, Environmental Science, Public Health, and Industrial Engineering have completed action research projects addressing Central South issues and problems."

Mercer also maintains an active partnership with the First Street Arts Center, "a model of inclusive education, bringing together children with and without disabilities in arts-rich educational environments." The program attracts volunteers from the federally-funded AmeriCorps program.

Student Financial Support for Service

Mercer offers four full-tuition ($22,000) Servant-Leader Scholarships annually to low-income students from inner-city Macon neighborhoods. "Students are expected to be active in the community during their four years at Mercer, working with third-graders in an after-school program 'to enrich their academic experience, guiding them to a mature adolescence and hopes of college.' To qualify, students must be eligible for a Pell Grant or be a first-generation college student, and graduate from a Bibb County high school."

SELECTIVITY

# of applicants	2,711
% of applicants accepted	85
% of acceptees attending	25

FRESHMAN PROFILE

Range SAT Verbal	530-640
Range SAT Math	540-640
Range ACT Composite	22-27
Minimum Paper TOEFL	550
Minimum Computer TOEFL	213
Average HS GPA	3.50
% graduated top 10% of class	38
% graduated top 25% of class	65
% graduated top 50% of class	91

DEADLINES

Regular admission	7/1
Regular notification by	rolling
Nonfall registration?	yes

FINANCIAL FACTS

Annual tuition	$22,050
Room and board	$7,060
Books and supplies	$800
% frosh rec. need-based scholarship or grant aid	69
% UG rec. need-based scholarship or grant aid	66
% frosh rec. need-based self-help aid	43
% UG rec. need-based self-help aid	46
% frosh rec. any financial aid	97
% UG rec. any financial aid	96

METROPOLITAN STATE UNIVERSITY

700 EAST 7TH STREET, ST. PAUL, MN, 55106-5000

ADMISSIONS: 651-793-1300 • FAX: 651-793-1310 • FINANCIAL AID: 651-793-1310

WEBSITE: WWW.METROSTATE.EDU

CAMPUS LIFE

Type of school	public
Environment	metropolitan

STUDENTS

Total undergrad enrollment	5,906
% male/female	40/60
% from out of state	2
% from public high school	85
% live on campus	0
% African American	12
% Asian	10
% Caucasian	74
% Hispanic	2
% Native American	1
% international	2
# of countries represented	23

ACADEMICS

Calendar	semester
Student/faculty ratio	17:1
% profs teaching UG courses	100
% classes taught by TAs	0
Most common lab size	20-29
Most common reg class size	20-29

Getting Involved

Metropolitan State University has become known nationally for its serious commitment to community partnerships. Community involvement is headquartered at the Center for Community-Based Learning, which "provides quality individual internships, group internships, applied research projects, service activities, courses with field components, and community partnerships which address mutually defined interests and build on the capacity of the community." Programs include "Academic Internship, K–12 Outreach, and Community Organizing and Development programs"; the university notes that "the center provides support for efforts across the university to integrate community-based learning with academic reflection through internships and courses which provide a meaningful experience beneficial to both the participating community organization or business and the student."

And the students' perspective on this? They tell us simply that "Metro offers great opportunities to give back to the community."

Campus Culture of Engagement

Sources of official notification for Metropolitan State's service-learning programs include "an online events-announcement site" (which, according to one student, "often doesn't include everything"), academic advisors, orientation events, the student senate and council, and "the Student Life and Leadership office on the first floor of Founder's Hall on the main St. Paul Campus." Observes one student: "Most of the time, students hear about an event from another student. There are many diverse student activity groups, and finding them is not difficult once one knows they exist."

While students agree that "civic engagement brings diversity to the campus experience," they also warn that "this is mainly a commuter school; most students are working full time and have family obligations, and you'll discover many just want to get their education and get out; they don't want to be involved." However, students add that "the people who do show up are generally enthusiastic and really want to do the job."

Connecting Service with the Classroom

In recent years, Metropolitan State University has developed a regional and national reputation for its community partnerships—programs organized through departments or through the Center for Community-Based Learning that connect faculty, staff, students, and alumni to community-based organizations and agencies. In the 2002–2003 school year, the university offered "150 separate course titles and 161 sections of courses that included a community connection. [A]n additional 48 courses have [subsequently] been identified by faculty. These courses are in all four colleges and within almost every department."

One example of service-learning is the university's program with the La Familia Guidance Center, "a nonprofit mental health agency which is the site of the Social Work Department's Community Learning Center in the Chicano-Latino community. The joint program is not just a short-term clinical experience for students; it is integrated into the very essence of what the social work department believes is essential instruction. The university provides financial and human resources to the organization; it pays for space, it provides materials, it provides faculty/counselors, and it provides students whose primary responsibility is to learn the theory and practice of social work by engaging in real community issues with real community members. Faculty members also often teach their classes at the community center. Social-work courses require students to engage in community-based research, including advocacy research. Community placements allow students to work in four communities of color—Hmong, Latino, African American, and Native American—to help residents appreciate and understand their community needs. La Familia exemplifies a program/sequence of courses that is not just about a one-semester experience. It is about a long-term relationship between the university and the community for the betterment of both."Other programs include:

- The Careership Program, which "was a 2004 Minnesota Carter Partnership Award Finalist." Explains the school, "there is a broad consensus that communities of color are underrepresented in community-based development processes and decisions in the Twin Cities. Twin Cities Local Initiatives Support Corporation (LISC) and Metropolitan State University have partnered to plan, manage and refine the 'Careership' program—a mid-career apprenticeship designed to train new leaders, particularly people of color, for professional positions in the field of community development."

- The East Side Community Outreach Partnership Center (COPC), a HUD-funded program that is jointly run by Metropolitan State, the University of Minnesota, and Macalester College. The COPC focuses on local issues such as housing, workforce development, leadership development, and healthcare.

- Project Shine (which stands for Students Helping in the Naturalization of Elders), through which students teach English and citizenship classes to older immigrants and refugees in the area.

Impact on Community and Students

Students involved in service at Metropolitan State University agree that "the urban community benefits because of the location of our university and whom is particularly invited" to participate. Students also benefit, they say: "Being engaged has sharpened my skills at communicating effectively, organizing, and speaking in a leadership capacity with brevity and relevance to vital issues. I see the big picture better and am able to communicate what can be done to improve things and bring those together to do them." Concludes one undergrad, "Good things are done for students and people in positions where they may not have opportunities or resources. Our school does its best to maximize community resources with limited funds and divergent schedules, and it does pretty well."

Student Financial Support for Service

Metropolitan State does not currently offer scholarships or other financial support for community/public service, but does offer a host of community work-study options.

MIAMI UNIVERSITY OF OHIO

301 S. CAMPUS AVENUE, OXFORD, OH 45056

ADMISSIONS: 513-529-2531 • **FAX:** 513-529-1550 • **FINANCIAL AID:** 513-529-8734

E-MAIL: ADMISSIONS@MUOHIO.EDU • **WEBSITE:** WWW.MUOHIO.EDU

CAMPUS LIFE

Type of school	public
Environment	village

STUDENTS

Total undergrad	
enrollment	15,011
% male/female	46/54
% from out of state	28
% live on campus	45
% African American	3
% Asian	3
% Caucasian	87
% Hispanic	2
% Native American	1
# of countries represented	40

ACADEMICS

Calendar	4-1-4
Student/faculty ratio	18:1
% profs teaching	
UG courses	100
% classes taught by TAs	25
Most common lab size	10-19
Most common	
reg class size	10-19

MOST POPULAR MAJORS

business administration/management
marketing/marketing management
zoology/animal biology

Getting Involved

Miami University, the school tells us, "has been unified over time in its mission of educating men and women for responsible, informed citizenship as well as meaningful employment. Citizenship and leadership are, therefore, developed through classroom and out-of-class involvement and are a part of the way [Miami University students] live and grow in this community." Service is central to the lives of many MU undergraduates who receive ample support in their efforts from the school: On campus, the Office of Service-Learning and Civic Leadership "strives to develop sustainable, reciprocal partnerships with area community-based organizations," and the newly-created Social Action Center "seeks to provide programs and resources for academic and co-curricular communities on campus interested in working for positive social change." The Center for Community Engagement in Over-the-Rhine (Cincinnati, Ohio), the Women's Center, the Cliff Alexander Office of Fraternity and Sorority Life and Leadership, the Buck Rodger's Leadership Program, and the Social Work Department provide additional support and opportunities for students to engage in hands-on, meaningful service.

Campus Culture of Engagement

MU offers myriad ways to keep up-to-date on service opportunities. Each fall, "the Office of Service-Learning and Civic Leadership hosts a Community Action Fair where local agencies and campus service organizations interact with students face-to-face to inform them of ways that they can serve in local communities. The Office of Service-Learning and Civic Leadership website (www.muohio.edu/servicelearning) is a hands-on resource students can utilize to search for service opportunities." And that's not all—students report "hundreds of posters, fliers, people handing out announcements, and signs all over campus," "announcements from professors and speakers coming to the classroom," and according to MU, "first-year students also have the option to live in the Residential Service-Learning residence hall or the Leadership, Excellence, and Community residence hall, two of many theme learning residence halls."

According to one student, "there are many different ways to get involved, and there is always some sort of activity" going on. As another student explains, "many of the sororities and fraternities do service projects. There is also a large non-Greek group on campus where female and male students do service work together. In addition, the progressive groups on campus do volunteer work such as working on low-income housing in Cincinnati with ReSTOC, in Hamilton at soup kitchens, or volunteering at a local no-kill animal shelter with the Progressive Animal Welfare Society. There is also an active Habitat for Humanity on campus." Students point out that service "is a fabulous way to meet new and different people that share the same interests as you. It can also open the door to other opportunities in the future."

Connecting Service with the Classroom

Miami University "continues to deepen its commitment to service-learning" with each passing year. "A growing number of faculty actively explore ways of including a service-learning component within their course curriculum. Students may also choose to participate in a residential service-learning course. This course is taught each fall in one of Miami's themed learning communities. At the heart of service-learning initiatives at Miami University is an effort to cultivate the dialectical relationship between class theories, knowledge, skills, resources, and the experience of connecting the campus community in the broader community."

Unique MU programs include:

- Empower, developed by a group of undergrads, is "a year-long program that blends service, leadership development, and education on social issues. The program is geared toward first- and second-year students. In addition to an intensive inter-group building experience, students engage biweekly in one-time service opportunities with partner agencies. The service covers a breadth of social agencies and issues."

- Design/Build Studio involves "a series of projects in close collaboration with community organizations in the Over-the-Rhine neighborhood of Cincinnati. The Design/Build Studio involves three primary modes of engagement. The first is design/build projects where students, in collaboration with low-income housing development organizations, provide design and construction skills to bring the buildings of the neighborhood back into use. The second takes the form of public interventions, named AGIT/PROPs. Students build artistic installations that AGITate and PROPagate points of view with regard to the neighborhood's history and political consciousness. The third mode of engagement includes providing design schematics for the Over-the-Rhine Housing Network in its proposals for Affordable Housing Tax Credit Financing."

Impact on Community and Students

MU is deeply involved in the Oxford, Butler County, and greater Cincinnati communities. The school explains that "in addition to the more than 50 area organizations that sponsor service projects, the university continues to deepen its commitment to eighteen community partner agencies. These organizations vary considerably in their missions, programs, and populations served. Due to Oxford's unique position as a rural community located near urban environments, students are able to engage with diverse communities. Social justice, affordable housing, race relations, hunger, immigration, education, family welfare, aging, and animal rights are among the social issues addressed at our partner agencies."

Students appreciate how service programs allow them "to be engaged in the Oxford community. Instead of just coming to the campus for school and taking so much from this university and town, civic engagement allows us to give back to the community." Adds one undergrad, "[Service] taught me how to relate to people who are different than me and to start to think beyond my own selfish wants and perspectives."

Student Financial Support for Service

Miami University reports that "currently, there are no scholarships designated specifically for community or public service." Students who demonstrate a deep interest in service may improve their chances for some departmental scholarships (e.g., social work) as well as for the university's Scholar Leader scholarships. Most financial awards at MU are need-based.

SELECTIVITY

# of applicants	14,977
% of applicants accepted	71
% of acceptees attending	33
# accepting a place on wait list	1,522
% admitted from wait list	24

FRESHMAN PROFILE

Range SAT Verbal	560-640
Range SAT Math	580-660
Range ACT Composite	25-29
Minimum Paper TOEFL	530
Average HS GPA	3.70
% graduated top 10% of class	37
% graduated top 25% of class	75
% graduated top 50% of class	97

DEADLINES

Regular admission	1/31
Regular notification by	3/15
Nonfall registration?	yes

FINANCIAL FACTS

Annual in-state tuition	$8,353
Annual out-of-state tuition	$18,103
Room and board	$6,680
Books and supplies	$800
Required fees	$1,334
% frosh rec. need-based scholarship or grant aid	14
% UG rec. need-based scholarship or grant aid	12
% frosh rec. need-based self-help aid	25
% UG rec. need-based self-help aid	25

MICHIGAN STATE UNIVERSITY

250 ADMINISTRATION BUILDING, EAST LANSING, MI 48824-1046

ADMISSIONS: 517-355-8332 • FAX: 517-353-1647 • FINANCIAL AID: 517-353-5940

E-MAIL: ADMIS@MSU.EDU • WEBSITE: WWW.MSU.EDU

CAMPUS LIFE

Type of school	public
Environment	village

STUDENTS

Total undergrad enrollment	35,107
% male/female	47/53
% from out of state	10
% live on campus	42
% African American	8
% Asian	5
% Caucasian	79
% Hispanic	3
% Native American	1
% international	3
# of countries represented	100

ACADEMICS

Calendar	semester
Student/faculty ratio	16:1
Most common lab size	10-19
Most common reg class size	20-29

MOST POPULAR MAJORS

communications studies/speech
communication and rhetoric
communications, journalism, and
related fields
psychology

Getting Involved

The cynosure of service at Michigan State University is the Center for Service Learning and Civic Engagement (CSLCE), an office "committed to empowering students with service and civic-based educational opportunities that extend beyond the classroom." MSU administrators inform us that "the mission of the CSLCE is to provide active, service-focused, community-based, mutually beneficial, integrated learning opportunities for students, building and enhancing their commitment to academics, personal and professional development, and civic responsibility."

To plug in to the service community, students should "keep an eye out for fliers posted on bulletin boards all over campus, watch for the many e-mails that get sent by service groups to student electronic mailing lists, and attend 'Party at the Aud,' which is a huge gathering at the beginning of the school year of many clubs and organizations on campus (it's a great way to learn about all the interesting groups you can be involved in)." Students also tell us that "there are plenty of helpful people and resources on campus for a first-year student" and especially praise the Service-Learning Center, where one can "discover numerous programs."

Campus Culture of Engagement

"There are plenty of opportunities" to get involved at MSU, students tell us, "and the best way to get involved is to check out the Service-Learning Center and find something that interests you." Students can choose from "a wide range of volunteer projects going on, both on and off campus" as well as from "many student organizations who do service," or they can fold service into their education through service-learning. Explains one student, "MSU is known for its service-learning program. We are very visible in the surrounding communities in many ways. We are involved in local hospitals, schools, and social work centers."

Connecting Service with the Classroom

MSU administrators report that the school "provides both curricular and co-curricular opportunities for students to become involved in service-learning and community and civic engagement. MSU begins offering academic service-learning and civic-engagement opportunities for first-year students through its first-year literature and composition course (Writing, Rhetoric, and American Cultures 135: Public Life in America), through the Service-Learning Writing Project, and through various required Integrative Studies in Social Science courses. [The school] continues to provide academic options throughout the undergraduate experience, both in Integrative Studies and through courses offered in a wide-range of academic majors." Overall, "approximately 120 to 130 courses are offered annually, taught by 90 to 100 faculty members. Departments offering service-learning courses include American Studies, Business/Accounting, Communications, Education, Engineering, English, Fine Arts, Foreign Language, Interdisciplinary courses, Music, Nursing, Philosophy, Physical Education, Psychology, Parks and Recreation/Tourism, Social Work, Urban Studies, and Women's Studies."

Students report that community service "takes place everywhere. For spring break, it took place in Mexico, Puerto Rico, and a few different states. During the year, it takes place in the hospitals, in the surrounding schools, in the community, and on campus."

More of MSU's outstanding civic engagement programs include MSU's Alternative Spring Break, "a week-long, immersive-living and working experience in which students perform service as requested by host agencies and organizations, while exploring the culture and history of the area where they are assisting. Seventeen trips, comprised of 300+ participants, were conducted during March 2004 in locations as far south as Mexico and Puerto Rico, as far north as Quebec, as far east as Massachusetts, and as far west as San Francisco. MSU ASB exemplifies student civic engagement, as the trips are student-planned and led, with CSLCE and faculty-staff support." YouVote is a program "designed to help inform the students of Michigan State University of the voting process in Michigan, and to provide appropriate, nonpartisan information leading to informed voting choices. The Center for Service Learning and Civic Engagement is a strong partner in YouVote, supporting both academic service learning and co-curricular student engagement related to this initiative." The Young Spartan Program is "a community partnership promoting academic achievement and career awareness through hands-on learning experiences between adults and elementary school children. Each semester between 275 and 325 MSU undergraduate students participate in service-learning placements in the nine partner schools. Additionally, nine students serve as in-school coordinators to ensure the integrity of the service placements within each building."

Impact on Community and Students

MSU has forged approximately 325 partnerships with local organizations in the fields of education, health, business, arts, communication, medicine, nutrition, human services, and government. One of the biggest involves the Ingham Regional Medical Center and Sparrow Health System, where "each semester, between 300 and 350 students participate on 30 different units such as the emergency department, radiology, oncology, pediatrics, and surgery/recovery." Students appreciate these opportunities, explaining that they "promote a well-rounded education. An education is much more than studying and writing papers. People must have real-world experience and must understand how many different lives people lead." Points out one student, "At worst, you are involved in a program that helps people and would look good on a resume. At best, you and the people you are helping are learning from each other, you feel better about yourself while helping others, and of course, it looks good on a resume."

Student Financial Support for Service

Michigan State University grants "a variety of scholarships to incoming students in which volunteer service is taken into consideration when making the selections." For example, the school notes that "the College of Human Medicine offers two scholarships annually for leadership in service performed during [one's] undergraduate career." Community-service jobs are among the many work-study opportunities available to students who qualify for the federally funded work-study program.

SELECTIVITY

# of applicants	21,834
% of applicants accepted	79
% of acceptees attending	44

FRESHMAN PROFILE

Range SAT Verbal	490-620
Range SAT Math	515-650
Range ACT Composite	22-27
Minimum Paper TOEFL	550
Minimum Computer TOEFL	213
Average HS GPA	3.55
% graduated top 10% of class	24
% graduated top 25% of class	61
% graduated top 50% of class	93

DEADLINES

Regular admission	
Regular notification by	9/1
Nonfall registration?	yes

FINANCIAL FACTS

Annual in-state tuition	$6,893
Annual out-of-state tuition	$17,640
Room and board	$5,458
Books and supplies	$826
Required fees	$812
% frosh rec. need-based scholarship or grant aid	25
% UG rec. need-based scholarship or grant aid	28
% frosh rec. need-based self-help aid	35
% UG rec. need-based self-help aid	35
% frosh rec. any financial aid	41
% UG rec. any financial aid	40

MIDDLEBURY COLLEGE

The Emma Willard House, Middlebury, VT 05753-6002

Admissions: 802-443-3000 • **Fax:** 802-443-2056 • **Financial Aid:** 802-443-5158

E-mail: ADMISSIONS@MIDDLEBURY.EDU • **Website:** WWW.MIDDLEBURY.EDU

CAMPUS LIFE
Type of school	private
Environment	rural

STUDENTS
Total undergrad enrollment	2,357
% male/female	48/52
% from out of state	93
% live on campus	97
% African American	3
% Asian	7
% Caucasian	70
% Hispanic	5
% international	8
# of countries represented	71

ACADEMICS
Calendar	quarter
Student/faculty ratio	10:1
% profs teaching UG courses	100
% classes taught by TAs	0

MOST POPULAR MAJORS
economics
English language and literature
psychology

Getting Involved

Service and community involvement at Middlebury College often originate at the offices of the Middlebury College Alliance for Civic Engagement, a "three-tier program that reports to the Vice President for Academic Administration/Dean of the Faculty, addressing not only community service but also service-learning and civic engagement." The busy folks at the Alliance handle a laundry list of chores that include running voter-registration drives, coordinating service-related seminars and trainings, organizing alternative-break projects for students, fundraising for local and national charities, promoting service learning, and much, much more. Students appreciate that "the Alliance for Civic Engagement office is located right in the Student Center, along with the Student Employment office," making it easy for undergraduates to combine service with work.

Chellis House, home to Middlebury's Women's and Gender Studies program, also contributes to civic engagement at the school by organizing lectures, films, and concerts, organizing educational events and demonstrations, and holding an annual "Feminist of the Year" award. Middlebury's Chaplains' Office runs numerous service and community-education events. The school's 130+ student organizations often coordinate their service efforts through the Center for Campus Activities and Leadership, which also provides the organizations with valuable advising, resources, and leadership training.

Some students are introduced to service at Middlebury through the Project for Integrated Expression: Exploring Collaboration and Community, a one-week pre-orientation program conducted in late August. The event "brings a small group together with faculty, staff, and student mentors to discuss what makes an effective community, and how each participant can have a lasting and powerful effect on Middlebury while reaping every possible benefit from the college experience." Students report that "Middlebury also stresses community service from the get-go of enrollment by offering pre-orientation community service trips that not only help orient students to Vermont life, but also introduce them to the wide array of service opportunities available at such a small, intimate college."

Campus Culture of Engagement

The Middlebury community "prides itself on giving back to the local community and reaching beyond the borders of Vermont." Students tell us that "there is a focus on the environment at Middlebury. Also, students do a lot to combat the rural poverty in the area and the low expectations for education. There is a large mentoring network that stretches for about 40 miles in every direction, encompassing schools all over Vermont and in upstate New York." Student organizations carry much of the burden: "Each organization has its own specialty and network of contacts which range from local schools, churches, and community care centers," say undergrads.

Politically, Middlebury leans well to the left. Writes one undergrad, "You often only get one side of the argument here. As most colleges go, this one is very liberal." The school's remote rural location means that "it is sometimes easy to forget the wide, messed-up world out there. For one who has a very high political or activist consciousness, there are times when the lack of political activity on campus is very frustrating."

Connecting Service with the Classroom

While Middlebury's earliest recorded service-learning course dates back to 1988 (in environmental studies), 2000 marked the creation of an office providing support for service-learning. At the time, "there were just a handful of faculty members who expressed interest in experimenting with this pedagogy," but today "that number has grown to about 35 or 40 faculty members, each typically teaching one or two service-learning courses." As a result, "it is estimated that about 350 to 400 students usually enroll in service-learning courses in an academic year. In the 2003 senior exit survey, 20 percent of the graduating seniors indicated that they had taken a service-learning course during their tenure at Middlebury." The school adds that "students can also pursue independent projects through endowed service-learning grants."

Service learning is available across the curriculum at Middlebury. Explains one undergrad, "For in-class service learning projects, we work with leaders of local organizations. We decide with them what the goals of our project will be: Each project is different and is tailored to be as helpful as possible to the community partner."

Middlebury is currently in the process of developing a Poverty Studies minor, which will include "an introductory course, several electives, a summer internship component, and a senior capstone course. Service-learning will be an important part of the pedagogy of the program. Given our institutional value for an international perspective, the focus of this program will make local, national, and international connections."

Impact on Community and Students

Middlebury partners regularly with 55 local organizations, as well as with numerous state and national government organizations and internationally based institutions. Partners include environmental and policy NGOs, social-service agencies, public-health institutions, and local schools.

The school's impact on its surrounding area can be seen in The Addison County Community Mapping Pilot Project. The project, "a partnership between Champlain Valley Head Start, Addison County United Way, and the Middlebury College Alliance for Civic Engagement," aims "to explore 'burning questions' identified by [Middlebury's] community partners about human and social services in our county. The needs relate to issues of poverty in our county and respond to the need for community mapping of both demographic and service-orientated information." The project takes advantage of the college's Geographical Information Systems (GIS) capabilities to "put a spatial face" on the results of the study.

Student Financial Support for Service

Middlebury does not offer any scholarships earmarked for service. It does, however, reward service through various employment opportunities; as the school explains, "Our off-campus federal work-study program has in the past few years comprised 16 percent to 19 percent of our total federal work-study program." In addition, there are "paid service-learning grants from our Academic Outreach Endowment," "paid internship opportunities coordinated by our Career Services Office," and opportunities through the Vermont Campus Compact part-time AmeriCorps Education Award Only program.

SELECTIVITY

# of applicants	5,122
% of applicants accepted	26
% of acceptees attending	44
# accepting a place on wait list	1,266
% admitted from wait list	6

FRESHMAN PROFILE

Range SAT Verbal	690-750
Range SAT Math	690-750
Range ACT Composite	28-32
% graduated top 10% of class	77
% graduated top 25% of class	96
% graduated top 50% of class	99

DEADLINES

Regular admission	1/1
Regular notification by	4/1
Nonfall registration?	yes

FINANCIAL FACTS

Books and supplies	$750
% frosh rec. need-based scholarship or grant aid	37
% UG rec. need-based scholarship or grant aid	42
% frosh rec. need-based self-help aid	37
% UG rec. need-based self-help aid	42

NORTH CAROLINA STATE UNIVERSITY

PO Box 7103, Raleigh, NC 27695

Admissions: 919-515-2434 • **Fax:** 919-515-5039 • **Financial Aid:** 919-515-2421

E-mail: UNDERGRAD_ADMISSIONS@NCSU.EDU • **Website:** WWW.NCSU.EDU

CAMPUS LIFE

Type of school	public
Environment	village

STUDENTS

Total undergrad enrollment	20,302
% male/female	58/42
% from out of state	7
% from public high school	90
% live on campus	33
% African American	10
% Asian	5
% Caucasian	81
% Hispanic	2
% Native American	1
% international	1
# of countries represented	103

ACADEMICS

Calendar	4-1-4
Student/faculty ratio	15:1
% profs teaching UG courses	100
% classes taught by TAs	6
Most common lab size	10-19
Most common reg class size	10-19

MOST POPULAR MAJORS

business administration/management
computer engineering
electrical, electronics and communications engineering

Getting Involved

As "the state's only research-extensive university in the land-grant tradition," North Carolina State University bears "a unique mission to serve the citizens of North Carolina through technical assistance, professional development, lifelong education, technology transfer, and other means of applying knowledge to 'real-world' issues and problems." To pursue this mission, the university created the Office of Extension and Engagement in 2001, charging it to develop "stronger integration of the academic and engagement missions of the university." One of the innovative ways this is done is by encouraging students and faculty to engage with the community through curriculum-based service-learning and other civic-engagement opportunities.

NC State is also home to a broad range of student-run organizations, many of which are grounded in service. The Center for Student Leadership, Ethics, & Public Service sponsors many of the service groups and service-related events on campus, including Alternative Breaks Trips, the Campus Pals (Big Brother/Big Sister Mentoring Program, and the Martin Luther King, Jr. Service Challenge. Other campus organizations include Greek houses, Amnesty International, Circle K, Engineers Without Borders, and Habitat for Humanity.

In addition, NC State hosts the newly-created Institute for Nonprofits, an innovative program housed in the College of Humanities and Social Sciences, which is "working to create additional opportunities for students to connect their interests in community issues with their academic pursuits." The institute is developing a new interdisciplinary minor in nonprofit studies designed to prepare the state's next generation of nonprofit leaders, both professional and volunteer. The school envisions the minor as "a unique opportunity for students to build competencies that will prepare them to successfully address challenges that face nonprofit leaders; it offers a specialized curriculum with developmentally sequenced, service-learning experiences that will expose students to a wide range of community-based nonprofits."

Campus Culture of Engagement

With approximately 30,000 students, NC State is "a large campus where there are a lot of interests; thus a lot of different groups in the community benefit from service performed by students." And because the school is broken into smaller divisions, "NC State combines a small-school feel within a larger university and a large city, so the campus offers opportunities to get involved on many levels, from small to big, local to national." Eclectic tastes are served by the fact that "the campus is diverse (probably the most diverse in all of NC), so there are plenty of ways to get involved and plenty of people to encourage you to do so."

Students report that the most prevalent service activities are found in "Greek life (social and non-social) fundraisers, volunteer work at schools, rest homes, food banks, and soup kitchens." They also note that "all the elite organizations such as the Honors Program, Scholars' Program, Park Scholars, and Caldwell Fellows very strongly encourage service." The chief obstacle to service at NC State? "Definitely transportation. It is hard to do some things if you don't have a car."

Connecting Service with the Classroom

NC State's Service-Learning Program was established in 1999. "The program has grown to support over 25 service-learning-enhanced courses," the school writes. Students should be aware that there are no spectators in this program: Students are asked from the beginning to play leadership roles after gaining experience with service-learning, acting as reflection leaders and community liaisons, for example. Administrators add that "the Program has supported courses especially designed for first-year students, upperclass capstone courses, and graduate-level courses; the service-learning components of these courses range from single-day service and reflection to semester-long, high-responsibility-level projects accompanied by multiple intensive-reflection mechanisms." Approximately 250 undergrads took service-learning courses in the 2002-2003 school year; that number increased to an estimated 350 in 2003-2004. In addition, "through the Alternative Spring Break program, CSLEPS supported approximately 70 students in co-curricular service-learning this year, and the range of academically-grounded civic-engagement opportunities for students is expanding."

Impact on Community and Students

NC State reaches out to the community through a number of annual events, such as ReCreate State ("a landscaping project run by the students"), Service Raleigh ("one of the largest events in the state run by students"), and the Martin Luther King, Jr. Service Activity, "which annually helps students to learn to be better service leaders and includes service opportunities."

Ongoing service includes Cooperative Extension projects "in every one of North Carolina's 100 counties plus the Cherokee Indian Reservation, reaching more than one million citizens annually." Writes the school, "traditionally, the College of Agriculture and Life Sciences has been at the heart of the University's extension mission, but in recent decades, other Colleges have developed strong extension and engagement initiatives." This expansion has meant that today NC State "collaborates with literally hundreds of partners to apply student and faculty expertise and cutting-edge research to such issues as technological innovation, economic development, K–12 education, environmental protection, sustainable communities, leadership development, and a variety of contemporary policy issues."

Typical of the school's community partnerships is the Service-Learning Computer Literacy Project, through which students "work with local assisted-living facilities to support computer access and literacy among the residents." Undergrads "solicit equipment donations, install it in convenient locations at the facilities, work with the facilities' staff on related funding issues, and teach the residents to use e-mail, access the Internet, and use various software packages for games and crafts."

Student Financial Support for Service

The Director of Financial Aid at NC State reports that the school offers no need-based scholarships related to community/public service. "It does, though, have two merit-based scholarship programs that strongly encourage or require service," the school adds. One is the Park Scholarships Program, which "awards a four-year scholarship covering tuition and fees, room, board, and academic expenses as well academic-enrichment activities such as retreats, seminars, and field trips." Park Scholars are selected as high-school seniors according to four criteria: "scholarship, leadership, service, and character,"and all scholars volunteer every semester. The other is the Caldwell Fellows Program, which "identifies highly motivated NC State students who have the ability and commitment necessary for lifelong learning, personal growth, stewardship, and servant leadership and provides them with a scholarship plus enrichment stipends and [an] experiential-learning community."

SELECTIVITY

# of applicants	13,947
% of applicants accepted	59
% of acceptees attending	47
# accepting a place on wait list	500
% admitted from wait list	20

FRESHMAN PROFILE

Range SAT Verbal	530-630
Range SAT Math	570-660
Range ACT Composite	22-27
Minimum Paper TOEFL	550
Minimum Computer TOEFL	213
Average HS GPA	3.09
% graduated top 10% of class	43
% graduated top 25% of class	83
% graduated top 50% of class	98

DEADLINES

Regular admission	2/1
Regular notification by	rolling
Nonfall registration?	yes

FINANCIAL FACTS

Annual in-state tuition	$3,505
Annual out-of-state tuition	$15,403
Room and board	$6,851
Books and supplies	$800
Required fees	$1,162
% frosh rec. need-based scholarship or grant aid	41
% UG rec. need-based scholarship or grant aid	38
% frosh rec. need-based self-help aid	33
% UG rec. need-based self-help aid	32
% frosh rec. any financial aid	67
% UG rec. any financial aid	53

NORTHWESTERN UNIVERSITY

PO Box 3060, 1801 Hinman Avenue, Evanston, IL 60204-3060

Admissions: 847-491-7271 • **Financial Aid:** 847-491-7400

E-mail: UG-ADMISSION@NORTHWESTERN.EDU • **Website:** WWW.NORTHWESTERN.EDU

CAMPUS LIFE

Type of school	private
Environment	village

STUDENTS

Total undergrad enrollment	7,988
% male/female	47/53
% from out of state	75
% from public high school	73
% live on campus	65
% African American	5
% Asian	17
% Caucasian	60
% Hispanic	5
% international	5
# of countries represented	51

ACADEMICS

Calendar	quarter
Student/faculty ratio	8:1
% profs teaching UG courses	100
% classes taught by TAs	2
Most common lab size	10-19
Most common reg class size	20-29

MOST POPULAR MAJORS

economics
engineering
journalism

Getting Involved

Northwestern undergrads tell us that "everywhere you turn, students are helping one another and the community." Community and civic action at Northwestern is coordinated through the Office of Student Community Service, which "advises eighteen student-[s1]service and philanthropy organizations; hosts a volunteer-opportunities search engine; sends out a monthly electronic mailing list with volunteer opportunities, conferences, internships, fellowships, and job opportunities; and organizes campus-wide events including two service days, a holiday gift drive, and National Volunteer Week recognition." The school is also home to "approximately 25 to 30 student groups" that "actively promote civic engagement, including the student government (ASG), service organizations, cultural organizations, and religious organizations. Residence Halls and Residential Colleges, Fraternities and Sororities also promote civic engagement as a means toward internal community-building."

Campus Culture of Engagement

Northwestern is the kind of place where "some of the service groups are among the most well-known organizations on campus: Dance Marathon, Suitcase Party, Special Olympics, and Alternative Student Breaks[s2]." Writes one senior, "This is a place I am proud to have called home for four years. Students are constantly helping one another find ways to learn and volunteer, and our administration is constantly helping us in this path." Political activity has heated up here recently; according to another senior, "Over my past four years here, I have been really impressed with the growing activism on campus. Service was always huge, but activism was very minimal; however, this had been changing."

Students single out the School of Education and Social Policy, which is "is filled with folks who want to make a difference and whose socio-political groups also host a number of panels, debates, and workshops to better inform the student population," and the Northwestern Community Development Corps (NCDC), "a large and active student group that had over 150 consistent volunteers this past year logging over 2,000 volunteer hours over the first two quarters," as two of the most important players in campus service. Undergrads here appreciate that "Chicago offers an incredible array of opportunities, facilitated by remarkable faculty and other students at Northwestern."

Connecting Service with the Classroom

You can get recognized for civic engagement at Northwestern with an academic program: They offer a Service-Learning Certificate Program that aims to "prepare students for a life of civic engagement and to build the academic skills to make a real contribution to the American community." This five-quarter program is flexible and unique, "completed over two years, [it] is designed for undergraduate students preferably in their freshman or sophomore years. [It] requires students to complete five credits of coursework starting with Introduction to Community Development, two additional elective courses and finishing with two quarters of work on the student's Capstone Project. Students perform 100 hours of community service over the five quarters and meet bi-weekly in facilitated reflection seminars." The program includes a Capstone Project that is "done in collaboration with a community organization with the purpose of making a concrete contribution to that organization's mission." The school reports that "past projects have taken the form of research papers, policy proposals, ethnographic studies, and program development."

Unique service opportunities at Northwestern, for-credit and otherwise, include the Undergraduate Leadership Program, "an interschool certificate program open to all Northwestern undergraduates. The program helps students understand the nature of leadership and prepares them to become leaders on campus, in the community, and in their professions." The Freshman Urban Program (FUP) is "a pre-orientation program built on the principles of Asset Based Community Development. Led by three student co-chairs and seventeen student counselors, 68 first-year students spend the week before orientation living in a hostel in downtown Chicago. The students learn about different social issues in various neighborhoods of Chicago and Evanston, complete service projects with different agencies in the various neighborhoods, and learn how they can affect change." The Alternative Student Breaks (ASB) program, a "completely student-run" endeavor, "sends over 250 students out to different places nationally and internationally each year. ASB coordinates a fall trip before school starts, seven to ten winter-break trips, and seventeen spring break trips, as well as spring and fall 'Community Connections Days,' where ASB students reconnect with the local community by participating in service projects that use the knowledge and skills they gained on their ASB trips. "The Freshman Emerging Leaders Program (FELP) offers freshmen a six-week course on developing leadership skills and introduces students to the Social Change Model of leadership, helping students find ways to lead ethically."

Impact on Community and Students

Civic engagement keeps Northwestern-an expensive, elite school-in close touch with quotidian communities in neighboring Evanston and Chicago. Among the school's many community partnerships are:

- The Freshman Urban Program, a pre-orientation program that introduces 68 incoming first-year students to the social issues in Chicago using the principles of Asset Based Community Development. Students learn to see the assets in the community and how they can affect change.

- The Northwestern Community Development Corps (NCDC), a "student organization that partners with over 20 sites in Chicago and Evanston, providing regular volunteers to the organizations each week. The organizations are diverse, covering many different social issues and working with many different populations. One of the best partnerships NCDC has is with Chicago and Evanston schools for Project Pumpkin, a one-day service event that provides children with a safe place to trick-or-treat," by bringing over 700 children from neighboring communities to campus for Halloween-themed games, celebrations, and candy.

Student Financial Support for Service

Northwestern informs us that the school "only gives out need-based financial aid. No scholarships are available for community/public service. However, students occasionally apply for and receive research grants to pursue projects within the community." Students eligible for work-study may request an off-campus service-related job with such organizations as America Reads, Friends of Battered Women and Their Children, McGaw YMCA, and Legal Assistance Foundation of Metropolitan Chicago. On campus, work-study students can also find positions in the Office of Student Community Service.

SELECTIVITY

# of applicants	14,137
% of applicants accepted	33
% of acceptees attending	41
# accepting a place on wait list	776
% admitted from wait list	13

FRESHMAN PROFILE

Range SAT Verbal	650-730
Range SAT Math	660-750
Range ACT Composite	29-33
Minimum Paper TOEFL	600
Minimum Computer TOEFL	250
% graduated top 10% of class	83
% graduated top 25% of class	97
% graduated top 50% of class	99

DEADLINES

Regular admission	1/1
Regular notification by	4/15
Nonfall registration?	yes

FINANCIAL FACTS

Annual tuition	$29,940
Room and board	$9,393
Books and supplies	$1,353
Required fees	$145
% frosh rec. need-based scholarship or grant aid	42
% UG rec. need-based scholarship or grant aid	41
% frosh rec. need-based self-help aid	43
% UG rec. need-based self-help aid	41
% frosh rec. any financial aid	60
% UG rec. any financial aid	60

OBERLIN COLLEGE

101 NORTH PROFESSOR STREET, OBERLIN COLLEGE, OBERLIN, OH 44074
ADMISSIONS: 440-775-8411 • FAX: 440-775-6905 • FINANCIAL AID: 440-775-8142
E-MAIL: COLLEGE.ADMISSIONS@OBERLIN.EDU • WEBSITE: WWW.OBERLIN.EDU

CAMPUS LIFE

Type of school	private
Environment	rural

STUDENTS

Total undergrad enrollment	2,807
% male/female	45/55
% from out of state	90
% from public high school	66
% live on campus	73
% African American	6
% Asian	8
% Caucasian	74
% Hispanic	5
% Native American	1
% international	6

ACADEMICS

Calendar	semester
Student/faculty ratio	12:1
% profs teaching UG courses	100
% classes taught by TAs	0

MOST POPULAR MAJORS

biology/biological sciences
English language and literature
history

Getting Involved

Oberlin proudly reports that "students who come to Oberlin find a variety of opportunities for civic engagement. The most obvious campus-community collaborations occur through the programs and activities of the Center for Service and Learning (CSL)," which "has created a student-run clearinghouse to link the campus, the City of Oberlin, and the broader region. Called the Community Service Resource Center (CSRC), it offers students and student organizations easy access to centralized information about local resources and available volunteer service opportunities."

The school also notes that "several academic departments and programs host occasional and on-going civic engagement efforts. Currently, the most active departments are Politics, History, Religion, African American Studies, and the Division of Music Education in the Conservatory of Music. Active interdisciplinary programs include Comparative American Studies, Environmental Studies, and Gender and Women's Studies. In addition, several campus offices promote civic engagement through internships, advocacy, and programs."

The school also is home to "a variety of student groups [that] directly sponsor and promote civic engagement, either through co-curricular programs or through Oberlin's Experimental College (ExCo), where students can teach courses on a variety of topics. Popular ExCo courses with service components that work with children include Oberlin Mentors, Students for Students, The Youth Energy Project (YEP), and Bikes and Kids. Additional ExCo courses that link activism with education include Grassroots Organizing, which does campaign work with the Ohio Public Interest Research Group (OPIRG), HIV Educators, Issues in Women's Health, Low Income Housing and Social Justice, and ESL Tutoring. Oberlin has more than 100 different student organizations, many of which are involved with the local community through service and other projects."

Campus Culture of Engagement

Oberlin undergrads, by their own account, are "very dedicated activists." Many choose Oberlin for its reputation; as one explained, "Oberlin is a fabulous institution because it is committed to civic engagement and has a long history of being an activist school. If one is interested in learning in a classic liberal-arts environment while also being involved in community betterment, Oberlin is a perfect choice." Adds one student, "I couldn't imagine a better place than Oberlin. When I looked at schools, this was the only one that actually recruited me because I performed community service in high school. I couldn't imagine a better place for finding a purpose for one's education."

Politically, Oberlin has an active student body with an overwhelmingly leftward orientation. One undergrad notes, "Oberlin students are not inclined to let an issue slip by quietly. Campus controversies are often discussed in the school newspapers, at forums that are run by student organizations, and students often hold information sessions to educate other students about relevant issues." Protests, sit-down strikes, and building occupations are not unheard of either. Recent controversies have focused on divestment of stock in companies that do business with Israel, student access to the school's operating budget, and gender-neutral campus housing.

Connecting Service with the Classroom

Oberlin "provides extensive opportunities for integrating classroom learning with service to the community." It provides these opportunities with an eye on understanding and addressing the root causes of problems-not simply serving the needy: "For example, organizing a grassroots anti-gun campaign, preparing a report on predatory lending, or providing educational assistance to children who read below grade level teaches lessons that can be brought into the classroom to be discussed alongside theoretical texts. Conversely, students apply classroom theories in the real world. Environmental studies students work with local teachers to implement educational programs centered on the local watershed; Geology students conduct mapping and geographic analysis with staff at the nearby Old Woman Creek National Estuarine Research Reserve and State Nature Preserve; politics students undertake community-based research for several northeastern Ohio policy organizations."

Between 2000 and 2003, Oberlin faculty taught "20 to 22 courses incorporating academically based community service or community-based research annually, with 25 offerings in 2003-2004 and 26 scheduled for 2004-2005."

Impact on Community and Students

Oberlin works with "over 200 nonprofit and community organizations in Northeast Ohio and beyond" to provide a wide range of services touching on "art, disability, racial diversity, ecological issues, grassroots organizing, public health, hunger and homelessness, senior citizens, women and gender, youth, and education."

Among the most exciting school-community partnerships are the Oberlin Design Initiative (ODI) and the Deaf and Deaf-Blind Committee on Human Rights (DDBCHR), both founded by Oberlin graduates. The school explains, "ODI began as a group of three Oberlin College students with an interest in planning ecologically and community-oriented housing. After graduating, they founded the nonprofit Oberlin Design Initiative with the primary goal of connecting local needs and issues with the energy and expertise of Oberlin College students. Through outreach and networking, they are creating projects with residents and students related to three main tenets: economic revitalization, social justice, and environmental stewardship. DDBCHR is unique in that it is one of the few groups in the nation run by deaf individuals for the deaf. Much of its work is done by volunteers, and Oberlin students are integral to its success."

Student Financial Support for Service

"Scholarship support specifically linked to community service is available through the Bonner Scholars Program," Oberlin writes, reporting that "15 first-year students are admitted to the program each year, through which students complete an average of ten hours of community service per week, for a total of 300 hours over the course of the academic year. Scholars are also expected to complete 280 hours of service each summer for two summers. Program benefits include a school year stipend of $2,100, summer support of up to $2,500 each summer, and a loan reduction check of up to $1,600 after graduation." The school also points out that "the CSL and the Office of Financial Aid collaborate to offer students the Community Service Work-Study Program. Students eligible for federal work-study awards can earn the awards by serving as an America Reads or America Counts tutor, or at one of over sixteen different off-campus community partner sites."

SELECTIVITY

# of applicants	4,824
% of applicants accepted	48
% of acceptees attending	32
# accepting a place on wait list	791
% admitted from wait list	8

FRESHMAN PROFILE

Range SAT Verbal	634-730
Range SAT Math	610-710
Range ACT Composite	26-31
Minimum Paper TOEFL	600
Minimum Computer TOEFL	200
Average HS GPA	3.55
% graduated top 10% of class	67
% graduated top 25% of class	85
% graduated top 50% of class	96

DEADLINES

Regular admission	1/15
Regular notification by	4/1
Nonfall registration?	no

FINANCIAL FACTS

Annual tuition	$30,925
Room and board	$7,643
Books and supplies	$734
Required fees	$188
% frosh rec. need-based scholarship or grant aid	54
% UG rec. need-based scholarship or grant aid	54
% frosh rec. need-based self-help aid	56
% UG rec. need-based self-help aid	55
% frosh rec. any financial aid	61
% UG rec. any financial aid	60

PITZER COLLEGE

1050 NORTH MILLS AVENUE, CLAREMONT, CA 91711-6101
ADMISSIONS: 909-621-8129 • **FAX:** 909-621-8770 • **FINANCIAL AID:** 909-621-8208
E-MAIL: ADMISSION@PITZER.EDU • **WEBSITE:** WWW.PITZER.EDU

CAMPUS LIFE
Type of school	private
Environment	village

STUDENTS
Total undergrad enrollment	942
% male/female	40/60
% from out of state	49
% live on campus	71
% African American	5
% Asian	10
% Caucasian	45
% Hispanic	13
% Native American	1
% international	3
# of countries represented	9

ACADEMICS
Calendar	semester
Student/faculty ratio	12:1
% profs teaching UG courses	100
% classes taught by TAs	0
Most common lab size	<10
Most common reg class size	10-19

MOST POPULAR MAJORS
fine arts and art studies
psychology
sociology

Getting Involved

Pitzer's large service and activist communities receive ample support from the school's Center for California Cultural and Social Issues (CCCSI), "an institutional structure that oversees issues of social responsibility." Currently, CCCSI's partnerships within the community "focus on themes of immigration, juvenile justice, homelessness, and health education for youth." The center utilizes a unique "'core' community partner model in which the school makes a minimum commitment of four years to an organization" and "works towards meeting collaboratively set goals with that organization. Due to its capacity-building nature, the core partner model invigorates the development of projects that grow from field-based courses into meaningful community partnership." All students here, regardless of their level of commitment to service, receive some exposure to community and social issues through a freshman seminar series "whose theme is social justice" and a curricular requirement in social responsibility (which typically entails experiential learning through community service).

Students report that it's easy to stay up-to-date on service activities. Writes one, "They are advertised nearly everywhere a student looks. E-mails, flyers, posters, announcements from teachers, incorporation into classes, clubs. With such a small, intimate campus, one would have to live in a cave not to find out."

Campus Culture of Engagement

For most undergrads at Pitzer, "a place for people who see injustices and want to take proactive steps to changing things," service and activism are high on their priority lists. As one student put it, "Even if you don't normally do much community service, you will come here and find a group of people that you truly connect with on a personal level and want to further serve, guaranteed." Observes another, "Students show genuine interest in participation, as well as commitment to particular activity."

Indeed, Pitzer is widely regarded as a leader in the area. As one student reports, "Pitzer is part of a ten-college collaborative called Project Pericles, and these ten colleges are supposed to be the best socially responsible in the country. Last May, I went to the first meeting of all ten schools as one of the student representatives, and Pitzer was by far the most socially responsible school there. The programs we have already established were years and years ahead of any of the other schools. It was quite obvious that we were there to help other schools develop their own programs."

Connecting Service with the Classroom

"Social responsibility is one of the four educational objectives of Pitzer College," and accordingly the school incorporates service into much of its curriculum. "Approximately one-half of our faculty engages in service-learning courses," the school tells us. "Most students will have service-learning classes at some point in their Pitzer career." Explains one undergrad, "service-learning takes place in the classroom and the communities. It takes the theory and tests it in the community. If you're learning in class about the effects of homelessness on a child's psychological development, then you must go work with and become a mentor to homeless children in the community." As this student says, it takes empathy to work "towards the community's goals, not ours."

Unique programs here include Pitzer's Alternative Semester in Ontario: Research, Action, and Cultural Immersion in a Local Setting, which "stresses civic engagement and cultural immersion in a city just ten miles east of Claremont. Students enter into semester-long internships with community-based organizations, engage in mutually beneficial action research projects, attend civic meetings, become involved with host families, and take classes at the Pitzer in Ontario House." And the Claremont International Studies Education Project (CISEP) sends Pitzer undergrads to "visit local schools and give lunch talks highlighting the country in which they studied abroad. This program is unique because it foregrounds a new direction for Pitzer-that of combining study abroad with action at home."

Impact on Community and Students

Pitzer participates in about 15 community partnerships, "one of which is a conglomerate of over 60 local organizations in the City of Ontario." Community partners "largely consist of local schools and community-based organizations. These deal with issues of immigration rights, health education, homelessness, financial literacy, media literacy, prison re-entry programs, juvenile detention, English as a second language education, literacy, tutoring, and more." Specific examples include:

- The Pomona Day Labor Center, which "is a place where workers can gather and act collectively to ensure safe, fair working conditions for its fellow worker members." The program engages in "training college students to teach ESL classes at the Center; developing a healthcare-needs assessment and networking healthcare services for laborers and their families; creating a mural project headed by acclaimed muralist Paul Botello; beginning a community garden project; organizing citizenship drives; negotiating labor disputes with employers; and holding educational workshops regarding workers' rights."

- Camps Afflerbaugh-Paige, "a juvenile court and community school administered through the Los Angeles County Office of Education that serves approximately 220 to 250 incarcerated youth. Since 2001, Pitzer College, CCCSI has collaborated with the Camp to form a structured Prison Literacy program. With the average student reading at the fourth grade level, the focus is on moving youth in the justice system toward literacy and academic achievement."

Observes one student, "At Pitzer, you will actually see hands on what you will study. You will interact with the community as a community member, not as an expert or educated person who's there to fix a problem. At Pitzer, we don't just talk about changing the world. We actually do it."

Student Financial Support for Service

Pitzer tells us that "if funding allows, we offer paid summer internships at local organizations and senior thesis awards for students doing community-based work."

SELECTIVITY

# of applicants	2,425
% of applicants accepted	50
% of acceptees attending	19
# accepting a place on wait list	195

FRESHMAN PROFILE

Range SAT Verbal	570-660
Range SAT Math	570-670
Range ACT Composite	22-28
Minimum Paper TOEFL	587
Minimum Computer TOEFL	240
Average HS GPA	3.58
% graduated top 10% of class	40
% graduated top 25% of class	70
% graduated top 50% of class	94

DEADLINES

Regular admission	1/15
Regular notification by	4/1
Nonfall registration?	no

FINANCIAL FACTS

Annual tuition	$26,640
Room and board	$7,796
Books and supplies	$900
Required fees	$3,154
% frosh rec. need-based scholarship or grant aid	37
% UG rec. need-based scholarship or grant aid	42
% frosh rec. need-based self-help aid	35
% UG rec. need-based self-help aid	41
% frosh rec. any financial aid	37
% UG rec. any financial aid	42

PORTLAND STATE UNIVERSITY

PO Box 751, Portland, OR 97207

Admissions: 503-725-3511 • **Fax:** 503-725-5525 • **Financial Aid:** 503-725-3461

E-mail: ADMISSIONS@PDX.EDU • **Website:** WWW.PDX.EDU

CAMPUS LIFE

Type of school	public
Environment	town

STUDENTS

Total undergrad enrollment	14,791
% male/female	46/54
% from out of state	11
% live on campus	10
% African American	3
% Asian	10
% Caucasian	66
% Hispanic	4
% Native American	1
% international	3

ACADEMICS

Calendar	semester
Student/faculty ratio	14:1
% profs teaching UG courses	87
% classes taught by TAs	4
Most common reg class size	10-19

MOST POPULAR MAJORS

business administration/management
fine/studio arts
psychology

Getting Involved

If you want a campus that makes an institutional commitment to civic engagement, Portland State University is your school. In almost every aspect, PSU puts into practice its motto "Let Knowledge Serve the City."

Portland State's Center for Academic Excellence (CAE), established in 1995 to "support and promote academic excellence in teaching, assessment, and community-university partnerships," is integral to the university's widely embraced mission to "contribute to the Portland metropolitan community." "Portland State University," says CAE, "is one of the very few universities in the country that requires a formal community-engagement course and project for graduation. This is fulfilled by over 200 community-based capstone courses annually, and comprises only a part of the over 400 courses annually that formally bring students and members of the community together." The school reports that "a unique element of CAE is the support it offers to faculty engaged with community-based teaching, research, and scholarship. The Community-University Partnerships program, a formal division of the CAE, is supported by the general budget and recognized as an integral part of the faculty development efforts that enhance teaching, learning, and community engagement at PSU. For potential community partners, CAE provides the entry point of access to PSU faculty. Since CAE's inception, over $1,500,000 in grant dollars have supplemented community-based learning and faculty development initiatives at PSU."

Student-run service organizations make their home at PSUs Student Activities and Leadership Programs (SALP) office. Students seeking service opportunities should check postings at the office and on its website and should also seek out organizations engaged in recruiting around campus. Undergraduates note that most students at PSU are initially involved in service through various curricular requirements (see "Connecting Service with the Classroom" below).

Campus Culture of Engagement

"PSU is a model campus for service and engagement," students agree. Writes one, "Regardless of your academic field or areas of interest, you will find a variety of service activities. Any student who feels that PSU lacks opportunities for civic engagement is simply not putting forth any effort to seek out opportunities." No less an authority on the subject than Harvard public-policy professor Robert Putnam recently visited the campus to "talk about how Portland was an exception to the normal downward trend in civic engagement in the U.S. Portland has a rising trend. Portland State University is a school that is committed to having its students be a part of service-learning and civic engagement."

Politically, PSU is very active. Observes one undergrad: "If you are looking for service-learning in a school loaded with liberal activism, come to PSU." Needless to say, conservatives can get a little lonely at PSU.

Connecting Service with the Classroom

Most students at PSU—over 80 percent, by the school's reckoning—undertake service as part of the school's required general-education (the "University Studies" program) Freshman Inquiry courses. And that's just the start of it; as one student explains, "the school requires Freshman and Sophomore Inquiry classes, which introduce students to various aspects of civic engagement and service-learning within the community. In the junior year, students take a series of classes that explore that area of interest within the community. Seniors engage in a capstone class/project that actively engages the community to promote positive change while providing a real-world environment in which to learn." This capstone requirement is "a six-credit community-based learning course designed to provide students with the opportunity to apply, in a team context, what they have learned in the major and in their other University Studies courses to a real challenge emanating from the metropolitan community. Interdisciplinary teams of students address these real challenges and produce a summation product under the guidance of a PSU faculty member."

All told, "there are over 400 service-learning courses offered at PSU, with over 7,000 students participating annually." These include courses offered within a single department, multi-disciplinary courses, and required general education courses. As if this all weren't enough, PSU "recently developed and approved a Minor in Civic Leadership [that] deepens and further integrates the university's commitment to sustained institutional engagement with the Portland metropolitan community and beyond."

Impact on Community and Students

"PSUs motto is to 'Let Knowledge Serve the City,'" students report, pointing out that "many classes and programs have 'community partners' with which students develop relationships that often continue after the class has ended." These include "several local municipal agencies, nonprofit organizations, local and regional educational institutions, neighborhood associations, neighborhood and nonprofit coalitions, national nonprofit service providers, PSUs community radio station (KPSU), student organizations, and partnerships with local businesses and philanthropists seeking sustainable and socially equitable change." In short, there are very few sectors of the community that PSU does not reach through its many service programs.

In an effort to increase further its commitment to its home city, PSU introduced the Engaged Department Initiative three years ago. Its purpose is to "embrace the development and institutionalizing of service-learning and civic engagement at the department level. The Engaged Department Initiative actively supports 12 academic units for one to three years to participate in an in-depth process designed to encourage collective community-university engagement." Many of these programs involve developing curricula and teaching in underserved area public schools and community centers.

Extracurricular service also has a major impact on the local community. Explains one undergrad, "Student groups on campus also reach out into the community. For example, there is a student group currently called the Portland Turkish and Greek Association that is concerned with the climate of Cyprus; they hold gatherings where individuals from the Portland community come together from those different backgrounds to develop relationships." PSUs nine Greek houses are also deeply involved in community service.

Student Financial Support for Service

In addition to helping federal work-study students work in community service, PSU provides financial support to service-oriented undergrads through its Student Leaders for Service program, through which "students commit to a nine-month term of five to ten hours per week and receive a variety of academic and community-based benefits from their work, including a small stipend." Participants also earn course credit; participation qualifies students to apply for AmeriCorps Education Awards of up to $2,362.

SELECTIVITY

# of applicants	3,344
% of applicants accepted	85
% of acceptees attending	54

FRESHMAN PROFILE

Range SAT Verbal	460-580
Range SAT Math	460-580
Range ACT Composite	18-24
Minimum Paper TOEFL	525
Average HS GPA	3.15

DEADLINES

Regular notification by	rolling
Nonfall registration?	yes

FINANCIAL FACTS

Annual in-state tuition	$3,240
Annual out-of-state tuition	$12,636
Room and board	$8,175
Books and supplies	$1,200
Required fees	$1,038
% frosh rec. need-based scholarship or grant aid	30
% UG rec. need-based scholarship or grant aid	35
% frosh rec. need-based self-help aid	40
% UG rec. need-based self-help aid	45

PRINCETON UNIVERSITY

PO Box 430, ADMISSION OFFICE, PRINCETON, NJ 08544-0430

ADMISSIONS: 609-258-3060 • **FAX:** 609-258-6743 • **FINANCIAL AID:** 609-258-3330

E-MAIL: UAOFFICE@PRINCETON.EDU • **WEBSITE:** WWW.PRINCETON.EDU

CAMPUS LIFE

Type of school	private
Environment	village

STUDENTS

Total undergrad enrollment	4,678
% male/female	53/47
% from out of state	85
% from public high school	55
% live on campus	98
% African American	8
% Asian	13
% Caucasian	63
% Hispanic	7
% Native American	1
% international	8

ACADEMICS

Calendar	semester
Student/faculty ratio	6:1
Most common lab size	10-19
Most common reg class size	10-19

MOST POPULAR MAJORS

English language and literature
history
political science and government

Getting Involved

For many incoming Princeton freshmen each year, service and activism commences before they even attend a class; through orientation's Community Action (CA) program, "40 upper-class students join more than 100 incoming freshmen who live and work in the community during the week before classes start. By living and working in one of eleven community partner sites, they get to know the community and each other, and discuss relevant issues to their community work with each other, the community partners, and Princeton faculty."

CA is sponsored by Princeton's Student Volunteer Council (SVC), a student-led organization that is the busy hub of much student service-related activity. Also available to would-be volunteers are the Pace Center for Community Service, which provides "funding for national and international service and internships (at nonprofits and NGOs), and funding for different student initiatives on campus," and Community House, "a diverse gathering of Princeton students and staff committed to responding to needs identified by the community to enrich, empower, and renew the lives of underserved children and families in the local community."

Campus Culture of Engagement

Princeton students agree that "opportunities for civic engagement, service, and activism at Princeton are so abundant that the most difficult part is choosing what to do." Many add, however, that "while there are many students interested in service and civic engagement, there is not a lot of political activism on campus." They also point out that "the hard part is navigating the university's decentralized structure. It may take more than a little effort to uncover the multitude of opportunities that exist." The good news is that those opportunities include "an entrepreneurial setting that facilitates student-initiated projects."

Students especially appreciate CA (a "very important gateway to engagement" that "introduces them to the community and to service at Princeton, right from the moment they arrive") and the SVC (brags one member, "We have 60 weekly projects, several hundred active volunteers, 70 project coordinators, and a student board and student administrators"). In addition, "Sororities/Eating Clubs/Residential Colleges all do various forms of community service, such as making sandwiches for soup kitchens, fundraisers, and hosting holiday parties for local low-income children." Undergrads note that "promotion of student activist groups is everywhere: e-mails, flyers, events," even "a scrolling marquee in front of the student center."

Connecting Service with the Classroom

The primary engine of service learning at Princeton is the Community-Based Learning Initiative (CBLI), which "links the community to the classroom and forces students to think critically about issues facing America domestically. The 'ivory tower' is bridged to the 'real world' in a setting that fosters the development of the intellectual as well as the civic. CBLI is an amazing program."

The school adds that "Princeton is a research university, and our community-based learning program focuses on community-based research. Faculty members across the disciplines, partnered with leaders of community organizations, develop community-based research projects for their students. Students apply the knowledge and analytic tools gained in the classroom to pressing issues that affect our local communities. Most important, they share their results and conclusions not just with their professors, but also with the organizations that can benefit from their research."

Unique programs include:

- Princeton in Africa, which aims to "create a constituency of young people committed to the emergence of Africa as a full partner in the developed world by offering service fellowships in connection with the humanitarian organizations and other agencies serving the African continent."

- The Princeton Justice Project, through which undergrads "research and address social injustice and inconsistencies in the United States [in order] to effect change by helping to give a voice to underrepresented sectors and raising awareness of unjust practices helping to facilitate disparities between American communities."

- Princeton WaterWatch, which works to "address water quality problems in New Jersey through education and service, [including] clean-ups, stream monitoring, environmental education, and community outreach."

Impact on Community and Students

Princeton justifiably brags that "an estimated 2,500 undergraduates participate each year in dozens of volunteer community service activities assisting thousands of residents in the Trenton/Princeton area. Nearly 1,000 faculty and staff take part in service programs." Most participants would agree with the student who wrote: "I feel that this civic engagement has been my education. It is what made me realize that I cannot just have a job that isolates me from the community. I want to be out there, working on the front lines, making a difference."

Student Financial Support for Service

Princeton writes that it "does not offer scholarships for undergraduates for community/public service. However, the Pace Center funds student organizations' service projects, and alumni organizations such as Project 55 and the Class of 1969 Community Service Fund provide funding for summer or post-graduate internships in service organizations and the nonprofit sector."

SELECTIVITY

# of applicants	13,695
% of applicants accepted	13
% of acceptees attending	68
# accepting a place on wait list	1,045
% admitted from wait list	8

FRESHMAN PROFILE

Range SAT Verbal	680-770
Range SAT Math	690-790
Average HS GPA	3.83
% graduated top 10% of class	94
% graduated top 25% of class	99
% graduated top 50% of class	100

DEADLINES

Regular admission	11/1
Regular notification by	4/4
Nonfall registration?	no

FINANCIAL FACTS

Books and supplies	$990
% frosh rec. need-based scholarship or grant aid	52
% UG rec. need-based scholarship or grant aid	49
% frosh rec. need-based self-help aid	52
% UG rec. need-based self-help aid	49
% frosh rec. any financial aid	52
% UG rec. any financial aid	50

ROCKFORD COLLEGE

OFFICE OF UNDERGRADUATE ADMISSION, 5050 EAST STATE STREET, ROCKFORD, IL 61108-2393

ADMISSIONS: 815-226-4050 • FAX: 815-226-2822 • FINANCIAL AID: 815-394-5289

E-MAIL: ADMISSION@ROCKFORD.EDU • WEBSITE: WWW.ROCKFORD.EDU

CAMPUS LIFE

Type of school	private
Environment	town

STUDENTS

Total undergrad	
enrollment	954
% male/female	37/63
% from out of state	5
% from public high school	87
% live on campus	42
% African American	5
% Asian	1
% Caucasian	57
% Hispanic	3
% international	2

ACADEMICS

Calendar	semester
Student/faculty ratio	10:1
% profs teaching	
UG courses	100
% classes taught by TAs	0
Most common lab size	20-29
Most common	
reg class size	20-29

MOST POPULAR MAJORS

computer and information sciences
education
nursing-registered nurse training
(RN, ASN, BSN, MSN)

Getting Involved

Rockford College wears its commitment to civic engagement like a badge of honor. Rockford proudly proclaims itself the alma mater of Jane Addams, and why shouldn't it? Addams, founder of Chicago's first settlement house, Hull-House and Nobel Peace Prize winner, is a legend of public service, and Rockford has admirably followed her lead in emphasizing the importance of experience-based learning and community involvement. The hub of service activity here is the aptly named Jane Addams Center for Civic Engagement (JACCE), founded in 2002. Its mission is to "integrate a range of institutional efforts: community-based learning (CBL), student voluntarism, campus ministry, a student fellows program, and a variety of college-community partnerships." To increase the breadth of its offerings, the JACCE is opening a field office at the Natural Land Institute, an environmental-advocacy organization.

The Office of Student Activities supports student-run service opportunities. Members of student organizations are required to conduct two community-service projects per semester. One project must be on campus; the other must serve residents of the city of Rockford. The administration reports that "students are going above and beyond their required service projects. Students at Rockford College are civic-minded and willing to go above and beyond for their community."

Student immersion in service starts during orientation. Explains one undergrad, "We have this thing during orientation called the Rockford Plunge. We wake up early in the morning and go out to different places in the community. We do all kinds of things: painting schools, cleaning parks, even cleaning up our own campus." The JACCE keeps students informed of all subsequent service opportunities.

Campus Culture of Engagement

According to faculty, "Rockford isn't just about service. At heart, the college is committed to helping students understand the obligations and responsibilities of citizenship from a practical point of view. Rockford challenges students to 'Think. Act. Give a damn,' an exhortation has raised eyebrows but neatly captures the college's essence."

According to students, Rockford "has only recently stressed service a lot, so it is still progressing. More and more people are starting to get involved. It will take a little time." Most new students are, as one undergrad noted, "carrying on the torch." Writes another student, "One thing that has been very successful on our campus is the alternative spring break trip, working for Habitat for Humanity in Starkville, Mississippi. Each year we have so many students express interest to go on the trip and help build a house that we have to turn away students. Last year we had to get two different building sites."

Connecting Service with the Classroom

Rockford reports that "during the spring 2004 semester, there were 35 courses with a Community Based Learning (CBL) component, with 455 students registered in them." The breakdown: "In the Social-Sciences division, there was one course in Sociology, one course in Business, 12 courses in Education, ten courses in Physical Education, five courses in Nursing, and four courses in Psychology. In the Natural-Science division, there was one course, and in the Arts and Humanities division, two courses."

Examples of service-learning classes include a speech class in which "students worked for the mayor of Rockford as a graffiti-abatement task force. Their first task was to research how other model cities in the United States try to solve their graffiti problems. Using their research material and their class knowledge of how to make informative and persuasive speeches, students presented formal speeches to the mayor and his staff arguing what would be the best graffiti-abatement solutions for our city to implement."

Another example is the Psychological Disorders class in which "students work annually with Shelter Care Ministries, an outreach ministry of Emmanuel Episcopal Church in Rockford" to serve the homeless and mentally ill. While serving, notes the school, "students are learning course concepts in an experiential format which complements classroom reading and discussion." Also, "the class throws an annual Halloween party for the Shelter Care clients, which the director says is a 'highlight in their lives.'"

Students observe that "many classes now require students to do a certain number of civic-engagement/service-learning hours to pass the course. This could include working at a mental-heath center or nursing home or soup kitchen, for example, depending on what the course material is about." For students hoping to experience service-learning abroad, Rockford also offers "several service-learning courses at its partner institution, Regents College in London, and more international sites for service-learning are planned."

Impact on Community and Students

College President Paul Pribbenow, the visionary architect of Rockford's civic innovations, has made impact on the community a commitment: "I'm concerned with how the college acts as a citizen and how it works with others," he says. Rockford maintains "more than 50 active community partnerships that cover a wide spectrum of organizations that support the arts, civic engagement, racial and gender equality, land conservation, literacy and education, as well as organizations that provide social and health services, children's development, and funding for community nonprofit organizations." Community service projects, such as Rockford College Plunge, Service Day, Hunger & Homelessness Awareness Week, and Thanksgiving Dinner at the Metro Christian Center keep Rockford undergrads in constant contact with, and constant service to, the area's neediest residents.

Student Financial Support for Service

The school tells us that "at Rockford College, our merit scholarship program is designed to attract students like Jane Addams—curious, creative, and determined to change the world." The school earmarks two awards, of up to $9,000 per year, for students "who demonstrate community involvement and civic service prior to joining our community." One is the Regent Co-curricular Award; the other is a fellowship in our Jane Addams' Center for Civic Engagement (JACCE). The latter are "highly sought-after positions [that] reward our students for continuing to be involved in community service by reducing housing costs in exchange for work within the JACCE."

SELECTIVITY

# of applicants	654
% of applicants accepted	59
% of acceptees attending	34

FRESHMAN PROFILE

Range SAT Verbal	460-570
Range SAT Math	490-550
Range ACT Composite	18-27
Minimum Paper TOEFL	560
Minimum Computer TOEFL	230
Average HS GPA	3.07
% graduated top 10% of class	18
% graduated top 25% of class	41
% graduated top 50% of class	77

DEADLINES

Nonfall registration?	yes

FINANCIAL FACTS

Annual tuition	$18,320
Room and board	$5,930
Books and supplies	$900
Required fees	$900

ROLLINS COLLEGE

Campus Box 2720, Winter Park, FL 32789-4499

Admissions: 407-646-2161 • **Fax:** 407-646-1502 • **Financial Aid:** 407-646-2395

E-mail: admission@rollins.edu • **Website:** www.rollins.edu

CAMPUS LIFE

Type of school	private
Environment	village

STUDENTS

Total undergrad enrollment	1,759
% male/female	40/60
% from out of state	51
% from public high school	58
% live on campus	66
% African American	5
% Asian	4
% Caucasian	74
% Hispanic	8
% Native American	1
% international	3
# of countries represented	43

ACADEMICS

Calendar	semester
Student/faculty ratio	12:1
% profs teaching UG courses	100
% classes taught by TAs	0
Most common lab size	10-19
Most common reg class size	10-19

MOST POPULAR MAJORS

economics
international business
psychology

Getting Involved

Four years ago, administrators at Rollins College decided to intensify the school's commitment to community service and civic engagement. Accordingly, the school created its Office of Community Engagement, "the one office on campus whose direct mission is to provide programs fostering civic engagement." The school hastens to point out, however, that the office "most certainly isn't the only department on campus that actively supports and initiates community and civic-engagement efforts. In fact, our collaboration with other divisions and departments is what makes Rollins College so unique." To bolster its efforts, for example, the Office of Community Engagement partners with the student-run Offices of Multicultural Affairs and Student Involvement and Leadership "to help bridge that gap that so often exists between Academic and Student Affairs."

Because of the combined efforts of these three offices, "prospective students should know that while they will receive a top-notch education at Rollins that will prepare them to make significant contributions in their field of study/choice of career, they will also receive an education that will prepare them to make significant contributions to their communities at large." Service opportunities, students report, "are everywhere, even during orientation. One of the first activities the freshman class participated in when we arrived on campus was volunteering within our community. The school also sends out e-mails for opportunities and involves service-learning in the classroom."

Campus Culture of Engagement

For many here, "Rollins is very much centered around community service. Every organization is required to do community service on and off campus in order to receive school funding. Many organizations voluntarily go above and beyond the required number of hours and strive to not only achieve hours, but to raise money and support for the community." Students contribute an above-average amount to these endeavors; explains one undergrad, "It seems that the majority of issues on campus are briefly discussed if teachers want to, but we are the ones who do the discussing and forming of groups." They also do a great job of getting the word out. "The only way a person might not be aware of these programs is if he walked around blindfolded all day and never once read his campus e-mail," observes one student.

Connecting Service with the Classroom

Writes the Rollins administration: "In keeping with the mission of the College to 'educate students for responsible citizenship and ethical leadership in local and global communities,' the Office of Community Engagement works closely with faculty, staff, and nonprofit agencies to bring service-learning opportunities into the curriculum." With much success: "since the 2001 fall semester (when the Office of Community Engagement was launched), the office has supported and helped close to 40 faculty integrate service-learning into their courses, and has worked with over 17 different academic departments," according to the school. Among the noteworthy successes has been the communications department's Small Groups and Leadership course; over 200 different service projects have been completed in the past three years. Also worth mentioning: "Spanish and Hispanic Studies are now even considering requiring a service-learning component for all of its majors. Over the past three years, several hundred students (close to 500) have participated in some type of traditional service-learning course."

And that's not all. Service-learning "has also become an important part of students' education outside of the traditional curriculum and classroom setting" at Rollins. The City of Winter Park Community Fellows program, for example, partners students with government and community leaders in the school's hometown to learn more about how to effect change on a local level. There are also "international service-learning courses in the Dominican Republic and Mexico" as well as a Habitat for Humanity course offered during the weeklong January intersession; the course "provides students the opportunity to help in the construction of a new Habitat home, as well as provides classroom time for students to learn about the mission and processes behind the Habitat organization."

Impact on Community and Students

Rollins "has partnered and collaborated with over 30 different community non-profits and organizations" over the past three years. Partners have included "organizations that help serve the needs of children and teens through education, the environment, refugee and immigrant families, and the local Winter Park government." Among the school's proudest accomplishments in this area is its work with Fern Creek Elementary School; involvement has grown from a mentoring program to a multi-faceted tutoring, enrichment, and research endeavor.

Arriving freshmen make their presence felt in the community through the school's Reach Out Day of Service Event, "a new and exciting part of orientation for all first-year students. Rollins now dedicates an entire day during orientation for service and outreach projects in the local community." The mandatory event "received more marks than any other event for the best event at orientation" in 2003, notes the school.

Student Financial Support for Service

Incoming freshmen at Rollins are eligible for Harriet W. Cornell and Peggy and Philip B. Crosby, Jr. Scholarships, which range from $10,000 to $17,000 per year; they are awarded "on the basis of leadership initiative, demonstrated community involvement, and sensitivity to diversity. Both scholarships are renewable annually." The scholarships require participation in the Crosby and Cornell Leadership Scholars Program, which, "in conjunction with LEAD (Leadership Education and Development), provides an exciting opportunity for students to further their academic and co-curricular pursuits. The program provides a unique support network and offers numerous opportunities for leadership and intellectual development, community involvement, and peer mentoring."

SELECTIVITY

# of applicants	2,598
% of applicants accepted	59
% of acceptees attending	31
# accepting a place on wait list	200
% admitted from wait list	15

FRESHMAN PROFILE

Range SAT Verbal	540-640
Range SAT Math	540-640
Minimum Paper TOEFL	550
Minimum Computer TOEFL	213
Average HS GPA	3.40
% graduated top 10% of class	39
% graduated top 25% of class	68
% graduated top 50% of class	91

DEADLINES

Regular admission	2/15
Regular notification by	4/1
Nonfall registration?	yes

FINANCIAL FACTS

Annual tuition	$26,910
Room and board	$8,570
Books and supplies	$550
Required fees	$790
% frosh rec. need-based scholarship or grant aid	40
% UG rec. need-based scholarship or grant aid	40
% frosh rec. need-based self-help aid	38
% UG rec. need-based self-help aid	38

SAINT ANSELM COLLEGE

100 SAINT ANSELM DRIVE, MANCHESTER, NH 03102-1310

ADMISSIONS: 603-641-7500 • **FAX:** 603-641-7550 • **FINANCIAL AID:** 603-641-7110

E-MAIL: ADMISSION@ANSELM.EDU • **WEBSITE:** WWW.ANSELM.EDU

CAMPUS LIFE

Type of school	private
Environment	village

STUDENTS

Total undergrad enrollment	1,960
% male/female	42/58
% from out of state	77
% from public high school	65
% live on campus	86
% African American	1
% Asian	1
% Caucasian	78
% Hispanic	1
% international	1
# of countries represented	15

ACADEMICS

Calendar	semester
Student/faculty ratio	15:1
% profs teaching UG courses	100
% classes taught by TAs	0
Most common lab size	10-19
Most common reg class size	20-29

MOST POPULAR MAJORS

business administration/management
nursing
psychology

Getting Involved

The Meelia Center for Community Service is the nerve center of Saint Anselm's bustling service community. The center, according to the school, "employs nearly 60 student service leaders, who in turn recruit, place, and support over 200 volunteers and 210 service learners each semester who perform weekly service in over 30 community agencies. An additional 350 volunteers serve in occasional one-day service events. Last year, the Meelia Center alone accounted for the coordination of 20,000 service hours by Saint Anselm students."

Not all service activity channels through the Meelia Center, though. The Office of Campus Ministry is also extremely active, running "three programs that provide opportunities for students to perform community service and become student-service leaders." The programs are Spring Break Alternative, which coordinates service projects "from Maine to Honduras" for 150 students; Urban Immersion, which sends groups of eight to ten students to service projects in the city for a weekend; and Road to Hope, a fundraising event in which "30 students raise money for local charities by walking 130 miles from Lewiston, Maine to Saint Anselm College in time for the start of the academic year. The program was initiated by a student and to date has raised more than $25,000 for various charitable organizations along the walking route."

Political junkies will enjoy the New Hampshire Institute of Politics, through which "students have tremendous access to guest speakers, which range from Nobel Peace Prize winners, presidential candidates, noted historians, novelists, renowned documentary filmmakers, pollsters, and the media elite." The institute has become a "must-stop" for presidential candidates, giving undergrads "unmatched opportunities to engage in the presidential primary process."

The school points out that "the extensive use of students as service leaders and the leadership model in which students are trained and supported to manage community partnerships" distinguishes the school's service programs from those of other schools. Another distinctive feature: "All new students are introduced to Saint Anselm's service commitment through the New Student Day of Service. As part of orientation, students are sent in teams of 30 to partnership sites and other community nonprofit agencies. Upperclassmen work throughout the spring and summer to organize the entire event, which involves ten to 15 sites in Greater Manchester."

Campus Culture of Engagement

Students come to Saint Anselm knowing that "part of our school mission is to learn through service. We at Saint Anselm believe that one can obtain knowledge from a book, but the true knowledge comes from both the books and experience. Through our service-learning/civic-engagement program, students learn skills necessary to challenge policy and work for social change." Undergraduates embrace the school's mission. In fact, not only do they serve enthusiastically, but they also spend additional time looking for ways to increase service opportunities. Explains one student, "This year, we initiated the Learning Liberty Program in which students, faculty, staff, [and] members of the monastic community met in study circles to address the issue of how civic engagement is being addressed at Saint Anselm."

Connecting Service with the Classroom

"Service-learning is one of the fastest growing things here," reports one student, adding that "students love the opportunity to not only learn in class but learn in real-life situations." According to the school, "11 academic departments and more than 20 courses at Saint Anselm offer service-learning opportunities. This includes the Social Sciences (Sociology, Psychology, Criminal Justice, and Nursing) and less traditional departments (Physics, Computer Science, Theology, and Humanities). 27 percent of this year's graduating class has had at least one service-learning experience during their four years."

The school is committed to developing its service-learning programs further. Administrators tell us that "for the past three years, Saint Anselm College has hosted a Student Service-Learning Conference where students, faculty, and community partners from around the state present their service-learning experiences. This opportunity to share models and strategies has been well received, especially by colleges looking to improve and develop new connections between service and academics."

Impact on Community and Students

Formal school-community partnerships at Saint Anselm include "one of the state's largest public child-care centers, several public schools, a large county nursing home, a facility for delinquent youth, an agency for homeless teens, and a soup kitchen for youth." The school has been recruiting new partners each year; the latest is the English for New Americans program, "which provides ESL and cultural-adjustment assistance to refugees and immigrants in Manchester. Currently over 150 ESL students from 32 countries are enrolled. Some Saint Anselm students actually teach classes under the supervision of the program director." Additional community partnerships are managed by Campus Ministry.

Saint Anselm has a major presence in local schools through the New Hampshire Alliance for Civic Engagement, founded by the New Hampshire Institute of Politics. This "statewide coalition of K-12 schools, youth-service organizations, colleges, universities, and public- and private-sector partners [works to] enhance civic engagement in New Hampshire by strengthening the knowledge, skills, and behaviors essential for active citizenship."

Student Financial Support for Service

Saint Anselm offers "a number of scholarships that reward good citizenship and public service," including the Trinity High School Scholarship, awarded to a graduate of the Manchester high school based on his/her academic and service records; the O'Farrill Scholarship, earmarked for Hispanic students active in service; and the Holmes Scholarship, "a full-tuition scholarship offered to one or two seniors who demonstrate leadership in public service, assistance to others, and exceptional involvement in College life." Also, "a variety of endowed scholarships offer funding for students who serve as Spring Break Alternative leaders." Finally, the school points out that "most of the student-leadership positions at the Meelia Center are filled by federal work-study students. Their leadership work is their campus job, although what they put into their work and what they gain from it far surpasses traditional work-study employment."

SELECTIVITY

# of applicants	3,214
% of applicants accepted	66
% of acceptees attending	25
# accepting a place on wait list	425
% admitted from wait list	31

FRESHMAN PROFILE

Range SAT Verbal	520-600
Range SAT Math	510-600
Range ACT Composite	22-26
Minimum Paper TOEFL	550
Minimum Computer TOEFL	213
Average HS GPA	3.14
% graduated top 10% of class	18
% graduated top 25% of class	56
% graduated top 50% of class	88

DEADLINES

Nonfall registration?	yes

FINANCIAL FACTS

Annual tuition	$22,700
Room and board	$8,580
Books and supplies	$750
Required fees	$750
% frosh rec. need-based scholarship or grant aid	74
% UG rec. need-based scholarship or grant aid	71
% frosh rec. need-based self-help aid	68
% UG rec. need-based self-help aid	67

St. Edward's University

3001 South Congress Avenue, Austin, TX 78704

Admissions: 512-448-8500 • **Fax:** 512-464-8877 • **Financial Aid:** 512-448-8523

E-mail: SEU.ADMIT@ADMIN.STEWARDS.EDU • **Website:** WWW.STEDWARDS.EDU

CAMPUS LIFE

Type of school	private
Environment	town

STUDENTS

Total undergrad	
enrollment	3,690
% male/female	43/57
% from out of state	5
% from public high school	74
% live on campus	39
% African American	5
% Asian	2
% Caucasian	55
% Hispanic	30
% Native American	1
% international	2
# of countries represented	38

ACADEMICS

Calendar	semester
Student/faculty ratio	15:1
% profs teaching	
UG courses	71
% classes taught by TAs	0
Most common lab size	10-19
Most common	
reg class size	<10

MOST POPULAR MAJORS
biology/biological sciences
communications and media studies
psychology

Getting Involved

St. Edward's University maintains two centers for civic engagement. The first, the Career Planning Office, "takes advantage of our location in the state capital and places student interns in legislative and state government offices as well as many local nonprofit organizations and for-profit companies. Through these internships, students live out the university's mission by working as part of the community." The Career Planning Office also promotes service-learning internships and national service opportunities and co-sponsors the university's Volunteer Fair. The Office of Student Life also manages and promotes community engagement by coordinating service and volunteerism outside the classroom. Student Life oversees more than 65 student organizations, nearly all of which incorporate service as part of their mission. As the university points out, "the mission statement of St. Edward's University calls every student to a life of civic engagement and service" by encouraging faculty "to confront the critical issues of society and to seek justice and peace" so that students "are helped to understand themselves, clarify their personal values and recognize their responsibility to the world community."

Students tell us that "the university does a great job of promoting student organizations on campus. It holds at least two involvement fairs a year. Also, organization leaders and members are always recruiting through e-mails and visits to classrooms."

Campus Culture of Engagement

"The campus really has a heart, and those organizing and participating in civic engagement activities aren't just doing it for the service hours, but for the advancement of our community," undergrads at St. Edward's tell us. Religion plays a major role in students' service; explains one undergrad, "our campus ministry helps our organizations so much. They participate and offer many opportunities for students to get involved with helping the community." In addition, "because SEU is a Catholic institution, there are several opportunities to participate in mission trips to many different countries throughout the year."

Another major factor is the school's College Assistance Migrant Program—"the longest continuously operating program of its kind in the country. St. Edward's was among the first four sites in the country to host the federally funded program and has provided college access and support to more than 2,250 students from migrant farm-worker families throughout the program's 30 year history."

Finally, there's the students' enthusiasm for service; as one tells us, "the most important strength of St. Edward's civic engagement efforts is the high level of participation. Although St. Edward's is significantly smaller than other major universities (like the University of Texas, which is also in Austin), there always appears to be obvious St. Edward's representation at many activities and rallies around the city."

Connecting Service with the Classroom

St. Edward's offered "service-learning courses in all schools and all disciplines for the Fall 2004 semester. Every school within the university has courses that incorporate required service-learning components. We estimate that approximately 200 to 300 students participate in academic-based service-learning each semester."

Among these service-learning opportunities is the Community Mentor Program, a charter AmeriCorps program that "matches 60 to 80 students from St. Edward's as mentors for elementary-school-age children each academic year. The majority of the mentors are migrant students, Hispanic, and bilingual in Spanish and English— uniquely-qualified role models for minority children at risk. All first-semester mentors enroll in a credit-bearing class taught by the CMP director called Service-Learning: Transformation Through Mentoring."

The university uses its Austin location to civic advantage, which allows for some government-related service-learning opportunities. Explains the university, "in the alternate years in which the state legislature is in session, most students enrolled in the very popular Legislative Process course intern with a member of the state legislature. After this experience, many students continue to volunteer or are hired part time and some launch full-time professional careers."

Undergrads report that many freshmen "participate in a one-day service-learning [experience], where they choose where they want to go and do it in groups. It's a great opportunity to meet people (since so many freshmen do it), and the faculty describes other clubs/school organizations that actively pursue service activities."

Impact on Community and Students

St. Edward's affects its surrounding community via two types of community partnerships: there are "those focusing on local pre-K-12 public and private schools," and "those that focus on local social-service agencies." The university points out that "both types frequently include area businesses." In addition, "Campus Ministry sponsors a number of projects [like] Alternative Spring Break immersion trips [or] Urban Plunge that put our students in service to the poor in our city, in our country, in our hemisphere and in our world."

Students see their lives intersect those of their Austin and global neighbors in numerous ways. Explains one, "it may be working at the Habitat for Humanity store or working on a low-income construction site. It may be picking up trash and cleaning creeks in the neighborhood parks. Many students choose to work in Mexico on school holidays with Campus Ministry. There are opportunities for students to live on the streets with the homeless to gain understanding of the situation and to work at service organizations that help these people." Through these experiences, undergrads "learn about the workings of the world, interacting with people, and what it means to be responsible. Getting out there and being 'civically engaged' is what all human beings could do to make the world a better place."

Student Financial Support for Service

At St. Edward's, "Incoming freshmen who have been involved in their communities may be offered named merit scholarships for that service. A condition of keeping that scholarship is continued public/community service." In addition, "there also is an annual scholarship for upper-division undergraduate students who have excellent academic credentials and are committed to community service." This award is granted based on a student's past community service, academic excellence, and a service project proposal submitted to the awards committee. The school adds that "awards are $5,000 for an academic year ($2,500 fall and $2,500 spring) and are one-time awards."

SELECTIVITY

# of applicants	1,943
% of applicants accepted	69
% of acceptees attending	45
# accepting a place on wait list	257
% admitted from wait list	25

FRESHMAN PROFILE

Range SAT Verbal	510-610
Range SAT Math	500-600
Range ACT Composite	21-26
Minimum Paper TOEFL	500
Minimum Computer TOEFL	173
% graduated top 10% of class	19
% graduated top 25% of class	52
% graduated top 50% of class	83

DEADLINES

Regular admission	6/1
Regular notification by	rolling
Nonfall registration?	yes

FINANCIAL FACTS

Annual tuition	$17,320
Room and board	$6,540
Books and supplies	$900
% frosh rec. need-based scholarship or grant aid	62
% UG rec. need-based scholarship or grant aid	54
% frosh rec. need-based self-help aid	48
% UG rec. need-based self-help aid	48
% frosh rec. any financial aid	86
% UG rec. any financial aid	77

St. Mary's University Texas

One Camino Santa Maria, San Antonio, TX 78228

Admissions: 210-436-3126 • **Fax:** 210-431-6742 • **Financial Aid:** 210-436-3141

E-mail: UADM@STMARYTX.EDU • **Website:** WWW.STMARYTX.EDU/

CAMPUS LIFE

Type of school	private
Environment	town

STUDENTS

Total undergrad enrollment	2,531
% male/female	41/59
% from out of state	4
% from public high school	74
% live on campus	41
% African American	3
% Asian	3
% Caucasian	20
% Hispanic	68
% international	5

ACADEMICS

Calendar	semester
Most common lab size	20-29
Most common reg class size	<10

MOST POPULAR MAJORS

biology/biological sciences
political science and government
psychology

Getting Involved

St. Mary's University has put substantial effort into their public mission for quite a long time now: "Since 1852," says the San Antonio-based school, "part of [our] enduring mission is to serve society as a beacon of access and educational transformation. Service and engagement at St. Mary's are based in the school's Service Learning Center (SLC), an office with a mission to "develop community-service projects and work with faculty members to integrate service into their courses." The SLC "also provides opportunities for students looking for a well-rounded, holistic education that is developed both in the classroom and in the community." The office's many endeavors include, among a host of special programs, the "supporting service-learning courses, attending and presenting at professional conferences (e.g., Texas Campus Compact), coordinating service projects for new-student orientation, co-sponsoring the nonprofit career fair and the creation of the Service Learning Intercollegiate Collaborative (SLIC), assisting the National Student Partnership (NSP), and coordinating the Purple Heart Project as well as the WINGS and Marianist Leadership programs." Administrators remind us that "the SLC, founded in 1994, is a national model supporting students in direct community-service work. St. Mary's is the first university in San Antonio and one of the first in the nation to have a service-learning center devoted to matching students with community-service projects."

The 21st Century Leadership Center of St. Mary's University, which "educates, trains, and resources future generations to lead ethically and effectively in the global community" for the benefit of "the underserved and underrepresented," also contributes substantially. Notes the school, "The 21st Century Leadership Center is distinctive because of its definition of [a leader as] a person engaged in a process of enabling and empowering others to accomplish shared objectives for the purpose of serving and benefiting the common good." In accordance with that definition, "the 21st Century Leadership Center collaborates with and supports more than 25 local, community-focused, servant-leadership programs operating in and around the underserved West Side of San Antonio, including pastoral, cultural, men's, women's, and worker-union leadership-development programs, city government agencies, private foundations, and local community activists and consultants."

Campus Culture of Engagement

Students are greeted at St. Mary's with an encouragement to serve; explains one undergrad, "There is a huge program at the beginning of each academic year that invites the whole campus to engage in a day of service. Students choose a service they would like, such as spending the day at the AIDS shelter or at the Humane Society bathing puppies. There's so many to choose from for that day." Momentum carries many into service throughout the school year. As one student puts it, "the strength of our program is that civic engagement becomes contagious because once a few students participate, all their friends want to join as well." Students also praise the "big hearts" of their classmates, observing that "the atmosphere seems to be one of service in general. It is not fake or proud, but humble and full of effort."

Connecting Service with the Classroom

According to the university, "service-learning at St. Mary's is a practical way to enable students to gain insight into classroom theory and appreciate volunteer work. Courses and programs cut across all disciplines, from the sciences to business and the humanities. Each semester, more than 300 students are enrolled in more than a dozen community-based service-learning courses." Service has "become an essential part of the Political Science major," the school writes, reporting that the department "supports community/civic engagement within the university and the community at large [through] civic engagement, leadership, political leadership, and community organizing. A course on civic engagement supports our commitment to activism and participation. Graduating seniors are expected to submit to the department a civic-engagement resume." Students note that throughout the curriculum, "service-learning takes place in required courses, student organizations, and the Marianist traditions in and around the community."

Impact on Community and Students

The university participates in "collaborative partnerships" with local business, government, nonprofit organizations, and neighborhood associations. Many serve local school-age children; ArtTeach, for one, provides children at a nearby low-income housing project with "the opportunity to express their feelings and ideas" through the arts. Undergraduates "help facilitate the program by organizing art-teachers' schedules and workshops and assisting the youngsters when they are working on art projects. St. Mary's students also assist the art teacher, who may have up to 25 children in one workshop."

Students training for careers in teaching often participate in the Communities in Schools program, which facilitates field placements at a local middle school. Notes the school, "Since much of the curriculum in teacher education is field-based, our students are groomed for the profession with a service-learning type of environment. Our pre-service educators are constantly tutoring and mentoring students and then reporting to their university professors how they contributed to the students' cognitive, affective, and psychomotor growth."

The student-run Get Out the Vote program helps empower San Antonians by "driving people to the polls, encouraging voter registration, and planning and moderating local political debates. Since the campaign vigorously began in 2000, more than 800 persons have been registered to vote in each year."

Student Financial Support for Service

At St. Mary's, "three scholarships totaling $225,000 channel funds to about 80 students who share in the spirit of community service" each year. USAA—one of San Antonio's largest employers-funds a Charitable Trust, which grants scholarships to "those students enrolled in the School of Humanities and Social Sciences who have demonstrated a commitment to community service." Those dedicated to service and leadership in the Hispanic community are eligible for the William "Willie" C. Velasquez Memorial Scholarship, named after the voting-rights advocate who is "one of St. Mary's most distinguished alumni." Finally, the Marianist Leadership Program provides $3,000 annually to students whose dedication to service embodies the Marianist tradition.

SELECTIVITY

# of applicants	1,619
% of applicants accepted	80
% of acceptees attending	36

FRESHMAN PROFILE

Range SAT Verbal	480-590
Range SAT Math	480-590
Range ACT Composite	19-24
Minimum Paper TOEFL	550
Minimum Computer TOEFL	300
Average HS GPA	3.10
% graduated top 10% of class	30
% graduated top 25% of class	62
% graduated top 50% of class	88

DEADLINES

Regular notification by	rolling
Nonfall registration?	yes

FINANCIAL FACTS

% frosh rec. need-based scholarship or grant aid	68
% UG rec. need-based scholarship or grant aid	63
% frosh rec. need-based self-help aid	63
% UG rec. need-based self-help aid	61
% frosh rec. any financial aid	78
% UG rec. any financial aid	73

SAN FRANCISCO STATE UNIVERSITY

1600 HOLLOWAY AVENUE, SAN FRANCISCO, CA 94132

ADMISSIONS: 415-338-6486 • **FAX:** 415-338-7196 • **FINANCIAL AID:** 415-338-7000

E-MAIL: UGADMIT@SFSU.EDU • **WEBSITE:** WWW.SFSU.EDU

CAMPUS LIFE

Type of school	public
Environment	town

STUDENTS

Total undergrad enrollment	22,291
% male/female	41/59
% from out of state	1
% from public high school	79
% live on campus	0
% African American	6
% Asian	31
% Caucasian	27
% Hispanic	13
% Native American	1
% international	5
# of countries represented	149

ACADEMICS

Calendar	semester
Student/faculty ratio	18:1
Most common lab size	10-19
Most common reg class size	10-19

Getting Involved

Volunteerism at San Francisco State University makes its home at the Community Involvement Center (CIC), a student-administered office that "offers students volunteer training and a full spectrum of volunteer internships and learning experiences on campus and the San Francisco Bay Area." Another key player in connecting students to the community is the San Francisco Urban Institute (SFUI), which administrators proudly describe as "a model of institutional engagement for the campus." SFUI is home to the Office of Community Service-Learning, which "sponsors a wide variety of community-based action projects, where SFSU faculty and students work with community-based and city agencies in the area of economic and social development, after-school and arts programming, and violence reduction in low-income neighborhoods." It is also the place "where faculty redesign courses to include community work," and—as if that weren't enough—"it is also the administrative headquarters for the San Francisco Head Start program, serving over 1,400 low-income families through nursing, early childhood development, nutrition, and education."

SFSU asserts that "the university is also unique in the degree to which it publicly acknowledges [service]; students taking community service-learning classes earn an extra course unit for those courses, community service-learning courses are formally designated in the catalogue and on transcripts, and the university formally lists the completed hours of community service on student transcripts."

Students can stay abreast of service opportunities by "checking out the SFSU website or asking at the info desk in our student center," but undergrads tell us that "visiting the Community Involvement Center and checking frequently posted flyers about on-campus events, clubs, and groups are the most direct, active, and truly beneficial routes to becoming involved."

Campus Culture of Engagement

Students believe that "San Francisco State is the place to be because the school is very active politically and socially and there is a lot of room for service-learning." Notes one undergrad, "SFSU has a tremendous number of amazing programs and groups on campus, waiting for students who want to be enlightened, educated, informed, resocialized, and awakened," adding that SFSU is "a remarkable university, set amidst the awesome culturally, ethnically, and socio-economically diverse city of San Francisco."

The large socially active population here utilizes the CIC, which "is virtually entirely student-run and very progressive. Everyone who is there really wants to be there, and it shows." CIC not only acts as a clearing house for organizations seeking volunteers, it also runs courses through which students can "share the experiences that we gain in the community through volunteering in a small classroom environment. It helps students grow as [people]. It's both highly professional and personal."

Connecting Service with the Classroom

SFSU has one of the largest community service-learning programs in the nation. In the 2003-2004 academic year, there were 320 community service-learning sections, enrolling over 7,000 students, independent of clinical and professional placements." The school tells us that "the university offers service-learning classes in each of its eight colleges. These are courses in virtually every academic major, in the arts and humanities, sciences and business, the social and health sciences." One unique program at SFSU is the Urban Curriculum, which offers courses that are team-taught by professors and local intellectual and political leaders and that require students to do research projects with community organizations.

Many students choose SFSU precisely because of its emphasis on service learning. Notes one, "the traditional classroom experience can only take you so far in your studies. You will need applicable, hand-on experience to both understand your area of study from the inside and the outside and to compete for jobs in this ever-increasingly competitive job market. Service-learning is amazingly rewarding, educational, and empowering. Don't miss out on your opportunity to get involved and make a difference in your life and others' lives. It could it will change your life!"

The many outstanding programs at SFSU include The Family Resource Center Stay-in-School project, "where student organizers run and operate a major resource center for low-income university student parents." Another is America Reads, through which "hundreds of San Francisco State students offer reading tutoring for elementary school students across the city, is a companion program to America Counts," an algebra-tutoring program. And the City Dancers projects "involves dance (and other arts-related) students at San Francisco State in the training and design of a major dance program for at-risk inner-city children. Working out of six public elementary schools, SFSU students recruit and train student dancers for two major performances each year, at the university theatre. These are major theatrical events, reaching a large public (as well as finding remarkably talented young dancers!)."

Impact on Community and Students

SFSU is deeply immersed in its home city through "formal Memoranda of Understandings with over 420 community-based and city agencies, ranging from clinical and service-learning placements to joint-venture community-action projects." The school has formed partnerships with "nonprofit and educational agencies, labor, small business and civic organizations, and municipal agencies." Students tell us that service is "a great way give back to the community. You get a lot out of helping another. You feel as though you are making a difference in someone's life as well as your own. And you meet a lot of nice people."

Student Financial Support for Service

SFSU "offers a variety of scholarship and stipend support for a variety of community-based activities," including Democracy Matters, "a national nonprofit program offering $1,500 stipends for students working on the role of money in public policy." Adds the school, "There are other programs as well."

SELECTIVITY
# of applicants	8,046
% of applicants accepted	151
% of acceptees attending	24

FRESHMAN PROFILE
Range SAT Verbal	430-570
Range SAT Math	450-570
Range ACT Composite	18-23
Minimum Paper TOEFL	550
Minimum Computer TOEFL	173
Average HS GPA	3.17

DEADLINES
Regular admission	rolling
Regular notification by	rolling
Nonfall registration?	yes

FINANCIAL FACTS
Annual in-state tuition	$2,520
Annual out-of-state tuition	$12,690
Room and board	$8,870
Books and supplies	$1,400
Required fees	$546
% frosh rec. need-based scholarship or grant aid	35
% UG rec. need-based scholarship or grant aid	35
% frosh rec. need-based self-help aid	35
% UG rec. need-based self-help aid	39
% frosh rec. any financial aid	65
% UG rec. any financial aid	42

Smith College

7 College Lane, Northampton, MA 01063

Admissions: 413-585-2500 • **Fax:** 413-585-2527 • **Financial Aid:** 413-585-2530

E-mail: admission@smith.edu • **Website:** www.smith.edu

CAMPUS LIFE

Type of school	private
Environment	village

STUDENTS

Total undergrad enrollment	2,682
% male/female	0/100
% from out of state	76
% from public high school	74
% live on campus	88
% African American	6
% Asian	10
% Caucasian	55
% Hispanic	6
% Native American	1
% international	7
# of countries represented	65

ACADEMICS

Calendar	semester
Student/faculty ratio	10:1
% profs teaching UG courses	100
% classes taught by TAs	0
Most common reg class size	10-19

MOST POPULAR MAJORS
political science and government
psychology
visual and performing arts

Getting Involved

Smith students turn to the office of the Service Organizations of Smith College (SOS) to obtain "long- and short-term community placements, assistance with the development of service-learning courses, and [training in] the fundamentals of operating a small nonprofit organization." Students tell us that the SOS's resources are "enormous! There are cars you can take out to work on projects that aren't within walking distance, there are people who will help you develop a project that interests you, and there is lots of information about all of the many organizations in the local community where you can volunteer."

Other offices at this midsize college also contribute to service and activism. Several offices, including the Office of Educational Outreach and the Department of Education and Child Study, coordinate educational partnerships between the school and the surrounding community. The Smith School for Social Work's Center for Innovative Practice "supports a number of community-centered initiatives via the academic-year placement of SSW clinical social work interns." The Lewis Leadership Program "provides high-achieving students with training in group dynamics, oral presentation, negotiation, and conflict management; participants then provide team and individual service to the surrounding community."

Many Smith undergrads are introduced to service through First Link, "a pre-orientation program combining short-term community projects with reflective discussion, introducing students to local community-service opportunities, and putting community needs into context. At the end of First Link, students may have helped build a house with Habitat for Humanity, harvested vegetables at the local Food Bank Farm, or refurbished a community center." Once involved, students find it easy to stay informed. Writes one, "Signs are posted everywhere, e-mails are frequently sent to the student body, and students write announcements in chalk on the paths and sidewalks. In addition, websites post events, and word of mouth gets messages around." And if that's not enough, "each house [i.e., dormitory] has a community-service representative that keeps the house informed."

Campus Culture of Engagement

Smith undergrads "are very conscious of the world and their surroundings. The average Smithie is very likely to be engaged in activist/service projects that are in some way related to their everyday lives. For example, as a progressive women's institution, Smith organized to have a large showing at the March for Women's Choice in Washington, DC. Also, within our smaller community, Smithies are fighting for living wages and adequate health care for our kitchen staff and housekeepers."

Connecting Service with the Classroom

Smith offers a smattering of classes that combine "elements of academic study with service placements and/or community-based research." These service-learning classes range from "Education in the City" to "Engineering and Global Development" to "Issues in Adolescent Gender-Role Development." The school adds that "summer and term-time student research internships, especially in science departments of the Clark Science Center, support faculty-supervised field research projects that engage students in community settings."

Students see the benefits. "Service has allowed me to apply my educational interests, Women's Studies and Sociology, with hands-on experience and learning," explains one. Writes another, "I think learning is more or less worthless if you can't extend some of it to your community at school and beyond. Community-based learning is usually very successful and keeps Smithies grounded and constantly learning new things that otherwise couldn't be learned in the classroom."

Impact on Community and Students

SOS "has established community partnerships with 64 agencies and programs," Smith reports. "The types of organizations working with SOS provide an array of community services including tutorial assistance at school programs, literacy projects, and language institutes; medical research at community health centers and hospitals; decisional training at county correctional facilities; [and] mentoring programs, counseling services, and legal advocacy at different sites."

Noteworthy partnerships include one with Hampshire County AIDS Care and the Between Family and Friends Center. The SOS board "created an enhanced outreach program for [these two] agencies, recognizing their vital community-service work. The students helped research the level of need in the local community for the types of services provided by the agencies. Also, they examined the impact of state budget cuts on the agencies' funding. The students addressed the agencies' needs by enhancing volunteer recruitment and informing the Smith College community about important HIV/AIDS issues. They accomplished this by creating agency placements in the community-based learning program, by organizing short-term projects at the individual agencies, and by holding informational meetings about HIV/AIDS medical and social issues. During the spring, SOS organized its annual Fund Drive around HIV/AIDS issues."

Smith service organizations hope to impact the global community as well as the local one. Undergrads are currently laying the groundwork for the China Project, through which they plan to become "actively involved in the development of a cross-cultural community service project with the People's Republic of China. The Project will create opportunities for five college students to engage in community-service internships in the People's Republic of China."

Student Financial Support for Service

At Smith College, "PRAXIS internships provide students with access to a one-time stipend of $2,000 to enable them to pursue an internship of their choosing, requiring clear learning goals and 220 hours of service to their host. Nearly 450 students pursue PRAXIS internships annually." In addition, "the Springfield Partnership, a program launched in 1999 to strengthen ties between the college and the largest city in western Massachusetts, provides up to three full-tuition, four-year scholarships annually to students from this nearby urban center. In 2003, these scholarships amounted to $27,330 each."

SELECTIVITY

# of applicants	3,304
% of applicants accepted	52
% of acceptees attending	37
# accepting a place on wait list	311
% admitted from wait list	14

FRESHMAN PROFILE

Range SAT Verbal	580-700
Range SAT Math	570-670
Range ACT Composite	25-30
Minimum Paper TOEFL	600
Minimum Computer TOEFL	250
Average HS GPA	3.80
% graduated top 10% of class	59
% graduated top 25% of class	88
% graduated top 50% of class	99

DEADLINES

Regular admission	1/15
Regular notification by	4/1
Nonfall registration?	no

FINANCIAL FACTS

Annual tuition	$27,330
Room and board	$9,490
Books and supplies	$1,500
Required fees	$214
% frosh rec. need-based scholarship or grant aid	59
% UG rec. need-based scholarship or grant aid	56
% frosh rec. need-based self-help aid	59
% UG rec. need-based self-help aid	56
% frosh rec. any financial aid	63
% UG rec. any financial aid	74

SOUTHWEST MISSOURI STATE UNIVERSITY

901 SOUTH NATIONAL, SPRINGFIELD, MO 65804

ADMISSIONS: 417-836-5517 • FAX: 417-836-6334 • FINANCIAL AID: 417-835-5262

E-MAIL: SMSUINF@SMSU.EDU • WEBSITE: WWW.SMSU.EDU

CAMPUS LIFE

Type of school	public
Environment	town

STUDENTS

Total undergrad enrollment	14,565
% male/female	44/56
% from out of state	7
% from public high school	93
% live on campus	24
% African American	3
% Asian	1
% Caucasian	87
% Hispanic	1
% Native American	1
% international	2

ACADEMICS

Calendar	semester
Student/faculty ratio	18:1
% profs teaching UG courses	94
% classes taught by TAs	9
Most common lab size	20-29
Most common reg class size	20-29

MOST POPULAR MAJORS

elementary education and teaching
management information systems
psychology

Getting Involved

"In 1995, the late Governor Mel Carnahan signed into law Southwest Missouri State University's statewide mission in public affairs (Senate Bill 340)," SMSU administrators inform us, explaining that the bill requires "the development of educated citizens for the democracy of Missouri [and] the United States, as well as citizens for the world." To accomplish its noble mandate, the university created several offices to oversee its efforts.

The Office of Citizenship and Service-Learning (CASL) is one; it administers service-learning opportunities by "engaging with each of the six colleges of the University in their academic goals. It is the mission of the CASL office to support the service-learning efforts of the faculty, to maintain reciprocal relationships with the University's community partners, and to provide direction, orientation, and service to students."

Many SMSU students are committed to service even when it doesn't bear college credit. For them, there's the Campus Volunteer Center, which "fills out the student-affairs side of the campus/community engagement equation. A key program of the Campus Volunteer Center is the work of the Student Community Action Team (SCAT). SCAT, using federal work-study money, partners students with community agencies."

SMSU undergrads also have numerous student-run entities available to them. Many "are very involved in student organizations, including the student-activities council, student government, [and] Greek life. There are so many organizations and so many opportunities to get involved." Undergrads learn about these opportunities through "numerous involvement fairs held throughout the year, especially at the beginning of the fall semester. These fairs offer information about becoming an engaged campus citizen as well as Getting Involved with organizations whose purposes are specifically geared to service and activism."

Campus Culture of Engagement

Students, like administrators, are acutely aware of SMSU's mission statement. Points out one undergrad, "The university mission revolves around public affairs, and that is stressed from day one through the Introduction to University Life course," a one-credit class that requires students to discuss such public-affairs issues as alcohol and drug abuse, sexually transmitted diseases, sexual dilemmas, and diversity. The course also "makes several efforts to emphasize the many different avenues to get involved in, such as the Association of Civically Engaged Students (ACES)."

SMSU must be pleased with the results of its efforts; students tell us that they yield a bumper crop of "great student leaders. It seems that a handful of organizations are the training grounds for these leaders. At the end of every year, strong leaders step down from their positions and equally effective leaders step up into those positions."

Connecting Service with the Classroom

"There are two types of service-learning on the SMSU campus," the school tells us. There's the traditional Integrated Service-Learning (ISL), through which "professors integrate a service-learning project into their regular course, making it one of the major assignments in their course, which all students must complete. With ISL courses, students will receive a special 'SL' designation on their transcripts, with an explanatory note which defines what this designation entails." Then there's the Optional 'Fourth Credit' mode, under which "students may elect to take an additional service-learning one-credit hour component with their regular course." Service-learning opportunities span the disciplines, ranging from Theater (impromptu shows at a local federal prison) to Psychology (consulting for a local nonprofit service organization) to Religious Studies (faith-based social service) to Political Science (students serve as "special court liaisons to the public").

Service learning is on the rise at SMSU. In 2001-2002, the school offered about 200 courses that could accommodate one of the two types of service learning; nearly 600 students took advantage of the option. Those numbers increased to 236 courses and 893 students in 2002-2003.

Impact on Community and Students

SMSU partners with hundreds of community organizations to make its presence felt in its region and throughout the state. Partners include prisons, churches, homeless agencies, courts, and all manner of social-service nonprofits (e.g., AIDS Project of the Ozarks, the Carol Jones Recovery Center for Women, and Disabilities Connection).

Typical of these partnerships is one created between the Citizenship and Service-Learning program and the local chapter of the American Cancer Society. It began when students in a Venue Management class volunteered to "apply their skills in event logistics management to coordinate arrangements for this partner's annual fundraising event." According to SMSU, the resulting program "has empowered students with activities ranging from securing custodial staff to follow-up thank-you letters." The results have been outstanding; "the American Cancer Society credits much of their record-breaking fundraising success to the CASL students who have served along side them in the fight to eliminate cancer," reports the administration.

Another successful program sends SMSU students to work with juvenile offenders at the Greene County Juvenile Court and the Missouri Division of Youth Services. This education-based program aims "to divert at-risk juveniles from further involvement with the legal system and to reintegrate young people coming from a residential program back into the community and to public schools" through tutoring and physical education activities.

Student Financial Support for Service

SMSU offers a number of service-related awards. Pepsi Cola sponsors five scholarships of $1,000 each, "awarded to undergraduate students enrolled at SMSU who have a demonstrated record of service, leadership, and qualities consistent with the goals of the public affairs mission." Then there's the Joseph A. Boyce Scholarship, given to one student "who has a demonstrated record of service, leadership, and qualities consistent with the goals of the public-affairs mission." Finally, there's the Hutchens/SGA Centennial Leaders Scholarship Program, a new scholarship for students who "have leadership potential. The amount of the scholarship will range from $1,250 to $2,500, depending upon financial need. Student recipients of the scholarship will participate in leadership-development opportunities and campus and community-service projects and activities."

SELECTIVITY

# of applicants	7,153
% of applicants accepted	77
% of acceptees attending	49

FRESHMAN PROFILE

Range ACT Composite	21-26
Minimum Paper TOEFL	500
Minimum Computer TOEFL	173
Average HS GPA	3.50
% graduated top 10% of class	20
% graduated top 25% of class	47
% graduated top 50% of class	79

DEADLINES

Regular admission	7/20

FINANCIAL FACTS

Annual in-state tuition	$4,620
Annual out-of-state tuition	$9,240
Room and board	$4,660
Books and supplies	$800
Required fees	$508
% frosh rec. need-based scholarship or grant aid	42
% UG rec. need-based scholarship or grant aid	42
% frosh rec. need-based self-help aid	43
% UG rec. need-based self-help aid	51
% frosh rec. any financial aid	54
% UG rec. any financial aid	58

SPELMAN COLLEGE

350 SPELMAN LANE, SOUTH WEST, ATLANTA, GA 30314

ADMISSIONS: 404-270-5193 • **FAX:** 404-270-5201 • **FINANCIAL AID:** 404-270-5212

E-MAIL: ADMISS@SPELMAN.EDU • **WEBSITE:** WWW.SPELMAN.EDU

CAMPUS LIFE

Type of school	private
Environment	town

STUDENTS

Total undergrad enrollment	2,063
% male/female	0/100
% from out of state	68
% from public high school	84
% live on campus	59
% African American	95
% international	2
# of countries represented	18

ACADEMICS

Calendar	quarter
Student/faculty ratio	14:1
% profs teaching UG courses	100
% classes taught by TAs	0
Most common lab size	10-19
Most common reg class size	10-19

MOST POPULAR MAJORS
biology/biological sciences
political science and government
psychology

Getting Involved

Spelman has a tradition of providing opportunities for service to women at this leading historically black college. Spelman's Office of Community Service coordinates volunteerism, providing support for NAACP voter-registration drives, community/civic engagement programs run through the Education and English departments, and similar programs. The school's center for Leadership and Civic Engagement also "promotes leadership development and civic-engagement programs for students," the school tells us. The university maintains a database of community-service opportunities at its website; the database is accessible only to current Spelman students. Spelman provides free van service to and from Atlanta for those engaged in service.

Students tell us that they stay apprised of service opportunities here by "simply being at school. There are so many things going on that are advertised all over campus that it is hard to miss the opportunities to engage in service." Reports one student, "Almost every group on our campus incorporates community service or activism."

Campus Culture of Engagement

Community service is part of every freshwoman's and sophomore's experience at Spelman. The school sees to that through its community-service requirement; explains one undergrad, "First- and second-year students are required to do community service." Adds another, "The standards per semester are very easy to fulfill. Usually students are only required to do two or three hours of service per semester. As such, students can pick one major event such as an AIDS Walk and be done with community service for the year." Many here "feel that the hours required could be increased, although most students do more than what is required anyway," and they agree that the requirement is beneficial. Writes one, "Because it is mandatory, everyone must participate. This gives people who would otherwise skip community service the chance to find a project they truly believe in and stick with it into their junior and senior years (when service is not required)."

Overall, Spelman "instills in all of her students that we are to be 'women who serve,'" leading many to assert that "it is not an option; it is your responsibility. To whom much is given, much is required. By having the opportunity to attend college, it is your responsibility to be a change-agent for those around you. We can be much more powerful, and there will be much less work for each person, if all get involved." Students here are also politically active; "we often have rallies and protests," they report. Recently those activities centered on rap artist Nelly, who cancelled a planned campus visit (in support of a bone marrow drive) when students protested negative portrayals of African American women in his most recent video.

Connecting Service with the Classroom

Much of Spelman's service-learning activity is coordinated through its LEADS Center (LEADS is an acronym for Leadership Development, Economic Empowerment, Advocacy through the Arts, Dialogue across Difference, and Service Learning and Civic Engagement). According to the school's website, the LEADS program offers curriculum-development workshops in its efforts to "encourage faculty members to create community-based learning opportunities." The office also stresses the importance of studying public policy issues in an effort to address the underlying causes of social problems.

Service-learning opportunities include translation services for Spanish speakers, after-school tutoring, and assisting in research for area health agencies; also, mentoring and tutoring services are offered at area schools through the Elementary Science Education Partners Program (ESEP), which is offered in conjunction with other area schools (Emory, Georgia Tech, Georgia State, Morehouse, and Clark). The LEADS Center's Global Peace Initiative also promises to provide compelling service-learning opportunities in the future.

Impact on Community and Students

Spelman tells us that "there are 95-plus organizations that we have partnerships with. Some of the organizations that we work with are the America Reads Program, Hands on Atlanta, AmeriCorps, the Neighborhoods Development Internship Project, and the Shepherd Poverty Alliance Program." Of the last, the school adds that "Spelman has a strong presence in the Shepherd Poverty Program. This program is a service-learning program that offers an opportunity for students to experience a new community by working full-time for a nonprofit organization. Not only does the student work at the agency, but she also lives in the community. Work becomes a learning experience. The focus of this program is poverty, and the alliances have been established between Spelman, Morehouse, Washington & Lee, Berea College, and the Bonner Foundation."

Other Spelman service opportunities include volunteer work at nearby Grady hospital, where students help sick patients and providing translation services for non-English-speaking patients; through this program, Spelman undergrads also work in the hospital's delivery room, assisting with both intake services and delivery. Other healthcare-related programs include SisterLove, which works to curtail HIV/AIDS in the African American community, and Outreach, which serves both male and female HIV/AIDS-infected populations. Student volunteers also work at Hammonds House, an Atlanta art museum devoted to the work of African American artists.

Students love knowing that they are contributing to the community. Those looking to work in public service after graduation reap an added benefit: "A lot of organizations come to our campus to recruit our students because our students have such a great history and reputation. A lot of people get involved on a consistent basis, and I think that's one of the best things about it," writes one undergrad.

Student Financial Support for Service

Spelman rewards select service-minded undergrads with its Bonner Scholars Program as well as a UPS Scholars Program. Writes the school, "Both programs provide scholarships for students who are involved in community service." Bonner Scholarships are available only to students who demonstrate financial need; the awards max out at $3,400 per year. UPS awards ten scholarships to students who, in return, tutor at an area elementary school. Students qualified for work-study jobs can seek employment through the school's Community Work Study program.

SELECTIVITY

# of applicants	4,345
% of applicants accepted	39
% of acceptees attending	29

FRESHMAN PROFILE

Range SAT Verbal	500-580
Range SAT Math	490-580
Range ACT Composite	20-24
Minimum Paper TOEFL	500
Minimum Computer TOEFL	250
Average HS GPA	3.40

DEADLINES

Regular admission	2/1
Regular notification by	4/1
Nonfall registration?	yes

FINANCIAL FACTS

Annual tuition	$12,700
Room and board	$8,040
Required fees	$2,240
% frosh rec. need-based scholarship or grant aid	83
% UG rec. need-based scholarship or grant aid	90
% frosh rec. need-based self-help aid	64
% UG rec. need-based self-help aid	83
% frosh rec. any financial aid	87
% UG rec. any financial aid	87

STANFORD UNIVERSITY

UNDERGRADUATE ADMISSION, OLD UNION 232, STANFORD, CA 94305-3005
ADMISSIONS: 650-723-2091 • **FAX:** 650-723-6050 • **FINANCIAL AID:** 650-723-0198
E-MAIL: ADMISSIONS@STANFORD.EDU • **WEBSITE:** WWW.STANFORD.EDU

CAMPUS LIFE

Type of school	private
Environment	village

STUDENTS

Total undergrad enrollment	6,500
% male/female	52/48
% from out of state	53
% from public high school	72
% live on campus	91
% African American	11
% Asian	24
% Caucasian	41
% Hispanic	12
% Native American	2
% international	6
# of countries represented	97

ACADEMICS

Calendar	semester
Student/faculty ratio	7:1
% classes taught by TAs	17
Most common lab size	20-29
Most common reg class size	10-19

MOST POPULAR MAJORS

biology/biological sciences
computer science
economics

Getting Involved

Consistently ranked among the top schools for service-learning, Stanford's Haas Center for Public Service has a proud tradition as one of the early leaders in the service movement and continues to be "the primary focal point for community and civic-engagement activities" for undergraduates. Even with the recent difficulty in retaining its early visionary leaders, according to the school, the center continues to connect "academic study with community and public service to strengthen communities and develop effective public leaders." In collaboration with other agencies of the school, the Haas Center "implements programs in five areas of work, including fellowships, courses, research, community programs, and leadership development." It also serves as campus headquarters to such programs as Stanford in Washington (School of Humanities & Sciences program), the Institute for Diversity in the Arts (Committee on Black Performing Arts and the Drama Department program), and VIA (Volunteers in Asia, a nonprofit cultural and educational-exchange program). Service- and civic-related student organizations also make Haas their home.

Numerous community centers organized around Stanford's ethnic, gender, and disability-focused subpopulations also provide service to the community-at-large. One example is Barrio Assistance, "which comes under the auspices of El Centro Chicano. Formed in 1971, it is the oldest ethnic center [and] community-service program on campus. Barrio Assistance is a community outreach, tutoring, and mentoring program for Latino grade school students in East Palo Alto and East Menlo Park."

Campus Culture of Engagement

Students agree that service is important in the lives of most Stanford undergrads. Writes one, "Most people I know have done or are doing some sort of service, many of them on a long-term basis. Those that aren't often feel guilty about not doing something." Points out another, "There are more than 70 student groups classified as 'community-service organizations' alone, not counting social/political-awareness organizations and service/activism groups run through the ethnic/community centers" or the many peer groups like the Bridge Peer Counseling Center. For the politically minded, "ASSU (Associated Students of Stanford University) is very active in promoting political engagement; the student-run Stanford in Government (SIG) regularly hosts distinguished political speakers, organizes issue-based discussions, and funds approximately 30 summer fellowships around the country and internationally every year; students of color are very active (Students of Color Coalition; SOCC); political groups (parties, issue groups) are very visible; and diverse political publications are published weekly."

Connecting Service with the Classroom

Service-learning is highly integrated into the Stanford curriculum. The school reports that "during every academic year, Stanford offers over 50 service-learning courses that provide students with a chance to engage in service while developing their intellectual capacities."

In addition, "each year, 160 students participate in an Alternative Spring Break (ASB), a student-led service-learning immersion experience that includes directed reading during winter quarter, a one-week trip during spring break, and leadership opportunities throughout the year. ASB is an entry point for many students." The Public Service Scholars Program (PSSP) can be a capstone service-learning experience during the senior year. "PSSP is a year-long academic program in which students research and write an honors thesis in an area related to service or political action. This opportunity to focus on research as a form of public service is available to students in all majors." Students brag that "there are opportunities to engage in a diverse spectrum of types of service. For example, Stanford has the nation's most developed undergraduate academic and extracurricular offerings in social entrepreneurship, bringing business skills to social causes."

And if that's not enough, other distinctive programs here include:

- The East Palo Alto Tennis and Tutoring program (EPATT), which for sixteen years has used "a unique blend of one-on-one academic tutoring and tennis instruction to enrich the academic, athletic, and social skills of its participants." The program "promotes leadership, discipline, hard work, and excellence through partnerships with families, area schools, local communities, and Stanford University." Approximately 130 Stanford students per year volunteer several hours a week as academic tutors.

- The Stanford Community Law Clinic (SCLC), "a vital community resource and a hands-on classroom for the many Stanford law students who volunteer there. SCLC offers free legal advice and services to low-income residents of several nearby communities." The clinic was "created through a partnership between Stanford University, Stanford Law School, the Legal Aid Society of San Mateo, and many local law firms" and utilizes the skills of both undergrads and Stanford law student who, "under the supervision of the clinic's attorneys, use their skills and legal knowledge to educate, counsel, and represent clients in a variety of areas of civil law."

- The Stanford Leaders for Public Service, "the Haas Center's leadership-development program for students wanting to devote a significant amount of time to exploring their own personal leadership styles and philosophies. The program aims to develop thoughtful, skilled, and reflective practitioners equipped to effectively lead their peers in public-service endeavors both here at Stanford and after graduation."

Impact on Community and Students

Stanford maintains over 100 partnerships with its surrounding community, running "the gamut from individual efforts to well-organized groups with over a hundred volunteers." Notes the school, "Stanford students play an active role in many of these community partnerships." Students as well as the community benefit from Stanford's partnerships; explains one student who coordinates a literacy program, "I've learned a lot about language, teaching philosophy, child psychology, and community. Civic engagement usually involves gaining knowledge, skills, and a sense that you're actually doing something with your education-all making for a more well-rounded person."

Student Financial Support for Service

Stanford puts resources into its students making a difference. Each year, ninety undergraduates receive fellowships for summer internships and self-designed projects in community organizations and government agencies in the U.S. and abroad. Stanford reports that "all financial aid is need-based. That said, the Community Service Work-Study program, co-administered by the Haas Center for Public Service and the Financial Aid Office, offers students eligible for work/study support the opportunity to do part-time community service work with a variety of local and national nonprofit and governmental organizations. In 2002, Washington Monthly ranked Stanford first among top universities using federal work-study money for community service. That data showed that 22.3 percent of students who earn federal work-study funding at Stanford do so through community service."

SWARTHMORE COLLEGE

500 COLLEGE AVENUE, SWARTHMORE, PA 19081

ADMISSIONS: 610-328-8300 • **FAX:** 610-328-8580 • **FINANCIAL AID:** 610-328-8358

E-MAIL: ADMISSIONS@SWARTHMORE.EDU • **WEBSITE:** WWW.SWARTHMORE.EDU

CAMPUS LIFE

Type of school	private
Environment	village

STUDENTS

Total undergrad enrollment	1,477
% male/female	47/53
% from out of state	84
% from public high school	57
% live on campus	93
% African American	7
% Asian	16
% Caucasian	53
% Hispanic	8
% Native American	1
% international	5
# of countries represented	46

ACADEMICS

Calendar	semester
Student/faculty ratio	9:1
% profs teaching UG courses	100
% classes taught by TAs	0
Most common lab size	20-29
Most common reg class size	10-19

MOST POPULAR MAJORS

biology/biological sciences
economics
political science and government

Getting Involved

Swarthmore College's "commitment to education for social responsibility is rooted in its Quaker heritage," and the Eugene M. Lang Center for Civic and Social Responsibility, which connects Swarthmore College to nearby communities (both literally and symbolically) is "the campus hub for activities [that] support Swarthmore's mission to 'help students realize their fullest intellectual and personal potential combined with a deep sense of ethical and social concern.'" The center is located at the Train Station Building, "where the campus meets the community. SEPTA trains make Philadelphia less than 30 minutes away. Within a few yards are bus stops for several other neighboring towns and smaller cities."

Students tell us that the Lang Center is "a great resource for helping students create their own projects and find funding and other support." They also report that since "Swarthmore is a small college with a great many ambitious programs, students are actively recruited to participate in a myriad of student organizations, service, and community action."

Campus Culture of Engagement

"Civic engagement at Swarthmore is strong because people are really passionate about learning and working, and people care," students tell us. Explains one undergrad, "Swarthmore is known for the outstanding service program it offers, and we have many staff members, like those of the Lang Center, who are professionals involved in civic engagement." Notes another, "I would say that the individual, student-run service groups vary in their levels of visibility, but that on the whole they are pretty accessible. There are some which I would not know about were I not involved with certain departments or if I did not know certain students, but I feel that if I were looking for a group, I could easily e-mail the Lang Center and ask them if it existed. If it didn't, there are most likely enough funds at Swarthmore to start that group."

Political activism is alive at Swarthmore on both the local and global level. Students tell us of a recent hot issue on campus: "the Living Wage campaign, which aimed to increase the salaries of our staff on campus. Students prepared reports, talks, speakers, and organized meetings with members of the board." Overall, the school is "amazingly engaged in the surrounding communities, and we are lucky to have such a good relationship with nearby Chester and organizations in Philadelphia." On the downside, many students feel "so pressed for time because of academics and all we do that it's hard to commit to going off-campus for service on a regular basis."

Connecting Service with the Classroom

The school reports that "Swarthmore offers service-learning courses in all three academic divisions, in both departmental and interdisciplinary programs. In the 2003-2004 academic year, service-learning courses were offered in Anthropology, Black Studies, Education, Engineering, Linguistics, Music and Dance, Political Science, Psychology, Public Policy, Sociology, and Women's Studies. In 2004-2005, courses will be added in Economics, History, and Religion. With the support of the Lang Center, new service-learning courses are added every year." Swarthmore is a Pilot Periclean, a founding member of Project Pericles, "a national organization of colleges and universities dedicated to education for social responsibility and participatory citizenship as an essential part of [education] in and out of the classroom."

Students point out that "many service-learning activities take place on campus, such as Upward Bound"—offering Swarthmore students the opportunity to tutor and mentor low-income and/or first-generation high school students preparing for college—"and Learning for Life, partnering students with staff members working together towards some education goal." Most activities, however, occur "in the nearby Chester and Philadelphia area and take the form of volunteering with organizations and internships, in addition to class discussions and support."

Unique opportunities at Swarthmore include:

- Learning for Life, "a campus-based program that joins students with members of the college environmental services and dining services staff in 'learning partnerships.' Partners meet at the beginning of the academic year and select the topics they plan to study. Currently there are 65 learning partnerships working on computing skills, writing, visual arts, history, genealogies, languages, adult basic literacy, GED preparation, and more."

- Dare to Soar, "an after-school program started by students who are affiliated with Swarthmore College's Black Cultural Center. Students work with elementary school students at several sites in the city of Chester, PA, offering a structured program that provides homework assistance, academic enrichment, cultural programming, and one-to-one mentoring."

- The Swarthmore Foundation, an in-house foundation that "provides small grants to students, faculty, and staff to implement community-based service projects and awards to students to enable them to take unpaid internships with nonprofit organizations. Most service projects are carried out in communities near the college or in grantees' home communities. Internships take place in a wide range of locations, both nationally and internationally. The Swarthmore Foundation has enabled students to create summer programs for children, build schools in India and Latin America, and intern in dozens of nonprofit organizations."

Impact on Community and Students

Swarthmore "has about 50 community partnerships, of which 15 are particularly close collaborations. The organizations range from small grassroots groups to major health demonstration and research institutions." Chief among them is the Chester Community Improvement Project (CCIP), whose mission is "to revitalize the city of Chester by building the base of homeownership through housing rehabilitation and mortgage counseling." Currently, CCIP is starting programs in financial literacy education to "support first-time home-buyers, and a collaboration with CCIP and five other community partners that will focus on workforce development for women in Chester." Students believe that their involvement with the community benefits them "because it creates well-rounded students who are not simply intellectually intelligent but socially aware, a necessary combination for anyone with a conscience."

Student Financial Support for Service

Summer of Service Internships offers stipends for students to "work with nonprofit organizations during the summer. The Lang Center staff assists students in finding internships to match their interests, provides orientation and reflection activities, and offers advising about ways to link internships to students' academic programs." In addition to Swarthmore Foundation grants, Swarthmore offers the Lang Opportunity Scholars Program, awarded to six sophomore students each year who demonstrate "strong commitment to service." The award includes a paid summer internship, a scholarship award of up to $1,000, and a budget of up to $10,000 to fund a student-designed project for the public good.

SELECTIVITY

# of applicants	3,908
% of applicants accepted	24
% of acceptees attending	40

FRESHMAN PROFILE

Range SAT Verbal	670-770
Range SAT Math	670-760
% graduated top 10% of class	92
% graduated top 25% of class	99
% graduated top 50% of class	100

DEADLINES

Regular admission	1/1
Regular notification by	4/1
Nonfall registration?	no

FINANCIAL FACTS

Annual tuition	$28,500
Room and board	$8,914
Books and supplies	$960
Required fees	$302
% frosh rec. need-based scholarship or grant aid	51
% UG rec. need-based scholarship or grant aid	49
% frosh rec. need-based self-help aid	48
% UG rec. need-based self-help aid	46
% frosh rec. any financial aid	53
% UG rec. any financial aid	51

SYRACUSE UNIVERSITY

201 TOLLEY, ADMINISTRATION BUILDING, SYRACUSE, NY 13244

ADMISSIONS: 315-443-3611 • FAX: 315-443-4226 • FINANCIAL AID: 315-443-1513

E-MAIL: ORANGE@SYR.EDU • WEBSITE: WWW.SYRACUSE.EDU

CAMPUS LIFE

Type of school	private
Environment	town

STUDENTS

Total undergrad enrollment	10,750
% male/female	44/56
% from out of state	55
% from public high school	80
% live on campus	73
% African American	6
% Asian	6
% Caucasian	71
% Hispanic	4
% international	3
# of countries represented	65

ACADEMICS

Calendar	semester
Student/faculty ratio	12:1
% profs teaching UG courses	98
% classes taught by TAs	6
Most common lab size	10-19
Most common reg class size	10-19

MOST POPULAR MAJORS

information science/studies
political science and government
psychology

Getting Involved

Syracuse administrators proudly point out that "civic engagement and service-learning are among of the main pillars of the SU Academic Plan and [are] an example of one of the best ways to truly engage students both in the university community and in their learning." The school told us that "a list of each specific office that actively supports civic engagement would be too long to include here" before providing us with the names of no fewer than 12 university offices and numerous other student groups that coordinate service on and around campus. Most important among these is the Mary Ann Shaw Center for Public and Community Service (MAS Center), which provides students with referrals to all manner of service opportunities. The MAS Center is also home to the Syracuse University Volunteer Organization, which organizes a number of service-related special events during the year.

Greek organizations are major contributors to extracurricular service at Syracuse, as are such organizations as Habitat for Humanity, the SU Child Advocacy Organization (SUCA), the Golden Key Honor Society, the National Association of Negro Business and Professional Women (NANBPW), and Black and Latino Information Studies Students (BLISTS). Service-minded students recommend Syracuse's Summer Start program, "a transition from high school [that provides] all of the resources to become involved during the freshman orientation class."

Campus Culture of Engagement

Syracuse undergrads "do so much for the community," by their own accounting. Reports one, "A huge number of students volunteer at local schools or after-school programs. In addition, there are various opportunities for freshman such as writing classes that tie in service-learning, as well as living-learning communities that perform service." The commitment to service is widespread; writes one woman, "Every student on my floor became civically engaged in some way. A lot of people became involved due to sororities, others through ROTC, the Asian Drumming Group, the local newspaper, or club and intramural athletics." And "once involved in service, SU students don't usually give it up. Even if one semester is too demanding to dedicate time, you can always see people returning to different service opportunities." Sometimes, the result is an embarrassment of riches; "our literacy corps job has to turn away student tutors because the interest has grown so much," one student told us.

Connecting Service with the Classroom

The MAS Center facilitates 25 courses through its office, on average, each academic year," Syracuse tells us; many other academic courses are offered that include a service component or requirement. "The estimated number of students who participate in service-learning classes in an academic year at SU is approximately 2,000," writes the school.

One of Syracuse's best-known community partnerships is the Syracuse University Literacy Corps (SULC), "a program born from President Clinton's America Reads/Counts challenge in 1997. [SULC] is a service-learning experience that mobilizes SU students to mentor and tutor students at area elementary schools and community-based organizations in Syracuse and Onondaga county. Tutors spend an average of ten to 12 hours per week tutoring at their sites. In 2003–04, 215 SULC tutors completed more than 32,600 hours of tutoring in the community, reaching close to 2,600 'at-risk' children. According to the assistant superintendent for curriculum and instruction at the Syracuse City School District (SCSD), the 12 percent rise in the children's state ELA test scores, as well as the improved confidence and motivation of more than 80 percent of the children with whom SULC tutors worked, is attributable in great measure to the participation of the SULC as a valued resource in the SCSD learning community."

Impact on Community and Students

Syracuse maximizes its contribution to the community by involving community members in all phases of service planning and execution. "The most unique aspect of Syracuse University's program is the collaborative model we use to develop all our programs," explains the school. "It involves bringing all stakeholders to the table–students, faculty, staff, and most importantly, community. Programs are developed around the needs of all, and all participate in the process. This requires a great deal more time, but results in much more powerful and successful programs." Despite the additional effort required, the school manages partnerships with "more than 400 nonprofit and public agencies in Syracuse/Onondaga County. The organizations range from public/private schools, to hospitals, to youth organizations, to food consortiums, to housing programs, to seniors programs, to nature centers, to churches, to literacy organizations, to health-related organizations, to hospice, to advocacy groups, funding organizations, and local foundations."

The school asserts that "our partnership with the Syracuse Boys and Girls Clubs is an excellent example of our many partnerships with community-based organizations. We work with administrators and staff to develop on-campus orientations in order to facilitate the intake of students, as well as to schedule and prepare our students to work at one of the three Boys and Girls Clubs' sites. We have MAS Center student-leadership interns assist Club staff with the recruiting and orientation of students; student van drivers help transport the student volunteers to the sites; Boys and Girls Club staff attend the MAS Center Annual Community Partner's Meeting. There are SU students working as mentors, tutors, recreation staff, administrative staff, program developers, IT support, grant writers, and public-relations assistants at the Boys and Girls Clubs."

Student Financial Support for Service

The MAS Center "offers a Public Service Intern Award, supported by the Robert B. Menschel Family, to up to five students each academic year to support students who have paid internships at nonprofits." The school tells us that "the purpose of the award is to encourage students to consider internships at nonprofits by making them more economically competitive with those in the private sector." Good news for future students: administrators point out that "students, faculty, and staff are involved in the process of developing the details of a community-service scholarship program."

TRINITY COLLEGE

300 SUMMIT STREET, HARTFORD, CT 06016

ADMISSIONS: 860-297-2180 • FAX: 860-297-2287 • FINANCIAL AID: 860-297-2046

E-MAIL: ADMISSIONS.OFFICE@TRINCOLL.EDU • WEBSITE: WWW.TRINCOLL.EDU

CAMPUS LIFE

Type of school	private
Environment	town

STUDENTS

Total undergrad enrollment	2,145
% male/female	49/51
% from out of state	78
% from public high school	43
% live on campus	92
% African American	5
% Asian	6
% Caucasian	66
% Hispanic	5
% international	2
# of countries represented	28

ACADEMICS

Calendar	semester
Student/faculty ratio	10:1
% profs teaching UG courses	100
% classes taught by TAs	0
Most common lab size	<10
Most common reg class size	10-19

MOST POPULAR MAJORS
economics
history
political science and government

Getting Involved

Trinity College "has been closely connected to the city of Hartford since its founding in 1823. The College even sold its original campus to provide a site for the new state capital," administrators tell us. Trinity's strong relationship with the city, coupled with the school's urban setting, means that there are "many opportunities for students to contribute passion and energy in volunteer efforts and to do research and classroom work that draws on its urban connections." Those opportunities include a curriculum that incorporates community and service-learning "in virtually every subject area." For example, "the Cities Program offers well-qualified entering students an opportunity to understand complex urban issues. The Health Fellows Program offers students an intensive semester-long experience combining research in local hospitals and health agencies with an academic seminar and a lecture series. Credit-bearing academic internships place students in the Connecticut Legislature, government offices, businesses, and nonprofit organizations."

Student volunteer activities are organized through the Office of Community Service and Civic Engagement. Reports the school, "More than 25 student groups on campus sponsor activities that bring students out into metropolitan Hartford, ranging from 'Do It Day,' which brought 350 students out for a Saturday of volunteer work, to the Praxis Dorm, where each resident does community-related work every week."

Campus Culture of Engagement

"We have so many students involved that you can ask any of them a question and if they can't answer it, they can refer you to a friend who can," Trinity undergrads tell us of the animated service scene here. Points out one, "It infiltrates all aspects of the campus, including the athletic arena, with our sports teams performing community-service activities together." The Trinity student body benefits from "committed and strong leaders; a variety of places to intern, volunteer, and work at; and a community-service office that is a great resource and offers places to volunteer according to your needs and wants." Students also cite the service dorm Praxis as a great asset.

Connecting Service with the Classroom

Trinity's Community Learning Initiative (CLI) "currently offers 30 to 35 community-learning courses a year, spanning almost all of our 20 departments and eight programs. One-third of our current faculty have taught one or more such courses. The courses are not required, but 50 to 60 percent of graduating seniors have taken one or more of them. Few colleges and universities offer this broad exposure," and "a Community-Action minor was created in 2000." CLI has also underwritten "several innovative community projects involving Trinity faculty and students with community in academically based cooperative experiences, such as creating an outdoor mural, exhibiting in an art gallery, and training middle-school students to build fire-fighting robots." Students brag that "because of Trinity's location in a city and its close proximity to suburbs, service-learning and civic engagement can look like whatever the student wants. The school is very open, flexible, and helpful in finding opportunities for civic engagement and service learning that really fit the student's wants and needs. Anything is honestly possible, and great strides will be taken by all of Trinity's staff to help a student accomplish her goals." Notes one undergrad, "In and outside the classroom, Trinity students constantly involve themselves with the community. Hartford Hospital, the Institute for Living, the Capitol building, various newspapers, and radio stations are just around the block!"

Impact on Community and Students

Trinity "has more than 200 community partnerships. This large number comes from the fact that so many different parts of our campus have relationships in the city. They include faculty and staff service on community boards, long-standing partnerships with groups in community-learning classes, community groups that have welcomed academic interns for decades, advocacy groups that collaborate with our Center for Neighborhoods, and local organizations that work with our Office of Community and Institutional Relations." Partnerships have been forged "in the government and corporate sectors, the arts community, the public school system, social service organizations, neighborhood advocacy groups, tenant organizations, social advocacy groups, refugee groups, health organizations, and more."

Perhaps most prominent among these partnerships is the Educational Studies Program at Trinity and schools in the Learning Corridor and elsewhere in Hartford, through which "students spend time assisting teachers in Learning Corridor classrooms, volunteer time as mentors for local youth in after-school and weekend mentoring programs, and participate with Trinity professors in research projects on magnet-school history and the effects of magnet schools on attitudes about racial diversity."

Another of Trinity's large community-centered operations is the Hartford Studies Project (HSP), which "documents, researches, and communicates the history of Hartford to Trinity students, the College community, Hartford residents, and the broader public. Faculty in Hartford Studies teach classes and coordinate research with a focus on Hartford's history, including classes on issues such as race, immigration, culture, labor, and local politics. HSP makes research resources available to students and faculty, and provides guidance on research projects both in the College community and in the city and region."

Yet another impressive project involves the Trinity Center for Neighborhoods (TCN), which "works with community groups in Hartford and specializes in community organizing and advocacy, particularly in the areas of health care and neighborhood issues. TCN works with students by providing internship opportunities for students eager to work with nonprofit community organizations, supervising students in independent study projects related to urban or health topics, and providing courses and training in the field of community organizing."

Student Financial Support for Service

Trinity College does not award scholarships in the public-service/community area. However, it does offer service awards at its Honors Day ceremony at the end of the school year and an endowment supports student and/or faculty projects with the surrounding community. Off-campus work-study assignments to non-profit organizations are available to work-study eligible undergraduates, and teaching assistantships are available to students in community-learning courses.

SELECTIVITY

# of applicants	5,510
% of applicants accepted	36
% of acceptees attending	28
# accepting a place on wait list	1,377
% admitted from wait list	1

FRESHMAN PROFILE

Range SAT Verbal	590-700
Range SAT Math	620-710
Range ACT Composite	25-29
Minimum Paper TOEFL	550
Minimum Computer TOEFL	210
% graduated top 10% of class	51
% graduated top 25% of class	81
% graduated top 50% of class	95

DEADLINES

Regular admission	1/15
Regular notification by	4/1
Nonfall registration?	no

FINANCIAL FACTS

Annual tuition	$28,740
Room and board	$7,810
Books and supplies	$850
Required fees	$1,490
% frosh rec. need-based scholarship or grant aid	43
% UG rec. need-based scholarship or grant aid	45
% frosh rec. need-based self-help aid	37
% UG rec. need-based self-help aid	38

TUFTS UNIVERSITY

BENDETSON HALL, MEDFORD, MA 02155

ADMISSIONS: 617-627-3170 • **FAX:** 617-627-3860 • **FINANCIAL AID:** 617-627-2000

E-MAIL: ADMISSIONS.INQUIRY@ASE.TUFTS.EDU • **WEBSITE:** WWW.TUFTS.EDU

CAMPUS LIFE

Type of school	private
Environment	village

STUDENTS

Total undergrad enrollment	4,888
% male/female	47/53
% from out of state	74
% from public high school	60
% live on campus	75
% African American	7
% Asian	13
% Caucasian	56
% Hispanic	8
% international	6
# of countries represented	65

ACADEMICS

Calendar	semester
Student/faculty ratio	10:1
% profs teaching UG courses	100
% classes taught by TAs	1
Most common reg class size	<10

MOST POPULAR MAJORS
economics
English language and literature
international relations and affairs

Getting Involved

If you're searching for civic ambition, Tufts University might be the place for you. At the forefront of service at Tufts University is the school's innovative and well-funded University College of Citizenship and Public Service, "a university-wide initiative to make the values and skills of active citizenship a hallmark of a Tufts University education." Launched in 1999 with a $10 million grant from the founder of eBay, the University College aims to "catalyze civic engagement and community building by identifying, generating, and supporting Tufts students, faculty, staff and alumni, and community partners who develop creative, effective approaches to active citizenship at the university and in communities around the world." In reviewing the program's first five years, the Boston Globe reported that "some believe [the University College] is the most ambitious attempt by any research university to make public service part of its core academic mission."

Tufts engages in numerous education outreach programs directed toward Boston's underprivileged population. The EPIIC (Education for Public Inquiry and International Citizenship) seeks "to educate individuals both within and outside the Tufts community to better understand and assume their responsibilities as global citizens." The Tufts Literacy Corps encompasses several programs, including reading, writing, and mathematics tutoring; book clubs; poetry writing workshops; and a book-distribution program. Students interested in other types of volunteer work may utilize the Leonard Carmichael Society, "a completely student-run volunteer organization with over 800 students participating in both one-day and long-term, sustained programs in the community." The Leonard Carmichael Society "boasts over 20 different service groups, such as Food Rescue, Habitat for Humanity, Shelters, Big Brothers, Kid's Day, UNICEF, Tutoring, AIDS Outreach, Blood Drives, and Cancer Outreach."

Campus Culture of Engagement

"The main strength of service at Tufts is the student body," undergrads here opine. "Tufts students are more engaged, both politically and in social service, than I have ever seen at any other university. Almost every student participates in some sort of community service or political action. Not only do they participate, but everyone has a passion for the issues that they are involved in, whether it be staying up all night for cancer, fasting to raise awareness about world hunger, volunteering once a week at a low-income preschool, or being completely involved in multiple positive organizations." Adds another student, "This is a university where people do not have to be involved in the Greek system to be doing community service on a regular basis. The community service organization here is the biggest club on campus, which really tells you something about the nature of the students here and the University itself."

Politically, Tufts is "mostly liberal, although there is some space for other views." Undergrads report that "the school is host to many rallies a year for women's rights, janitors' rights, for and against the war in Iraq, for Sudan," and plenty of others.

Connecting Service with the Classroom

"Departments as diverse as Environmental Engineering and Child Development include active citizenship components," Tufts reports, noting that "there is a wide range of opportunities for students that includes research, advocacy, activism, and service." An example of such coursework was offered last year through Media and Communications Studies; the course, "Producing Television Programs for Social Change," was "taught by an Emmy-Award-winning former producer of Dateline; [it taught] students how to create actual video stories on social issues and includes camera work, editing, interview skills, production skills, and publicity."

Other service-learning opportunities include Education for Active Citizenship, "a course for freshman that provides skills training, civic dialogues, self-exploration, reflection, and opportunities for change." There's also Peace and Justice Studies, which "provides an interdisciplinary structure for examining the obstacles, conditions, and paths to achieving a just global peace. The program brings intellectual and experiential inquiry to the fundamental interrelationship of peace and justice." And there's also Community Health, an interdisciplinary program that "includes the study of Anthropology, Medicine, History, Sociology, Psychology, Economics, Ethics, Political Science, Public Health, and Biology as they affect our understanding of communities' strategies to promote health and cope with disease." Sums up one student, "There are many classes with a focus on public service and active citizenship. These amazing classes are well publicized and give students the opportunity to learn about activism in an academic and practical manner."

Impact on Community and Students

Boston and its surrounding areas provide numerous opportunities for Tufts to impact the community in a positive way. The school singles out several, among them "a partnership with the Mystic River Watershed Association (MyrWA) that is multi-faceted [and] includes student projects, faculty research, course-based learning, student internships, community events, and celebrations. Recent developments are students creating of a community-asset map of river access points for ten watershed communities, and the participation of key MyrWA staff in university dialogues on community partnerships."

The school also points to its Building Bridges Program, through which "students are working with key Chinatown community-based organizations to provide services while increasing student understanding of needs and issues. Through a course with Professor Jean Wu, students combine human services work with academic curriculum. Other Chinatown work includes public-health research such as asthma in Asian youth, assisting with research on bias and hate crimes, and serving as tutors in the Chinatown public school."

Student Financial Support for Service

"The University College of Citizenship and Public Service offers the Citizenship and Public Service Scholars Program; in the fall of freshman year, 20 students are selected to participate in a spring semester course called Education for Active Citizenship. Successful completion of this course allows students to apply to the Scholars Program. Scholars are given $6,000 scholarships per year for their sophomore, junior, and senior years. They are expected to complete long-term, sustainable projects, engage other students, and inspire others to become active citizens. The program offers Scholars funding for projects, weekly meetings, training workshops, retreats, and advising."

SELECTIVITY

# of applicants	14,728
% of applicants accepted	27
% of acceptees attending	32

FRESHMAN PROFILE

Range SAT Verbal	640-730
Range SAT Math	650-740
Range ACT Composite	27-32
Minimum Paper TOEFL	200
Minimum Computer TOEFL	300
% graduated top 10% of class	74
% graduated top 25% of class	94
% graduated top 50% of class	99

DEADLINES

Regular admission	1/1
Regular notification by	4/1
Nonfall registration?	no

FINANCIAL FACTS

Annual tuition	$28,859
Room and board	$8,640
Books and supplies	$800
Required fees	$734
% frosh rec. need-based scholarship or grant aid	36
% UG rec. need-based scholarship or grant aid	37
% frosh rec. need-based self-help aid	34
% UG rec. need-based self-help aid	37
% frosh rec. any financial aid	39
% UG rec. any financial aid	40

TULANE UNIVERSITY

6823 St. Charles Avenue, New Orleans, LA 70118

Admissions: 504-865-5731 • **Fax:** 504-862-8715 • **Financial Aid:** 504-865-5723

E-mail: UNDERGRAD.ADMISSION@TULANE.EDU • **Website:** WWW.TULANE.EDU

CAMPUS LIFE

Type of school	private
Environment	town

STUDENTS

Total undergrad enrollment	7,952
% male/female	47/53
% from out of state	70
% live on campus	65
% African American	8
% Asian	3
% Caucasian	56
% Hispanic	3
% international	2
# of countries represented	100

ACADEMICS

Calendar	quarter
Student/faculty ratio	9:1
% classes taught by TAs	0

MOST POPULAR MAJORS

business/commerce
engineering
social sciences

Getting Involved

Tulane administrators recognize their university's unique role as a leading institution in a major metropolis, telling us that "New Orleans is a dynamic, interesting, culturally rich city with a dramatic history, a unique blend of cultures, and also, with deep and challenging problems experienced by a population characterized by poverty and low education levels. Tulane University is actively involved with many community agencies, through service-learning and volunteer activities, program-development efforts, and research. Thus, there are many opportunities for students to become involved with the community in meaningful and productive ways." There's service-learning, for one, as well as the doings of the student-run Community Action Council of Tulane University Students (CACTUS), which coordinates volunteer and service activity at Tulane. There are also one-day events such as Outreach Tulane, which in 2003 saw over 400 students, faculty, and staff volunteer to serve lunch at homeless shelters, clean public facilities, landscape a run-down cemetery, paint and repair public schools, and work at an animal shelter.

Students interested in service are advised to attend an activities fair in the fall where "every club has a booth with brochures; it is at this time students can choose to sign up to be on an activity's electronic mailing list." In addition, "we have chalked sidewalks and kiosks advertising events. The university sends out a daily e-mail as well."

Campus Culture of Engagement

"Tulane has a lot of opportunities for civic engagement, service, and activism," writes one student, adding that "there are a lot of people (faculty, students, and staff) who are very passionate about their work and love getting new students involved." Students praise the service-learning office, which "helps to acquaint students with the community. They have bookcases full of books and brochures about what students can do to get involved in the community and ways to help students in their goals at their community-service learning sites. They also offer rap sessions where students can ask questions and give advice to other students." For those who seek non-credit-bearing volunteer work, Tulane is affiliated with "hundreds of community-action programs within the community and continues to expand each year with new organizations." Sums up one undergrad, "There are many opportunities for civic engagement offered on campus throughout the year that last for long and short periods of time, allowing for greater collaborative efforts that fit into the student's schedules and interests."

Connecting Service with the Classroom

Service-learning has really taken off at Tulane in the past three years, during which more than 50 service-learning courses have been offered to more than 800 participating students annually. The school reports that "service-learning courses [are] offered by faculty from 14 departments in the Liberal Arts and Sciences (LAS), as well as by faculty in the Business School, the School of Engineering, and the Graduate School. LAS departments and programs offering service-learning include African and African Diaspora Studies, Biology, Communication, Education, English, Latin American Studies, Linguistics, Music, Political Science, Psychology, Sociology, Spanish, Theater and Dance, and Women's Studies." In addition, "during 2002-2003, five departments offered internships administered through the Office of Service-Learning. 74 students completed internships: 38 students did their internships at nonprofits, 14 were in education settings, nine in government agencies, ten in health settings, and three worked in media-related sites."

Tulane's Office of Service-Learning (OSL) runs the show, seeking "to engage faculty members and students in an endeavor that combines community service with academic learning. OSL Program Coordinators work closely with faculty and community site representatives from the beginning of planning for an academic course to the reporting of final grades. Students are carefully oriented to each community site's needs and goals, and projects are monitored closely by the Program Coordinators."

Especially worthy of note is the partnership between the Urban Conservancy (UC) and the Office of Service Learning (OSL), which places students in semester-long service assignments. In the past, the project has resulted in "presentations that promote smart growth development and a Stay Local! campaign to support local small businesses. Together, they developed a survey and inventoried local small businesses along commercial corridors in four mixed-use neighborhoods."

Impact on Community and Students

Tulane impacts its surrounding community through its many service-learning projects. The school tells us that "community sites working with the service-learning program include schools, hospitals, environmental-activism agencies, city government offices, and a range of social-service agencies. During the spring of 2004, for example, Tulane students [carried] out service-learning activities in 51 sites. These sites include public schools serving families living in public housing in the city, a community center serving a neighborhood of low-income families, medical facilities and support programs for persons with AIDS/HIV," and local schools, served through the partnership of Tulane Upward Bound and the Tulane Service Learning program.

Through both volunteer work and service-learning, students also participate in "efforts to support local small businesses, organizations dealing with environmental matters, organizations providing job training, savings incentives, legal assistance, and community development efforts for low-income persons, non-discriminatory practices in housing, efforts to prevent violence against women; groups supporting the arts, and organizations aiming to preserve and further develop the unique cultural heritage of New Orleans."

Student Financial Support for Service

School administrators inform us that "Tulane does not offer scholarships for community/public service, but a large number of scholarships are awarded to students, with approximately 75 percent of enrolled freshmen receiving some form of financial aid." In addition, "Tulane's Student Employment Office awards almost 10 percent of federal work-study grants to community-based work study. This rate is higher than the 7 percent that is required by federal regulations. These students work in area schools and nonprofits and contribute to the functioning of the service-learning program."

SELECTIVITY

# of applicants	17,572
% of applicants accepted	45
% of acceptees attending	21
# accepting a place on wait list	2,337

FRESHMAN PROFILE

Range SAT Verbal	628-725
Range SAT Math	603-700
Range ACT Composite	28-32
Minimum Paper TOEFL	550
Minimum Computer TOEFL	213
Average HS GPA	3.60
% graduated top 10% of class	59
% graduated top 25% of class	75
% graduated top 50% of class	100

DEADLINES

Regular admission	1/15
Regular notification by	4/15
Nonfall registration?	no

FINANCIAL FACTS

Annual tuition	$28,900
Room and board	$7,925
Books and supplies	$800
Required fees	$2,310
% frosh rec. need-based scholarship or grant aid	47
% UG rec. need-based scholarship or grant aid	39
% frosh rec. need-based self-help aid	29
% UG rec. need-based self-help aid	29
% frosh rec. any financial aid	92
% UG rec. any financial aid	91

UNIVERSITY OF ALASKA ANCHORAGE

3211 PROVIDENCE DRIVE, ANCHORAGE, AK 99508-8046

ADMISSIONS: 907-786-1480 • **FAX:** 907-786-4888 • **FINANCIAL AID:** 907-786-1586

E-MAIL: ENROLL@UAA.ALASKA.EDU • **WEBSITE:** WWW.UAA.ALASKA.EDU

CAMPUS LIFE

Type of school	public
Environment	town

STUDENTS

Total undergrad enrollment	9,341
% male/female	37/63
% from out of state	5
% from public high school	95
% live on campus	25
% African American	4
% Asian	5
% Caucasian	70
% Hispanic	4
% Native American	10
% international	2
# of countries represented	35

ACADEMICS

Calendar	semester
Student/faculty ratio	14:1
% profs teaching UG courses	94
% classes taught by TAs	0
Most common lab size	20-29
Most common reg class size	10-19

Getting Involved

The University of Alaska Anchorage offers exceptional urban and outdoor service opportunities to its many public-minded students. As the school points out, "by participating in UAA clubs, service projects, and academic-university partnerships, students can raise awareness, advocate for their causes, and promote creativity through their learning. With its academic and service leadership resources, proximity to the Alaskan wilderness, and strong programs (Nursing and Public Health, Engineering Management, Social Work, Biological Science, Environment and Natural Resources, Aviation, and Psychology), UAA is a college with opportunities for active learning and service."

Academic service finds its home at the Center for Community Engagement and Learning at UAA. This office "stands ready to help students create even more fruitful and lasting relationships with community partners and University faculty" by stimulating "opportunities for engaged learning so that students can serve as catalysts of social change." Students keep apprised of service activity "mostly through flyers and the school newspaper *The Northern Light*," e-mail announcements, bulletin boards, and their professors, who are "very instrumental in presenting service-learning opportunities."

Campus Culture of Engagement

UAA is "unlike many schools," undergraduates here tell us, because "many students have lives that are already integrated into the community. Most are from the local community, have been raised in the area, have family in the community, and take pride in and care about the special place they live in." As a result, "UAA has a very active student body and campus club roster. There is something for every person who wishes to become involved in extra activities and develop professional experience." It's a good thing that students are so dedicated, because Anchorage, "like many large cities, has many needs. Universities bring young people with new ideas and passion for change to many of these problems. UAA has benefited by being the central crossroads for all of Alaska's varying cultures."

Connecting Service with the Classroom

"UAA is recognized as a statewide center of excellence in community-based research, engaged learning, and public service," the school reports, pointing out that "our mission integrates community service with research and instructional programs by increasing partnerships with Alaska Native corporations and social service agencies, and fostering stronger communities." The school offers "approximately 35 service-learning courses reaching over 600 students each academic year. Service-learning courses are found across nearly all schools and colleges," including in the departments of Biological Sciences, Philosophy, Social Work, Sociology, Environmental Science, Music, Special Education, Psychology, Justice, Computer Information and Office Systems, and the Honors Program.

Prominent among the school's service-learning options is the Chester Creek Watershed Project, "a unique collaboration of 23 courses, predominately in the natural sciences, that provides students an opportunity to provide community service while learning hands-on applications for promoting environmental sustainability. Faculty and students have been collecting baseline water-quality data from a popular urban stream, Chester Creek, to be compiled into a database, accessible by the community."

UAA's Alaska Native Science and Engineering Program (ANSEP) teams Alaska Native students with professionals "from their first indication of an interest in science or engineering. ANSEP is aimed at effecting a systemic change in the hiring patterns of Alaska Natives in the professions [through] a comprehensive suite of high-school outreach, recruitment, university retention, and placement strategies designed to help students fulfill their potential in college, sustain their interest in science, technology, engineering, and math, and develop an interest in graduate study. According to the National Science Foundation, the national average retention rate for Native Americans in engineering programs is 27 percent. This program's life retention rate is 73 percent."

Students love all the opportunities available here. Says one, "I have learned more through my applied service-learning projects than I ever could have through academic learning alone. I have been able to apply abstract theoretical concepts to actual community situations. I have learned to step outside of my comfort zone and contact individuals in the community. And I have learned invaluable lessons in leadership and team participation."

Impact on Community and Students

Each year, "UAA connects with over 150 community organizations. A sample of our partnerships includes community-based organizations (the Nature Conservancy of Alaska), businesses and business organizations (HiTech Alaska), cultural groups (Alaska Humanities Forum), museums, schools, health-care centers (Alaska Regional Hospital, Southcentral Foundation's Traditional Healing Program), tribal councils or governments (Cook Inlet Tribal Council), and public agencies (Alaska Department of Environmental Conservation)."

Among the university's high-impact endeavors is the Community Health Nursing program, which presents "Healthy Choices Carnivals" to local elementary schools. Through these events, "UAA Nursing students gain an important presence and visibility within the schools [and] provide excellent role modeling and a true glimpse into the role of nurses working in the community with a population at risk. This community partnership has evolved into a true win-win situation for all involved."

Student Financial Support for Service

The university reports that "UAA's Center for Community Engagement and Learning offers tuition waivers to students to play key roles in the development and delivery of community-based learning and research." These students "assist faculty in community-based projects, community partnership development, and student leadership in disciplinary-based community engagement." In addition, the Union of Students at UAA (USUAA) offers ten $1,000 Leadership Scholarships per year; the "criteria for these scholarships include community and public service, but eligible students must also demonstrate leadership involvement and possess a 2.0 cumulative GPA."

SELECTIVITY

# of applicants	2,516
% of applicants accepted	76
% of acceptees attending	76

FRESHMAN PROFILE

Range SAT Verbal	440-570
Range SAT Math	450-570
Range ACT Composite	18-24
Minimum Paper TOEFL	450
Average HS GPA	2.92
% graduated top 10% of class	9
% graduated top 25% of class	27
% graduated top 50% of class	57

DEADLINES

Regular admission	8/1
Nonfall registration?	yes

FINANCIAL FACTS

Annual in-state tuition	$3,232
Annual out-of-state tuition	$8,962
Room and board	$6,430
Books and supplies	$923
Required fees	$352

UNIVERSITY OF CALIFORNIA—BERKELEY

OFFICE OF UNDERGRADUATE ADMISSIONS, 110 SPROUL HALL #5800, BERKELEY, CA 94720-5800

ADMISSIONS: 510-642-3175 • **FAX:** 510-642-7333 • **FINANCIAL AID:** 510-642-6442

E-MAIL: OUARS@UCLINK.BERKELEY.EDU • **WEBSITE:** WWW.BERKELEY.EDU

CAMPUS LIFE

Type of school	public
Environment	town

STUDENTS

Total undergrad enrollment	23,205
% male/female	46/54
% from out of state	6
% from public high school	85
% live on campus	35
% African American	4
% Asian	41
% Caucasian	30
% Hispanic	11
% Native American	1
% international	3

ACADEMICS

Calendar	semester
Student/faculty ratio	17:1
% profs teaching UG courses	100
% classes taught by TAs	0
Most common lab size	10-19
Most common reg class size	20-29

MOST POPULAR MAJORS
computer engineering
English language and literature
political science and government

Getting Involved

University of California—Berkeley has a justly earned reputation for its students' dedication to service and activism, and the university maintains a plethora of offices to serve this community. At the top of the list is the Cal Corps Public Service Center, dedicated to "coordinating a variety of activities and programs for students, faculty, and staff by providing training, advising, and support. The center is home to a number of programs that connect students and the campus with their communities in meaningful ways, including Alternative Breaks, a program that allows students to create and lead their peers on co-curricular service immersion trips, and Cal in Berkeley, an internship program that places undergraduates with Berkeley and Oakland government and nonprofit organizations." Students tell us that Cal Corps' website is the best place to look for service opportunities (they also rely on Calapalooza, a recruiting event held during Welcome Week, and the activists in Sproul Plaza "who set up tables and pass out fliers every day").

Also serving Berkeley's socially conscious undergrads are the Center for Educational Outreach, which "is charged with improving academic preparation and expanding educational opportunities for middle school, high school, and community college students" in the region; the Service Learning Research and Development Center; and the Center on Politics at UC Berkeley's Institute of Governmental Studies, which "brings together students, faculty, politicians, activists, and policymakers on a nonpartisan basis to stimulate and nurture their interest and participation in politics and public service and to promote better understanding and cooperation between the campus and the world of politics, government, and public affairs."

Campus Culture of Engagement

"There are over 50 student groups that do work directly in the community" at UC Berkeley among the "over 600 registered student groups" on campus. "Most students are engaged in community activities," students report, adding that "almost all student groups on campus have a community-service component." Observes one student, "The great thing about the [service opportunities here] is that many of them are student-run, giving students the hands-on experience of getting things done themselves." And get things done they do; "our school also won a Rock the Vote contest for registering the most voters before the 2002 elections," boasts one student.

Many UC Berkeley groups "specifically focus on engaging students in electoral politics" and political causes. Politics is huge here; asked what provokes controversy in and around campus, one student responded, "Everything. This is Berkeley, after all-affirmative action, abortion rights, Israel-Palestine, our chancellor re-landscaping the middle of campus in the middle of the year, 'standards of community'-this list could go on for pages." As one student put it: "Berkeley is activism, period!!" CalPIRG is among the biggest political players on campus along with the Cal Berkeley Democrats and the Berkeley College Republicans, we're told, but there are tons of organizations covering nearly every issue and running the ideological gamut from far left to far right (the majority of students, it should be noted, lean well to the left of center).

Connecting Service with the Classroom

UC Berkeley administrators point out that "as part of the campus's recent accreditation review by the Western Association of Schools and Colleges (WASC), service-learning was identified as a key component for advancing teaching and learning initiatives on the campus." These initiatives manifest themselves in "approximately 150 service-learning courses in 45 departments [at the university]. It is estimated that approximately 2,800 students participate in service-learning courses each year." The school elaborates that "the campus's service-learning faculty policy committee has designated three types of service-learning courses: service-based internships (culminating courses usually offered in graduate programs), academic service-learning (discipline-based courses that count towards a students' major), and co-curricular service-learning (service-based courses for which students receive credit for an affiliated learning component; typically these are elective courses that do not count towards a students' major).

Educational outreach is a major component of UC Berkeley's service-learning courses. Undergraduates in such classes visit local schools to teach and tutor in a wide range of subjects. Governmental and nonprofit agencies and hospitals also provide key venues for service-learning.

Impact on Community and Students

UC Berkeley has "over 200 formalized partnerships with the community," partnering with "nonprofit agencies that serve a wide variety of community needs, as well as with local school districts, community development agencies, and government offices." These include Cal in Berkeley, "a year-long internship program for students in the local city department, and school district administrative offices." Cal in Berkeley "offers interns an opportunity to be involved in broad policy projects that will meaningfully address community needs, while taking a related seminar course. Cal in Berkeley is among a small group of partnerships recognized by Berkeley's chancellor as an outstanding example of the University's work with the community-these 'University-Community Partnership Awards' are given out each fall."

Students feel that their work beyond campus "contributes to a more just and caring society, the kind we ought to be living in. Contrary to the rampant stories of 'youth apathy' and a cold and uncaring world, students, professors, staff, and community members are making a positive difference in the local communities where they serve." Students benefit, too; in addition to "offering an inside perspective on what's happening in other parts of the community that we might not otherwise know" and "putting a face on abstract issues," outreach work helps "to make the school smaller and our experience more worthwhile by teaching us what cannot be learned in large lecture halls."

Student Financial Support for Service

UC Berkeley offers "approximately 200 AmeriCorps positions every year for students are interested in being involved in public service; students in these positions receive $1,000 to support their education for 300 hours of service."

SELECTIVITY

# of applicants	36,580
% of applicants accepted	25

FRESHMAN PROFILE

Range SAT Verbal	580–710
Range SAT Math	620–740
Minimum Paper TOEFL	550
Minimum Computer TOEFL	213
Average HS GPA	3.93
% graduated top 10% of class	98
% graduated top 25% of class	100
% graduated top 50% of class	100

DEADLINES

Regular admission	11/30
Regular notification by	Decisions available on website by 3/31
Nonfall registration?	yes

FINANCIAL FACTS

Annual in-state tuition	N/A
Annual out-of-state tuition	$23,686
Room and board	$11,630
Books and supplies	$1,240
Required fees	$5,956
% frosh rec. need-based scholarship or grant aid	50
% UG rec. need-based scholarship or grant aid	49
% frosh rec. need-based self-help aid	39
% UG rec. need-based self-help aid	38

UNIVERSITY OF CALIFORNIA—LOS ANGELES

405 HILGARD AVENUE, BOX 951436, LOS ANGELES, CA 90095-1436

ADMISSIONS: 310-825-3101 • **FAX:** 310-206-1206 • **FINANCIAL AID:** 310-206-0400

E-MAIL: UGADM@SAONET.UCLA.EDU • **WEBSITE:** WWW.UCLA.EDU

CAMPUS LIFE

Type of school	public
Environment	town

STUDENTS

Total undergrad enrollment	24,946
% male/female	43/57
% from out of state	5
% from public high school	80
% live on campus	35
# of countries represented	132

ACADEMICS

Calendar	semester
Most common lab size	20-29
Most common reg class size	20-29

MOST POPULAR MAJORS

economics
political science and government
psychology

Getting Involved

"There are three major units that support civic engagement at UCLA," the school reports: "The UCLA Center for Community Partnerships, which is the administrative home of the Chancellor's new UCLA in LA initiative; the Center for Community Learning, an educational unit under the Vice Provost for Undergraduate Education; and several units under the sponsorship of the Student Affairs Organization." The goal of the Center for Community Partnerships, administrators add, "is to nurture development partnerships between community groups and UCLA that produce joint efforts to improve the quality of life for area residents." The Center for Community Learning "is part of our Undergraduate Education Initiative program. The mission of this Center is to engage UCLA undergraduates, faculty, and community partners in programs that integrate teaching, research, and service. In collaboration with academic departments, the Center offers UCLA undergraduates the opportunity to participate in a variety of structured and rigorous academic courses that link theory and practice."

Finally, the Student Affairs Organization (SAO) "supports and oversees a wide range of offices and programs that promote students' community service and volunteerism outside the academic arena." The SAO oversees the Center for Student Programming, which "coordinates opportunities for involvement throughout the campus and the greater Los Angeles Community," and the Community Programs Office, which "administers over 25 student-initiated community service projects, six retention projects, and seven outreach projects." Undergrads here agree that "there are multiple centers where a student can find out about civic engagement, from established centers to student organizations to conferences."

Campus Culture of Engagement

"The sheer number of campus organizations on campus is our greatest strength," students tell us. "That and the enthusiasm from organizers and volunteers." Undergrads appreciate that "many endeavors are completely student-run, making the efforts an empowering process." Writes one, "Outreach efforts are very passionate primarily because students, especially students of color and working-class students, know the most and care the most about making UCLA and other higher-education campuses accessible to all."

Because "Los Angeles is a large and diverse city, civic-engagement efforts have a great population to work with, and hence many different types of opportunities are presented." As one student puts it, "From organizing a rally during the Democratic National Convention in 2000 to working with homeless persons in finding shelters to having dance marathons to fundraise for children who have cancer, there are multiple ways to get involved."

Connecting Service with the Classroom

UCLA points out that its Center for Community Learning is "a unique organization among research universities, offering students 'one-stop shopping' for courses and programs that include both meaningful work in the community and the opportunity to earn academic credit." Many here opt for participation in the Early Academic Outreach Program, "one of many co-curricular opportunities students have to help students prepare for college, partnering with community and faith-based organizations. CBOP program staff members teach the undergrads, the undergrads teach the pre-college students, and they, in return, will teach younger students."

UCLA's Community Based Research Institute offers Immigration Issues in Los Angeles, "a unique, intensive, interdisciplinary program that includes two concurrent upper-division courses in Honors and Sociology. Students learn research methods while conducting a piece of community-based research that has been commissioned by one of six nonprofits that work full-time on immigration issues. Months before the courses begin, community partners meet with faculty from the Center for Community Learning to come up with a question they need to have answered; these become the students' research questions." The resulting research "is used in real-world applications, empowering [students] to deliver useful and high-quality research."

In addition to these options, "UCLA offers a wide range of service-learning courses for everyone from first-year students to graduating seniors. These include courses for first-year students in Gerontology and in Labor Issues. The campus also has service-learning courses in Social Welfare, Chicana/o Studies, Spanish and Portuguese, Russian, Engineering, Statistics, Psychology, Asian American Studies, Sociology, Community Health Science, and the Honors Collegium. Nearly 1,000 students enrolled in the 2003-2004 academic year, with new courses already planned that will significantly increase that number in the future."

Impact on Community and Students

"Prospective students should be aware that UCLA has a long history of maintaining community service projects that are entirely student-run," administrators here report. "For example, the 52 projects that are funded by the student-run Community Activities Committee (CAC) involve thousands of undergraduates and provide various community services to tens of thousands of people in greater Los Angeles. CAC's service recipients include incarcerated youth, homeless people, people living in poverty, children striving to learn in traditionally under-represented socio-economic communities, day laborers, and many more."

The school also tells us that "UCLA's Center for Community Learning partners with nonprofit and governmental organizations for service-learning courses and the research institutes. The Center has approximately 500 partners, and roughly 3,000 students participate in programs through the Center for Community Learning each year." The UCLA BruinCorps "has 30 engaged community partnerships with nonprofit organizations, such as child-development centers, elementary schools, middle schools, community-based organizations, and faith-based organizations."

Student Financial Support for Service

UCLA rewards service-oriented students through its various AmeriCorps programs, which "offer students educational vouchers upon completion of their service commitment in return for their work in the communities of Los Angeles. Students in these programs can work in a variety of settings such as educational institutions, including tutoring and mentoring programs in schools and after-school programs, in self-help legal clinics and family law centers, or in programs that focus on health care and related issues. All provide service scholarships that can be used for a student's education, including the costs of tuition or books."

SELECTIVITY

# of applicants	43,199
% of applicants accepted	23
% of acceptees attending	37

FRESHMAN PROFILE

Range SAT Verbal	570-690
Range SAT Math	610-720
Range ACT Composite	24-30
Minimum Paper TOEFL	550
Minimum Computer TOEFL	220
Average HS GPA	3.12
% graduated top 10% of class	97
% graduated top 50% of class	100

DEADLINES

Regular admission	11/30
Regular notification by	rolling
Nonfall registration?	no

UNIVERSITY OF COLORADO—BOULDER

552 UCB, BOULDER, CO 80309-0552

ADMISSIONS: 303-492-6301 • FAX: 303-492-7115 • FINANCIAL AID: 303-492-5091

E-MAIL: APPLY@COLORADO.EDU • WEBSITE: WWW.COLORADO.EDU

CAMPUS LIFE

Type of school	public
Environment	village

STUDENTS

Total undergrad	
enrollment	25,942
% male/female	52/48
% from out of state	33
% live on campus	23
% African American	2
% Asian	6
% Caucasian	77
% Hispanic	6
% Native American	1
% international	1
# of countries represented	104

ACADEMICS

Calendar	semester
% profs teaching	
UG courses	90
% classes taught by TAs	16
Most common lab size	20-29
Most common	
reg class size	20-29

MOST POPULAR MAJORS

English language and literature
journalism
psychology

Getting Involved

University of Colorado at Boulder offers a number of university- and student-run facilities for the service-minded. Those seeking to incorporate service into their curricula should take note of the Service-Learning Center, which "awards small grants for course development and implementation to faculty and provides support and consultation for any instructor on campus wishing to incorporate service learning." The center also administers the AmeriCorps Education Award Program.

Students should also look into the Puksta Scholars Program, "a premier University of Colorado scholarship program for undergraduate students who have a deep commitment to civic engagement, [and] who demonstrate strong academic goals and want to further their knowledge and skills. Each scholar is provided a substantial scholarship and must develop a year-long intensive civic-engagement project either individually or with a small group." Or they might wish to consider the innovative Farrand Residential Academic Program, "a coeducational liberal arts program with approximately 400 first- and second-year students who share a living-learning environment. Farrand emphasizes service-learning classes which integrate academic study with volunteer work for communities in need."

For those who simply want to add service to their extracurricular rosters, the student-run Volunteer Clearing House "works to link up interested students with volunteer programs that best fits their individual interests and needs. Among its programs [are] Best Buddies of America, designed to promote friendships between university students and persons with developmental disabilities; Service Days, sending students to work in community activities; and Alternative Breaks, placing teams of students in week-long service projects during spring and winter recesses." Other student-centered service agencies include Engineers Without Borders, a group "dedicated to helping disadvantaged communities improve their quality of life through implementation of environmentally and economically sustainable engineering projects" that was founded at CU.

Campus Culture of Engagement

CU is a huge campus, so it plays host to activists across a wide swath of interests. Students tell us that "we have many political groups that promote involvement in politics and civic activities," "the biggest student-run environmental center in the nation (and it rocks!)," a "great service-learning major," and a student government that "controls the most amount of money of any student government in the nation." All told, "civic engagement is very encouraged and visible" here. Writes one undergrad, "CU is everywhere in Boulder. Using campus money, space, and programs, there are all kinds of events that take place."

Students tell us that "the best way is through the Buff Bulletin, an e-mail sent out to students every week. It tells about all the activities on campus that week. Summer Orientation is also a great place, as there is an activity fair to let students know about what to do on campus."

Connecting Service with the Classroom

CU offers "approximately 120 courses that focus on ethical and civic engagement" each year, noting that "while the national trend is for service-learning courses to cluster in the social sciences, CU Boulder is noteworthy for having a more equal distribution among sciences, humanities, and the law, business, and engineering schools as well." Students report that "there are service-learning practica as well as courses that offer a service-learning component."

Prominent among CU's service-learning opportunities is the two-year INVST Community Leadership Program, in which second-year students "design and implement year-long service-learning projects as organizing models for their lifetime endeavors." Participants "work in partnership with community-based organizations to identify community needs and fulfill relevant goals and objectives." A recent project "worked to increase awareness and dispel myths about sexual assault in Boulder County. In collaboration with the nonprofit Moving to End Sexual Assault (MESA), [students] created a six-week long art show with an opening performance that involved 32 visual and performing artists. Over 200 people attended the opening night, and approximately 5,000 viewed the exhibit during the time that it was displayed."

Impact on Community and Students

CU has "developed hundreds of community partnerships spanning a wide-range of nonprofit organizations. Our database at the Volunteer Clearing House includes over 400 listings." Administrators point out that "many of our community partnerships have been initiated through student involvement. Often students begin as volunteers individually, but then become so committed to a program that they establish mechanisms and programs to involve other students."

Successful outreach programs in 2003-2004 include the Spangler Elementary Homework Club and Books as Mentors Program, which "brings together CU School of Education students and faculty with local elementary school students and their teachers in an after-school academic environment. The program works to enhance homework skills and improve standardized test scores. It involves a literacy component that works to engage at-risk students in reading and writing both in school and at home, improve English proficiency of native Spanish-speaking students, and foster a greater sense of community in and around the school."

Among those going farther afield are the "exceptional" Engineers Without Borders, who "are committed to spending several months in other cultures, where they not only receive direct experience in applying their technical skills but also learn a great deal about the cultures themselves. The concept and organization have spread nationwide, with CU Boulder as its center."

Student Financial Support for Service

CU makes a number of service-related awards available to undergraduates. The President's Leadership Class, for example, offers 50 to 60 entering freshman a $2,000 to $9,000 merit scholarship; these students follow a "four-year curriculum of strong academic and experiential components designed to orient scholars to the theory and practice of leadership. Service-learning is an integral part of the program and is required for all students.

Also three $500 scholarships are awarded annually to entering freshmen, sophomores, or juniors who demonstrate commitment to community." Other awards are given by the Puksta Program (see above), the CU-Lead program, the INVST Community Leadership Program, and the AmeriCorps Education Award program.

SELECTIVITY

# of applicants	20,920
% of applicants accepted	80
% of acceptees attending	34
# accepting a place on wait list	1,007
% admitted from wait list	18

FRESHMAN PROFILE

Range SAT Verbal	530-630
Range SAT Math	550-650
Range ACT Composite	23-28
Minimum Paper TOEFL	500
Minimum Computer TOEFL	173
Average HS GPA	3.52
% graduated top 10% of class	24
% graduated top 25% of class	57
% graduated top 50% of class	91

DEADLINES

Regular admission	1/15
Regular notification by	rolling
Nonfall registration?	yes

FINANCIAL FACTS

Annual in-state tuition	N/A
Annual out-of-state tuition	$19,508
Room and board	$6,754
Books and supplies	$1,163
Required fees	$828
% frosh rec. need-based scholarship or grant aid	19
% UG rec. need-based scholarship or grant aid	19
% frosh rec. need-based self-help aid	23
% UG rec. need-based self-help aid	25
% frosh rec. any financial aid	61
% UG rec. any financial aid	51

UNIVERSITY OF KANSAS

OFFICE OF ADMISSIONS AND SCHOLARSHIPS, 1502 IOWA STREET, LAWRENCE, KS 66045

ADMISSIONS: 785-864-3911 • **FAX:** 785-864-5017 • **FINANCIAL AID:** 785-864-4700

E-MAIL: ADM@KU.EDU • **WEBSITE:** WWW.KU.EDU

CAMPUS LIFE

Type of school	public
Environment	town

STUDENTS

Total undergrad enrollment	20,766
% male/female	48/52
% from out of state	24
% live on campus	23
% African American	3
% Asian	4
% Caucasian	84
% Hispanic	3
% Native American	1
% international	3
# of countries represented	113

ACADEMICS

Calendar	semester
Student/faculty ratio	15:1
% profs teaching UG courses	98
% classes taught by TAs	20
Most common lab size	<10
Most common reg class size	10-19

MOST POPULAR MAJORS

business administration/management
journalism
speech and rhetorical studies

Getting Involved

When the University of Kansas' Jayhawks want to know about service opportunities, they turn first to the Center for Community Outreach (CCO) for guidance. This "student-run, student-funded organization comprised of 14 volunteer programs and partnerships" functions as a "referral agency for community and national service organizations, and provides group or one-time opportunities for KU Students." The organization serves "more than 7,000 students annually" who provide "over 31,000 hours in the community."

All told, "about one-third of the students who come to KU participate in some sort of service or service-learning experience. This happens through student groups, internships for their majors, student living communities, and through faculty who offer service-learning options in their classrooms." Greek houses contribute heavily to service at KU, as do "places like the ECM (Ecumenical Christian Ministries), the Women's Resource Center, and the Multicultural Center," according to students. Reports one, "There is a lot of emphasis on community service in the Greek community, and most campus organizations are service-based."

For those who seek a 24/7 focus on service, there's Lewis Hall, "a unique student-living environment which focuses on community involvement in the areas of community service, diversity, and leadership." Residents here must "agree to be involved in one of these three areas: community service, multicultural and leadership experiences, and personal development."

In order to bolster service-learning opportunities, KU created the Center for Teaching Excellence (CTE), which "puts together ongoing monthly faculty seminars on service-learning. These meetings highlight existing service-learning in KU courses, help interested faculty members prepare to include service-learning in their courses, provide a forum for discussion of what learning is appropriate in service-learning, and invite outside speakers who promote the service-learning agenda on campus. The goal is the establishment of a coherent faculty voice asking for more central coordination of opportunities and communication with local agencies."

Campus Culture of Engagement

Because the CCO is student-run, undergrads at KU bear an unusual degree of responsibility for service activity both on and off campus. Funding is handled by the Student Senate, "one of the most powerful in the nation," students tell us. When this puissant parliament stumbles or grinds to a halt, there's always the liberal Delta Force to shove it back into line. Delta Force, students explain, "was found[ed] eight years ago from progressive roots to create change in administration, campus, and in the legislature. The activities this group has done involves massive changes to KU, protests, and rallies of all kinds. It really shows an ideal grassroots political activist organization. It counters stagnancy in Senate and the oft-linked administration."

Students at KU are especially proud of their Alternative Breaks programs, which "send over 300 students a year on over 40 curriculum-based service-learning trips around the country." Overall, the school fosters "a strong tradition of activism in community service and civic engagement. With 41 volunteers, KU was 25th in the nation among large colleges and universities for the number of Peace Corps volunteers produced in 2003. KU was one of two universities to host the national Tenth Annual Alternative Break Citizenship School in 2003 and hosted the national Campus Greens Convention in 2002."

Connecting Service with the Classroom

At KU, "many departments offer service-learning as a component of individual classes. Examples of areas who have offered service-learning opportunities at the undergraduate and graduate levels are English, Human Development and Family Life, College of Liberal Arts and Sciences, Psychology, Journalism, Sociology, Engineering, Communication Studies, and Education." The school reports that "in the past, we have not tracked the number of service-learning courses" but adds that "in the next academic year, KU is developing a mechanism to be used to certify service-learning experiences. A designation of service-learning participation will be added to the transcript."

Alternative Breaks is perhaps the most prominent of KU's service-learning opportunities. The program "offers a one- or two-credit courses in which service-learning and social justice issues are discussed in an academic setting, the culmination of which is a week-long trip over either winter or spring break, in which the student volunteers in combating a social issue of their choice." Following the trips, students "write reflection papers on each topic and hold group discussions over the issues."

Impact on Community and Students

"A large network of formal and informal partnerships exists" between KU and the community-at-large, university administrators tell us; this network includes elementary schools, youth-service organizations, mental-health providers, food kitchens, tutoring programs, crisis counseling centers, domestic abuse-prevention centers, environmental-awareness groups, and housing providers such as Habitat for Humanity. Student groups also work closely with the United Way on an annual joint project as well as blood drives, Adopt-a-School, and the United Way Campaign.

KU impacts the community with a vast range of programs. Among its most concerted efforts is Into the Streets Week, during which over 20 activities are offered for both the student body and the surrounding community. Events and activities include a community garden project, outreach programs to the developmentally disabled, arts projects, a community dance, and several outreach projects to the homeless. KU's presence is also strongly felt in Lawrence-area schools, where students and faculty participate in a variety of ESL, Math, and Science programs.

The impact of these activities on students is profound. As one explains, "I have had the opportunity to connect with the Lawrence community in a way that I hadn't thought possible. Coming a new city was initially intimidating, but I knew that I could count on the Center for Community Outreach to help me transition. Once I became established, I began to see a world outside of academics, one in which I could seamlessly use skills acquired in the classroom in a real-world situation."

Student Financial Support for Service

The University of Kansas does not earmark any grants or scholarships for service.

SELECTIVITY

# of applicants	10,442
% of applicants accepted	69
% of acceptees attending	59
# accepting a place on wait list	126
% admitted from wait list	74

FRESHMAN PROFILE

Range ACT Composite	21-27
Average HS GPA	3.40
% graduated top 10% of class	28
% graduated top 25% of class	54
% graduated top 50% of class	86

DEADLINES

Regular admission	4/1
Regular notification by	rolling
Nonfall registration?	yes

FINANCIAL FACTS

Annual in-state tuition	$4,163
Annual out-of-state tuition	$12,117
Room and board	$5,126
Books and supplies	$750
Required fees	$574
% frosh rec. need-based scholarship or grant aid	31
% UG rec. need-based scholarship or grant aid	28
% frosh rec. need-based self-help aid	29
% UG rec. need-based self-help aid	29
% frosh rec. any financial aid	48
% UG rec. any financial aid	45

UNIVERSITY OF MARYLAND—COLLEGE PARK

MITCHELL BUILDING, COLLEGE PARK, MD 20742-5235

ADMISSIONS: 301-314-8385 • FAX: 301-314-9693 • FINANCIAL AID: 301-314-9000

E-MAIL: UM-ADMIT@UGA.UMD.EDU • WEBSITE: WWW.MARYLAND.EDU

CAMPUS LIFE

Type of school	public
Environment	village

STUDENTS

Total undergrad enrollment	24,590
% male/female	51/49
% from out of state	24
% live on campus	33
% African American	12
% Asian	14
% Caucasian	58
% Hispanic	6
% international	2
# of countries represented	169

ACADEMICS

Calendar	trimester
Student/faculty ratio	13:1
Most common lab size	20-29
Most common reg class size	10-19

MOST POPULAR MAJORS

computer science
criminology
political science and government

Getting Involved

The University of Maryland, administrators tell us, "has many centers and departments that actively support community and civic engagement." Among the most important is the Office of Community Service-Learning, which "offers, promotes, and supports numerous opportunities for students to engage in community service-learning, including highly structured one-day events, Federal Work-Study Community Service positions through America Reads/America Counts, introductory and discipline-based service-learning courses, student organization service, and several curricular and co-curricular means to explore and develop the connections between service, civic engagement, and leadership."

Also crucial to organizing Maryland's service community are the school's living-learning programs. CIVICUS, for example, is "a living-learning program for first- and second-year students who define and build their own civil society as they discuss social issues in both academic and real-world contexts. CIVICUS Associates (students in the program) create their own service projects and participate in internships at the university or in the Washington, DC area." Maryland offers numerous other living-learning situations.

A huge university, Maryland supports "over 100 student organizations [that] are deeply involved in service and civic-engagement activities," including Greek houses, "a very active MaryPIRG chapter that engages in several major annual activities around hunger and homelessness," a recycling program, and "many faith-based service-learning opportunities out of the campus chaplaincies."

Campus Culture of Engagement

Maryland's Greeks play a special function in the university's service orbit. That's because of the school's "ground-breaking Greek vision plan," under which "fraternities and sororities are required to engage in service as well as the traditional philanthropy." Students observe that "Greek life is often at the center of the social scene. Even if most students are not part of frats or sororities, we are very aware of them and attend their events. So it would only natural that we are also aware of their community-service requirements." This awareness creates a snowball effect; even students outside the Greek system are more likely to become involved in service because of their exposure to service through the Greeks. As a result, "there is always a good turnout at whatever civic-engagement event is happening."

And the need for engagement is strong, because "we have a community surrounding us that is in need of a lot of services. Parks need to be cleaned up, trees need to be planted, schools need to have tutors for students, kids need to learn to read and speak and understand English, homeless need to be fed and clothed, and so much more." All this service helps mend the rifts between campus and community caused by College Park's "famous basketball riots" and the school's frequent clashes with city and county officials.

Connecting Service with the Classroom

"Experiential education, including service-learning, is firmly embedded" in the College Park experience. The university offers "a wide range of service-learning courses. At the discretion of the instructors, more and more freshman seminars are incorporating service learning, including all sections of the freshman seminar for incoming Honors students. Service-learning capstone courses are also offered in living-learning programs, including Beyond the Classroom and College Park Scholars." The school also reports that "many discipline-based service-learning courses exist, ranging from introductory to advanced levels. Approximately 30 service-learning courses are offered each semester, with approximately 1,500 students participating annually." The school reminds us that College Park "is located nine miles from the U.S. capital. Federal government offices, national associations, and embassies are all convenient to the campus by Metrorail. The university has well-developed relationships with all these entities to offer outstanding experiential learning opportunities for students."

Among the school's largest service-learning offerings is Team Maryland, "a three-credit service-learning course at the intersection of leadership, service-learning, social change, and education, is open to juniors and seniors. Students provide 'life and leadership' training to middle and high school students weekly and mentor a youth for the duration of the semester."

Impact on Community and Students

"At the most basic level, over 900 community-based organizations (CBOs) are listed in our ServiceLink searchable web-based database of service and community-engagement opportunities," the university tells us, adding that "the Office of Community Service-Learning works more closely with approximately 25 CBOs whose volunteer coordinators regularly come to campus to participate in volunteer fairs, trainings, and other activities."

One of the school's closer partnerships is with the community of Langley Park. Through the student-established Beyond These Walls programs, undergrads become "involved deeply in the community of Langley Park, just one mile from campus but worlds apart in many ways. Community members are primarily recent immigrants from Central America, speak little or no English, are unemployed or underemployed, and live in poverty in very crowded conditions." Beyond These Walls brings arts and literacy programs, soccer programs, an adult ESL program, and other such services to these neighbors. "Each year, Beyond These Walls adds at least one additional program to meet a need identified by their community partners," the school writes.

Through service projects, students find themselves "cleaning campus or a nearby park, helping at risk school children with art projects or soccer practice, making sandwiches for a soup kitchen, serving at a soup kitchen, toiletries and clothes drives, or befriending elderly at a nursing home." Observes one undergrad, "Maryland is a world unto itself, and it's easy to only pay attention to what's going in this isolated bubble. By reaching beyond the campus, you learn that the world doesn't revolve around you."

Student Financial Support for Service

"There are no [service-related] scholarships per se," Maryland administrators tell us, "but active community service and civic engagement are essential criteria for selection for the major university scholarships." Students eligible for the federal work-study program may participate in the America Reads/America Counts programs.

UNIVERSITY OF MASSACHUSETTS—AMHERST

UNIVERSITY ADMISSIONS CENTER, AMHERST, MA 01003-9291

ADMISSIONS: 413-545-0222 • **FAX:** 413-545-4312 • **FINANCIAL AID:** 413-545-0801

E-MAIL: MAIL@ADMISSIONS.UMASS.EDU • **WEBSITE:** WWW.UMASS.EDU

CAMPUS LIFE

Type of school	public
Environment	village

STUDENTS

Total undergrad enrollment	18,064
% male/female	50/50
% from out of state	17
% from public high school	90
% live on campus	59
% African American	4
% Asian	7
% Caucasian	76
% Hispanic	3
% international	1
# of countries represented	98

ACADEMICS

Calendar	semester
Student/faculty ratio	18:1
% profs teaching UG courses	88
% classes taught by TAs	12
Most common lab size	10-19
Most common reg class size	10-19

MOST POPULAR MAJORS
biology/biological sciences
communications studies/speech
communication and rhetoric
psychology

Getting Involved

Consistently rated as one of the top activist schools in the country, University of Massachusetts—Amherst earns its reputation. "UMass—Amherst is a highly engaged campus that contradicts the dominant notion of college campuses as centers of apathy and cynicism," university administrators here tell us, pointing out that "myriad opportunities for students to get involved in politics, community affairs, and social change range from conventional and formal outlets like student government and campus political clubs to campaigns centered on single issues (UMass, for example, mobilized the largest turnout in the nation for the anti-war protests in Washington, DC prior to the start of the most recent war in Iraq) to several unique comprehensive programs."

A matrix of offices sustains all this activity. The Office of Community Service-Learning (OCSL), for example, "helps students find service-learning courses and community-service opportunities, helps students create their own individualized service-learning courses, helps faculty develop new CSL courses, and helps community organizations work with faculty and students." The Student Activities Office "supports a host of Registered Student Organizations (RSOs) with a high degree of civic engagement, including Campus Democrats, the Republican Club, the Radical Student Union, MassPIRG (Massachusetts Public Interest Research Group), SHARE (Students Helping Area Reach-Out Efforts), Alpha Phi Omega, Circle K" and more. The Student Government Association "provides a vehicle for influencing university policies and funds a wide range of student organizations." Finally, the Office of ALANA Affairs "is an advocate for inclusiveness in public higher education and supports ALANA (African, Latino/a, Asian/Pacific Islander, and Native American) RSOs as they develop programs that promote awareness of the cultural, ethnic, racial, and social diversity of our campus community."

Campus Culture of Engagement

"If you want a school that offers a million different types of service, activism, and ways to be engaged, UMass is the place," writes a typical student. Explains another, "Since our campus is so large, there is guaranteed to be an initiative that a new student will find exciting. There are constantly outside lecturers, conferences, rallies, vigils, teach-ins, and every kind of organization imaginable. We also have student-run cooperative businesses here on campus, which are really unique." Location is also a plus; as one student points out, "UMass has the benefit of sitting in a very active area. In coordination with four other colleges, the Pioneer Valley offers weighty discussions of the world and the people who shape it. Arguably, UMass takes the lead." Students here caution that "you'll find the type of group that your comfortable with (because there are so many groups), but you need to find them. They won't come and find you."

The student body appreciates "a deep reservoir of opportunities for activism," as many in this left-leaning student body are anxious to take advantage of such opportunities; writes one undergrad, "UMass and the Amherst community is incredibly in tune with political issues, social issues, and the dedication to social change. It is a whirlwind of ideas and hope."

Connecting Service with the Classroom

Service-learning courses at UMass "are offered as introductory general-education courses, as elective courses, and as advanced courses in many majors. They are found in departments ranging from Anthropology to Plant and Soil Science to Marketing to Community Health Studies." Students can take the initiative to "create one- to two-credit service-learning 'add-on' courses connected to any course they are taking, with the approval of the instructor; they can also create free-standing service-learning courses up to six credits with the approval of a faculty sponsor and a community advisor." All in all, the school reports that "30 or more service-learning courses are offered and over 1,000 students participate in them" each semester.

Unique service-learning opportunities here include the Citizen Scholars Program, "a two-year academic service-learning program that aims to produce leaders who have the knowledge, the skills, and the will to successfully address problems and advocate for social justice in their own communities and beyond. Students in the program take four courses in sequence and a fifth elective, engage in at least 60 hours of community service each semester, work on projects aimed at promoting structural change and social justice, and build a community of support with one another." Over the past two years, students in the program have partnered with Hampshire Community United Way to "research the impact of proposed growth at UMass on the availability of affordable housing in the region."

Impact on Community and Students

"Faculty at UMass—Amherst develop many community partnerships individually or in small groups; last year faculty were involved in more than 1,100 community-based projects," the school tells us. In addition, "the Office of Community Service Learning maintains contact with over 100 community-based organizations in the Pioneer Valley and endeavors to maintain close partnerships with about ten." As a result, the university has a huge impact on the region; as one undergrad observes, "students volunteer at a myriad of nonprofit organizations around the area. Legal counseling, veterinary care, economic development, education and mentoring, homelessness, public safety, and veteran services are a sample of the areas in which students can serve the community."

Student Financial Support for Service

UMass offers numerous service-related awards. Among them are the DiGiammarino Summer Service Internship (up to $1,500), given "to a Citizen Scholar [in the Commonwealth College] who does a summer internship with a community-service organization." There's also the Class of 1941 Humanitarian Award, the Lawrence Payne Class of 1977 Public Service Scholarship, and the Commonwealth College Alumni Public Service Fellowship, all two-year grants of $1,000 per year "awarded to Commonwealth College students who have done outstanding community service." Citizen Scholar students also receive a $500 award each semester to help them make time for community engagement.

UNIVERSITY OF MASSACHUSETTS—BOSTON

100 MORRISSEY BOULEVARD, BOSTON, MA 02125-3393
ADMISSIONS: 617-287-6000 • **FAX:** 617-287-5999 • **FINANCIAL AID:** 617-287-6300
E-MAIL: UNDERGRAD@UMB.EDU • **WEBSITE:** WWW.UMB.EDU

CAMPUS LIFE

Type of school	public
Environment	town

STUDENTS

Total undergrad	
enrollment	8,666
% male/female	42/58
% from out of state	4
% African American	11
% Asian	8
% Caucasian	35
% Hispanic	5
% international	3
# of countries represented	64

ACADEMICS

Calendar	semester
Student/faculty ratio	15:1
% profs teaching	
UG courses	100
% classes taught by TAs	0
Most common lab size	20-29
Most common	
reg class size	10-19

MOST POPULAR MAJORS

business/commerce
education
social sciences

Getting Involved

University of Massachusetts—Boston is home to the College of Community and Public Service, a unique school that promotes full participation in society through educational programs and professional practice." But public service at UMass—Boston is not isolated to one college; on the contrary, the school reports that "community outreach is fundamental to all areas of UMass—Boston's academic, student, civic, and administrative centers. All seven of our colleges and schools sponsor service-learning or civic-engagement projects as part of their curriculum."

Extracurricular service is coordinated through the Office of Service-Learning and Community Outreach, which "serves as a clearinghouse on campus to connect students with community-service projects. Students volunteer for community-service projects that are integrated into the regular academic curriculum. Among these have been a Helping Hands Toy Drive, through which students, faculty, and staff contribute gifts and time to benefit children served at the Hyde Park DSS Office; Good Neighbor Day activities, which have included serving at local food pantries, cleaning up playgrounds, visiting local day-care centers, and tutoring; and an annual Community Service Fair."

Campus Culture of Engagement

At the forefront of UMass—Boston's service community is the College of Public and Community Service, a school "entirely devoted to service-learning. [It] is extremely accessible to students from all walks of life and has a great track record of producing community leaders." Students here "learn from experience and paper-writing," a great "non-traditional setting" that suits both their needs and the needs of the many Bostonians who benefit from their services.

There are also "plenty of [other] community-service based organizations on campus, including honor societies such as Golden Key, Psi Chi, and Delta Sigma Pi, and the Joiner Center for the Study of War and Its Social Consequences." Overall, "there is a huge amount of awareness and interest on campus among students, administrators, and faculty to be involved in the world around them. There are always people willing to take time out of their busy schedules and make an effort to be involved. Nowhere do you find more dedicated and interested people than here. The creative efforts made by students, and the support they receive from the faculty and administration, is unparalleled."

Connecting Service with the Classroom

The UMass—Boston administration tells us that "there is an average of 15 classes offered each semester that offer service-learning courses through areas such as the College of Community and Public Service, the College of Nursing, and the Graduate College of Education." The administration notes that "UMass—Boston the university forges linkages between research and service [to] bring the intellectual, technical, and human resources of the university community to bear on the economic and social needs of metropolitan regions: for example, through public-policy analysis and applied problem solving in areas such as environmental quality, city planning, tax policy, the schools, and economic development, especially in ethnic and minority communities."

The university's many service-oriented programs include the Beacon Leadership Project, an academic program that helps "students develop and enhance their leadership skills. Final projects have included the launch of a parish nursing program, creation of trauma-indicators brochures for grade school teachers, recruitment volunteers for a local disabilities center, and sponsorship of an on-campus play examining domestic violence." Another program, the Healthy Initiative Collaborative, "brings students from the College of Public and Community Service (CPCS) together with youth from a low-income housing facility near campus. CPCS students meet weekly with the youth residents to create solutions to local community problems. Results of the collaboration include a book drive for a local boys and girls club, a voter registration drive, reorganizing and staffing a community computer center, and a holiday gift drive."

Students add that service-learning "takes place under the supervision of extremely learned and qualified professors who then direct us to civic organizations where our expertise can benefit the civic organization." Writes one undergrad, "One of the things that is wonderful about service-learning at my school is that the school develops and promotes projects that appeal to a wide variety of people and interests."

Impact on Community and Students

According to the school's administration, UMass—Boston students "have the opportunity to contribute a real world impact-whether working on a survey of worldwide attitudes towards people with disabilities for the Special Olympics, engaging in community nursing outreach programs for local neighborhood centers, helping inactive youth enjoy exercise in a local community fitness program, or teaching kids from neighboring communities how to sail in a special summer program." The school participates in "more than 100 community activities a year. We host approximately 70 community groups on campus and work with organizations such as local YMCAs, Boys and Girls Clubs, Board of Trades, nonprofit agencies, neighborhood groups, and Chamber of Commerce."

Student Financial Support for Service

UMass—Boston offers "a number of merit-based scholarships for which students interested in service-learning and public service are top candidates." Students may also apply for "mini-grants and scholarships offered through the Massachusetts Campus Compact, of which UMass—Boston is an active member. The compact is an organization of colleges and universities committed to promoting community service and service-learning as critical components of higher education." Finally, "the Division of Student Affairs offers the STARS mini-grant program that seeks to award up to $2,000 for initiatives that enhance the university and improve student life. The mini-grant program provides resources for collaborative efforts between students, faculty, and student-affairs staff members."

SELECTIVITY

# of applicants	2,903
% of applicants accepted	53
% of acceptees attending	36

FRESHMAN PROFILE

Range SAT Verbal	460-570
Range SAT Math	470-570
Minimum Paper TOEFL	500
Average HS GPA	3.00

DEADLINES

Regular admission	11/1
Regular notification by	rolling
Nonfall registration?	yes

FINANCIAL FACTS

Annual in-state tuition	$1,714
Annual out-of-state tuition	$9,758
Required fees	$6,310
% frosh rec. need-based scholarship or grant aid	52
% UG rec. need-based scholarship or grant aid	50
% frosh rec. need-based self-help aid	35
% UG rec. need-based self-help aid	47

UNIVERSITY OF MICHIGAN—ANN ARBOR

1220 STUDENT ACTIVITIES BUILDING, ANN ARBOR, MI 48109-1316
ADMISSIONS: 734-764-7433 • **FAX:** 734-936-0740 • **FINANCIAL AID:** 734-763-6600
E-MAIL: UGADMISS@UMICH.EDU • **WEBSITE:** WWW.ADMISSIONS.UMICH.EDU

CAMPUS LIFE

Type of school	public
Environment	town

STUDENTS

Total undergrad enrollment	24,680
% male/female	49/51
% from out of state	31
% from public high school	80
% live on campus	37
% African American	8
% Asian	12
% Caucasian	63
% Hispanic	5
% Native American	1
% international	5
# of countries represented	117

ACADEMICS

Calendar	semester
Student/faculty ratio	17:1
% profs teaching UG courses	72
% classes taught by TAs	0
Most common lab size	10-19
Most common reg class size	10-19

MOST POPULAR MAJORS
economics
English language and literature
mechanical engineering

Getting Involved

A number of community-service and civic-engagement programs and initiatives at University of Michigan—Ann Arbor are headquartered at the Edward Ginsberg Center for Community Service and Learning, which, the school writes, "engage students, faculty, and community members in learning together through community service, service-learning, and civic participation in a diverse democratic society." Through the center, "thousands of students each year are involved in community service, service-learning, and social action efforts." Opportunities to serve include "academic courses, student organizations, and University-sponsored programs." Information about civically-engaged student organizations is coordinated by the Civic Mapping Team, while collaboration amongst these groups is the goal of the Community Justice Council, which consists of "various student advocacy groups working together for social justice." Students seeking community involvement on their own "may consult the Volunteer Connection [a school-run online database of volunteer opportunities] to identify a suitable community placement."

Incoming freshmen can plug into the activist scene through Festifall, "an annual event that showcases many student groups on campus, not just the progressive/social justice organizations. This happens within the first two weeks of school." Subsequently they can check in through Maize Pages, "an online resource that lists groups by issue," Volunteer Connection, and by visiting the Ginsberg Center.

Campus Culture of Engagement

"Whatever your interests are, you will find people at U of M that share your passions," students report, observing that "involvement at U of M is widespread and diverse in its methods. Those interested in social engagement will find what they're looking for, whether that be tutoring troubled students, working against war, connecting art and social change, working in prisons, or volunteering one's time somewhere else." The Ginsberg Center, students tell us, "is primarily service-oriented. It's harder to do truly progressive work through the center." There are, however, "numerous political-advocacy groups" here; "U of M and Ann Arbor are known for their presence at the forefront of social movements," students remind us, adding that "whether it was affirmative action or labor unions, this university provides students with an opportunity to see how they can affect change on campus, as well as at a local, state, and national level."

Undergrads here report that their co-curricular activities are "well-organized and well-intentioned. Many, if not most, students who become involved with civic engagement and service learning at U of M are profoundly affected by the experience." Their efforts include "many high-profile and high impact events, including Affirmative Action protests, Detroit Project Day, involvement in marches on Washington for women's reproductive rights, and the list goes on and on."

Connecting Service with the Classroom

"Virtually all departments, schools, and colleges that comprise the University offer service-learning courses," U of M administrators tell us, adding that "some departments and schools at the university require a service-learning course for graduation." There are also "ample opportunities to become involved in community-based research, through classes or working with an individual professor." Offerings encompass more than 70 courses enrolling over 1,000 undergrads. Points out one student, "service-learning takes place around Ann Arbor, in Detroit, and all over the U.S. Some examples are teaching children, building houses, working on organic farms, volunteering at homeless shelters and food kitchens, and working with people seeking political asylum."

The Alternative Spring Break (ASB) program, reports the school, "involves 400 students in service-learning in 25 different states. In contrast to most Alternative Spring Break programs across the nation which run for only one week, the University of Michigan's ASB program runs from November through March. Peer leaders and students prepare for months before the actual one-week trip." Alternative Weekends program and an Alternative Summer Breaks program are also available.

Project Community, a peer-facilitated seminar, is "one of the oldest service-learning courses in the nation. The weekly seminars are taught by undergraduates who are previous course participants and have been through an extensive training program."

The Michigan Community Scholars Program (MCSP) is a "living-learning program that brings together students and faculty who have a commitment to community service, social justice, and academic study. Through small courses, service projects, leadership opportunities, social programs, study groups and tutors, students model an ideal community in terms of friendship, responsibility, diversity, celebration, collaboration, and caring."

The Arts of Citizenship program partners with local schools, museums, libraries, and arts organizations "to produce cultural products such as history and art exhibits, educational websites, performance pieces, curricula, and park designs."

Impact on Community and Students

"There are more than 150 community partners with which the University of Michigan works to improve the quality of life for those in disenfranchised communities," writes the school. "Approximately 80 of them are with school-based or after-school programs. We also work with community-based organizations on such issues as urban poverty, rural poverty, Native American issues, mental health issues, criminal justice, health, homelessness, HIV/AIDS, lesbian, gay, bisexual and transgender people, domestic violence, community and economic development, chemical dependency, aging, and disabilities." Students observe that "Detroit is a great place to work. It obviously is an impoverished community, but more importantly, the spirit of the people is remarkable. I know that students learn sooo much from interacting with the Detroit community."

Student Financial Support for Service

The university writes that while it "does not offer scholarships for community service, the Ginsberg Center offers one scholarship each year for a local Washtenaw County high school graduate who attends the University of Michigan. In addition, about a dozen U of M students each year are Ginsberg Fellows and receive a stipend for undertaking a community-based initiative." The school offers service-related work-study jobs to those who qualify for the federally funded program, and a school-supplied budget of about $75,000 (administered by the undergraduate student government) keeps the school's community service and student organizations solvent.

SELECTIVITY

# of applicants	21,293
% of applicants accepted	62
% of acceptees attending	46
# accepting a place on wait list	4,100

FRESHMAN PROFILE

Range SAT Verbal	580-680
Range SAT Math	630-720
Range ACT Composite	26-30
Minimum Paper TOEFL	570
Minimum Computer TOEFL	230
Average HS GPA	3.72
% graduated top 10% of class	90
% graduated top 25% of class	99
% graduated top 50% of class	100

DEADLINES

Regular admission	2/1
Regular notification by	rolling
Nonfall registration?	yes

FINANCIAL FACTS

Annual in-state tuition	$8,294
Annual out-of-state tuition	$25,460
Room and board	$6,704
Books and supplies	$938
Required fees	$187
% frosh rec. need-based scholarship or grant aid	24
% UG rec. need-based scholarship or grant aid	24
% frosh rec. need-based self-help aid	50
% UG rec. need-based self-help aid	44
% frosh rec. any financial aid	50
% UG rec. any financial aid	44

University of Minnesota—Twin Cities

240 Williamson Hall, 231 Pillsbury Drive SE, Minneapolis, MN 55455-0213

Admissions: 612-625-2008 • **Fax:** 612-626-1693 • **Financial Aid:** 612-624-1665

E-mail: Admissions@tc.umn.edu • **Website:** admissions.tc.umn.edu

CAMPUS LIFE

Type of school	public
Environment	town

STUDENTS

Total undergrad enrollment	28,103
% male/female	48/52
% from out of state	18
% live on campus	22
% African American	4
% Asian	8
% Caucasian	80
% Hispanic	2
% Native American	1
% international	2

ACADEMICS

Calendar	semester
Student/faculty ratio	15:1
Most common lab size	10-19
Most common reg class size	10-19

Getting Involved

University of Minnesota—Twin Cities' Career and Community Learning Center (CCLC) is the main office coordinating the school's large and active service community. The CCLC "engages students, faculty, and staff in sustained and mutually-beneficial involvement with local communities in a variety of ways, including neighborhood organizing, teaching or tutoring English with immigrants and refugees, working in area health-care facilities, and spending time with children in after-school programs or in connection to area social-service or grassroots-organizations programs."

The CCLC is hardly the only entity supporting service, however. In fact, the enterprise requires an intricate matrix of offices at this large university. The nationally-renowned Center for Democracy and Citizenship (CDC), housed at the Humphrey Institute, involves students in "public work" projects with youth and immigrant communities. The Center for Urban and Regional Affairs (CURA) houses the Neighborhood Planning for Community Revitalization (NPCR) program, and the College of Education and Human Development manages the Literacy Initiative, UMTC's America Reads early-literacy tutoring program. The University YMCA "seeks to develop the ethical leadership capacities of students in the context of social issues by combining cross-cultural and community-based experiences with reflection sessions" In addition to other university offices and numerous student organizations, "many academic departments across campus encourage students to be actively engaged in the community, working to address public issues." Incoming students also have the opportunity to live in the Service-Learning House, an on-campus housing option dedicated to service and social change. Students in the house take courses with service components together and reflect on their work in the classroom as well as the dorm.

Campus Culture of Engagement

"We have an organization representing nearly every interest" at UMTC, students tell us—"everything from religious and faith groups to ballroom dancing to fishing to frats and sororities, all kinds of political clubs, a math club; the list goes on and on." The students also point out that "many organizations [in the Twin Cities] that have partnerships with the University are close to campus or have campus liaisons in order to keep a visible presence on campus. My own experience has been that the organizational aspect is well-run." Further enhancing matters is the sense that "the community-at-large seems very receptive of students coming to work in a civic environment." Observes one student, "UMTC has built strong connections to the Twin Cities community. Although we are a large campus, we are not in a bubble."

Political activism here "is fairly moderate compared to the University of Wisconsin or Macalester College in St. Paul, but there are a lot of political student groups (from College Republicans all the way to the Socialist Alternative) that shamelessly promote their ideas."

Connecting Service with the Classroom

UMTC administrators explain that "academic service-learning provides a way to unite the tripartite mission of the university: teaching, research, and public engagement. With the Twin Cities' campuses located in the heart of an increasingly diverse urban area, faculty members and students have an excellent opportunity to engage in partnership with local nonprofit and governmental organizations through community service-learning or community-based research to address local issues through the curriculum." For those who wish to focus their educations on service, "a Leadership minor is available to undergraduate students at UMTC through the joint efforts of the College of Education and Human Development, the Humphrey Institute of Public Affairs, and Student Affairs. Coursework in the minor includes civic-learning requirements through several courses building to the leadership practicum course."

UMTC's Community Engagement Scholars Program, slated to start up in spring 2005, will require "400 documented hours of service which addresses community needs, nine credit hours of service-learning courses, a series of reflections tied to community work, and completion of an integrative community-engagement project based on community-identified needs and the student's academic interests. Students completing the program will receive Community Engagement Scholar notation on official academic transcripts, public recognition at a reception for the scholars, acknowledgement of their accomplishments in their college commencement program, and a cord of distinction to wear at commencement."

The school tells us that "in a typical academic year, over 70 courses in nine colleges (Liberal Arts; Natural Resources; Agricultural, Food, and Environmental Sciences; Human Ecology; Education and Human Development; General College; Architecture and Landscape Architecture; Biological Sciences; and the Carlson School of Management) provide the opportunity for over 1,750 students to participate in service-learning." Students appreciate the convenience of UMTC's service-learning opportunities; writes one, "the service-learning takes place in the metro area of St. Paul and Minneapolis. There are many near-campus locations that make it feasible to do service-learning without having a car or bus pass. It's a few hours a week to connect to the community in which you live."

Impact on Community and Students

The University of Minnesota "takes its public missions seriously" and has "hundreds of partnerships with community groups across the Twin Cities and throughout Minnesota," including "nonprofit groups and local, county, state, and federal governmental organizations; [among them] social-service agencies, schools, recreation centers, grassroots issue-oriented groups, advocacy organizations, non-partisan political groups, faith-based groups, neighborhood associations, community economic-development programs, libraries, nature centers, arts organizations, youth programs, and health and wellness organizations." Of the school's many programs, the Literacy Initiative arguably has the biggest impact, "approximately 30 schools and community centers in Minneapolis and St. Paul are [our] community partners. Over 650 students were placed in 2003-2004, serving over 2,500 elementary students," the school reports.

Students also interact with the community through Public Achievement, a program sponsored by the Center for Democracy and Citizenship "in which teams of youth are coached-often by college students-in doing public work projects around issues that they have chosen such as gangs, teen pregnancy, the environment, and school policies."

Student Financial Support for Service

While the University of Minnesota doesn't offer community-service scholarships, it has funding opportunities for research and engagement through the Undergraduate Research Opportunities Program (UROP).

SELECTIVITY

# of applicants	14,724
% of applicants accepted	74
% of acceptees attending	47

FRESHMAN PROFILE

Range SAT Verbal	540-660
Range SAT Math	550-670
Range ACT Composite	22-28
Minimum Paper TOEFL	550
% graduated top 10% of class	30
% graduated top 25% of class	65
% graduated top 50% of class	92

DEADLINES

Regular admission	
Regular notification by	rolling
Nonfall registration?	yes

FINANCIAL FACTS

Annual in-state tuition	$5,420
Annual out-of-state tuition	$15,994
Room and board	$5,696
Books and supplies	$730
Required fees	$860
% frosh rec. need-based scholarship or grant aid	37
% UG rec. need-based scholarship or grant aid	34
% frosh rec. need-based self-help aid	40
% UG rec. need-based self-help aid	40

UNIVERSITY OF MONTANA—MISSOULA

103 LODGE BUILDING, MISSOULA, MT 59812

ADMISSIONS: 406-243-6266 • **FAX:** 406-243-5711 • **FINANCIAL AID:** 406-243-5373

E-MAIL: ADMISS@SELWAY.UMT.EDU • **WEBSITE:** WWW.UMT.EDU

CAMPUS LIFE

Type of school	public
Environment	town

STUDENTS

Total undergrad enrollment	10,943
% male/female	47/53
% from out of state	21
% live on campus	22
% Asian	1
% Caucasian	88
% Hispanic	1
% Native American	4
% international	2

ACADEMICS

Calendar	semester
Student/faculty ratio	19:1
Most common reg class size	<10

MOST POPULAR MAJORS

business, management, marketing, and related support services
education
English language and literature

Getting Involved

In beautiful Missoula, Montana, UM's Office for Civic Engagement (OCE) provides the center point for the university's service community. The office coordinates such student volunteer programs as "America Reads/America Counts, Alternative Breaks, and Earth Day Clean Start; AmeriCorps and AmeriCorps*VISTA programs, including Campus Corps, the Montana Technology Corps, and Missoula-based Campus Compact VISTA; American Humanics, a national nonprofit management certification program; engaged scholarship such as academic service learning and community-based research; and Academic Learning Integrated with Volunteer Experience (ALIVE), designed to engage national service participants in credit-based service-learning projects connected to their service."

Academic departments also contribute to campus service. Writes the school, "several campus departments actively support civic engagement through the use of academic service learning and community-based research." In addition, "several student organizations also directly support and promote civic engagement activities. For example, the Associated Students of the University of Montana provide funding to various students organizations to carry out community service projects and develop community-based partnerships designed to further strengthen students' commitment to service." UM is home to student-run chapters of Volunteers in Action, Golden Key, Circle K, MontPIRG (Montana Public Interest Research Group), a Women's Center, the Kyi-Yo Native American Student Association, and a variety of Greek organizations, among others.

Campus Culture of Engagement

Environmental issues are important to most UM undergrads; explains one, "This campus is very aware of how we treat the environment, and the student body takes an active role in protecting it." Adds another, "Between river cleanups and noxious weed pulls, the presence of environmental service opportunities is constantly visible." The environment isn't the only thing on UM students' minds, though; the school offers "lots of options, opportunities, and positions (paid and unpaid), work-study and non-work study, independent studies, internships, and practicums, regardless of your political ideology. "

UM is known as a liberal campus within Montana, but students suggest that outsiders keep that characterization in perspective. "Despite being known as a liberal school, our College Republicans are the strongest in the state," writes one campus liberal. Reports another, "there are student groups such as MontPIRG, the College Democrats, the Women's Center, and the College Republicans (to name a few) who are quite interested in the political issues of the day and will be happy to have your help. You are welcome on this campus as an activist if you are a conservative or a liberal."

Connecting Service with the Classroom

According to UM, "service-learning courses are offered in a variety of departments across campus. Each semester, approximately 22 service learning courses are offered in classes such as Literacy Studies, Addiction Studies, Organizational Communication, Dance Methods, Explorations in Gerontology, Business and Society, Public Health in Pharmacy, Environmental Science, Applied Ecology, Creative Writing, Health Promotion, Contemporary Art, School Counseling, Teaching Elementary Math, Marketing Communications, Geology Curation

Techniques, and Methods of Teaching Drama. During the academic year 2002-2003, more than 1,200 students provided 30,856 hours of service through academic service learning courses."

One unique service-learning opportunity is available through the Program in Ecological Agriculture and Society (PEAS). The program "combines traditional academic learning with hands-on work on a 6.5-acre urban farm. Students are involved in everything from managing the farm's greenhouse in February to harvesting pumpkins in October. In the past six years, more than 600 UM students have produced tens of thousands of pounds of organically-grown vegetables for distribution to low-income members of our community."

Impact on Community and Students

UM "partners with dozens of community agencies and the local K-12 school district" in partnerships that "involve faculty and students working collaboratively with schools and organizations to help address identified needs through academic service learning and extracurricular volunteer service." UM's community partners include the Salvation Army, Habitat for Humanity, the Missoula Food Bank, the Poverello Homeless Shelter, Headstart, and the Missoula Urban Demonstration Project, to name a few.

Among the school's noteworthy endeavors is its partnership with the Missoula Flagship program, which "provides after-school enrichment activities that build protective factors for K-12 youth. UM students play a vital role in the success of the program by providing thousands of hours of volunteer time to coordinate and implement educational, fun after-school activities for Flagship youth participants."

"Another important community partnership that UM students are involved in is with the Missoula YWCA," the school tells us. "Student members of the Student Assault Resource Center (SARC) partner with the local YWCA to share resources in order to advocate and respond to the needs of victims of abuse." The SARC works to "raise awareness of sexual and domestic violence, and provide education and support services to victims of violence." Its members "also provide crisis counseling to victims who are receiving medical services from the hospital."

Student Financial Support for Service

"The University of Montana offers scholarships and awards for students and student groups involved in community service," the school reports, citing "the Outstanding Student Leader Award offered each semester to a student who exhibits extraordinary leadership and service to the campus and local community; the award includes a tuition waiver for one semester. In addition, a $500 annual cash award is given to an outstanding student organization that exhibits a high level of community service and a demonstrable impact from the service." Also, "through UM's affiliation and membership in The Montana Campus Compact, UM students are eligible to receive a $500 community-service scholarship for outstanding service, and student athletes are eligible to receive the Montana Athletes in Service Award. The latter recognizes student athletes from all sports and from academic disciplines who have demonstrated exemplary service to their community." Participation in the Compact also qualifies students for the national Howard Swearer Humanitarian Award.

SELECTIVITY

# of applicants	3,987
% of applicants accepted	96
% of acceptees attending	51

FRESHMAN PROFILE

Range SAT Verbal	490-600
Range SAT Math	460-570
Range ACT Composite	20-25
Average HS GPA	3.18
% graduated top 10% of class	14
% graduated top 25% of class	33
% graduated top 50% of class	66

DEADLINES

Regular notification by	rolling
Nonfall registration?	yes

FINANCIAL FACTS

Annual in-state tuition	$3,125
Annual out-of-state tuition	$10,725
Room and board	$5,292
Books and supplies	$800
Required fees	$1,135
% frosh rec. need-based scholarship or grant aid	40
% UG rec. need-based scholarship or grant aid	42
% frosh rec. need-based self-help aid	47
% UG rec. need-based self-help aid	48

UNIVERSITY OF NORTH CAROLINA—CHAPEL HILL

OFFICE OF UNDERGRADUATE ADMISSIONS, JACKSON HALL 153A - CAMPUS BOX #2200, CHAPEL HILL, NC 27599

ADMISSIONS: 919-966-3621 • **FAX:** 919-962-3045 • **FINANCIAL AID:** 919-962-8396

E-MAIL: UADM@EMAIL.UNC.EDU • **WEBSITE:** WWW.UNC.EDU

CAMPUS LIFE

Type of school	public
Environment	village

STUDENTS

Total undergrad enrollment	15,711
% male/female	41/59
% from out of state	18
% from public high school	85
% live on campus	44
% African American	11
% Asian	6
% Caucasian	76
% Hispanic	2
% Native American	1
% international	1
# of countries represented	102

ACADEMICS

Calendar	semester
Most common lab size	10-19
Most common reg class size	20-29

MOST POPULAR MAJORS
biology/biological sciences
mass communications/media studies
psychology

Getting Involved

The University of North Carolina at Chapel Hill is a massive university; its size explains the need for a central office to coordinate the school's many service-related activities. That office is the Carolina Center for Public Service, "a pan-university center with the mission to 'lead the university in its engagement efforts and service to the state of North Carolina and beyond by connecting the energy and expertise of students, faculty, and staff to the needs of the people.'"

UNCs Campus Y, "one of the oldest and largest student organizations on campus," is also a major player, an organization that is "fully devoted to its mission: 'the pursuit of social justice through the cultivation of pluralism.' The Campus Y believes that everyone has a responsibility to foster cultural understanding and interaction while maintaining the individuality of all cultural groups."

Students also organize service-learning opportunities through APPLES (Assisting People in Planning Learning Experiences in Service), whose goal is "to foster socially aware and civically involved students through participation in an enriched curriculum and hands-on experiences that address the needs of North Carolina communities." University-sponsored service occurs through the School of Government, which "works to improve the lives of North Carolinians by engaging in practical scholarship that helps public officials and citizens understand and improve state and local government."

The administration points out that "in addition to these units, there are countless additional student groups and university programs that actively support community/civic engagement through the university's tri-partite mission of teaching, research, and service." Students report that "there are so many ways to find out about activities: at orientation during the summer, Fall Fest during the first week of school, Activities Fair on Polk Place, activities and message boards in the Pit, and message boards in the dorm. There are also multiple electronic mailing lists students can be added to."

Campus Culture of Engagement

Students are "impressed with Chapel Hill's level of dedication to service. We have basically every service organization represented on campus, plus our own unique Chapel Hill service organizations, such as APPLES, which is service-learning, and the Carolina Public Service Scholars program, which recognizes students for their dedication to community service if they fulfill certain requirements by graduation." Students identify the Campus Y, Circle K, and the professional fraternities as important contributors; they also report that many students volunteer at the "huge hospitals on campus."

No matter where students choose to serve, they agree that "civic engagement makes Carolina lively and happy. Students and professors get excited about the issues they're involved in. It gives the university an importance beyond its basic goal of education; it gives it color and rounds it out. It makes the university worldly." Warns one student, "Be prepared for the onslaught of opportunities! Know what you want to do and don't over-commit, because there are so many cool opportunities out there!"

Connecting Service with the Classroom

Service-learning at UNC is "well integrated into undergraduate courses throughout a variety of Academic Affairs departments, addressing the university's three-pronged mission of teaching, research, and service. Roughly 900 students are engaged in service-learning programs (i.e., courses, internships, fellowships, or break trips) hosted by the APPLES program each academic year." APPLES academic courses "are geared towards undergraduates. Generally, 40 courses are offered each year in over 20 departments, involving roughly 800 students. Some of the classes are designed as first-year seminars, while others are capstone courses, honors independent-study courses or courses required for major credit." The school also points out that "beginning in the fall of 2006, the new Experiential Education requirement may be satisfied by participating in an approved service-learning course that requires at least 30 hours of supervised service and meets community-identified needs."

Impact on Community and Students

UNC is deeply engrained in the Chapel Hill community through its work with "hundreds of community agencies and governmental entities. Many of the partnerships are long standing; others continue to develop in response to the changing needs and priorities of the community." UNCs partnerships join the school with "a variety of entities that include, but are not limited to, health-related organizations, public schools, social-service agencies, and youth-serving organizations, and they address a myriad of topic issues such as Hispanic/Latino outreach, arts enrichment, disaster recovery, homelessness, domestic violence, literacy, and access to health care."

The school also reaches beyond its immediate surroundings to the rest of the state, the nation, and the world. When deadly hurricanes struck North Carolina in recent years, the school and its undergraduates were there to "go to the areas hardest hit and conduct a rapid assessment of impact and needs. Subsequently, four trips (including two over Fall Break) were organized to help with clean-up and repair. Students at the School of Government provided consultation to local and county governments to help with federal procedures and applications."

Student Financial Support for Service

UNC provides "numerous opportunities for students to pursue financial support for community/public service." Among these are the Robert E. Bryan Fellowship Program, "a summer fellows program of the Carolina Center for Public Service." Recipients must work on public-service projects "that address identifiable needs within North Carolina." The school also offers Social Entrepreneur Fellowships through the APPLES Service-Learning Program; recipients are awarded service-learning grants "to assess community needs and design innovative service projects that address those needs. The program provides monetary support, community links, and assistance with volunteer recruitment." There's also the Burch Fellows Program, administered by the Johnston Center for Undergraduate Excellence; this program "recognizes undergraduate students at the university who possess extraordinary ability, promise, and imagination. The fellowships support self-designed off-campus experiences that will enable students to pursue a passionate interest in a way and to a degree not otherwise possible."

SELECTIVITY

# of applicants	17,591
% of applicants accepted	37
% of acceptees attending	55
# accepting a place on wait list	1,671
% admitted from wait list	13

FRESHMAN PROFILE

Range SAT Verbal	590-690
Range SAT Math	600-700
Range ACT Composite	25-30
Minimum Paper TOEFL	600
Minimum Computer TOEFL	250
Average HS GPA	3.14
% graduated top 10% of class	70
% graduated top 25% of class	94
% graduated top 50% of class	99

DEADLINES

Regular admission	1/15
Regular notification by	1/31, 3/31
Nonfall registration?	no

FINANCIAL FACTS

Annual in-state tuition	$2,955
Annual out-of-state tuition	$14,803
Room and board	$6,045
Books and supplies	$800
Required fees	$1,117
% frosh rec. need-based scholarship or grant aid	27
% UG rec. need-based scholarship or grant aid	25
% frosh rec. need-based self-help aid	13
% UG rec. need-based self-help aid	17
% frosh rec. any financial aid	53
% UG rec. any financial aid	51

UNIVERSITY OF NOTRE DAME

220 MAIN BUILDING, NOTRE DAME, IN 46556

ADMISSIONS: 574-631-7505 • FAX: 574-631-8865 • FINANCIAL AID: 574-631-6436

E-MAIL: ADMISSIO.1@ND.EDU • WEBSITE: WWW.ND.EDU

CAMPUS LIFE

Type of school	private
Environment	village

STUDENTS

Total undergrad enrollment	8,322
% male/female	53/47
% from out of state	87
% from public high school	50
% live on campus	76
% African American	4
% Asian	5
% Caucasian	78
% Hispanic	8
% Native American	1
% international	4
# of countries represented	100

ACADEMICS

Calendar	4-1-4
Student/faculty ratio	13:1
% profs teaching UG courses	94
% classes taught by TAs	7
Most common lab size	10-19
Most common reg class size	30-39

MOST POPULAR MAJORS

business administration/management
engineering
pre-medicine/pre-medical studies

Getting Involved

Like many Catholic schools, Notre Dame takes its commitment to service-learning seriously. As the school reminds us, its mission statement requires the school to "seek to cultivate in its students not only an appreciation for the great achievements of human beings but also a disciplined sensibility to the poverty, injustice, and oppression that burden the lives of so many. The aim is to create a sense of human solidarity and concern for the common good that will bear fruit as learning becomes service to justice." Accordingly, students here have ample opportunity to participate in both service-learning and extracurricular service. Both are coordinated through Notre Dame's Center for Social Concerns, whose staff of approximately 20 "has at the heart of its mission conducting and supporting community-based learning (CBL) at the university."

The school stresses the importance of service to students before they even arrive in South Bend. Explains one undergrad, "From the first packet of information you receive from Notre Dame, you'll start to get ideas about activism and service opportunities on campus. The best way to find out what fits you best is to do make a stop at the Center for Social Concerns, and to attend Activities Night [at the beginning of the fall term], where all clubs and organizations are represented."

Campus Culture of Engagement

There is a culture of social commitment at Notre Dame "exemplified by the fact that 85 percent of students engage in some form of service or service-learning.". As one student explains, "Service and civic engagement have really stood out to me as what distinguishes Notre Dame from other schools. Here, involvement is so ubiquitous and encouraged. In fact, I just recently was talking to friends at state schools about all of my involvement this summer in service and they were shocked. They hadn't even heard of anyone doing summer service projects at their school." According to the university, "by graduation, approximately 10 percent of Notre Dame seniors commit to one or more years of full-time service in the United States and abroad."

Notre Dame's traditionally conservative student body has received an infusion of liberalism in recent years, which has manifested itself in increased political activism. In 2003-2004, more than 100 students conducted hunger strikes to protest the school's contract with a major fast food chain accused of mistreating farm workers. Support for gay students has also grown more visible; the underground student organization Gay-Straight Alliance recently staged an event at which over 2,000 attendees wore the group's "Gay? Fine by me" t-shirts to show support for ND's homosexual community.*

Connecting Service with the Classroom

Notre Dame reports that "approximately 90 service-learning courses are offered each year, about 20 being conducted directly by the Center for Social Concerns. Service-learning courses are offered in most disciplines. Such offerings include courses in Anthropology, Computer Applications, Latin American Studies, Philosophy, Psychology, Sociology and Theology, Accountancy, Management, Civil Engineering and Geographical Sciences, Computer Science and Engineering, First-Year Composition, and Law. Some of these courses are primarily experiential in nature; others offer regular direct-service, research, organizing, and community-development opportunities."

Outstanding service-learning opportunities include Urban Plunge, "a one-credit seminar through which roughly 150 students yearly spend 48 hours in a U.S. city between semesters to investigate urban challenges with individuals working to address those challenges." Notre Dame also offers a variety of one-credit Social Concerns Seminars "through which students travel to over 20 sites [in the U.S. and abroad] over fall/winter/spring/summer breaks. Students focus on topics such as children and poverty, the experiences of migrant workers, rural poverty, border issues, and more." Several excellent summer options exist; the Summer Service Project Internship (SSPI) sends "about 200 students to spend eight to ten weeks each summer in a city in the U.S. engaged in some form of community involvement, as part of a three-credit course," while the International Summer Service Learning Program (ISSLP) "facilitates community experiences for about 38 students in 12 countries in Africa, Asia, and Latin America for eight to ten weeks during the summer."

Impact on Community and Students

According to the university, "The Center for Social Concerns is able to maintain relationships with about 65 partner organizations. The organizations vary in terms of the services they offer (homelessness prevention, health care for the medically indigent, AIDS education, etc.), their missions to and within the community (neighborhood organizations, coalitions, city offices), and in their access to resources, both human and financial."

One of ND's most successful community partnerships involves the Robinson Community Learning Center (RCLC), located "in a neighborhood just south of campus. [At first] it facilitated many meetings of neighborhood residents and in other ways attempted to learn what kind of center the residents would value in their area. The RCLC works with students at ND in many capacities. Students tutor children and work with senior citizens in RCLC programs. ND classes visit the RCLC to learn how such an entity affects and works with children and the neighborhood. Students live in the neighborhood and have been members of the area's neighborhood organization." Students also proudly report that "ND has helped build the Center for the Homeless in South Bend."

Student Financial Support for Service

Notre Dame administrators remind us that "civic engagement, social action, and leadership are often criteria for scholarships given by various departments/entities." The school offers several examples: "The Hesburgh Public Service Program has funded an internship with the Kensington Welfare Rights Organization in Philadelphia and is funding a local community based research student project this summer (2004); the Institute for Latino Studies, the Notre Dame Vocation Initiative, and the Higgins Labor Research Center are contributing funds to student internships this summer with the National Interfaith Committee on Worker Justice. The Arts and Letters Honors Program is funding a student to do a community-based research project this coming summer with the Service Employees International Union in Boston." The school also notes that "students participating in the Summer Service Learning Internship receive $2,000 tuition scholarships for the following year."

*confirming source: www.siecus.org/controversy/cont0030.html

SELECTIVITY

# of applicants	11,490
% of applicants accepted	30
% of acceptees attending	57
# accepting a place on wait list	840
% admitted from wait list	15

FRESHMAN PROFILE

Range SAT Verbal	630-730
Range SAT Math	650-740
Range ACT Composite	30-33
Minimum Paper TOEFL	550
Minimum Computer TOEFL	230
% graduated top 10% of class	85
% graduated top 25% of class	95
% graduated top 50% of class	100

DEADLINES

Regular admission	12/31
Regular notification by	4/1
Nonfall registration?	no

FINANCIAL FACTS

Books and supplies	$850
% frosh rec. need-based scholarship or grant aid	44
% UG rec. need-based scholarship or grant aid	38
% frosh rec. need-based self-help aid	37
% UG rec. need-based self-help aid	35

UNIVERSITY OF PENNSYLVANIA

1 COLLEGE HALL, PHILADELPHIA, PA 19104

ADMISSIONS: 215-898-7507 • **FAX:** 215-898-9670 • **FINANCIAL AID:** 215-898-1988

E-MAIL: INFO@ADMISSIONS.UGAO.UPENN.EDU • **WEBSITE:** WWW.UPENN.EDU

CAMPUS LIFE

Type of school	private
Environment	town

STUDENTS

Total undergrad enrollment	9,719
% male/female	50/50
% from out of state	81
% from public high school	57
% live on campus	64
% African American	6
% Asian	18
% Caucasian	49
% Hispanic	6
% international	9
# of countries represented	109

ACADEMICS

Calendar	semester
Student/faculty ratio	6:1
Most common lab size	20-29
Most common reg class size	10-19

MOST POPULAR MAJORS

business administration/management
economics
finance

Getting Involved

The University of Pennsylvania reports that "the Center for Community Partnerships (CCP) is Penn's main vehicle for linking academic work and community issues and partners." According to the school's website, this office's mission is to "improve the internal coordination and collaboration of all university-wide community-service programs, create new and effective partnerships between the University and the community, encourage new and creative initiatives linking Penn and the community, and create and strengthen local, national, and international networks of institutions of higher education committed to engagement with their local communities." The center has worked for over a decade to make Penn a national leader in community/university partnerships.

Complementing CCP is the more student-centered Civic House, the school's "hub for student community service and advocacy work." Civic House "provides extensive training and education opportunities and advises the wide range of student-led service and advocacy programs on campus. Additionally, Civic House works with Penn's Career Services office and other partners to support students pursuing careers in the public interest." Civic House also coordinates PennCORP, a four-day pre-orientation program designed to introduce first years to available service opportunities.

Campus Culture of Engagement

Students at Penn are regularly reminded of the school's many service opportunities. All they have to do is stroll down Locust Walk (simply 'The Walk' to cognoscenti); as one student explains, "A student would have to try pretty hard to avoid The Walk on any given day, and community-service groups make themselves very obvious on The Walk frequently during the year." Not that most undergrads need reminding; many, in fact, chose Penn for its numerous service opportunities. As the school reminds us, "one of the most compelling reasons for committed, engaged students to attend Penn is its urban setting in Philadelphia, which both informs and makes possible an unlimited number of campus-community partnership activities."

Students here report that "in terms of political activism, there are groups such as the coalitions for people of color who establish their presence among students with events like fairs while also making their presence known in campus decision-making by holding seats on the University Council."

Connecting Service with the Classroom

Penn tells us that "academically based community service (ABCS), supported by the Center for Community Partnerships, is service rooted in and intrinsically linked to teaching and/or research. These academic programs find synergy in the combination of scholarship and service, in their integration of practice and theory." The school reports that "to date, over 150 ABCS courses representing diverse schools and disciplines across the university have been created. During the 2003-2004 academic year, 39 undergraduate courses across 18 departments and 14 graduate courses involving five of the professional schools were engaged in community-based problem-solving research and learning-by-teaching. Nearly 1,500 Penn students were involved in ABCS over the two semesters."

One student explains how Penn service-learning courses work: "The academic classes involved with community service are based around small seminars where the professor teaches you for part of the course hours and the other part is field work"—for example, "it could be working at local schools, with Habitat for Humanity, or doing an internship at a nonprofit."

Impact on Community and Students

Through its unique West Philadelphia Initiative, Penn coordinates with community leaders to improve the neighborhood surrounding the school. As a result of the program, over 300 partnerships have developed between the school and "a range of community-based organizations, including schools, healthcare providers, neighborhood organizations, and a variety of other nonprofit organizations." The multidimensional program addresses issues of street safety and sanitation, public education, housing and home ownership, commercial development, and economic opportunity.

Penn's greatest impact on the community lies in its commitment to education writ large. Coordinated by CCP, the Sayre Health Promotion Disease Prevention Program, for example, is "a comprehensive, multi-component school day, after-school, and evening program" whose goal "is to integrate the activities of the health promotion center with the educational programs and curricula at both Sayre [a local public middle school in transition to becoming a high school], which enrolls nearly 1,000 predominately African American eighth through tenth graders in 2004-2005, and the University. Currently, nearly 70 Penn students in Medicine, Dentistry, Nursing, Law, Social Work, Design, Graduate Education, and Arts and Sciences work in Sayre classrooms." Penn students have also worked to "develop community schools that engage Penn and K-16 students in real-world problem-solving curriculum and development of projects to address community needs. [These schools] support a range of after-school and evening programs for children, youth, their parents and community members." CCP's Digital Divide program helps bring modern technology to the community by "refurbishing computers coming off-line across the campus and then creating computer labs at local schools, community organizations, and communities of faith." The program also provides computer training to volunteers and staff from these organizations.

Student Financial Support for Service

"Alumni support several scholarships for students (usually juniors or seniors) with financial need who have done exemplary work in Center for Community Partnerships programs," the university tells us. "The competitively-selected Penn Program for Public Service Summer Internship provides a stipend, tuition for a summer-research course, and housing" for students to engage in school and community-based projects. Penn's Civic House "oversees the Public Interest Internship Funds, which enable students who rely on summer earnings to accept public interest internships that provide little or no compensation." Finally, "qualifying students receiving financial aid may apply for the Summer Waiver Program, which can waive summer earnings requirements for students in low-paying or unpaid public or community-service internships."

SELECTIVITY

# of applicants	18,282
% of applicants accepted	21
% of acceptees attending	63

FRESHMAN PROFILE

Range SAT Verbal	650-740
Range SAT Math	680-760
Range ACT Composite	28-33
Minimum Paper TOEFL	600
Minimum Computer TOEFL	250
Average HS GPA	3.84
% graduated top 10% of class	93
% graduated top 25% of class	99
% graduated top 50% of class	100

DEADLINES

Regular admission	1/1
Regular notification by	4/1
Nonfall registration?	no

FINANCIAL FACTS

Annual tuition	$27,544
Room and board	$8,918
Books and supplies	$830
Required fees	$3,172
% frosh rec. need-based scholarship or grant aid	42
% UG rec. need-based scholarship or grant aid	39
% frosh rec. need-based self-help aid	45
% UG rec. need-based self-help aid	42
% frosh rec. any financial aid	64
% UG rec. any financial aid	58

UNIVERSITY OF RHODE ISLAND

UNDERGRADUATE ADMISSIONS OFFICE, 14 UPPER COLLEGE ROAD, KINGSTON, RI 02881

ADMISSIONS: 401-874-7100 • **FAX:** 401-874-5523 • **FINANCIAL AID:** 401-874-9500

E-MAIL: URIADMIT@ETAL.URI.EDU • **WEBSITE:** WWW.URI.EDU

CAMPUS LIFE

Type of school	public
Environment	rural

STUDENTS

Total undergrad	
enrollment	10,957
% male/female	44/56
% from out of state	39
% from public high school	90
% live on campus	39
% African American	4
% Asian	3
% Caucasian	76
% Hispanic	4
# of countries represented	53

ACADEMICS

Calendar	semester
Student/faculty ratio	18:1
% profs teaching	
UG courses	83
% classes taught by TAs	8
Most common lab size	10-19
Most common	
reg class size	10-19

MOST POPULAR MAJORS

communications studies/speech
communication and rhetoric
nursing-registered nurse training
(RN, ASN, BSN, MSN)
psychology

Getting Involved

The service community at University of Rhode Island owes a lot to local philanthropist Alan Shawn Feinstein, whose donations created and endows a small universe of service-related offices. There's the Feinstein Center for Service-Learning, for one, which promotes the integration of service with academic study through the Feinstein Enriching America Program, the service-learning component of URI's freshman seminar. The center is home to the Feinstein Engaged Department Program, which "supports academic departments that integrate a service component into their curricula, publish and/or present on service-learning, conduct community based research, and include students in the process," plus engage in other related activities. Another Feinstein endowment supports the Feinstein Center for Hunger Free America, "an educational center that develops solutions to the problem of hunger in RI and nationwide." URI's Clearinghouse for Volunteers, which "coordinates several on-campus service projects each month [and] works with students and the campus community to assist them in planning and coordinating volunteer projects both on and off campus," and Jumpstart URI, "a national nonprofit organization that engages young people in service to work toward the day every child in America enters school prepared to succeed," are also housed at the Feinstein Center.

Feinstein's peer in promoting service is John Hazen White Sr., a wealthy industrialist with a lifelong interest in ethics in business and government. The John Hazen White Sr. Center for Ethics and Public Service sponsors "workshops and selective academic seminars wherein faculty link issues of citizens' responsibility and community service with academic-based learning," endows ethics-related fellowships, and sponsors student internships in public service and government.

URI is also home to a universe of service-related student organizations, including Greek houses, Habitat for Humanity, URI Students for Social Change, and the Kingston Volunteer Fire Department.

Campus Culture of Engagement

High-profile endowments, students report, mean that service at URI is "well-supported by the university." The dual forces of the Feinstein Center and the John Hazen White Sr. Center keep undergrads highly conscious of service opportunities. So too do "events promoting service learning and civic engagement, which take place on and off campus." The efforts of the big university-sponsored offices are supplemented by "the many student-run groups on campus that promote civic engagement, including Students for Sustainable Peace, Students for Social Change, and a Republican group, among others."

Undergrads benefit as much as do the recipients of these services. Writes one student, "Service brings together a diverse group of students that would probably never work together. It is a great feeling to be involved." Agrees another, "Working together allows the students to get to know each other on a personal level; in return, the students become committed to making the campus a better place for everyone." "Don't wait for the opportunities to come to you, though," explains one undergrad, "There are plenty of opportunities to get involved, but like any situation, they are not going to fall into your lap. You need to go out and become an active member of the URI community."

Connecting Service with the Classroom

By the reckoning of URI's administration, "48 service-learning courses exist in 17. Additional courses are added each year. All students participate in at least one service-learning course." To keep abreast of these offerings, each year the Feinstein Center for Service Learning "surveys the faculty on campus to find out about new service-learning courses." The school adds that "such courses receive the Service Learning designation in the Course Catalog."

URI students may choose to pursue a minor in Leadership Studies through the Center for Student Leadership and Development. This minor "prepares students with opportunities to develop and enhance a personal philosophy of leadership. The goal is to prepare students for leadership roles and responsibilities on campus and in career, community, and family leadership roles." Students love it; writes one, "We have an amazing leadership minor here at URI that has impacted many lives by bridging the gap between different organizations, ethnic groups, and diverse students on this campus."

Impact on Community and Students

URI works with over 70 community partners all over Rhode Island, providing a range of services to the underprivileged, sick, and disabled. Among the university's high-impact endeavors is its work with Providence's St. Patrick's Meal Kitchen, where students "regularly volunteer, serving food and eating and visiting with clients." The two also partner for the annual Hunger Banquet, in which "each participant randomly becomes a member of a worldwide economic class and eats a meal appropriate for that class" in order to increase awareness and raise funds.

Local schools receive a huge windfall from URI services. The university's Mentor-Tutor internships provide "disengaged youth and children with a safe haven to explore social and academic issues. URI student mentors assist students in discovering their goals and support the process of attaining those goals." The Science Math Investigative Learning Experiences (SMILE) program works to " increase the number of underrepresented minority and low-income students who graduate from high school qualified to go on to higher education and pursue careers in science, math, engineering, and health professions."

Student Financial Support for Service

URI's Scholarships for Service program allows undergrads to "join AmeriCorps and provide 300 hours (about ten hours per week) of community service through federal work-study, volunteer work, and/or involvement in the Raise Your Voice campaign. Participants earn $1,000 to repay student loans or to finance their education, meet other community-oriented students in Rhode Island, participate in optional trainings related to issues they care about, and become a part of a national service program." In addition, the Robert A. Weygand Scholarship is awarded "for citizenship, [recognizing] that good citizens are good students," and the University Citizen Scholarship, established by the Dean of University College and the President, is awarded "for contributions to the university community."

SELECTIVITY

# of applicants	13,110
% of applicants accepted	70
% of acceptees attending	29

FRESHMAN PROFILE

Range SAT Verbal	510-600
Range SAT Math	520-610
Minimum Paper TOEFL	550
Minimum Computer TOEFL	213
% graduated top 10% of class	18
% graduated top 50% of class	89

DEADLINES

Regular admission	2/1
Regular notification by	rolling
Nonfall registration?	yes

FINANCIAL FACTS

Annual in-state tuition	$4,680
Annual out-of-state tuition	$16,266
Room and board	$7,810
Books and supplies	$800
Required fees	$2,072
% frosh rec. need-based scholarship or grant aid	55
% UG rec. need-based scholarship or grant aid	51
% frosh rec. need-based self-help aid	50
% UG rec. need-based self-help aid	46

UNIVERSITY OF SAN DIEGO

5998 ALCALA PARK, SAN DIEGO, CA 92110-2492

ADMISSIONS: 619-260-4506 • **FAX:** 619-260-6836 • **FINANCIAL AID:** 619-260-4514

E-MAIL: ADMISSIONS@SANDIEGO.EDU • **WEBSITE:** WWW.SANDIEGO.EDU

CAMPUS LIFE

Type of school	private
Environment	town

STUDENTS

Total undergrad enrollment	4,904
% male/female	39/61
% from out of state	38
% from public high school	65
% live on campus	49
% African American	2
% Asian	7
% Caucasian	68
% Hispanic	15
% Native American	1
% international	2
# of countries represented	63

ACADEMICS

Calendar	semester
Student/faculty ratio	18:1
% profs teaching UG courses	100
Most common lab size	20-29
Most common reg class size	10-19

MOST POPULAR MAJORS

business administration/management
communications studies/speech
communication and rhetoric
psychology

Getting Involved

Service at University of San Diego is inextricably bound up with the school's mission to "embrace the Catholic moral and social tradition" through a "commitment to serve with compassion, to foster peace and to work for justice, and prepare leaders dedicated to ethical conduct and compassionate service." USD maintains a number of offices to facilitate these goals. The Center for Community Service-Learning "engages USD students, faculty, staff, and alumni to learn in partnership with the community" through "course-based service-learning, student-run co-curricular service, America Reads/Counts work-study tutoring, and a campus-wide Social Issues committee which sponsors an annual conference as well as speakers and special events."

Another key player is University Ministry, which offers students "opportunities for service and reflection [such as] cross-border immersion opportunities, delivering meals to AIDS patients, service at a soup kitchen, and 'Hunger and Homelessness Week,' which includes a night without shelter." The organization's new facility, the Romero Center for Faith in Action, "focuses on educating the campus community on important social issues in our community and in our world and on providing immersion programs for students." The center "relies almost exclusively on student leadership for vision and programming."

Extracurricular volunteerism finds a home at USD's Center for Awareness, Service, and Action (CASA), which "combines opportunities for service and activism, and encourages students to connect their community service to social issues and advocacy." Its student-run projects include not only "well-known national programs such as Habitat for Humanity, Special Olympics, and Best Buddies" but also "many unique to our neighborhood such as the Linda Vista Kids program."

Campus Culture of Engagement

Students love the support network USD provides; of those who run the offices, undergrads tell us that "they are so positive and they reach out to all people and all areas. The leaders we have here on campus are so amazing, and you are able to build such great bonds with them." They also appreciate how "the variety of projects allows everyone to find something they could enjoy. Also relating the projects to classes brings both life and learning a new aspect." Religious organizations, of course, play a major role; "people who like working with Christian groups, regardless of personal faith choice, will find a fantastic community at USD," writes one student. Political groups are less active; complained one undergrad, "As an International Relations student, I find many people on our campus do not volunteer or care about political issues."

Most of all, students appreciate how service opens their eyes to the big picture. Explains one, "What I have learned is that the world as I know it is not limited to what life is like at USD where BMWs, Hummers, and Ferraris are almost standard cars for students. That there are those out there with close to nothing yet still manage to hold on and hope for better days."

Connecting Service with the Classroom

Service learning at USD "formally began in 1994 with support from a 'Learn and Serve' grant from the Corporation for National Service," the school reports, adding that "since then, over 150 courses, from a broad spectrum of disciplines, have included the component, and 100 do so on a continuing basis." Over 1,600 students participate in service-learning courses annually.

USD professors, the university tells us, "have shown remarkable creativity in designing projects that meet both curricular objectives and the needs of the community. These programs include such things as an annual middle-school health fair, math family night, cross-border weekends, community research with students, a course with participation of middle-school students, media-criticism workshops, marketing projects for nonprofits, working with youth organizing and other 'action for change' organizations, and major project management through extensive house renovations."

Students note that "service learning takes place not only in the Linda Vista Community (where USD is located), but all over San Diego county; it also crosses the border to Mexico. It takes the form of students tutoring at many schools in Linda Vista, volunteering at Juvenile Hall, helping out with events in the community, working at Migrant Outreach, going to Tijuana, Californians for Justice, [and] working with homeless shelters."

Impact on Community and Students

Through its various service-learning courses and extracurricular projects, USD "works with approximately 50 ongoing partnerships, 20 of which are in our immediate neighborhood." Service recipients include "schools and after-school programs, and projects with detainees in Juvenile Hall, teen parents, migrants, cross-border communities, persons who are homeless, and environmental work," as well as "emerging grass-roots organizations and community organizing projects."

Among the beneficiaries of USD's good works are members of the Linda Vista community, which surrounds the campus. This unique neighborhood includes "a large number of Southeast Asian immigrants (especially Vietnamese, Hmong, and Lao) as well as a growing Latino population." Because nearly two-thirds of the children attending local schools speak English as a second language, "USD students work to teach English, tutor in all subject areas, and provide enrichment activities in arts, science, and preparation for college." Each semester, "over 300 students work in seven schools, seven after-school programs, Head Start, and engage in numerous community projects" throughout Linda Vista.

USD undergrads also perform service in Mexico to participate in "four rewarding cross-border partnerships," including "a Catholic community center located in a growing but very poor group of ten neighborhoods on the east side of Tijuana." Notes one student, "Living in a large city (San Diego), as well as next to the international border (Tijuana), provides an ideal location to engage in diverse settings with which to serve."

Student Financial Support for Service

USD annually offers $15,000 in scholarships to "upperclassmen who have taken on leadership roles in community service. Students are selected by the Community Service-Learning staff on the basis of need, commitment, and leadership ability." In addition, "between ten and 20 students each year are recruited for a part-time AmeriCorps position, which includes an educational award upon completion of their commitment to service."

SELECTIVITY

# of applicants	7,623
% of applicants accepted	66
% of acceptees attending	23
# accepting a place on wait list	458
% admitted from wait list	1

FRESHMAN PROFILE

Range SAT Verbal	530-620
Range SAT Math	550-640
Range ACT Composite	23-28
Minimum Paper TOEFL	550
Minimum Computer TOEFL	213
Average HS GPA	3.66
% graduated top 10% of class	34
% graduated top 25% of class	70
% graduated top 50% of class	95

DEADLINES

Regular admission	1/5
Regular notification by	4/15
Nonfall registration?	yes

FINANCIAL FACTS

% frosh rec. need-based scholarship or grant aid	52
% UG rec. need-based scholarship or grant aid	49
% frosh rec. need-based self-help aid	41
% UG rec. need-based self-help aid	43
% UG rec. any financial aid	69

UNIVERSITY OF SOUTHERN CALIFORNIA

ADMISSIONS OFFICE: STUDENT ADMINISTRATIVE SERVICES, 700 CHILDS WAY, LOS ANGELES, CA 90089-0911

ADMISSIONS: 213-740-1111 • FAX: 213-740-6364 • FINANCIAL AID: 213-740-1111

E-MAIL: ADMITUSC@USC.EDU • WEBSITE: WWW.USC.EDU

CAMPUS LIFE

Type of school	private
Environment	town

STUDENTS

Total undergrad enrollment	16,271
% male/female	49/51
% from out of state	32
% from public high school	59
% live on campus	36
% African American	7
% Asian	21
% Caucasian	48
% Hispanic	13
% Native American	1
% international	9
# of countries represented	148

ACADEMICS

Calendar	semester
Student/faculty ratio	13:1
% profs teaching UG courses	75
% classes taught by TAs	0
Most common lab size	10-19
Most common reg class size	10-19

MOST POPULAR MAJORS

business administration/management
communications studies/speech
communication and rhetoric
psychology

Getting Involved

"Unlike most universities, in which service and volunteer programs are housed under one roof, USC uses a decentralized model," the university tells us, explaining that "many independent centers on the university's two campuses actively support civic engagement on the part of faculty, students, and staff." These include the Joint Educational Project (JEP), "one of the oldest and largest nationally recognized service-learning programs in the country," which "places more than 2,000 service-learning students in the neighborhood." Also among them is the USC Volunteer Center, which "supports students in search of meaningful volunteer experiences on and off campus [by maintaining] a searchable database of short- and long-term volunteer opportunities at more than 300 community organizations."

USC's Civic and Community Relations (CCR) focuses on "enhancing the quality of life of people who live and work in the neighborhoods surrounding USC's University Park and Health Sciences campuses." The Civic Engagement Initiative, "a partnership of the School of Policy, Planning, and Development and the Jesse M. Unruh Institute of Politics, seeks to build bridges across scholarly disciplines and across communities to study the theory and practice of civic engagement, share theoretical and practical knowledge with others, and promote a robust civic culture." Finally, the Experiential Learning Office "conducts internship programs and workshops throughout the academic year." With so many options, it's no wonder students tell us that "the possibilities here are truly endless."

Campus Culture of Engagement

"It is definitely the 'cool' thing to be engaged on campus. Our service programs are quite popular and many students of various backgrounds participate," students at USC agree, noting that their school "prides itself on making a concerted effort to reach out into the surrounding community. There are numerous student-run and university-run organizations that target community service for citizens of all ages and demographics, with a focus on youth and adolescents in USC's low-income surrounding area. Many students at USC see Getting Involved in service-learning as part of their duty as Trojans." Their actions go a long way toward dispelling the "prevailing stereotype that USC [undergrads] are rich white students who care very little for a neighborhood that is poorer minorities."

Connecting Service with the Classroom

According to USC, "in 2004, service-learning can be found in some 25 departments across the university, from Anthropology to Music, Physics to Social Work, Women's Studies to Architecture. Students are involved in research activities such as a recent group of undergraduates from a course on Race and Ethnic Relations in a Global Society who investigated the impact that immigration and sexuality had on the work of health-care providers in Mexico. Their findings were used in a proposal to fund an AIDS education center and clinic on the border between the U.S. and Mexico. Other students are engaged in direct service activities, such as dental students who visit local elementary school in the Mobile Dental Van, assisting volunteer dentists in free dental check-ups for children."

Overall, "Service-learning is a component in over 80 classes. Each year, some 3,000 [students]-or 18 percent of all undergraduate students-participate in these courses, all receiving course credit for their community assignment and the reflective work that they do (e.g., a weekly journal, group discussions, or analytical papers)." Students point out that "at USC, service-learning looks like a fascinating mixture of large-scale projects and one-on-one involvement, mostly geared with an academic emphasis (i.e., tutoring, mentoring, or providing pseudo-child care). The implicit message is that no one person can change everything, but touching one person in need can have a huge impact."

Impact on Community and Students

USC's presence is felt in Los Angeles through "approximately 250 community partners ranging from 20 K-12 public and parochial schools to an assortment of nonprofit organizations that emphasize everything from providing parenting education to civic engagement as vehicles for improving quality of life." Chief among these projects is the Joint Educational Project (JEP), a service-learning program through which "students are drawn from about 50 different courses each semester and placed in over two dozen community sites, from local schools to a shelter for battered women and their families. These 'JEPers' (as they're known) receive training, guidance, and assistance in bridging theory and practice from [organization] staff, who also monitor students' progress in the field and help community supervisors in evaluating students' work." Through JEP, USC students tutor underprivileged students, volunteer in local hospitals and clinics, and provide other valuable services to the community.

USC also impacts its surrounding community through "several campus-wide events such as Swim with Mike, which is an annual fundraiser for physically disabled athletes in which students are sponsored to swim laps; and Spirits in Action, which is a Special-Olympics-type event for area children. There are also events held on campus to raise awareness, such as Take Back the Night, raising awareness of sexual violence; teach-ins on a variety of hot button issues; and academic retreats, in which a small number of students accompany a professor off campus for a weekend to discuss various topics that combine culture and academics."

Student Financial Support for Service

USC offers the following awards to students involved in service: the Norman Topping Student Aid Fund, which "[focuses] on low-income students who demonstrate community awareness and engagement with their community," with priority given to local students; the Dean Joan Metcalf Schaefer Endowed Scholarships, for continuing students "who have demonstrated a continuous love for learning and scholarly excellence while addressing social, artistic, educational, health, or public-service issues" within the greater community; the Grace Ford Salvatori Community Service Scholarships; and the Henry Martin Lederman Award for Servant Leadership, "given to an exceptional first-year or transfer student who, upon arriving at USC, has generously shared his or her time and talents with neighbors in the community surrounding the USC campuses."

SELECTIVITY

# of applicants	29,792
% of applicants accepted	27
% of acceptees attending	34

FRESHMAN PROFILE

Range SAT Verbal	620-710
Range SAT Math	640-730
Range ACT Composite	27-31
% graduated top 10% of class	84
% graduated top 25% of class	94
% graduated top 50% of class	100

DEADLINES

Regular admission	1/10
Regular notification by	4/1
Nonfall registration?	yes

FINANCIAL FACTS

Annual tuition	$29,988
Room and board	$8,998
Books and supplies	$650
Required fees	$524
% frosh rec. need-based scholarship or grant aid	42
% UG rec. need-based scholarship or grant aid	42
% frosh rec. need-based self-help aid	47
% UG rec. need-based self-help aid	47
% frosh rec. any financial aid	72
% UG rec. any financial aid	66

UNIVERSITY OF VERMONT

ADMISSIONS OFFICE, 194 SOUTH PROSPECT STREET, BURLINGTON, VT 05401-3596

ADMISSIONS: 802-656-3370 • FAX: 802-656-8611 • FINANCIAL AID: 802-656-5700

E-MAIL: ADMISSIONS@UVM.EDU • WEBSITE: WWW.UVM.EDU

CAMPUS LIFE

Type of school	public
Environment	village

STUDENTS

Total undergrad enrollment	8,143
% male/female	45/55
% from out of state	63
% from public high school	70
% live on campus	52
% African American	1
% Asian	2
% Caucasian	93
% Hispanic	2
% international	1
# of countries represented	40

ACADEMICS

Calendar	4-1-4
Student/faculty ratio	15:1
% profs teaching UG courses	85
% classes taught by TAs	2
Most common lab size	10-19
Most common reg class size	<10

MOST POPULAR MAJORS

biology/biological sciences
business administration/management
psychology

Getting Involved

The University of Vermont's sizeable service community is supported by three main offices: The Office of Community-University Partnerships and Service-Learning (CUPS), the Department of Student Life, and Career Services. CUPS "supports individuals and groups on and off campus that collaborate to provide opportunities for community-based scholarship and service-learning."

UVM's Department of Student Life houses the Office of Community Service Programs, "which involve everything from day-long service events each fall and spring semester, to one-shot service opportunities, extended-commitment volunteer opportunities, Community Service TREK (a pre-first year orientation week of community service), and Alternative Spring Break." The department also serves as headquarters for Volunteers In Action (VIA), "the largest student group on campus." VIA sponsors adaptive sports for the disabled, alternative breaks, big buddy programs, ESL outreach, a therapy-dog program, and outreach projects serving the homeless, infirm, and elderly. In addition, "there are community-service opportunities in Greek Affairs, the Department of Residential Life, and the Department of Judicial Affairs."

Career Services, the university reports, "houses two programs that support students interested in service-learning and eventual careers in the not-for-profit sector." The Service-Learning Internship Program (SLIP) "supports students as they search for, choose, and are placed in local, state, national, and even international internships in nonprofit, governmental, and other social-justice internships." The Nonprofit Program "assists students in their search for and placement in post-graduate employment and/or further education in the not-for-profit, governmental, and social-justice fields."

Campus Culture of Engagement

"There are a lot of visible communities that anyone can be involved in, from environmental-justice organizations to equal-rights programs" at UVM, a campus that "is very civically engaged because the clubs are always out there, getting the word out, and they don't let themselves fade into the background. There are always various activities, and they usually include food, which helps to draw even non-civically engaged students, and then they become interested and stick around."

Politically, "UVM is one of the most liberal schools in the country and the issues of social change are quite important. Many clubs support liberal views." Students brag that "Burlington is a great place and offers a lot of civic services both here and around the world. Very environmentally friendly too." The huge student population means that there is "plenty of variety. There are so many groups doing so many things, and if there is something that you believe should be getting done or getting more attention, then it is really easy to start a new group yourself. Everyone is so supportive and helpful. People interested in community service really thrive."

Connecting Service with the Classroom

UVM, "one of the first schools in the country to offer academic credit in relationship to service-learning," maintains a strong commitment to credit-bearing service. In fact, service-learning offerings have increased substantially in recent years; writes the school, "According to [an] end-of-grant evaluation [following up a four-year service-learning grant], the disciplines experienced a 155 percent increase in the number of service-learning courses (from 33 to 84), a 123 percent increase in the number of professors who teach service-learning (from 34 to 76), and a 100 percent increase in the number of academic departments that offer service-learning courses (from 14 to 28) in the four-year grant period."

The results include an English class that "works with teens in the Teen Futures Program at the King Street Youth Center to expand their use of the web, poetry, and creative writing," a community Psychology class that collaborates with the City of Burlington Community and Economic Development office "to survey specific neighborhoods about community involvement and leadership, and create recommendations for community leaderships training," and a Natural Resources senior seminar that is working with the local transit authority to study emissions reductions. Students point out that "many introductory first-year classes now include a service-learning section of the class."

Impact on Community and Students

UVM's Volunteers in Action provides myriad contact points between students and the surrounding community. Its eighteen service-oriented programs "provide services to the community to address a wide variety of social, educational, physical, and environmental concerns in the local, state, national, and international communities. Whether it is feeding local citizens in need of a hot meal every week, teaching children the joy of creative expression through writing, or helping the area's young people learn how to respect and care for the environment, the UVM students involved in VIA are committed to and passionate about making a positive contribution to the world."

Students also provide valuable EMT services through UVM Rescue, "started in the spring of 1972 when a few students who were Emergency Medical Technicians began riding on the campus security vehicles carrying a kit with emergency supplies to assist anyone who may have needed emergency medical care." Today the group has "more than 30 full-time members [and] is a state-certified emergency-ambulance service completely staffed and operated by University of Vermont students 24 hours a day, 365 days a year."

Student Financial Support for Service

First-year and transfer students at UVM are eligible for a Vermont Community Service Scholarship, awarded to those "who demonstrate, through their admissions materials, essays, and recommendations, a commitment to community service. Recipients are awarded a minimum merit-based scholarship of $1,250 annually." All students are eligible for the Fishman Scholarship, which "recognizes one student per semester who exemplifies excellence in the Service-Learning Internships Program through Career Services."

SELECTIVITY

# of applicants	11,384
% of applicants accepted	76
% of acceptees attending	23
# accepting a place on wait list	977
% admitted from wait list	9

FRESHMAN PROFILE

Range SAT Verbal	530-620
Range SAT Math	530-630
Range ACT Composite	22-27
Minimum Paper TOEFL	550
Minimum Computer TOEFL	213
% graduated top 10% of class	23
% graduated top 25% of class	57
% graduated top 50% of class	93

DEADLINES

Regular admission	1/15
Regular notification by	3/31
Nonfall registration?	yes

FINANCIAL FACTS

Annual in-state tuition	$9,088
Annual out-of-state tuition	$22,728
Room and board	$7,016
Books and supplies	$832
Required fees	$1,138
% frosh rec. need-based scholarship or grant aid	52
% UG rec. need-based scholarship or grant aid	50
% frosh rec. need-based self-help aid	48
% UG rec. need-based self-help aid	47
% frosh rec. any financial aid	81
% UG rec. any financial aid	77

UNIVERSITY OF WISCONSIN—MADISON

RED GYM AND ARMORY, 716 LANGDON STREET, MADISON, WI 53706-1481

ADMISSIONS: 608-262-3961 • FAX: 608-262-7706 • FINANCIAL AID: 608-262-3060

E-MAIL: ONWISCONSIN@ADMISSIONS.WISC.EDU • WEBSITE: WWW.WISC.EDU

CAMPUS LIFE

Type of school	public
Environment	town

STUDENTS

Total undergrad enrollment	28,217
% male/female	47/53
% from out of state	29
% live on campus	24
% African American	2
% Asian	5
% Caucasian	84
% Hispanic	3
% Native American	1
% international	3
# of countries represented	110

ACADEMICS

Calendar	semester
Student/faculty ratio	13:1
% profs teaching UG courses	90
% classes taught by TAs	25
Most common lab size	20-29

MOST POPULAR MAJORS
history
political science and government
psychology

Getting Involved

Central to the mission of the University of Wisconsin—Madison is the Wisconsin Idea that "a tradition of service that originated with university leaders over 100 years ago when they declared, 'The boundaries of the campus are the boundaries of the state.'" That concept has expanded as the world has grown smaller, administrators tell us, explaining that "today, the Wisconsin Idea calls us to extend our boundaries beyond the state to the global community. This tradition underpins many University of Wisconsin-Madison civic-engagement activities across campus."

The lynchpin of service here is the Morgridge Center for Public Service, which coordinates volunteer service, academic credit-based service-learning and community-based research, and civic-engagement activities. This office maintains an "online, searchable database listing hundreds of local volunteer opportunities [and] resources on national and international service opportunities and programs." It also organizes Volunteer Fairs at the beginning of each semester, manages the Undergraduate Peer Advisor program "to help students find volunteer opportunities or assist in developing group or individual service projects" and manages "grants to assist registered student organizations implement service activities."

Campus Culture of Engagement

"Engagement, service, and activism are pretty much constants at our university," UW—Madison undergrads agree. Another reports, "From the first day that a student walks to class, there will be a group outside soliciting support for their cause or recruiting new members." Adds another, "The Wisconsin Idea specifically states that the boundaries of the state are the boundaries of the university and that the university is to engage with the community in order to create a mutually beneficial relationship. Almost every major makes service learning a priority!" Furthermore, because "the opportunities are numerous" here, "students of all backgrounds and areas of interest are able to participate in projects that are suited specifically to the individual."

University administrators point out that "UW—Madison has a long history of student activism and community involvement, including support for civil and gender rights, activism against the Vietnam War, and protests concerning sweatshop labor. For the tenth year in a row, UW—Madison has the highest number of alumni serving as Peace Corps volunteers (142). We are also among the top campuses that have alumni serving in Teach For America." Students concur; advises one, "Come to Madison if you really want to get involved on a political or civic issue. Students here are very proactive at taking on issues and getting results." Adds another, "The location just a few blocks from the state capitol and the traditions of student involvement and student activism on campus make the UW—Madison an excellent place to be involved and make a real difference."

Connecting Service with the Classroom

The UW—Madison administration tells us that "there are approximately 80 service-learning courses taught at UW—Madison in a range of departments. The number of service-learning courses has increased threefold in the last few years, and we anticipate it will keep growing." These courses "are extremely varied; some have an ongoing, direct service requirement, some have a one-time service-project option, some require an indirect-consultation project. The courses also address a variety of social needs, including education, race relations, small-business development, women's issues, individuals with disabilities, affordable housing, poverty, the environment, and health care, to name a few." Explains one student, "Service-learning needs to start in the classroom, but it always ends up outside of the traditional classroom. It involves becoming informed about the situations and then actively engaging in those environments to get a first-hand view of what is going on."

Impact on Community and Students

"In a university of our size and complexity," write UW—Madison administrators, "there are dozens-if not hundreds-of partnerships on campus and in local, national, and international communities." One of the most significant, in terms of impact on the local community, is the Volunteer Income Tax Assistance Program (VITA) in South Madison, which assists low-income individuals and families, the elderly, and disabled people in filing their income-tax returns. It is a partnership with the Internal Revenue Service, the Wisconsin Department of Revenue, the university, and the UW-Extension Dane County. Last year, nearly 4,000 returns were filed by 120 volunteers, over half of whom were university students." Notes the school, "Literally millions of dollars-especially through the earned-income tax credits-were returned to people who need them the most. This is an example of just one of the programs which have been developed through the Campus-Community Partnerships Initiative."

Students report that undergrads in many departments contribute significantly to communities in Madison and greater Wisconsin. Explains one, "Most engineers design a contraption that will be used in the community (swing sets, climbing walls, pet shelter cages), Premed/life scientists participate in a Biological Aspects of Conservation project. Physical and applied mathematicians set up service education. Business students offer finance seminars to the public. The list goes on and on."

Student Financial Support for Service

UW—Madison exceeds the minimum requirement for community work study by five percentage points. In addition, the school's "most prestigious awards for juniors and seniors, the Meyerhoff Undergraduate Awards for Service, Leadership and Scholarship and the Herfurth Kubly Awards (established 75 or 80 years ago) require significant service in the community for consideration. Finally, there are Wisconsin Idea Undergraduate Fellowships, which "support innovative projects where undergraduate students, faculty/instructional staff and community organizations collaborate in service activities and/or research designed to meet a community need while enhancing student learning."

SELECTIVITY

# of applicants	20,495
% of applicants accepted	66
% of acceptees attending	42

FRESHMAN PROFILE

Range SAT Verbal	560-670
Range SAT Math	600-700
Range ACT Composite	26-30
Minimum Paper TOEFL	550
Minimum Computer TOEFL	213
Average HS GPA	3.68
% graduated top 10% of class	58
% graduated top 25% of class	93
% graduated top 50% of class	99

DEADLINES

Regular admission	2/1
Regular notification by	rolling
Nonfall registration?	yes

FINANCIAL FACTS

% frosh rec. need-based scholarship or grant aid	12
% UG rec. need-based scholarship or grant aid	14
% frosh rec. need-based self-help aid	24
% UG rec. need-based self-help aid	27

VANDERBILT UNIVERSITY

2305 WEST END AVENUE, NASHVILLE, TN 37203

ADMISSIONS: 615-322-2561 • **FAX:** 615-343-7765 • **FINANCIAL AID:** 615-322-3591

E-MAIL: ADMISSIONS@VANDERBILT.EDU • **WEBSITE:** WWW.VANDERBILT.EDU

CAMPUS LIFE

Type of school	private
Environment	town

STUDENTS

Total undergrad enrollment	6,231
% male/female	49/51
% from out of state	76
% from public high school	60
% live on campus	83
% African American	7
% Asian	6
% Caucasian	73
% Hispanic	4
% international	2
# of countries represented	52

ACADEMICS

Calendar	semester
Student/faculty ratio	8:1

MOST POPULAR MAJORS

engineering science
psychology
sociology

Getting Involved

Vanderbilt houses a host of offices serving to coordinate students' and faculty's community and civic service. One undergrad advises incoming students to "seek out the good stuff"—and sure enough, there's plenty to seek out. Volunteerism is headquartered at the Office of Active Citizenship and Service, whose "fundamental aim is to promote, through active citizenship and service work, the value of social justice, public awareness, service-learning, and lifelong civic involvement." Service-learning also finds a home at the Office of the Assistant Provost for Service Learning, which is "committed to the preparation of undergraduate and graduate students, faculty, and community partners to become, in part through a strong university-wide service-learning program, the next generation of community builders who will move Nashville, and the nation, toward a more democratic society." The Center for Health Services, the Community Outreach Partnership Center, and the Community Research and Action Doctoral Program all also contribute.

Students describe a cornucopia of ways to stay in touch with the campus activism scene. Explains one, "It's all around. From the freshmen move-in crew made solely of volunteers to tons of various student-organization and service-organization fairs at the start of the semester, from the trillions of fliers and banners all over campus to the hundreds of extremely helpful and creative staff in both the Student Organization Office and the Office of Volunteer Activities, it would be near-impossible to miss out on a great opportunity."

Campus Culture of Engagement

"There are nearly 40 student-run service organizations" at Vandy "that do everything from tutoring at-risk youth to GLBT advocacy nationwide, to Meals on Heels locally, to working with AIDS/HIV patients in Africa and India, to even promoting cross-cultural dialogue in the Middle East." Observes one student, "There is so much money at Vanderbilt that is put into outstanding projects for the students; for example, there are political speakers from all different parties throughout the year. There is voter registration in the cafeteria. The administration and students are very dedicated to creating a culture of growth and personal development, including active citizenship and service to others."

The overall political vibe on campus is conservative but, notes one aspiring lefty, "We have a growing liberal population that is interested in activism and empowering others."

Connecting Service with the Classroom

Vanderbilt reports that "both the Chancellor and the Provost have strongly tied service-learning to the academic mission of the university and have included service-learning as one of the university's top priorities in its overall strategic plan. Over the past three years, we have trained over 30 faculty and more than 25 graduate students in year long service-learning seminars. This has resulted in the development of over 40 service-learning courses. In addition, other faculty have integrated service-learning into their courses and it is estimated that over 50 service-learning courses currently are taught on the campus across each of the undergraduate and professional schools." During a typical semester "it is estimated that 400 to 800 students will be enrolled in a service-learning course on the campus." The school also points out that "students have had a key role in the service-learning movement on our campus. Their efforts, and the efforts of many other students, continue to move our faculty and administration toward the institutionalization of service-learning on our campus."

Impact on Community and Students

"The Office of Volunteer Activities has relationships with over 150 local nonprofit agencies," Vandy tells us, adding that "faculty and students engage numerous agencies in service-learning partnerships." Says the school, "Our goal is to create long-term sustainable relationships with our community partners and to integrate both volunteer service, service-learning, and community research and action to best meet community defined needs."

Noteworthy endeavors here include a partnership between the Community Outreach Partnership Center and three neighborhood associations to implement programs in "crime prevention, community organizing, and health promotion." This program incorporates the efforts of many different sectors within the university: the Department of Human and Organizational Development, the Blair School of Music, and the Nursing School, for example, all contribute through health-related service-learning classes. The Medical Center and the Owen Graduate School of Management contribute "expertise in both children's health initiatives and economic development issues." And "the Office of Active Citizenship and Service has provided volunteer groups for special projects to the North Nashville agencies."

Vandy's Mayfield Living Learning Lodge program, "established in 1988-1989, has gained national recognition among service-learning programs." The program sets aside residences for "groups of ten students who live together in order to pursue a self-directed, yearlong program of educational activities, including community-service projects. This year, the program included 140 students in 14 lodges organized around topics ranging from the homeless to women's health to Nashville's multicultural history."

Student Financial Support for Service

Vanderbilt offers several awards to students involved in community and public service. Among them is the distinguished Ingram Scholarship Program, which requires that recipients "design and implement projects that address significant societal needs. The Ingram Scholarship Program provides: a) full tuition support each year to entering freshmen; b) half-tuition support each year to current Vanderbilt students; c) stipends for special summer projects; d) project expense budgets."

SELECTIVITY

# of applicants	11,170
% of applicants accepted	38
% of acceptees attending	37

FRESHMAN PROFILE

Range SAT Verbal	620-710
Range SAT Math	650-730
Range ACT Composite	28-32
Minimum Paper TOEFL	570

DEADLINES

Nonfall registration?	yes

FINANCIAL FACTS

Annual tuition	$29,240
Room and board	$9,736
Books and supplies	$1,030
Required fees	$750
% frosh rec. need-based scholarship or grant aid	40
% UG rec. need-based scholarship or grant aid	37
% frosh rec. need-based self-help aid	27
% UG rec. need-based self-help aid	27

WILLIAMS COLLEGE

33 STETSON COURT, WILLIAMSTOWN, MA 01267

ADMISSIONS: 413-597-2211 • FAX: 413-597-4052 • FINANCIAL AID: 413-597-4181

E-MAIL: ADMISSION@WILLIAMS.EDU • WEBSITE: WWW.WILLIAMS.EDU

CAMPUS LIFE

Type of school	private
Environment	rural

STUDENTS

Total undergrad enrollment	1,931
% male/female	50/50
% from out of state	84
% from public high school	54
% live on campus	93
% African American	10
% Asian	9
% Caucasian	67
% Hispanic	8
% international	6
# of countries represented	63

ACADEMICS

Calendar	38078
Student/faculty ratio	11:1
% profs teaching UG courses	100
% classes taught by TAs	0
Most common reg class size	<10

MOST POPULAR MAJORS

art/art studies
economics
political science and government

Getting Involved

The location of Williams College, administrators observe, provides a unique opportunity to the school's service-minded undergrads. Explains the school, "Among the most important ingredients of a Williams education are the challenges and struggles of this region. Our poor and working-class neighbors are being left behind as Berkshire County struggles to transition from a manufacturing to a service/tourism economy. If ever there was a time for Williams students to join in local struggles and to play a role in leading the region back toward health and sustainability, that time is now."

The Office of Community Service handles much of the heavy lifting at Williams. It "supports a wide range of student initiatives in community service and civic engagement, in more than 30 established community-service programs and in continual fomentation of new projects and new ways of thinking about our relationships to the surrounding community." The office "serves as a clearinghouse for information from the community" and "produces a wide array of alternative winter-break and spring-break trips, provides resources for faculty and staff interested in volunteering, and helps to promote and coordinate activities and events between and among student groups."

The Chaplain's Office also contributes substantially; it "is the point of departure for many service ventures, both faith-based and secular. Many student initiatives that don't have a home in an already-existing group seek support and guidance from [the Chaplain's Office]." Classwork-related service is headquartered in the Office of Experiential Education. Academic service also operates from specific departments; the popular Center for Environmental Studies, for example, offers classes "that involve extensive research in the natural and human landscape and have pioneered some of the more imaginative ventures in experiential education." The school also points out that "virtually every student group on campus is involved, in some way and at some point in the year, in community-service or civic-engagement projects."

Campus Culture of Engagement

Students groups at Williams are involved in everything from AIDS care, to the environment, to the arts, to politics across the spectrum. Students report that "opportunities are certainly there if one chooses to take advantage of them" and that "whether you are liberal or conservative, Christian or secular, male or female, you can find a campus organization that enables you to be actively involved in your community." Better still, "anyone who wishes to participate in projects or create their own can approach the board." A substantial international community focuses students on global as well as local issues.

To keep students posted of service opportunities, "each week, the council puts a flyer in everyone's mailboxes describing the service events for the week and who to contact if a person is interested." Also, "tabling (groups set up with information in the student center during lunch hours) for community service-events is very helpful." Students love "the vans specifically reserved for community service, which are a huge plus: You don't need a car or special funding to work on something away from campus."

Connecting Service with the Classroom

Williams offers approximately 20 service-learning courses "involving community work, ranging from those designed around intensive fieldwork such as the Berkshire Farm Internship Course (Anthropology/Sociology) to those that feature one half-day of community service such as the Humans in the Landscape Course (Environmental Studies)." Many of these courses are offered in psychology, anthropology, sociology, and environmental studies, although they are spread through other disciplines as well. Undergraduates "are also encouraged to develop their own independent-study projects involving fieldwork. In 2003-2004 alone, over 200 students have either taken a fieldwork course or designed their own study involving some form of community work."

The school points out that "the recent addition of a coordinator of experiential education will further develop this program at Williams, and benefits can already be seen. The 2004-2005 academic year promises an even more exciting menu of experiential and community-based coursework."

Impact on Community and Students

Williams supports a Social Choice Fund, a socially- and environmentally-responsible investment option for alumni giving initially created by student activists. The fund is an important model that invests in socially-responsible stocks and in the local community. Williams also boasts "an impressive array of partnerships both within the region and throughout the world" that serve as "a ready resource for any students interested in learning more about and engaging deeply with social and political issues, whether as students, researchers, volunteers, interns, or employees." Among the contact points between Williams and the community is the Pownal (Vermont) Elementary School, to which Williams provides over 30 America Reads and America Counts tutors every year. Undergrads also provide mentoring services, after-school enrichment, multicultural education, and an early college-awareness program "to make Pownal students aware of the many possible futures that lie ahead."

Williams students are also a consistent presence at the Williamstown Youth Center, which "relies on committed students as sports coaches, tutors, summer-camp leaders, art and dance instructors, computer-network administrators, and administrative interns."

Student Financial Support for Service

Williams "does not offer scholarships exclusively for community service, though it does manage several endowed funds to recognize the service provided by financial-aid students." Among the school's aid offerings are the Herbert Lehman Scholarships, the Class of 1957 Scholarships, and the Williams Scholarships, all "awarded each year to approximately two dozen financial-aid students who have made significant contributions to the community."

SELECTIVITY

# of applicants	5,705
% of applicants accepted	19
% of acceptees attending	49

FRESHMAN PROFILE

Range SAT Verbal	660-760
Range SAT Math	670-760
% graduated top 10% of class	85
% graduated top 25% of class	97
% graduated top 50% of class	100

DEADLINES

Regular admission	1/1
Regular notification by	4/9
Nonfall registration?	no

FINANCIAL FACTS

Annual tuition	$29,786
Room and board	$8,110
Books and supplies	$800
Required fees	$204
% frosh rec. need-based scholarship or grant aid	41
% UG rec. need-based scholarship or grant aid	40
% frosh rec. need-based self-help aid	41
% UG rec. need-based self-help aid	42
% frosh rec. any financial aid	64
% UG rec. any financial aid	70

STUDENT PROFILES

Adam Reich
Senior, Brown University

MAJOR

Public Policy and American Institutions

HOMETOWN

Cambridge, MA

Which groups and organizations have you been involved in throughout college?

Student groups

The People's School Student Project

The Next Left

Student-Labor Alliance

Community groups

The People's School

AS220's Broad Street Studio

The Rhode Island Training School for Youth

RI Governor's Select Committee on Race and Police-Community Relations

Direct Action for Rights and Equality

Prison Roundtable Group

Carnegie Foundation's Political Education Project

What's your favorite class been so far?

My favorite class has actually been one at Harvard's Kennedy School of Government. The class is called "Organizing: People, Power, and Change" taught by Marshall Ganz. I had the good fortune this semester of working as a teaching fellow with Professor Ganz, having never taken the class. It's a whirlwind of history and theory of organizing in which each student engages in his or her own organizing project. I spent the semester working with ten students, coaching these students individually and facilitating weekly sections.

What advice about starting school would you give a prospective student?

I would recommend that a first-year student keep her eyes peeled for older students and professors who inspire her, take a deep breath, and ask those people to sit down for a cup of coffee and a one-on-one conversation. Finding meaningful community work, I've found, is largely about forming personal relationships with people who are already engaged in this sort of work. Not only can these people serve as bridges to communities outside the school, but they can serve as important mentors as a student begins her own independent work.

How is your civic engagement related to your education?

Over the last three and a half years, I have led writing workshops with young people inside and recently released from the Rhode Island Training School—the state's only juvenile corrections facility. The conversations I have had and the relationships I have formed as a result of my work have transformed my worldview as well as my academic trajectory.

My work at the Training School intensified and personalized my interest in the juvenile justice system. I have witnessed the struggles of the young people who are sent to and released from the facility. While I have been inspired by those few young people who found a way out of the cycle of crime and incarceration, I have been devastated to see so many young people returning to the Training School time and again.

I have also come to see the importance of community work to academic research. This past spring, I wrote a senior thesis about juvenile justice policy. My research consisted of extensive interviews with the young people I knew from my work in the facility, and the depth of my analysis was greatly enhanced by the honesty with which I was able to talk to the young people I interviewed. The thesis recounted the young offenders' experiences and drew lessons about how to improve juvenile justice from their stories. My work in the juvenile prison deepened my education and allowed me to bring the experiences of a marginalized group to the academy.

Laura Cazares
Senior, California State University—Monterey Bay

MAJOR

Social and Behavioral Science

HOMETOWN

Chula Vista, CA

Which groups and organizations have you been involved in throughout college?

Student groups

Social and Behavioral Science Association

Service organizations

Monterey County AIDS Project

United Farm Workers Union

Tellus/Diganos

Student-government bodies

Inter-Club Council Representative

Others

Residential Life

What's your favorite class been so far?

My favorite class so far has been "The Social and Environmental History of California." This class provided me with the opportunity to become a volunteer with the United Farm Workers Union. As a volunteer, I walked door to door to mobilize Latino/a voters in an area that historically has low voter participation rates.

I went into this project with a slightly broken spirit and emerged enlightened and invigorated. When I first began this project, I expected to encounter a lot of apathy, but I have learned that despite the low voter turnout in many past elections, the community does indeed care about their own political participation. I documented my experience and combined it with historical research on voting rights in California for a paper that has since been accepted to a peer-reviewed journal. This class enriched my understanding of the past and prepared me to work for change in the future.

Which activities, groups, or projects are you involved in on campus and in your community? Which is most important to you and why?community? Which is most important to you and why?

I first became a Community Health Outreach Worker at the local AIDS project as part of my campus' service-learning requirement. I worked with people who were at high risk for infection due to drug use, sex work, or homelessness, providing HIV and hepatitis-C prevention services on the streets, in homes, and at the local prison. I continued to educate myself about HIV and through my firsthand experiences was able to become an expert in my community, and I combined my experience with the theory taught inside the classroom to write my senior capstone paper. The highlight of my experience as a health educator was being invited to present at a national AIDS conference. As a result of my classroom and service-learning, I am more confident as a public speaker and have a firmer understanding of how information shared in the classroom will be applied in the real world.

Mehran M. Heravi
Senior, Florida State University

MAJOR

Exercise Physiology / Biology

HOMETOWN

[unspecified], Iran

Which groups and organizations have you been involved in throughout college?

Student groups

International Medical Outreach

Community Medical Outreach

What's been your biggest success so far?

A few years ago, I joined six other pre-medical students on a ten-day medical outreach trip to serve underprivileged people in the country of Haiti. During this trip, I was inspired to start a similar organization serving underprivileged communities in the United States. I envisioned a program in which promising premedical students would be provided with intense, hands-on medical experience and in which underprivileged communities would be provided with much needed free medical care.

I began organizing a group that I called Community Medical Outreach (CMO) when I returned to the United States. I soon ran up against the regulations in this country that restrict anyone who is not already a doctor from providing medical care. The obstacles of insurance and accreditation were daunting, and some people advised me not to waste my time and effort. Instead of giving up, I set up dozens of meetings with administrators who could give me technical advice and administrative support.

In the end, we found ways to work within the complex regulations. A select group of students work side by side with physicians and assist them in providing medical care. In the past three years, CMO has served 760 patients/farm workers, and it has raised over $12,000 for six medical mission trips to Dade City and Quincy, Florida.

How is your civic engagement related to your education?

I returned to college after eights years in business to pursue my dream of becoming a doctor. I work hard in my classes and maintain good grades, but getting into medical school today requires extracurricular service as well as high academic achievement. I knew that I had to demonstrate my commitment to medicine both inside and outside of the classroom. I created the Community Medical Outreach program because it is reciprocal: Communities in need obtain medical care, and premed students like me obtain valuable educational experience.

Christopher Percopo
Junior, George Washington University

MAJOR

Human Services

HOMETOWN

Holmdel, NJ

Which groups and organizations have you been involved in throughout college?

Student groups

Pi Kappa Phi Fraternity

Inter-Fraternity Council

Service organizations

Washington Civic and Leadership Fellow

Neighbors Project

Volunteer Coordinator for pre-kindergarten and elementary education sites

Martin Luther King Jr. Day of Service

Student-government bodies

Judicial and Legislative Affairs

Rules Committee

Special Committee to Investigate Budget Shortfall for 2002–2003 Academic Year

Student Association Senate

What advice did you receive about getting involved in college?

I went to college and after being overly committed in high school, I thought that it might be about time that I stopped focusing on my volunteering and extracurricular activities and just be a student. Bad idea! When my sister heard that I was not enjoying my college experience, she swooped right in. I got a call from California, and the wise words of my older sister, Lissa, came through the phone. She told me about how she had gone through the same thing her freshman year and how she had sworn off outside-the-classroom-activities at college, and it was not the right choice for her. Like many other students, my sister and I need to be busy, and the education we get in the classroom is simply not enough. I heeded her advice and took a good long look at what made me enjoy high school so much. With that I went to our student union and got involved. I started volunteering again, became involved in student government, decided to stick with the fraternity that I had helped found, and tried every other organization that could use my help.

How is your civic engagement related to your education?

Much of my education has consisted of the lessons that I have learned through serving. In the classroom, I learned that there is a defined sociological structure to which all humans fall victim. Some people are born poor, others are born into the lap of luxury, and only in the rarest incidents does someone born into one of these categories transition into the other. Reading in a textbook about the living wage and unequal education teaches me the basic theories as they related to the perpetual cycle of poverty and the achievement gap in education. While this is useful, my time serving as a teacher's aide is far more applicable to real life. The inherent problem with minimum-wage laws become truly apparent as I sit with the six-year-old I tutor whose parents both work two jobs but still have trouble keeping him from going to bed hungry. Reading an article about schools "failing their students" only gives me numbers that show students are performing poorly on standardized tests.

Margaret MacWhirter
Junior, Georgetown University

MAJOR

International Politics

HOMETOWN

Gaithersburg, MD

Which groups and organizations have you been involved in throughout college?

Student groups

School of Foreign Service Peer Advisor

HoyaSibs

Club Field Hockey

Service organizations

Hoya Outreach Programs and Education (HOPE)

Online Housing Resource Project (OHRP)

First-Year Orientation to Community Involvement (FOCI)

Just One Day Poverty-Awareness Event

National Student Campaign Against Hunger and Homelessness

Student-government bodies

Volunteer and Public-Service Advisory Board

School of Foreign Service Academic Council Social-Action Committee

What's your favorite class been so far?

"Human Rights: A Culture in Crisis." Taught by three professors (and weekly guest speakers), this class approached the topic of human rights from perspectives of literature, law, and philosophy.

What advice about starting school would you give a prospective student?

In your first weeks, and continuing through to graduation, be willing to question how things are done within existing groups. One of the benefits of student organizations is that every four years, they are made up of completely new people with fresh ideas. Don't be afraid to ask tough questions about how a group functions. You could help improve the group's efficiency and effectiveness, and you will certainly learn a lot about the organization and begin to feel invested in its success.

How does your service and activism connect to your social life?

The closest friends I have made in college have been those with whom I share extracurricular experiences. A group in which students share common values and all commit time and energy to work toward common goals is a perfect environment for developing friendships. I have found that my friendships based on common activities last long after we leave the office or finish the project. These are the people I call to make weekend plans, go to for advice or help, have a great time with at parties, and know will be in my life way past graduation.

In addition, being involved often includes a large commitment of time and energy to a group or cause, a dedication in working towards common goals, and many opportunities to problem solve and learn from mistakes. All of these experiences increase your sense of belonging to a group and help to form bonds with other active students. On a more obvious level, if you like the people with whom you are working, the meetings, the hard work, and the planning processes are much more fun!

Eliana Machuca
Junior, Humboldt State University

MAJOR

Environmental Science

HOMETOWN

Stockton, CA

Which groups and organizations have you been involved in throughout college?

Student groups

Food Not Waste

Dance Project

Acción Zapatista

Service-Learning Club

Humboldt State Committee for Conscientious Objection

Service organizations

Friends of the Dunes

Food Not Bombs

Service-Learning Center

Charlie Richards Goat Backyard Circus

Service-Learning/Experiential-Education Committee

What has been your biggest success in your service or activism?

My biggest success was helping to plan a town-hall meeting on three key political issues. We discussed (1) whether our local government should take a stand on national issues like the Patriot Act, (2) whether to support a state bond initiative for education, and (3) whether to recall our local district attorney. The meeting was held at the local high school and was open to all community members. First, city officials and Humboldt students led a panel discussion and presented on both sides of each issue. Once the panelists had presented information on each issue, the audience split up to discuss the issues and form opinions in small groups.

The meeting was a huge success. All of participants left with a better understanding of the issues, and I got great feedback on how to improve town meetings in the future. Many of the participants asked to help organize the next town-hall meeting.

Why was Humboldt a good choice for you?

Most of the classes are fairly small, and many professors encourage students to do work in the community that is related to readings or lectures. While the classes are generally good, the students are what make the campus wonderful. Humboldt students are very active and passionate; we have over 100 clubs, a student-run volunteer organization, and an excellent service-learning center. With so many different programs to choose from, it was easy for me to get my feet wet and find a program that fit my interests.

Off campus, I have become very involved in local community politics. Arcata (where Humboldt State is located) is a liberal town, and there are many opportunities to learn from liberal community organizations. People in Arcata are used to students, and community organizations usually welcome student members. I have had great experiences working with local high schools and with local environmental groups. Over the past few years, Arcata has become my home—not just a place I go to school.

Stephanie Raill
Sophomore, Macalester College

MAJOR

Theater

HOMETOWN

Hamilton, New Zealand

Which groups and organizations have you been involved in throughout college?

Student groups

Mac Catholics

Mac Bike

Macalester International Organization

Environmental Funk

Amnesty International

Mac Fair Trade

Mac Peace and Justice/Student Labor Action Coalition

Mac Players

Mac Soup

Service organizations

Arts for Social Change

How do you balance academic work and civic engagement?

At 4:00 on Saturday afternoon, I'm shivering in the biting wind at the conference cross-country championship and panicking. Somehow the results have gotten mixed up, and the award ceremony is running way late. I'm supposed to be at a nearby café, setting up for a big fundraising event, and then I can't even stay to see it unfold because I have a compulsory performance to see for my dance class! What am I going to do?

Balancing varsity athletics, schoolwork, and civic engagement is a huge challenge for me. It often seems like all the deadlines happen at once. It's important to me that whatever I choose to do, I do well.

Here are some suggestions to help achieve the right balance:

- Don't take on more than you can handle. There's a difference between being active and being overwhelmed.

- Talk to your teachers, coaches, and supervisors if you have a scheduling conflict. Nine times out of ten, they will help you work out a compromise.

- Aim for good grades, but don't freak out if that paper you didn't revise because you were at a homeless shelter for the night gets a B+ instead of an A-. In the real world, it's experience that counts—for employers as well as in your own life.

How did your civic interests affect which college you chose?

Macalester became part of my life because of a poster on the wall of my high-school cafeteria featuring Kofi Annan, the U.N. Secretary General and a Macalester alum. At the time, I aspired to work in international relations—I wanted to be Secretary General myself someday! So I thought, if Macalester could help a young man from Ghana go on to lead the United Nations, it was certainly the school for me.

Ross Meyer
Senior, Miami University of Ohio

MAJOR

Interdisciplinary Studies

HOMETOWN

Cincinnati, OH

Which groups and organizations have you been involved in throughout college?

Student groups

Raise Your Voice Student Civic-Engagement Campaign

Amnesty International

Campaign for Racial and Economic Justice

Students for Peace and Social Justice

Fair-Trade Campaign

United Students Against Sweatshops

Service organizations

Miami University Office of Service-Learning and Civic Leadership

Empower Program in Service-Learning and Social Justice

Over-the-Rhine Weekend Experience Program

Others

Miami University Social-Action Center

Witness for Peace

What's your favorite class been so far?

My favorite course was "Human Rights Theory and Practice," which I took at the International Human Rights Exchange in Cape Town, South Africa. The program brought together 80 students from around the world to study human rights in Cape Town for a month.

What has been your biggest success in your service or activism?

Throughout high school, I was deeply engaged in service and advocacy work in Cincinnati's impoverished Over-the-Rhine community. Upon entering Miami University, I created a program in Over-the-Rhine, Cincinnati, entitled "Over-the-Rhine Weekend Experience: An Introduction to Urban America." On the two-day experience, students visit and work in a homeless shelter, work on low-income housing rehabilitation, tour the neighborhood and community agencies, meet community activists and leaders, and reflect on their experience. To date, I have coordinated and led 20 trips, involving more than 300 students.

Student participants often recount that the experience was one of the most powerful learning experiences they had while attending Miami University. Faculty report that the students who participated in the program were more engaged in the course material following the experience. After the weekend, many students also remain involved in volunteer work in the community. Some even take on a more substantive involvement, through internships or research with community agencies.

How did your civic interests affect which college you chose?

I was highly involved in service and activism in high school, and I wanted to find a college that would be supportive of my work.

While I could have gone to a nearby college that had a strong institutional commitment to civic engagement, I felt that there was more potential for change at Miami University. If I had gone to a college with a strong activist culture, I would have merely blended in with the crowd and my contribution would have been minimal. Perhaps the administration at an activist college would have been jaded, burned-out, and resistant to new ideas.

I found the faculty, administration, and students at Miami receptive, supportive, and encouraging of new ideas and eager for change. I feel that I have made a significant contribution to building a socially-conscious campus at Miami, perhaps more than I could have at a college known for activism.

Kelli Hamann
Senior, Portland State University

MAJOR

Social Science

HOMETOWN

Seattle, WA

Which groups and organizations have you been involved in throughout college?

Other

Practicum for ED 420

Practicum for UNST 421

Special Research Project at Martin Luther Elementary School

What activities or projects are most important to you and why?

A fellow student and I organize a music and literacy project at a local elementary school. We spend four hours each week in classrooms, teaching basic literacy skills through music, movement, and visual aids. We also write all of the songs and create all of the visual aids for the classes ourselves. I have seen how a program that integrates music into classwork teaches young students to read. Children, especially those who are easily bored by rote learning, enjoy the musical lessons, and they remember the songs that we teach them.

How is your work off campus related to your education?

A college campus can consume all of a student's energy. Service reminds me that there is a world beyond the classroom. It is a psychological and emotional break from the pressures of the classroom. I remember that the goal of education is not simply to do well on tests and papers. Rather, the purpose of education is to prepare to be an active, involved member of our society.

How do you balance academic work and socially-responsible work?

We all find the time to do the things that we deem most valuable and important to us. As a mother of four and a full-time student, finding time for any community activities is nearly impossible. But when I prioritize my work in the community, I make the time to participate. Because I truly see the value of my community work, I incorporate it into my life.

James R. Williams
Sophomore, Princeton University

MAJOR

Public and International Affairs

HOMETOWN

Portland, OR

Which groups and organizations have you been involved in throughout college?

Student groups

Student Volunteers Council

Religious Life Council

Bridge Club

College Democrats

Princeton Justice Project's Education Committee

Service organizations

Community-Based Learning Initiative

Student-government bodies

U-Council

USG Senate

Student groups

Recognition Committee.

Others

Priorities Committee

What's your favorite class been so far?

"United States History Since 1920." This class had an incredible professor, made me see modern U.S. history in a totally new light, and has allowed me to place myself—and this era—within this nation's historical framework.

Why was Princeton a good choice for you?

"In the nation's service and in the service of all nations" stands as a proud motto for Princeton and exemplifies the reason why I chose to attend. I hoped for a school where I would be able to freely explore political and social action and have the opportunity to enjoy both outstanding academics as well as immersion in a community of engaged and active students. At Princeton, I have found both.

How is your civic engagement related to your education?

At Princeton, the notion of an "ivory tower," separate and apart from the outside world, remains strong and entrenched. Many believe that work in the community is antithetical to high-quality scholarship and true academic work. However, I have found that it is the lack of involvement outside the classroom that stifles learning and inhibits my understanding of how theories relate to the real world.

My civic-engagement work has been absolutely vital to my learning within the classroom at Princeton. I have found that I am able to deepen conversations with peers and professors by bringing in relevant outside material to enrich the academic discussion based on readings and lectures. Especially in my department, Public Policy and Public Affairs, it has been incredibly helpful to understand firsthand how political policy is implemented and how it affects people's daily lives.

How have the skills you've gained outside of the classroom helped you in your academics?

I have always found that I gain a deeper appreciation for the struggle and depth required by academic problems through the firsthand knowledge of and application in the community (or by trying to put into practice) of the theory and ideas gleaned from the classroom. Civic engagement-by including personal connections with people from the community, political, and social connections through real-world policy, advocacy, and activism, and an understanding of place-leads to a rich and relevant education. In my experience at Princeton, much of my academic success has been because of my ability to break out of the bubble and join others in civic efforts off and on campus.

Stephen Chan
Senior, Stanford University

MAJOR

Public Policy

HOMETOWN

San Diego, CA

Which groups and organizations have you been involved in throughout college?

Student groups

Future Social Innovators Network (FUSION)

Stanford in Government

Service organizations

Side by Side

Project AIYME

Alternative Spring Break

Community Organizations

Greenbelt Alliance

California Campus Compact

Haas Center for Public Service

U.S. Department of Justice, Civil Rights Division, Housing and Civil-

Enforcement Section Office of California State Assembly Member Joe Simitian

Northern California Grantmakers

What's your favorite class been so far?

My favorite class has been Public Policy 182A/B: "Policy-Making and Problem Solving at the Local, Regional Level." This service-learning course is a two-quarter-long experience, using Silicon Valley as a case study. The first quarter focuses on the problems of the Valley and how they are interrelated, while the second quarter focuses on innovative approaches to solving these problems.

What activities are most important to you?

With so many entrepreneurial students on campus, student groups proliferate. At a place like Stanford, it is important to facilitate cooperation among the hundreds of socially-responsible groups. I coordinate the "Youth and Education Network," a coalition of the 40 to 50 different groups on campus that work with youth or in education. The goal of the coalition is simply to make sure that each organization knows what the others are doing. At one meeting, for example, I introduced the leader of the Pediatric Interest Group, a children's-health student organization, to Barrio Assistance, a tutoring/mentoring program. Apparently, each group independently held fairs every spring and brought groups of underprivileged children campus. Because of the meeting, the groups' leaders decided to collaborate on a single spring fair in the future.

Why was Stanford a good choice for you?

Heading into Stanford, I knew little about the opportunities for civic engagement, but I couldn't have made a better choice. The best part about the Haas Center is that it truly supports a spectrum of service, including direct service, advocacy, electoral politics, philanthropy, social entrepreneurship, and research. Students are not forced into a certain path but are challenged to examine how their academic interests and career goals fit into a type of social responsibility.

Personally, I have been involved in a wide range of activities, groups, and projects that reflect the diversity of ways in which one can have a positive social impact. I have been involved in community service, mentoring at-risk Asian youth, and singing to seniors at nursing homes. I also spent a quarter learning about government in Washington when I worked with the Department of Justice's civil rights agency. With the support of the Haas Center for Public Service, I was also able to spend a summer interning in a nonprofit advocacy group.

Tara Germond
Sophomore, University of Rhode Island

MAJOR

Environmental Science and Management

HOMETOWN

North Providence, RI

Which groups and organizations have you been involved in throughout college?

Student groups

Students for Environmental Action

Intercollegiate Organization for Nonviolence

Students for a Sensible Drug Policy

Promotion for the Awareness of Gender Equality (PAGE)

Student Senate

Service organizations

Clearinghouse for Volunteers

Feinstein Center for Service Learning

Others

NAACP chapter

Latin American Student Association

BRIDGES

Sustainable Initiatives on Campus

Jumpstart.

What's your favorite class been so far?

"Community Planning 300: Introduction to Global Issues and Sustainable Development." The class, which was structured as if we, the students, were an NGO working to solve a community-based problem in Nicaragua, focused on the role of the United States in development assistance to foreign nations. Topics included foreign aid, sustainable development, transfer of technology, and international career opportunities.

What has been your biggest success in your service or activism?

My greatest accomplishment was coordinating a program entitled "Boxes and Walls." The program was an interactive diversity-education tour that illustrated how discrimination affects many different groups of people.

In each room on the tour, a different group's experience of discrimination was represented. These groups included African Americans, Arab Americans, people with disabilities, women, gays and lesbians, and Latin Americans. As people entered each room, they were placed in situations that personalized oppression and illuminated the types of hate that exist in our society. The tour helped students to empathize with others and to reexamine their own perceptions and stereotypes.

I consider this program my greatest success because it brought together students, staff, and faculty from diverse backgrounds and experiences to work in collaboration with one another. 70 students from a dozen student groups and numerous faculty and staff members from various departments all volunteered substantial time and effort to create this program. In the end, over 400 students and members of the community attended the tours, and the program received great reviews.

How did you become active on campus or in your community?

I became active on my campus through a fellowship position with the Raise Your Voice Campaign out of Campus Compact. I spent the first month of my fellowship mapping all of the allies and resources available to me on campus.

I contacted professors, student organizations, and administrative departments to inform them of the programs I had planned for the year and to ask about their plans. I attended organizational meetings and arranged one-on-one conversations. I did my best to network with as many groups and people on campus as possible. Mapping my campus allowed me to see what was already being done and to find the people who could best support my work.

Carlos Silva
Senior, Williams College

MAJOR

Political Economy and Environmental Studies

HOMETOWN

Farmington, CT

Which groups and organizations have you been involved in throughout college?

Student groups

Greensense

Advisory Committee on Shareholder Responsibility

Campus Environmental Advisory Committee

Town-College Greenhouse Gas Reduction Committee

Service organizations

Elementary-school tutor

How do you balance academic work and civic engagement?

I have often had the amazing opportunity to pursue my civic ambitions through my classes. In my environmental-planning class, I did consulting work for the local town government and designed a redevelopment plan to turn an old dilapidated mill in town into affordable housing for area residents. In a class on the global carbon cycle, my final project was an analysis of how Williams College could participate in a market for the buying and selling of greenhouse gases, which will soon be presented to the college administration.

But even with classes that promote community involvement, balancing academic work and civic engagement is tough. Your heart and passions impel you toward spending enormous amounts of time each week organizing to improve your campus, local community, and the world at large. Yet I think it is absolutely necessary to maintain the highest level of academic performance possible. In the end, academic performance will open up opportunities to become an even more effective force for making the world a better place.

Why was Williams a good choice for you?

I could not have made a better choice than Williams for pursuing civic engagement. Making change at a small institution is, in many ways, very good preparation for making change in the world at large. A small institution is a much easier to understand, more manageable version of the world at large.

Changing the status quo requires meeting with people in control of the power levers, and at a place as small and intimate as Williams, I can stop by their office to discuss ideas face-to-face. I know the president and vice president of the college. I know administrators in the Buildings and Grounds and Dining Services Departments on a first-name basis. I even know the mayor of our town and a number of local town officials. I doubt that I would know these types of wonderful and influential people in my community if I were at a large institution with several thousands or even tens of thousands of students.

Community Colleges

If you are using this book, you're most likely searching for four-year public or private institutions beyond your local community, and these are the types of schools we've profiled in this book. However, some of the most engaged campuses are actually local two-year community and technical colleges. Schools like Miami Dade College, Chandler-Gilbert Community College, Kapi'olani Community College, Mount Wachusett Community College, Minneapolis Community and Technical College, and Brevard Community College are among the hundreds of two-year institutions providing amazing, innovative opportunities for civic engagement and campus-community partnerships.

To help you get a sense of what's possible at a community college, we've included profiles of students from Miami Dade College and North Eastern Oklahoma A&M. Harold Silva, the SGA president at Miami Dade, and Joseph Blundell, the 2004 winner of Campus Compact's Swearer Humanitarian Award, embody the wonderful socially-responsible work being done by thousands of community-college students around the country.

Harold Silva
Miami Dade College—Kendall Campus

MAJOR

International Relations

HOMETOWN

Hialeah, FL

Which groups and organizations have you been involved in throughout college?

Student groups

Model United Nations

Phi Theta Kappa-International Honor Society

Service organizations

Service for Peace

Hands on Miami

Student-government bodies

Student Government Association

Florida Junior/ Community Colleges Student Government Association

Others

Florida Youth Action Council

Of the activities, groups, and projects you're involved in on campus and in your community, which is the most important to you and why?

Since the beginning of college, I've been involved with the Student Government Association (SGA) on my campus. I began as a senator my first year, and I held a number of other positions before I was elected as state president of the Florida Junior Community Colleges Student Government Association. That means I serve 800,000 Florida community college students. As state president, my responsibilities include presenting community college students' concerns to local and national legislators and chairing the meetings of SGA presidents across the state.

Why was Miami Dade a good choice for you?

One of the best decisions that I have made was to attend Miami Dade College. Miami Dade College is the largest community college in the nation, but professors still set aside time to talk to students about class assignments or to chat about the student's career plans. The professors are passionate about what they teach, and they often offer students many opportunities to do hands-on work that relates to a class. When I took "American Federal Government," I interned at a state senator's office, and when I took "International Relations," I worked with the Model United Nations program. Now I am taking "Conflict Resolution," and I volunteer as a mentor for middle- and high-school students.

Joseph T. Blundell
Northeastern Oklahoma A&M

MAJOR

1. Native American History

2. Psychology

3. Art

4. Communications

HOMETOWN

Pittsburg, KA

Which groups and organizations have you been involved in throughout college?

Student groups

Native American Student Association

Philosophy club

Psychology club

Service organizations

The city of Cliff Village

What has been your favorite class so far?

Pottery. It is the ultimate example of building something from nothing—from clay to a gift to give with just a little bit of sweat, fire, and getting your hands dirty.

Of the activities, groups, and projects you're involved in on campus and in your community, which is the most important to you and why?

The most important of all my endeavors at Northeastern Oklahoma A&M Community College has been my involvement with the Native American Student Association. Over the past few years, we have held Gourd Dances to honor Native American veterans and pow-wows to celebrate the elaborate culture and customs of the plains Indians.

These celebrations have showed me power of tradition and taught me to have pride in my heritage. I have come to believe that as Native American customs and ideas are lost due to repression or assimilation, the entire American [culture] is impoverished. A society with a diversity of worldviews and an open interchange of ideas would be a stronger, more perceptive society.

What has been your biggest success in your service and/or activism?

My greatest achievement has been helping a small town in Missouri win access to clean water. When I started college, I had recently moved to a small town named Cliff Village. The village has only 48 people, but an alarmingly high proportion of those people had developed rare cancers. I soon discovered that a large factory had been dumping a toxic chemical upstream from the aquifer that filled the residents' wells. Inspired by a horticulture class I was taking, I began a campaign to test the well water for contamination and to get the village clean water.

After meeting with resistance from the Environmental Protection Agency, the residents of the town decided to elect me as mayor of the village, and my new political position did help me convince the EPA to test the wells. The tests proved that the wells were contaminated, but due to budget shortfalls, no money was available to alleviate the situation.

Fortunately, I was able to resolve the issue with a local water company that was sympathetic to our plight. I am happy to report that new water lines are coming to our village in the summer of 2005. Until then, I will be working on other projects that I started as mayor, including a community greenhouse project and a low-income housing project.

SCHOOL SAYS

In this section you'll find colleges with extended listings. This is your chance to get in-depth information on colleges that interest you. The Princeton Review charges each school a small fee to be listed, and the editorial responsibility is solely that of the college.

CONCORDIA COLLEGE—NEW YORK

171 WHITE PLAINS ROAD, BRONXVILLE, NY 10708

PHONE: 914-337-9300 E-MAIL: ADMISSION@CONCORDIA-NY.EDU FAX: 914-395-4636 WEBSITE: WWW.CONCORDIA-NY.EDU

THE COLLEGE AT A GLANCE

Concordia College is a four year, coeducational liberal arts institution in the Lutheran tradition. The historic 33-acre campus is located in suburban Westchester County, New York, one-half hour north of New York City by commuter train. While the campus has a distinctly Christian atmosphere, students from all faiths are welcome and attend here. As members of a close-knit community representing 30 states and 30 nations, Concordia students are mentored by a dedicated faculty and staff, most of whom live on or near campus. All classes and labs are taught by faculty—not teaching assistants.

ACADEMIC PROGRAMS

A Concordia College education strengthens students intellectually, socially, and spiritually by building on a solid foundation of value-oriented, faith-based liberal arts. Concordia's academic program, The Concordia Experience, places a significant emphasis on critical thinking and communication skills. Students complete requirements in the Concordia Distinctive, an integrated array of liberal arts courses forming the core curriculum. A concentration area is selected from among seven programs: Biology, Business, Education, English/Communications, Liberal Studies, Social Sciences, Social Work, and a multi-disciplinary field from among 15 concentrations. Each of programs encompasses experiential learning—encompassing education outside the traditional classroom such as "city as text," study abroad, professional internships, and research opportunities.

The Business Program has two specializations. International Management prepares students for global careers with input from a community advisory board of senior executives. Sports Management students benefit from unique professional internship opportunities with NYC professional teams. Concordia Business graduates are known for their core values and ethical approach to business.

Education students benefit from the College's Professional Development School run in conjunction with the Chapel School, a K-8 Lutheran school located adjacent to campus. Students gain classroom experience, work in small group settings with children, and volunteer for Professional Development School programs and events.

The Social Work Program is accredited by the Council on Social Work Education—affording Concordia Social Work graduates advanced standing in graduate degree programs. This allows graduates to obtain the MSW degree in one year rather than two.

SERVICE-LEARNING

Experiential learning offers students an opportunity to connect Concordia's value-oriented curriculum with real-world needs. Participation and service-learning are part of the campus culture. Opportunities for service abound at Concordia through student life organizations, volunteer programs in Westchester County and the five boroughs of New York City, church and Lutheran benevolence programs, and through the curriculum.

Popular service activities include Midnight Runs which provides food and clothing for the homeless in New York City; City Squash brings inner city youth to campus for games of squash and tutoring by Concordia students; and Youth Day—a Fall event where city youth visit campus for healthy outdoor activities and mentoring .

Service opportunities available at Concordia—New York provide a dynamic, interactive, and integrated dimension to the college experience.

SCHOOL SAYS . . .

CORNELL COLLEGE

OFFICE OF ADMISSION, 600 FIRST STREET WEST, MOUNT VERNON, IA 52314

PHONE: 800-747-1112 **E-MAIL:** ADMISSIONS@CORNELLCOLLEGE.EDU **FAX:** 319-895-4215 **WEBSITE:** WWW.CORNELLCOLLEGE.EDU

THE COLLEGE AT A GLANCE

Very few colleges are truly distinctive like Cornell College. Founded in 1853, Cornell is recognized as one of the nation's finest liberal arts colleges. It is Cornell's combination of special features, however, that distinguishes it. It boasts an attractively diverse residential college of 1,150 students. Cornell places special emphasis on service leadership. Foremost, it is a place where theory and practice are brought together in exciting ways through the college's One-Course-At-A-Time (OCAAT) academic calendar. The college's beautiful, hilltop campus is one of only two campuses nationwide listed on the National Register of Historic Places. Located in the charming town of Mount Vernon, Cornell is also within commuting distance of Iowa City (home of the University of Iowa) and Cedar Rapids. It is within a three to five hour drive of major Mid-western metropolitan areas such as Chicago, Minneapolis, Milwaukee, St. Louis, and Kansas City.

ACADEMIC PROGRAMS

With OCAAT, there is no interference from competing classes, and the lively pace keeps students focused and engaged by their studies. Students enjoy learning as they immerse themselves in a single subject for a three-and-a-half week term. Cornell's student-faculty ratio of 13:1 enables its exceptional faculty to provide students with highly personalized attention. Students choose from more than 40 majors or create individualized majors; two-thirds graduate with double majors. Internships and study abroad programs are also common pursuits, as OCAAT provides a powerful and flexible structure for off-campus study. Alumni say their Cornell experience gave them an advantage in the workplace and in graduate school.

SERVICE-LEARNING

Cornell students are cause-oriented and globally aware. The majority of students are eagerly engaged in community service at any given time. One student recently launched a collection drive for shoes to send to orphans in Afghanistan. Another petitioned county officials to set up voter registration in the college library. Others organized a day of fasting to fund donations to local shelters. Some students even "eat, live, and sleep" service via the Living and Learning Community program, which enables student groups to live together in a residence hall while sharing a service-learning experience. Each year, a number of students continue their service through Alternative Spring Break, building houses in Alabama, working at a homeless shelter in Nashville, Tennessee, and assisting low-income families in Virginia. In general, service projects are managed by student organizations with assistance from the college's Leadership and Service Office (LSO). LSO coordinates the New Student Orientation service day, introducing students to service and to their new community beyond the campus, forging bonds that can continue throughout college. Community service offers Cornell students valuable experience by working in teams, teaching them community dynamics, and providing insight into interpersonal relations. Students learn how organizations work, how to rally people to get things done, and how to be leaders. Leadership at its best is service.

DePaul University

1 EAST JACKSON BOULEVARD, CHICAGO, IL 60604-2287

PHONE: 312-362-8300 E-MAIL: ADMITDPU@DEPAUL.EDU FAX: 312-362-5749 WEBSITE: WWW.DEPAUL.EDU

DePaul University is nationally recognized for its innovative academic programs that enable students' personal and professional growth through hands-on learning and individual attention. Its pragmatic, experiential approach draws accolades from guidebooks and employers. All courses are taught by professors, not assistants, and class sizes are kept small, underscoring DePaul's primary commitment to teaching. The university's location in Chicago—a world-class center for business, finance, government, law, and culture, as well as home to a thriving nonprofit sector—provide students with exceptional career-related job experiences, internships, mentors, and cultural opportunities.

DePaul, the nation's largest Catholic university, has a diverse student body of more than 23,500 enrolled on two primary and several suburban campuses. Founded in 1898 by followers of St. Vincent de Paul, the university incorporates community-based service-learning throughout its curriculum, giving students practical experience while developing their ability to make a difference in the world.

Two important centers that focus on university-community collaborations are Irwin W. Steans Center for Community-based Service Learning (CbSL), whose core purpose is to develop community-based service-learning courses at DePaul, and University Ministry, which coordinates numerous service opportunities. Their activities are complemented by DePaul's centers and institutes, many of which involve undergraduate students in community service and/or community-based research.

The Steans Center is an endowed, nationally recognized center that collaborates with faculty and community organizations to develop and sponsor approximately 120 CbSL courses annually. The center matches more than 1,600 DePaul students with community placements, projects and research in more than 100 community-based organizations every year. The Steans Center also sponsors three CbSL study-abroad programs in the undergraduate curriculum and develops opportunities for students to use their federal work-study funds for jobs with community-based organizations.

University Ministry sponsors a wide range of service opportunities, including 13 one- or two-week annual service trips involving more than 150 students. Every year it organizes and sponsors two service days during which the university community performs approximately 7,000 hours of service. University Ministry houses the DePaul Community Service Association, an alliance of service and justice-oriented student organizations, through which about 1,000 volunteers provide 3,000 hours of service per quarter.

At DePaul, students can find service and justice woven throughout the university's curricula. Service-oriented academic programs include the Environmental Studies major; the Peace, Conflict Resolution, and Social Justice minor; the Community Service Studies minor; and the Religious Studies Concentration in Ethics and Social Justice. Many of DePaul's 150-some student organizations provide opportunities to engage with Chicago's communities.

Many scholarships support service-oriented students. The Steans Center offers the Community Service Scholars Program ($5,000 per year for up to four years), the Meister Community Service Scholarships ($1,000) and the McCormick-Tribune Community Internships ($1,000). Additional scholarships include 36 University Ministry St. Vincent de Paul Community Service Scholarships ($1,000 –$3,000) for DePaul Community Service Association coordinators, Amate House need-based scholarships for volunteers, Mayor's Leadership, Monsignor Egan Hope Scholarships, and the Vincentian Endowment Fund (VEF), which supports "student-led initiatives and faculty-student initiatives that have a direct community service or social justice objective."

LESLEY UNIVERSITY

ADMISSIONS OFFICE, 29 EVERETT STREET, CAMBRIDGE, MA 02138

PHONE: 800-999-1959 EXT. 8800 OR 617-349-8800 E-MAIL: UGADM@LESLEY.EDU WEBSITE: WWW.LESLEY.EDU/LC

THE UNIVERSITY AT A GLANCE

Since its founding in 1909, Lesley's mission has always been to provide programs that will positively impact the lives of its students, and enable them to make a positive impact on the lives of others and on the world at large. This commitment to putting people first continues to make Lesley University the top choice for individuals seeking leadership positions in education, management, human services, liberal arts, environmental studies, and the arts.

Undergraduate programs offered through Lesley College and The Art Institute of Boston combine experiential learning (students complete between 450–650 hours in significant work and service learning situations), with inquiry-based classroom discussions, studio work, and small seminars. Through this unique approach, Lesley students gain a critical understanding of real world demands within their profession, and the leadership skills to succeed in it.

ACADEMIC PROGRAMS

Lesley offers a variety of undergraduate programs on its Cambridge and Boston campuses. Lesley College offers traditional undergraduate students the unique appeal of a small liberal arts/professional studies college that's located in a vibrant urban setting, providing enormous opportunities for community involvement. Through the Audubon Expedition Institute at Lesley, students have the opportunity to spend an entire semester in a travel-study program, learning about the world's ecosystems and how to protect them. Lesley also offers travel-study programs to Tibet, Ecuador, Cuba, and Peru that emphasize cultural understanding. In addition, Lesley is the foremost educator of teachers in the country, offering programs in over 20 states.

SERVICE-LEARNING

Beginning their freshman year, Lesley students participate in internships and service-learning opportunities. The University is an active partner with many local and national organizations including the AIDS Action Committee, Boston Area Rape Crisis Center, Cambridge Peace Commission, Boston Department of Social Services, Franciscan Children's Hospital, Big Brothers/Big Sisters of Greater Boston, Literacy for All, as well as dozens of area schools where all students, not just teachers in training, have an opportunity to contribute in "classrooms." In addition, Art Institute of Boston students provide pro bono design services for many of the nonprofit organizations that are supported by The United Way.

The university's positioning line, "Let's wake up the world!" reflects the commitment of Lesley's faculty, students, and alumni to work collaboratively for constructive change and advocating civic engagement by all individuals.

QUINNIPIAC UNIVERSITY

275 MOUNT CARMEL AVENUE, HAMDEN, CT 06518

PHONE: 203-582-8600 E-MAIL: ADMISSIONS@QUINNIPIAC.EDU FAX: 203-582-8906 WEBSITE: WWW.QUINNIPIAC.EDU

THE UNIVERSITY AT A GLANCE

Quinnipiac University, founded in 1929, is a private, coeducational, nonsectarian institution of higher education. It is primarily a residential campus in a uniquely attractive New England setting. Quinnipiac's student body of 5,200 undergraduates and 2000 graduates comes from most of the United States and around the world. Quinnipiac's mission is to provide a supportive and stimulating environment for the intellectual and personal growth of undergraduate, graduate, and continuing education students.

ACADEMIC PROGRAMS

Quinnipiac offers broad range of undergraduate programs and specialized graduate programs. Undergraduate programs in the Schools of Business, Communications, Health Sciences, and the College of Liberal Arts prepare students for career entry or advanced studies through an integrated liberal arts and professional curricula. Graduate programs are designed to provide professional qualifications for success in business, education, health sciences, communications, and law.

An education at Quinnipiac embodies the university's commitment to its three core values: excellence in education, sensitivity to students, and a spirit of community. Academic programs and services are offered in a highly personalized learning environment featuring small classes and ready access to faculty. This reflects the university's commitment to excellence in teaching, as well as support for scholarship and professional development. The university's collegial atmosphere fosters a strong sense of community, identity, and purpose among faculty, staff, and students.

Quinnipiac strives to prepare graduates who manifest critical and creative thinking, effective communication skills, informed value judgments, and who possess an educational foundation for continued growth and development in a changing world of diverse cultures and people. Through public service and cultural events, Quinnipiac extends its resources to the professions and communities which it serves.

SERVICE-LEARNING

Quinnipiac's strong service-learning program empowers students to revitalize communities and focus on issues of social justice, culture, and society as a whole. Through the Albert Schweitzer Institute, affiliated with Quinnipiac, students and faculty travel to other parts of the world for short-term educational and humanitarian experiences. One recent trip brought Quinnipiac students and faculty to Nicaragua to help build an expansion to an overcrowded school. Another group traveled to Barbados where some taught computer skills to inhabitants of a women's shelter, while others shared physical and occupational therapy skills with professionals on the island.

The student organization, Community Action Project, encourages students to join in community service on campus and reach out and assist in meeting the needs in the Greater New Haven area. Quinnipiac is also affiliated with the Highville Mustard Seed School in Hamden, Connecticut, a chartered school that develops experimental forms of education for children from international or disadvantaged backgrounds. The school uses an innovative "global community education" approach where each classroom focuses on a different national culture, and the children develop their own rules to resolve conflicts through a United Nations General Assembly.

SCHOOL SAYS . . .

RANDOLPH-MACON WOMAN'S COLLEGE

2500 RIVERMONT AVENUE, LYNCHBURG, VA 24503-1526

PHONE: 434-947-8100 E-MAIL: ADMISSIONS@RMWC.EDU FAX: 434-947-8996 WEBSITE: WWW.RMWC.EDU

OVERVIEW

Founded in 1891, Randolph-Macon Woman's College offers women a rigorous education in the liberal arts and sciences. R-MWC is committed to excellence in the education of women and offers students from around the globe a challenging and inspiring environment in which to learn, pursue personal growth, and prepare for their futures.

R-MWC's 760 students come from 43 states, the District of Columbia, and over 40 countries and territories. Nine percent are international, eight percent are of black/non-Hispanic descent, four percent are of Hispanic descent, and three percent are of Asian/Pacific Islander descent. NAFSA: Association of International Educators has selected R-MWC as one of only 16 institutions nationwide to be honored for the internationalization of its campus, and the College is a member of the International 50—the top 50 schools in the United States whose graduates are most likely to pursue internationally oriented careers.

ACADEMICS

The College offers more than 60 majors, concentrations, and programs, most of which can be supplemented by departmental, interdisciplinary, or independently designed concentrations (minors). R-MWC also offers pre-professional programs (in law, medicine, and business) and cooperative career programs in engineering and nursing. Ninety-two percent of the R-MWC full-time faculty hold the highest degree in their fields, the average class size is 12, and the student/faculty ratio is 9:1. The College awards Bachelor of Science and Bachelor of Arts degrees.

Students also use The Macon Plan, an individualized, systematic plan that helps to define their personal, educational, and professional goals. Working with faculty and staff, students move confidently through a series of steps to identify the many courses, internships, study-abroad opportunities, clubs, and activities that constitute a coherent plan to meet their goals.

GLOBAL INITIATIVES

The College's many global initiatives include:

- Approximately 40 percent of R-MWC students study, work, or do service internationally during their four years at the College.

- R-MWC students study abroad through affiliated programs in England, the Czech Republic, Denmark, France, Germany, Greece, Ireland, Italy, Japan, Mexico, and Spain.

- The Gravely-Hampson Scholarship Fund provides support annually to 20 to 30 students for study abroad, either during the academic year or over College breaks.

- Students and faculty recently traveled to Bali, Costa Rica, El Salvador, Guatemala, Japan, Russia, Senegal, South Africa, Tunisia, Italy, and Spain on R-MWC-sponsored International Summer Study Seminars.

- Students study many languages on campus, including French, Spanish, Russian, German, Japanese, Chinese, Latin, Arabic, and Greek.

- Over 300 of our alumnae live in countries other than the U.S., including Turkey, Hong Kong, Ecuador, Switzerland, Ethiopia, Malaysia, Ghana, and the United Arab Emirates, to name just a few.

- R-MWC students participate in Model U.N., Model African Union, and Model European Union events each year.

- R-MWC brings international scholars to campus each year as Quillian International Professors to teach, present their research, and interact with our community. Recent scholars have hailed from Malaysia, India, Ghana, Egypt, the West Indies, China, Nigeria, and Croatia.

SEATTLE UNIVERSITY

ADMISSIONS OFFICE, 900 BROADWAY, SEATTLE, WA 98122-4340

PHONE: 206-296-2000 E-MAIL: ADMISSIONS@SEATTLEU.EDU FAX: 206-296-5656 WEBSITE: WWW.SEATTLEU.EDU

Seattle University, a Jesuit Catholic university of 6,800 students, prides itself on putting its mission to "empower leaders for a just and humane world" into action. Students state "SU walks the talk of social justice."

In February 2005, Seattle University hosted a "tent city"—a temporary encampment providing safety and shelter for the homeless—on its campus. Students helped the tent city's 100 residents in a variety of ways—from preparing hot meals and raising donations, to organizing legal and health clinics. During that month, educational visits and forums involving the tent-city residents and homelessness advocates augmented the university's year-long focus on consumption and poverty.

Academic, personal, and community engagement is at the heart of the SU experience. The university attaches enormous importance to the benefits of service-learning, and it is integrated into all of the university's eight schools. Examples include:

- College of Science and Engineering students participate in programs like Engineers Without Borders where they apply their skills to meet routine daily needs in developing countries such as Tibet and Thailand.

- The College of Education's Children's Literacy Project mobilizes hundreds of Seattle University students to tutor low-income children at local schools.

- Students and faculty in the School of Law's Community Justice Project provide free legal education and advice to members of the region's under-served communities.

- All Nursing students participate in community based nursing—providing support to those lacking adequate access to healthcare.

- Accounting majors from the Albers School of Business and Economics assist hundreds of low-income individuals and families prepare their tax returns through the Volunteer Income Tax Assistance (VITA) Program.

The university Center for Service is the fulcrum for service-learning activity. In 2004–2005, the center supported 45 courses that engaged 1,000 students in meaningful work with community organizations. It also sponsors co-curricular opportunities, including an "Alternative Spring Break" service-immersion trip and an intensive year-long service and leadership program, Student Leaders for the Common Good.

Seattle University's students are connected to the broader world through study and service abroad and service programs in Mexico, Belize, Calcutta, Nicaragua, Africa, and Europe. Included among those SU has selected for honorary degree recognition are some of the world's most respected humanitarian leaders: Nelson Mandela, Corazon Aquino, Archbishop Desmond Tutu, and the Dalai Lama.

Through service, students develop values and sensibilities to enrich a lifetime.

As one student described her six months volunteering in Calcutta "I've begun to see myself as more than just an American citizen, but also a global citizen."

"Education should be a transforming experience," notes the university's president Stephen V. Sundborg, S.J., "one that challenges and supports students in their intellectual, personal and spiritual growth. We are proud of the difference we make in our students' lives, and in the difference our alumni make in the world."

SIMMONS COLLEGE

OFFICE OF UNDERGRADUATE ADMISSION, 300 THE FENWAY, BOSTON, MA 02115

PHONE: 617-521-2051 FAX: 617-521-3190 E-MAIL: UGADM@SIMMONS.EDU WEBSITE: WWW.SIMMONS.EDU

OVERVIEW

Decades before American women gained the right to vote, Simmons College was founded with a revolutionary idea: prepare women to earn independent livelihoods and contribute in meaningful ways to their professions, families, and communities. Located in a vibrant Boston neighborhood near theatres, museums, stadiums, cafes, public gardens, other colleges, and medical and research institutions, Simmons is a small university that emphasizes intellectual leadership, professional preparation, and civic engagement.

Simmons continues its mission by putting students first, honoring their passion for learning, commitment to community, and determination to make a difference in the world.

ACADEMICS

Simmons offers a strong liberal arts foundation integrated with professional preparation, interdisciplinary study, service learning, and community service. While the curriculum is challenging, small classes and collaborative environment facilitate student success.

Undergraduates choose from more than 40 majors and programs, including Africana studies, arts administration, biochemistry, education, environmental science, information technology, nutrition, psychology, sociology, and women's studies. Students enrich their classroom work with independent study and service-learning options, and acquire a global outlook by studying languages, cultures, and foreign policies, and by taking advantage of foreign study and service learning opportunities. There are also opportunities to participate in a wide variety of student organizations ranging from academic language and culture, community service, student government, and publications, to music, multicultural, and multi-faith associations.

As a women's college, Simmons offers its students a sense of empowerment. Learning in the company of other women offers many advantages such as a supportive environment that promotes full participation. At Simmons, there are a lot of confident women—in the classrooms, on the playing fields, in the laboratories, and at the podium.

SERVICE-LEARNING

Simmons has a long-standing commitment to community service, with a special focus on children. The Scott/Ross Center is comprised of two major programs: Simmons Community Outreach (SCO), which is student-run, and the Office of Service Learning. SCO organizes volunteer efforts in the local community, addressing problems of homelessness, hunger, and the environment, as well as working with the elderly and youth. The Office of Service Learning collaborates with faculty and community organizations to incorporate the pedagogy of service-learning into course curricula. Each semester, several courses throughout the curriculum provide service-learning opportunities; the College recently introduced a Social Justice minor. In addition to service-learning courses, the Office plans Alternative Spring Break, a program that sends a team of students and staff to a community around the country to engage in a week of service.

Underscoring the college's commitment to community service, Simmons was ranked as one of the top colleges in the United States with more than $100,000 spent on work-study community service—devoting 34.6% of its budget to that area.

Simmons's long tradition of social responsibility led it to become the first college in Massachusetts to offer full four-year scholarships to two Afghan women who were previously denied the right to an education under the Taliban.

SUNY COLLEGE AT OLD WESTBURY

ADMISSIONS OFFICE, PO BOX 210, OLD WESTBURY, NY 11568-0210

PHONE: 516-876-3073 FAX: 516-876-3307 E-MAIL: ENROLL@OLDWESTBURY.EDU WEBSITE: WWW.OLDWESTBURY.EDU

THE COLLEGE AT A GLANCE

SUNY College at Old Westbury is a small, public college that teaches students leadership for the work place, the community, and life. In an environment that demands academic excellence and offers close interaction among students, faculty members, and staff members, Old Westbury weaves intercultural understanding into the very fabric of its liberal arts and professional programs. The college's student body of 3,300 comes primarily from New York State, but approximately 22 nations are also represented. In fact, Old Westbury is among the most diverse student bodies in the Northeast. Students learn in small classes (17:1 student-to-faculty-ratio) from a faculty recognized for its excellence in teaching. Located on the historic North Shore of Long Island, Old Westbury is a short drive from commercial centers and is less than 20 miles from the excitement, culture, and real-world educational opportunities of New York City.

ACADEMIC PROGRAMS

Through its School of Business, School of Education, and nine individual academic departments in the arts and sciences, Old Westbury offers 47 undergraduate degrees programs, in fields ranging from American Studies to Accounting, Chemistry to Criminology, Economics and Society to Visual Arts. The Old Westbury curriculum is carefully designed to enable students to compete in the global economy or to pursue further studies at the finest graduate and professional schools. Although all students focus on a major program of study, the College believes it is equally important for students to acquire a broad base of general knowledge and to develop strong analytical and creative skills.The core is a general education program structured into seven domains (basic communication, creativity and the arts, the western tradition, the American experience, major cultures, foreign languages, natural sciences, and mathematics) and three knowledge areas (humanities, social science, and diversity). All freshmen enroll in the First Year Experience program, which provides students with the academic and personal support needed to succeed as first-year students.

A COMMITMENT TO SOCIAL JUSTICE

Since its founding in 1965, Old Westbury has maintained, through its curriculum and activities, a commitment to engendering in its students a passion for learning and a commitment to social justice. Courses and on-campus activities regularly reflect on issues and themes as viewed from across socioeconomic, cultural, age, and gender lines. The College's widely diverse student body enables students to experience Old Westbury as a microcosm of the world. Students are urged to bring this understanding to fruition through service-learning, internship, and field experience opportunities available in virtually every discipline. Old Westbury's educational mission is carried about by students, faculty, and an alumni family 17,000 strong, active in civic engagement through community-based research and programming, and exhibiting leadership in the business and civic communities of our region, state, and nation.

WARREN WILSON COLLEGE

PO Box 9000, Asheville, NC 28815-9000

Phone: 828-771-2073 **E-mail:** ADMIT@WARREN-WILSON.EDU **Fax:** 828-298-1440 **Website:** WWW.WARREN-WILSON.EDU

A TRUE PIONEER IN SERVICE-LEARNING

For 40 years new students—freshmen and transfers alike—have come to Warren Wilson College knowing that service-learning is one of the three components of the WWC Triad. Perhaps it's no surprise that before even their first day of classes, incoming students join hands with faculty and staff to participate in the college's annual Service Day in the Asheville area.

Service Day, despite its scale, is only a start for students who understand that service-learning is at the core of what Warren Wilson College is about. In addition to being a major part of Orientation Week each August, Service Day serves as an introduction to the college's service-learning program that calls upon each undergraduate student to work a minimum of 100 service hours as a graduation requirement. Many students go well beyond the minimum, as evidenced by the fact that each year Warren Wilson students give well over 20,000 hours of service to community.

The numbers tell only a small part of the service-learning story at Warren Wilson. The impact students can have in the local community and beyond is often immeasurable. "Students can make a big difference to a project struggling to improve the lives of people," says Carolyn Wallace, Warren Wilson College dean of service. "I always envision students involving themselves passionately with critical community issues, leading to bold, joint ventures between students and communities."

Warren Wilson College has a number of service-learning community partners, including a regional food bank, homeless day shelter, an after-school tutoring program, and a community garden. But service for Warren Wilson students extends far beyond the Asheville-area community, and school breaks are likely to find students in places such as Jacksonville, Fla., where they have worked for organizations ranging from Habitat for Humanity, to Heifer Project International.

Warren Wilson College's service activities often focus on international situations and projects Service is often a major part of courses offered through the college's WorldWide Program, which affords students the opportunity to travel off-campus on a cross-cultural educational experience.

On a recent course titled, "Peru: Native Peoples of the Andes," students painted a school in a Peruvian village. During another course that traveled to Sri Lanka and India, students worked with a Gandhian institute for community development in the western Indian state of Gujarat. In Russia, living and serving in a children's orphanage in the middle of Moscow, students applied social work and cross-cultural communication skills.

Each of these courses offers a good example of how Warren Wilson seeks to integrate the three elements of the Triad – academics, service and work – into student learning both at home and abroad.

"Students can better serve communities when they speak with residents, read local papers and talk with area leaders," Wallace says. "Good service begins with listening—learning as much as possible about problems and strengths in a community, and then addressing both short- and long-range solutions to the problems."

INDEXES

ALPHABETICAL INDEX

INDEX BY SCHOOLS

STUDENT PROFILES

INDEX BY LOCATION

ALASKA

CALIFORNIA

COLORADO

CONNECTICUT

DISTRICT OF COLUMBIA

FLORIDA

GEORGIA

ILLINOIS

APPENDIX

CAMPUS COMPACT MEMBERS

UNITED STATES

ALABAMA

Birmingham-Southern College

Samford University

ALASKA

University of Alaska—Anchorage

ARIZONA

Arizona State University

Chandler Gilbert Community College

Gateway Community College

Paradise Valley Community College

Pima County Community College

Prescott College

Yavapai College

ARKANSAS

University of Arkansas—Little Rock

University of Arkansas (main campus)

CALIFORNIA

Azusa Pacific University

Barstow Community College

Butte College

California College of the Arts

California Lutheran University

California Maritime Academy of California State University

California Polytechnic State University— San Luis Obispo

California State Polytechnic University— Pomona

California State University—Bakersfield

California State University—Channel Islands

California State University—Chico

California State University—Dominguez Hills

California State University—Fresno

California State University—Fullerton

California State University—Hayward

California State University—Long Beach

California State University—Los Angeles

California State University—Monterey Bay

California State University—Northridge

California State University—Sacramento

California State University—San Bernardino

California State University—San Marcos

California State University—Stanislaus

City College of San Francisco

Dominican University of California

Evergreen Valley College

Glendale Community College

Humboldt State University

Loyola Marymount University

Mills College

MiraCosta College

Mount Saint Mary's College

Notre Dame de Namur University

Occidental College

Pitzer College

Saint Mary's College (CA)

San Diego State University

San Francisco State University

San José City College

San José State University

Santa Clara University

Scripps College

Sonoma State University

Stanford University

University of California—Berkeley

University of California—Davis

University of California—Los Angeles

University of California—San Diego

University of California—San Francisco

University of California—Santa Barbara

University of California—Santa Cruz

University of Redlands
University of San Diego
University of San Francisco
University of Southern California
University of the Pacific
Westmont College
Whittier College

COLORADO
Colorado Christian University
Colorado State University
Colorado College
Colorado State University—Pueblo
Fort Lewis College
Mesa State College
Naropa University
Regis University
University of Colorado—Boulder
University of Colorado—Colorado Springs
University of Colorado—Denver
University of Northern Colorado

CONNECTICUT
Asnuntuck Community-Technical College
Briarwood College
Connecticut College
Eastern Connecticut State University
Mitchell College
Naugatuck Valley Community College
Quinnipiac University
Three Rivers Community-Technical College
Trinity College (CT)
Tunxis Community College
University of Connecticut
University of Hartford
Yale University

DELAWARE
University of Delaware

DISTRICT OF COLUMBIA
American University
Georgetown University

FLORIDA
Barry University
Brevard Community College
Broward Community College
Central Florida Community College
Chipola College
Daytona Beach Community College
Eckerd College
Florida A&M University
Florida Atlantic University
Florida Community College at Jacksonville
Florida Gulf Coast University
Florida Hospital College of Health Sciences
Florida Institute of Technology
Florida International University
Florida Keys Community College
Florida Southern College
Florida State University
Hillsborough Community College
Indian River Community College
Jacksonville University
Miami Dade College
New College of Florida
North Florida Community College
Nova Southeastern University
Palm Beach Community College
Pasco-Hernando Community College
Pensacola Junior College
Ringling School of Art & Design
Rollins College
Saint Leo University
Santa Fe Community College
South Florida Community College
Southeastern College of the Assemblies of God
St. Petersburg College
St. Thomas University
Stetson University
Tallahassee Community College
University of Central Florida
University of Florida
University of Miami
University of North Florida

University of South Florida

University of Tampa

University of West Florida

Valencia Community College

Warner Southern College

GEORGIA

Agnes Scott College

Berry College

Brenau University

Columbus State University

Darton College

Emory University

Georgia College & State University

Georgia Southwestern State University

Kennesaw State University

Mercer University

Morehouse College

North Georgia Technical College

Piedmont College

Spelman College

University of Georgia

Wesleyan College (GA)

HAWAII

Brigham Young University (HI)

Chaminade University of Honolulu

Hawaii Pacific University

University of Hawaii—Hilo

University of Hawaii—Manoa

University of Hawaii—West Oahu

IDAHO

Boise State University

University of Idaho

ILLINOIS

Augustana College (IL)

Aurora University

College of DuPage

College of Lake County

Columbia College Chicago

DePaul University

Dominican University (IL)

Elmhurst College

Eureka College

Illinois College

Illinois Institute of Technology

Illinois State University

Illinois Wesleyan University

John A. Logan College

Lake Forest College

Lewis University

Loyola University of Chicago

McKendree College

Millikin University

National-Louis University

North Central College

Northwestern University

Oakton Community College

Rend Lake College

Rockford College

Roosevelt University

Saint Xavier University

Southern Illinois University—Carbondale

Southern Illinois University—Edwardsville

Trinity Christian College

University of Illinois—Chicago

University of Illinois—Springfield

University of Illinois—Urbana-Champaign

Western Illinois University

INDIANA

Ball State University

Butler University

DePauw University

Earlham College

Franklin College

Goshen College

Holy Cross College

Indiana University-Purdue University
  Fort Wayne

Indiana State University

Indiana University—Bloomington

Indiana University—East

Indiana University—Kokomo

Indiana University Northwest

Indiana University South Bend

Indiana University Southeast

Indiana University-Perdue University Indianapolis

Manchester College

Marian College (IN)

Martin University

Purdue University—West Lafayette

Purdue University—Calumet

Purdue University—North Central

Saint Mary's College (IN)

Taylor University—Upland

Taylor University—Fort Wayne

University of Evansville

University of Indianapolis

University of Notre Dame

The University of Saint Francis (IN)

University of Southern Indiana

Valparaiso University

IOWA

Buena Vista College

Central College

Clarke College

Coe College

Cornell College

Des Moines Area Community College

Dordt College

Drake University

Grand View College

Iowa Western Community College

Luther College

Morningside College

Northwestern College (IA)

Simpson College (IA)

University of Iowa

Wartburg College

KANSAS

Allen County Community College

Baker University

Butler County Community College

Cloud County Community College

Fort Hays State University

Fort Scott Community College

Garden City Community College

Highland Community College

Independence Community College

Johnson County Community College

Kansas State University

Kansas Wesleyan University

Labette Community College

Seward County Community College

Southwestern College

University of Kansas

University of Saint Mary

KENTUCKY

Bellarmine University

Berea College

Eastern Kentucky University

Northern Kentucky University

Thomas More College

Transylvania University

Union College (KY)

University of Kentucky

LOUISIANA

Baton Rouge Community College

Bossier Parish Community College

Delgardo Community College

Louisiana Delta Community College

Louisiana State University

Louisiana State University—Alexandria

Louisiana State University Health Sciences Center

Louisiana State University—Shreveport

Louisiana Tech University

Louisiana Technical College

Loyola University New Orleans

McNeese State University

Nicholls State University

Northwestern State University

Nunez Community College

Our Lady of the Holy Cross College

Our Lady of the Lake College

River Parishes Community College

South Louisiana Community College

Southeastern Louisiana University

Southern University at New Orleans

Southern University at Shreveport

Southern Univesity and A&M College

Tulane University

University of Louisiana—Lafayette

University of Louisiana—Monroe

Xavier University of Louisiana

MAINE

Andover College

Bates College

Bowdoin College

Colby College

Eastern Maine Community College

Kennebec Valley Community College

Maine College of Art

Saint Joseph's College (ME)

Southern Maine Community College

Unity College

University of Maine

University of Maine—Augusta

University of Maine—Farmington

University of Maine—Fort Kent

University of Maine—Machias

University of Maine—Presque Isle

University of New England

University of Southern Maine

York County Community College

MARYLAND

Anne Arundel Community College

Frostburg State University

Johns Hopkins University

Loyola College in Maryland

Maryland Institute College of Art

Morgan State University

Mount Saint Mary's College

Salisbury University

University of Maryland, Baltimore County

University of Maryland, College Park

MASSACHUSETTS

Amherst College

Assumption College

Babson College

Bentley College

Berklee College of Music

Berkshire Community College

Boston College

Brandeis University

Bridgewater State College

Bristol Community College

Bunker Hill Community College

Cape Cod Community College

Clark University

College of Our Lady of the Elms

College of the Holy Cross

Eastern Nazarene College

Emerson College

Emmanuel College (MA)

Endicott College

Fitchburg State College

Gordon College

Greenfield Community College

Hampshire College

Harvard University

Holyoke Community College

Lasell College

Lesley University

Massachusetts Bay Community College

Massachusetts College of Art

Massachusetts College of Liberal Arts

Massachusetts Institute of Technology

Massasoit Community College

Merrimack College

Middlesex Community College

Mount Holyoke College

Mount Ida College

Mount Wachusett Community College

North Shore Community College
Northeastern University
Northern Essex Community College
Pine Manor College
Quincy College
Quinsigamond Community College
Regis College
Simmons College
Simon's Rock College of Bard
Smith College
Springfield College
Stonehill College
Suffolk University
Tufts University
University of Massachusetts—Amherst
University of Massachusetts—Boston
University of Massachusetts—Dartmouth
Wellesley College
Wentworth Institute of Technology
Western New England College
Wheaton College (MA)
Wheelock College
Williams College
Worcester State College

MICHIGAN

Adrian College
Albion College
Alma College
Andrews University
Aquinas College (MI)
Baker College—Jackson
Calvin College
Central Michigan University
Davenport University
Eastern Michigan University
Ferris State University
Grand Rapids Community College
Grand Valley State University
Hope College
Jackson Community College
Kalamazoo College

Kirtland Community College
Lansing Community College
Madonna University
Marygrove College
Michigan State University
Northwood University
Olivet College
Saginaw Valley State University
Schoolcraft College
Spring Arbor University
University of Michigan—Ann Arbor
University of Michigan—Flint
University of Michigan—Dearborn
Wayne State University
Western Michigan University

MINNESOTA

Alexandria Technical College
Anoka Technical College
Augsburg College
Bemidji State University
Bethany Lutheran College
Bethel College (MN)
Capella University
Carleton College
Century College
College of Saint Benedict
College of St. Catherine
The College of Saint Scholastica
Concordia College—Moorhead
Concordia College—St. Paul
Crown College
Dakota County Technical College
Dunwoody College of Technology
Fond du Lac Tribal & Community College
Gustavus Adolphus College
Hamline University
Hennepin Technical College
Inver Hills Community College
Lake Superior College
Luther Seminary
Macalester College

Metropolitan State University

Minneapolis College of Art and Design

Minneapolis Community and
Technical College

Minnesota State University—Mankato

Normandale Community College

North Hennepin Community College

Northeast Higher Education District

Northland Community and Technical College

Northwestern College

Northwestern Health Sciences University

Rochester Community and Technical College

South Central Technical College

Southwest State University

St. Cloud Technical College

Saint John's University

Saint Mary's University of Minnesota

St. Olaf College

University of Minnesota—Crookston

University of Minnesota—Duluth

University of Minnesota—Morris

University of Minnesota—Twin Cities

University of Saint Thomas

William Mitchell College of Law

MISSISSIPPI

Alcorn State University

Delta State University

Jackson State University

Mississippi Valley State University

Tougaloo College

University of Southern Mississippi

MISSOURI

Central Methodist College

Central Missouri State University

Columbia College (MO)

Cottey College

East Central College

Fontbonne College

Jefferson College

Lincoln University (MO)

Linn State Technical College

Missouri Western State College

North Central Missouri College

Northwest Missouri State University

Ozarks Technical Community College

Rockhurst University

Southeast Missouri State University

Southwest Missouri State University—
Springfield

Southwest Missouri State University—
West Plains

St. Charles County Community College

St. Louis Community College—
Florissant Valley

St. Louis Community College—Forest Park

St. Louis Community College—Mcramec

Truman State University

University of Missouri—Columbia

University of Missouri—Kansas City

University of Missouri—Rolla

University of Missouri—Saint Louis

Washington University—Saint Louis

Webster University

Westminster College (MO)

MONTANA

Carroll College (MT)

Flathead Valley Community College

Miles Community College

Montana State University College
of Technology—Great Falls

Montana State University—Billings

Montana State University—Bozeman

Montana State University—Northern

Montana Tech of the University of Montana

Rocky Mountain College

Salish-Kootenai College

University of Montana—Missoula

University of Montana College
of Technology—Helena

The University of Montana—Western

University of Great Falls

NEBRASKA

Creighton University

University of Nebraska—Omaha

NEVADA

Nevada State College

NEW HAMPSHIRE

Antioch New England Graduate School

Chester College of New England

Colby-Sawyer College

College for Lifelong Learning

Daniel Webster College

Dartmouth College

Franklin Pierce College

Keene State College

McIntosh College

New England College

New Hampshire Institute of Art

New Hampshire Technical Institute

New Hampshire Community Technical
  College—Berlin

New Hampshire Community Technical
  College—Claremont

New Hampshire Community Technical
  College—Laconia

New Hampshire Community Technical
  College—Manchester

New Hampshire Community Technical
  College—Nashua

New Hampshire Community Technical
  College—Stratham

Plymouth State College

Rivier College

Saint Anselm College

Southern New Hampshire University

University of New Hampshire

NEW JERSEY

Montclair State University

Princeton University

Richard Stockton College of New Jersey

Rutgers, The State University of New Jersey

NEW MEXICO

Crownpoint Institute of Technology

New Mexico State University

San Juan College

University of New Mexico

University of New Mexico—Gallup

NEW YORK

Adelphi University

Barnard College

Buffalo State College

City College of New York

Colgate University

Cornell University

Corning Community College

Daemen College

DeVry Institute of Technology

Hamilton College

Hartwick College

Hobart and William Smith Colleges

Hofstra University

Houghton College

Ithaca College

Keuka College

Long Island University

Le Moyne College

Molloy College

Mount Saint Mary College (NY)

Nassau Community College

Nazareth College of Rochester

Niagara University

Onondaga Community College

Pace University

Rensselaer Polytechnic Institute

Roberts Wesleyan College

Rochester Institute of Technology

Saint John Fisher College

St. John's University (NY)

St. Lawrence University

Sarah Lawrence College

Skidmore College

St. Joseph's College

State University of New York at Brockport
State University of New York at Buffalo
State University of New York at Cortland
State University of New York at Cobleskill
State University of New York at Fredonia
State University of New York at Geneseo
State University of New York at Oswego
State University of New York at Plattsburgh
State University of New York at Stony Brook University
State University of New York at Potsdam
State University of New York at Purchase
Syracuse University
The College of Saint Rose
University of Rochester
Vassar College
Wagner College
Wells College

NORTH CAROLINA

Appalachian State University
Catawba College
Central Piedmont Community College
Duke University
East Carolina University
Elon University
Gardner-Webb University
Greensboro College
Guilford College
Johnson C. Smith University
Lenoir-Rhyne College
Meredith College
North Carolina Central University
North Carolina State University
Peace College
Pfeiffer University
University of North Carolia—Pembroke
University of North Carolina—Chapel Hill
University of North Carolina—Greensboro
University of North Carolina—Wilmington
Wake Forest University
Warren Wilson College

NORTH DAKOTA

Dickinson State University
North Dakota State University
University of North Dakota

OHIO

Antioch College
Ashland University
Baldwin-Wallace College
Bowling Green State University
Capital University
Case Western Reserve University
Central Ohio Technical College/
    The Ohio State University Newark
Chatfield College
Cleveland State University
The College of Wooster
Columbus State Community College
Cuyahoga Community College
Defiance College
Denison University
Heidelberg College
Hiram College
Hocking College
John Carroll University
Kent State University
Lourdes College
Marietta College
Mercy College of Northwest Ohio
Miami University
Mount Union College
Muskingum College
Oberlin College
Ohio Dominican University
Ohio Northern University
Ohio State University
Ohio University
Ohio Wesleyan University
Otterbein College
Shawnee State University
Sinclair Community College
University of Akron

University of Cincinnati
University of Dayton
University of Findlay
University of Toledo
Urbana University
Walsh University
Wilberforce University
Wilmington College (OH)
Wittenberg University
Wright State University
Xavier University (OH)

OKLAHOMA

Cameron University
Carl Albert State College
Connors State College
East Central University
Eastern Oklahoma State College
Langston University
Murray State College
Northeastern Oklahoma A&M College
Northeastern State University
Northern Oklahoma College
Northwestern Oklahoma State University
Oklahoma Baptist University
Oklahoma Christian University
Oklahoma City Community College
Oklahoma City University
Oklahoma Panhandle State University
Oklahoma State University
Oklahoma State University—Oklahoma City
Oklahoma State University Technical Branch—
   Okmulgee
Oral Roberts University
Redlands Community College
Rogers State University
Rose State College
Saint Gregory's University
Seminole State College
Southeastern Oklahoma State University
Southern Nazarene University
Southwestern Oklahoma State University

Tulsa Community College
University of Central Oklahoma
University of Oklahoma
University of Science and Arts of Oklahoma
University of Tulsa
Western Oklahoma State College

OREGON

Central Oregon Community College
Eastern Oregon University
Lewis & Clark College
Linfield College
Linn-Benton Community College
Oregon State University
Pacific University
Portland Community College
Portland State University
Reed College
Southern Oregon University
University of Portland
Western Oregon University
Willamette University

PENNSYLVANIA

Albright College
Allegheny College
Alvernia College
Arcadia University
Bloomsburg University of Pennsylvania
Bryn Mawr College
Bucknell University
Cabrini College
Cedar Crest College
Chatham College
Cheyney University of Pennsylvania
Clarion University of Pennsylvania
College Misericordia
Community College of Philadelphia
Delaware Valley College of Science
   and Agriculture
DeSales University
Dickinson College
Duquesne University

East Stroudsburg University of Pennsylvania
Edinboro University of Pennsylvania
Elizabethtown College
Franklin & Marshall College
Gannon University
Gettysburg College
Gwynedd-Mercy College
Juniata College
Keystone College
King's College (PA)
Kutztown University of Pennsylvania
Lafayette College
LaSalle University
Lehigh University
Lock Haven University of Pennsylvania
Luzerne County Community College
Lycoming College
Mercyhurst College
Messiah College
Millersville University of Pennsylvania
Montgomery County Community College
Moravian College
Muhlenberg College
Neumann College
Northampton County Area Community College
Pennsylvania State University Main Campus
Rosemont College
Saint Francis University (PA)
Saint Joseph's University (PA)
Shippensburg University of Pennsylvania
Susquehanna University
Swarthmore College
Temple University
Thiel College
University of Pennsylvania
University of Pittsburgh
The University of Scranton
University of the Sciences in Philadelphia
Ursinus College
Villanova University
Washington & Jefferson College

Waynesburg College
West Chester University of Pennsylvania
Widener University
Wilkes University
Wilson College

RHODE ISLAND
Brown University
Bryant University
Community College of Rhode Island
Johnson & Wales University
New England Institute of Technology
Rhode Island College
Rhode Island School of Design
Roger Williams University
Salve Regina University
University of Rhode Island

SOUTH CAROLINA
Benedict College
Clemson University
College of Charleston
Converse College
Furman University
South Carolina State University
University of South Carolina
Winthrop University
Wofford College

SOUTH DAKOTA
South Dakota School of Mines & Technology

TENNESSEE
Belmont University
East Tennessee State University
Maryville College
Tennessee State University
Tusculum College
Vanderbilt University

TEXAS
Austin Community College
Brookhaven College

Collin County Community College District

Del Mar College

Huston-Tillotson College

Northwest Vista College
   (Alamo Community College District)

Our Lady of the Lake University

Palo Alto College
   (Alamo Community College District)

Richland College

St. Edward's University

St. Mary's University (TX)

San Antonio College
   (Alamo Community College District)

Southern Methodist University

Southwestern University

St. Philip's College
   (Alamo Community College District)

Texas Christian University

Texas Tech University

University of Texas—Brownsville and
   Texas Southmost College

Trinity University

University of Houston

University of Houston—Downtown

University of St. Thomas (TX)

University of Texas—Arlington

University of Texas—El Paso

University of the Incarnate Word

UTAH

Brigham Young University (UT)

College of Eastern Utah

Dixie College

LDS Business College

Salt Lake Community College

Snow College

Southern Utah University

University of Utah

Utah State University

Utah Valley State College

Weber State University

Westminster College of Salt Lake City

VIRGINIA

Appalachian School of Law

Norfolk State University

Tidewater Community College

Virginia Polytechnic Institute & State University

VERMONT

Bennington College

Burlington College

Castleton State College

Champlain College

Community College of Vermont

Goddard College

Green Mountain College

Johnson State College

Lyndon State College

Marlboro College

Middlebury College

New England Culinary Institute

Norwich University

Saint Michael's College

Southern Vermont College

Springfield College of Human Services

Sterling College

University of Vermont

Vermont Law School

Vermont Technical College

Woodbury College

WASHINGTON

Antioch University Seattle

Bellevue Community College

Cascadia Community College

Central Washington University

Eastern Washington University

Edmonds Community College

Everett Community College

The Evergreen State College

Gonzaga University

Grays Harbor College

Heritage College

North Seattle Community College

Northwest Indian College
Seattle Central Community College
Seattle Pacific University
Seattle University
Skagit Valley College
Spokane Community College
Spokane Falls Community College
University of Washington
University of Washington—Tacoma
Washington State University
Western Washington University
Whitworth College

WISCONSIN

Alverno College
Cardinal Stritch University
Carthage College
Edgewood College
Gateway Technical College
Lakeland College
Lawrence University
Madison Area Technical College
Marian College of Fond du Lac
Marquette University
Milwaukee Institute of Art and Design
Northland College
Ripon College
St. Norbert College
University of Wisconsin Colleges
University of Wisconsin—Eau Claire
University of Wisconsin Extension
University of Wisconsin—Green Bay
University of Wisconsin—La Crosse
University of Wisconsin—Madison
University of Wisconsin—Milwaukee
University of Wisconsin—Oshkosh
University of Wisconsin—Parkside
University of Wisconsin—River Falls
University of Wisconsin—Stevens Point
University of Wisconsin—Stout
University of Wisconsin—Superior
University of Wisconsin—Whitewater

Viterbo University
Waukesha County Technical College
Western Wisconsin Technical College
Wisconsin Lutheran College

WEST VIRGINIA

Bethany College (WV)
Concord College
Concord University
Davis & Elkins College
Fairmont State Community and Technical
College
Fairmont State University
Glenville State College
Marshall University
Potomac State College—West Virginia
University
University of Charleston
West Virginia State College
West Virginia State University
West Virginia University
West Virginia University—Institute of
Technology
West Virginia University—Parkersburg
West Virginia Wesleyan College
Wheeling Jesuit University

INTERNATIONAL

AMERICAN SAMOA

American Samoa Community College

GUAM

Guam Community College

IRELAND

National University of Ireland, Galway

PUERTO RICO

Universidad del Sagrado Corazón

Notes

Notes

MORE BOOKS FOR YOUR
COLLEGE SEARCH

Best 361 Colleges
2006 Edition
0-375-76483-6 • $21.95/C$29.95

America's Elite Colleges
The Smart Buyer's Guide to the
Ivy League and Other Top Schools
0-375-76206-X • $15.95/C$23.95

Complete Book of Colleges
2006 Edition
0-375-76482-8 • $26.95/C$37.95

Guide to College Majors
2005 Edition
0-375-76469-0 • $21.00/C$28.00

The Internship Bible
10th Edition
0-375-76468-2 • $25.00/C$35.00